STEAL THIS DREAM

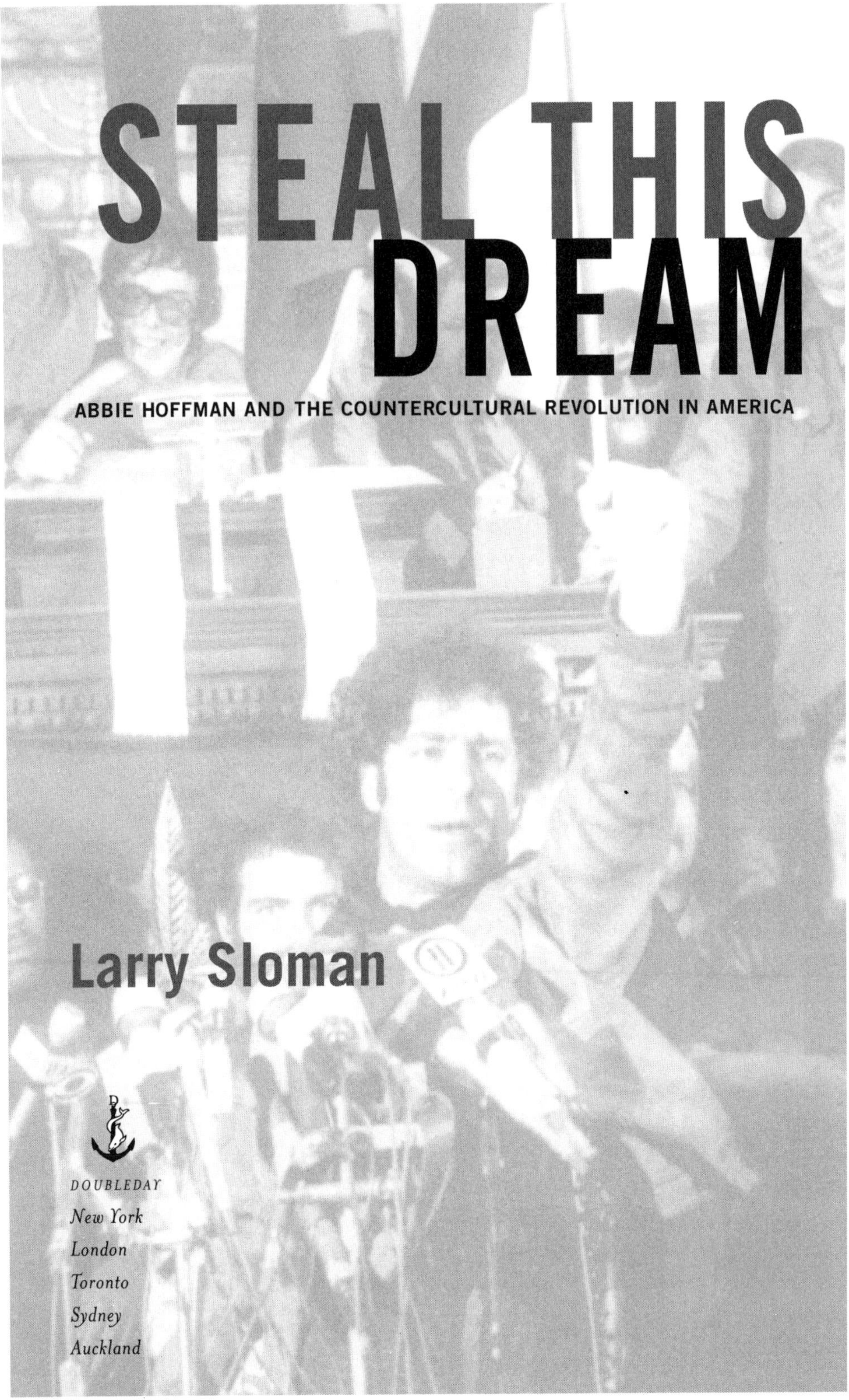

STEAL THIS DREAM

ABBIE HOFFMAN AND THE COUNTERCULTURAL REVOLUTION IN AMERICA

Larry Sloman

DOUBLEDAY
New York
London
Toronto
Sydney
Auckland

PUBLISHED BY DOUBLEDAY
a division of Bantam Doubleday Dell Publishing Group, Inc.
1540 Broadway, New York, New York 10036

DOUBLEDAY and the portrayal of an anchor with a dolphin
are trademarks of Doubleday, a division of Bantam
Doubleday Dell Publishing Group, Inc.

Design by Leah S. Carlson

Library of Congress Cataloging-in-Publication Data
Sloman, Larry.
Steal this dream : Abbie Hoffman and the countercultural revolution in America / Larry Sloman. — 1st ed.
p. cm.
1. Hoffman, Abbie. 2. Radicals—United States—Biography. 3. Radicalism—United States. 4. Popular culture—United States. 5. Social history—1960–1970. 6. Social history—1970– 7. United States—Civilization—1970– I. Title.
HN90.R3S57 1998
303.48′4—dc21
[B] 98-12791
CIP

ISBN 0-385-41162-6

Printed in the United States of America
August 1998
First Edition

10 9 8 7 6 5 4 3 2 1

For my mother, Lilyan, who helped instill an independent spirit in me, and for Christy, who fans the flames—

and for my father, Jack, who's up there kibbitzing with Abbie.

CONTENTS

Chapter Four: **CHICAGO, CHICAGO, THAT TODDLIN' TOWN** 119

In which the antiwar forces survive the battle of Chicago during the 1968 Democratic National Convention, only to be charged with treasonous acts.

Chapter Five: **HOFFMAN *V.* HOFFMAN** 160

In which Abbie and the rest of the Chicago 7 are put on trial for upsetting the status quo of American life.

Chapter Six: **REBEL WITHOUT A PAUSE** 221

In which countercultural heroes Abbie and Jerry Rubin are betrayed by their own movement.

Chapter Seven: **MAD ABOUT MOOLAH** 276

In which Abbie succumbs to the temptations of drugs and is busted by undercover agents for attempting to deal cocaine, ultimately resulting in his decision to flee underground.

Chapter Eight: **QUOTES FROM UNDERGROUND** 317

In which Abbie, having assumed a new identity, travels across America through much of the 1970s, conducting interviews, doing good, and yearning for his former prominence.

LIST OF CONTRIBUTORS

The following list includes everyone who was interviewed and quoted in Steal This Dream, *placed at the place or event at which he or she met Abbie Hoffman. The list is not strictly chronological within each section.*

Abbie's road began in Worcester, Mass.

Family:
Florence Hoffman
Jack Hoffman
Sidney Schanberg
Burt Aisenberg

Friends:
Haskell Morin
Burt Chandler
Ron Siff
Milton Frem
Tony Aaronson
Stuart Freedman

Associates:
Rabbi Joseph Klein
Herbie Gamberg

	Harold Rader Florence Zuckerman
continued at Brandeis University (Waltham, Mass.)	Jeremy Larner Esther Kartiganer Ellen Maslow Manny Schreiber Ira Landess
and the University of California, Berkeley	Marty Kenner Marshall Efron
then back to Worcester for work	Don Broverman Bob Baker
and the beginnings of his activism	Bob Solari Hal Gordon John Schezinsky Dan Dick Father Bernie Gilgun D'Army Bailey Hank Chaiklin Angela Dorenkamp Ruby Jarrett Bob Zellner Howard Zinn Terri Priest Elaine Edinburgh Gloria Solari
Near Biloxi, Miss., he met	Jerome Washington
in Worcester, he did drugs with	Marty Carey Susan Carey
and divorce proceedings in Worcester were handled by	Bob Weihrauch Seymour Weinstein

Moving to the Lower East Side of New York City, he met	Bill Kunstler
	Jim Fouratt
	Paul McIsaac
	Robin Palmer
	Anita Hoffman
	Truusje Kushner
	John Eskow
	Grace Slick
	Tuli Kupferberg
	Rudi Stern
	Allen Ginsberg
	Howie Glatter
	Captain Joe Fink
	Art Goldberg
	Paul Krassner
	Randy Wicker
	Ed Sanders
	Jean-Jacques Lebel
	Keith Lampe
	Bob Fass
	Stew Albert
	Andy Kent
	Jeff Nightbyrd
	Kate Coleman
	Jerry Rubin
	Danny Schechter
and in the Haight-Ashbury section of San Francisco was	Peter Coyote
whose fellow Digger Abbie met in Michigan at the SDS conference	Peter Berg
along with	Todd Gitlin
Also in New York City in this period he met	John Garabedian
	Country Joe McDonald

Jeff Jones
Lynn Freeman House
Tom Neumann
Sal Gianetta

In Newark, N.J., he met Tom Hayden

At the Pentagon demonstration in Washington, D.C., he met Superjoel
Bill Zimmerman
Cora Weiss

Still others he knew on the Lower East Side were the mayor's subordinates Sid Davidoff
Barry Gottehrer
Teddy Mastroianni
Sandy Garelik

and still more people he met on the Lower East Side were Dennis Dalyrimple
Jerry Brandt
George DiCaprio
Michael O'Donoghue
John Gerassi
Wolfe Lowenthal
Steve Tappis
Larry Sloman
John Fisk
Jacques Levy
Jay Levin
Al Kooper

and even more people he met on the Lower East Side were Laura Cavestani
Frank Cavestani
Joie Davidow
A. J. Weberman
Dana Beal
Aron Kay

Mike Brownstein
Steve Ben Israel
Gus Reichbach
Faye Schreibman
Mayer Vishner
Wavy Gravy
Viva
Timothy Leary
Spain Rodrigues
Jack Newfield
Dr. Eugene Schoenfeld

Chicago introduced him to
Mike Rossman
Rennie Davis
Abe Peck
John Schultz
Lee Weiner
John Zitek
Ron Kaufman
"Honeyman"
Bob Zmuda
Michael Shamberg
John Sack
Paul Sills
Carol Sills
Joe LoGuidice

Returning to New York City, he came into contact with
"J.P."
Len Weinglass
Danny Fields

and at Woodstock with
Richie Havens
Peter Townshend
Ken Kelley

In New York City around that time he also met
Alex Ducane
Chris Cerf

	Roger Lowenstein Charles Garry Norman Mailer
On the road in Kansas he met	Sue Williamson
and in Paris with Anita conceived	america Hoffman
Back in New York again there were	Paul Solomon Ron Rosen Alex Bennett Fred Jordan Daniel Ellsberg John Giorno David Peel Coca Crystal Lola Cohen Gabrielle Schang Velocity (Andrea Vaucher)
Then Abbie traveled to Miami, where there were	Walter Philbin Gerry Rudoff Ellis Rubin Steve Berticelli Carol Realini Jeff Fogel
And once more back in New York he met up with	John Lobell Mimi Lobell Jerry Lieberman Patsy Cummings Stella Resnick "Boxman" "Sportsman" Diane Peterson

	Arthur Nascarella Stanley Bard
While underground in Texas he was with	Kinky Friedman
in Woodstock with	Eric Anderson
and in the Thousand Islands with	Annie Gefell Rick Spencer Bea Schermerhorn David Maloney
In hiding in Miami he saw	Mimi Rubin
and in New York City met	Catherine Revland
and in Worcester	Joe Abooty
and was in touch with	Dennis Roberts Dave Lubell David Fenton Sam Mitnick
and in L.A. saw	Oscar Janiger Mike Elias Peggy Farrar
Once Abbie resurfaced, and in New York City he came to know	Ramsey Clark Jill Seiden Don Epstein Kenny Rahtz George Lois Rennie Gross Bruce Paskow Elli Wohlgelernter
On college campuses he debated	G. Gordon Liddy

and while involved with the pump he worked in Delaware with	Al Giordano Fred Duke
and on several projects in New York with	Jon Silvers
In the new student movement he met	Mark Caldiera Christine Kelly Elliot Katz Betsy Tomlinson David Kirshenbaum
In connection with some film projects he met	Nancy Cohen Jeremy Kagan
and working on Nicaragua he met	Art D'Lugoff Abby Fields
and on another film met	Oliver Stone
and was counseled by	Abby McGrath
After his death, he was spoken of by	Mary
and memorialized by	Whoopi Goldberg Andy Soma

FOREWORD
BY HOWARD STERN

The guy who wrote this book is my friend Ratso. He asked me to write a foreword and I'm really pissed because I don't want to. Not that I'm not honored, but I've been kind of busy lately and I'd rather just avoid the extra work. If I had the ability to say no, then I wouldn't be doing this. Lately everyone asks me to write a foreword because they believe it will help sell their book. I hate to break it to Ratso, but I don't think my foreword is going to really help. No one buys the book for the foreword.

I think the decent thing to do is to get a real close friend of Abbie's to write the foreword, or maybe his kid, Zowie, could have written it. As you know, Zowie Hoffman later changed his name to Joey because he didn't like his hippie name. Wait, I'm wrong, that was David Bowie's kid who hated his hippie name. Abbie's kid was America. Or is it Amerika? Well, "Americka" should have written the foreword.

Ratso gave me the manuscript for the book over a year ago. It appeared to be seventeen thousand pages long. Ratso is very thorough. Looking over this giant manuscript, I thought, "Jeez, Ratso must have chronicled Abbie's every bowel movement. How lucky for Abbie that Ratso wrote this, because nothing will be missed."

I have only read three or four books during my entire life and I wrote two of them. I read the first ten pages of this book and then I gave up. My reading comprehension is very low. Reading is not my thing. Most times that I try to read a book I zone out and then I give up and watch TV. Some people might say I have attention deficit disorder, but I think I'm just stupid. Even Abbie Hoffman used to say I was shallow and an "empty head with a wagging tongue."

Let me assure you that I know this is a great book, even though I haven't read it. I know it's great because Ratso is really smart and he's a good writer. I know that because Ratso has written other good books that I haven't read. I know Ratso's books are good because Ratso tells me they are good. Ratso tells me over and over again that his book about hockey is the best book ever written on hockey. And Ratso is an expert on hockey, so he knows. Whatever.

* * *

Look, it's not like I didn't know Abbie. I knew him. He appeared on my radio show several times. We weren't close friends and I didn't know him outside of the radio studio, but I was fortunate enough to have interviewed Abbie for many hours toward the end of his life.

What I want you to know is, I loved Abbie. You couldn't help but love Abbie because he was so damned entertaining and brilliant. When he visited my show I was mesmerized by the man and truly enjoyed his company. He was odd, irresponsible, and disgusting (he blew his nose straight into my garbage pail the first time he came in my office), but he was a sensational interview and a true intellectual. A fiery human being who cared about the environment and the human condition.

The day he died I was heartbroken because we had lost one of our brightest-shining stars. But I didn't always feel that way.

I had always assumed Abbie was another insincere jerk just trying to get famous and get laid. It turned out he was a passionate, sincere human being who was just trying to get laid.

I first became aware of Abbie Hoffman when I was in high school. Now here I was scared shitless that I was going to end up in the military in a year or two and get my fucking head blown off in Vietnam. Instead of realizing that Abbie was out there fighting for guys like me, I figured he was out there just trying to get girls. When others were scrambling to find careers, Abbie was putting his future on hold, getting arrested, and devoting himself to the antiwar movement. I just figured this must be some weird performance art or there had to be a cash angle to what Abbie did. I told you I wasn't very deep.

I was afraid of Abbie back in my high school days. He seemed dangerous. He looked and sounded like a guy who had nothing to lose and who just might go off and do something really bizarre. Abbie fit into no particular category. He was famous for what? He looked and sounded like a rock star but didn't play a song. He just . . . well, he just protested. With Abbie I couldn't figure out his angle, and that made him a real revolutionary. It was safe to love rock stars, but Abbie . . . what the fuck was he all about?

I was jealous of Abbie, too. What right did he have to capture America's attention? He became famous for protesting the war. Hell, any idiot could do that. I could do that. I didn't believe he deserved all the attention he was getting. But there he was, the talk of the town for no apparent reason. Why did he get to be a spokesman? Who appointed him boss of the revolution? I was envious. I used to hate the loudmouths in high school who got to lead the protest and hold the megaphones when we marched against the war. A couple of the real popular kids got to organize and boss the other dweebs around. I was one of the dweebs. Guys like Abbie got to hold the megaphone and get the chicks.

Years later, when I had Abbie on the show for the very first time, I was curious, nervous, and intrigued. I had a lot of feelings about Abbie, preconceived notions from my high school days, but in walked this odd loudmouth who had an opinion on everything. I instantly liked him. No topic was off-limits. I admired his honesty, his ability to tell a story, and the out-of-control energy that surrounded him. Politics was his passion, but at the same time he could be compelling on just about any subject.

Lots of great images of various Abbie appearances flood my memory as I write this. Like when we did this routine with Abbie called the "homo room." The idea was that we would go in the room and admit all our gay fantasies. Most celebrities would reluctantly get roped into this bit and nervously play along. Abbie was the first celebrity to participate in this bit, and rather than make fun of homosexual stereotypes, he volunteered that he once tried having sex with a man. He was proud and had no problem with our dissecting every kinky detail of his one-time homosexual experiment. He was fascinated with our childish approach to gay sex. He had a great sense of humor as he belly-laughed his way through this "way too personal" interview. He was fun. He was interesting. He knew how to roll with the situation.

Abbie always seemed to have a million different causes to champion and would storm the studio with a whirlwind of rebellious thought. One day he announced that he was suing an airline. He wasn't just suing an airline, he was going to sue the airline to set the injustices of the system straight. We spent an entire program going over every detail of Abbie's plane adventure and how he planned to teach the airline a lesson. The airline had accused him of smoking pot on the plane, but Abbie claimed it was just a cigarette. He was incensed that they threw him off the plane. We believed in his cause. He was fighting for us all. Abbie could make it all sound so urgent. Vietnam all over again!

While Abbie brought me so much joy, what I remember most is the sadness in Abbie's eyes each time I saw him. Although he was passionate, I sensed a weariness. I felt protective around him because he seemed so fragile. You could sense his depression. I took great joy in the fact that Abbie would leave my show happy and energized. He always made a point of telling me how all of my listeners were congratulating him on the street after an appearance, and that the fans thought he was one of the best guests. It made him feel good that he was recognized by people in such a positive way, a new way, not as that guy from the sixties but as that guy who made them laugh and think on the Howard Stern show.

Each time I saw Abbie, I made sure to thank him for his leadership role in our history, for dedicating his life to so many great causes. I wanted him to know that I had great respect and admiration for him, and that I knew he needed to be thanked and his ideals appreciated. I figured that strange look in his eyes meant he missed the old days, fighting the good fight where his struggles were news. It pained him that he was no longer the center of attention. I think he had thought that at this point in his life, he would be treated as a scholar and a true revolutionary, who instead of speaking with Howard Stern would be courted by Ted Koppel and *60 Minutes* for his opinion on world events.

I miss Abbie Hoffman. I think about how sad he looked the last time I saw him. My wife leaves me little notes when she goes to sleep that I read early in the morning when I get up to do my show. Usually the notes are about what the kids did the previous night or what bills we haven't paid. But one morning I picked up the note and read that Abbie was dead. I got real freaked out. He was the first friend of the show that ever died. The thought of Abbie dying tucked away in some house in Pennsylvania was depressing. The obituary said, "Hoffman, 52, was discovered at about 8:15 PM fully dressed, under the covers of his bed. He had a blanket and a quilt on." The reports said his "hands were tightly clasped around his face." I felt bad that this unique voice would no longer be around to stir things up to get us thinking. It doesn't seem right to me that a man who stood up against the establishment and saved tens of thousands of men from dying in a senseless war should die alone, sad, and ignored. Abbie deserved a televised funeral with a flag wrapped around his coffin and a twenty-one gun salute, because Abbie was a patriot, Abbie was a hero. That's right, a hero. The day he died I announced to Robin during my radio show that "anybody who helped bring down the Vietnam War is a hero, and Abbie was on the front line." And that's the truth . . . I'm so glad I got to know Abbie for a while. It turns out that the guy with the megaphone at the protest march wasn't there just to get laid . . . it turns out he really cared.

PROLOGUE

"Are you not letting us up because we're Jewish?"

Larry Sloman I'll never forget the first time I met Abbie Hoffman. It was in the summer of 1967. This was a strange time for a nice Jewish nineteen-year-old boychick from Queens, New York. A year or two earlier, I would have been working for the accountant down the hall from my parents' apartment, trying to reconcile the checkbook of a neighborhood pizza place. At nights, I would have hung out with Ronnie Simon or Joey Abelson, my roller hockey teammates. So how did I wind up in the dank offices of an underground newspaper, the *East Village Other,* a tabloid put out by a small crew of longhaired, dope-addled, visionary artists and writers who were in temporary residence of the bohemian stream known as the Lower East Side of New York City?

I guess you could blame Bob Dylan. My parents probably did. They were unwitting accomplices the night in 1965 they drove me to Alexander's Department Store in Flushing to pick up a copy of an album (on sale for $1.88!) called *Highway 61 Revisited.* I was late to Dylan, so this was my first exposure. What a dose. "Like a Rolling Stone," "Tombstone Blues," "Ballad of a Thin Man," "Desolation Row." These weren't songs, these were cultural manifestos. Countercultural, that is. All delivered with a sneering, fiercely hip, too-cool-for-the-room Attitude. And there was Dylan on the album cover, wearing a Triumph motorcycle T-shirt and an Op Art shirt over it, his hair Medusa-like. Right then, the sixties began for me.

The next day I quit my part-time accounting job. And I discovered the Village. My new friends from Queens College and I would drive into the city over the Williamsburg Bridge and go down to MacDougal Street. There was a small hole-in-the-wall store there that sold all sorts of shocking buttons like "Fuck Communism," "Kill for Peace," and "Make Love, Not War." And right across the street, at the Players Theatre, we went to see the Fugs play.

The Fugs were a group of beatnik peacenik poets who decided to subvert the impressionable minds of the baby boomers through the rock and roll medium. The three principals in the group, Ed Sanders, Tuli Kupferberg and Ken Weaver, weren't really players (although Ken banged the drums), but they enlisted some of their Lower East Side musician friends, like Steve Weber and Peter Stampfel of the Holy Modal Rounders, to provide some semblance of musical accompaniment.

But the Fugs were more than just music. Sanders would croon antiwar ditties while Kupferberg, dressed in army surplus, would smash doll heads with bayonet butts. Ed would do a great tent-meeting evangelist selling "3-D picktures of Jee-sus with eyes that follow you from the bedroom to the living room to your pickup truck as you go serve your Lord, Savior, Jesus Christ." Then there were the songs of wild sexual abandon: "Coca-Cola Douche," "Slum Goddess from the Lower East Side," "Saran Wrap" ("After the prom, and you ain't got no scumbag, Saran Wrap, Saran Wrap"). It was a total assault on straight culture—sex, drugs and rock and roll incarnate.

So I followed the Fugs to their haunts, the Lower East Side (or the East Village, as it was becoming known). Ed Sanders ran a small bookshop on the perimeter of Tompkins Square Park called the Peace Eye. That's where you could pick up Paul Krassner's pioneer satirical countercultural magazine, the *Realist,* or Ed's own mimeographed rag, *Fuck You—A Magazine of the Arts,* or the new underground paper servicing this nascent community, the *East Village Other.* Before long, I found myself hanging out at the *EVO* offices over Bill Graham's Fillmore East, working as a sort of quasi-mascot/cub reporter.

That's where I encountered Abbie. I had read about him, of course, in *EVO* and the *Village Voice.* He was the most visible "leader" of the new hippie community of the East Village. Which meant you could often find him on the corner of Second Avenue and St. Mark's Place in front of Gem Spa, home of the world's greatest egg cream, handing out street sheets, harassing the pigs, steering runaways to crash pads, or just generally tripping out.

But that day in August 1967, he bounded into the *EVO* offices, a bundle of hyperkinetic curly-haired energy.

"C'mon, we're going to the stock exchange today," he said in his thick New England accent. "Why don't you cover it?"

In a flash, Abbie split. One of the editors, Peter, and I went over to the exchange at the appointed time. About twenty hippies had congregated outside. There was also a phalanx of reporters from the straight newspapers. Apparently, Abbie didn't notify just *EVO*.

After a few minutes of clowning around outside, the group tried to blend in with the usual tourists and make their way upstairs to the visitors' gallery. They got as far as the security guard, who seemed shocked to see a group of hippies waiting to tour the exchange. He detained them and conferred with a superior.

Abbie interrupted their deliberations in a loud voice. "Hey, are you not letting us up because we're Jewish?"

That did it. Jews banned from the stock exchange gallery! Fearing a scandal, the guard immediately ushered us upstairs. Now Abbie went to work. He pulled out a huge wad of dollar bills and handed them out to his comrades and to the straight tourists too. Suddenly, at a prearranged signal, the hippies rushed to the edge of the balcony and began throwing the money down to the stock exchange floor, shouting, *"Free!* It's *free!"*

At first, there was a stony surreal silence as the brokers looked up and saw a shower of currency gently wafting down. Then, as the bills hit the ground, pandemonium broke out. The brokers started scrambling, pushing each other, grabbing for the money. When the avalanche subsided, they actually looked up at the gallery and demanded "More!" But Abbie and his friends had run out of bills, so they started throwing some pocket change down. The brokers booed.

Upstairs, chaos reigned. The straight press had surrounded Abbie and some of the other leaders. "What did you hope to accomplish?" "Why are you throwing money?" "Who are you people?"

"I'm only talking to the underground press," Abbie pronounced, and walked through the crowd to where Peter and I were standing. Abbie then began a monologue about "guerrilla theater" and "exposing the money changers" and "It's all *free.*" The straight scribes surrounded us and scribbled down his words.

Then the hippies made a quick exit to the street. A number of camera crews from the local network stations were waiting there. Abbie did a quick handstand and then he and a few of his friends burned some bills that somehow weren't launched onto the floor. Again, Abbie was surrounded by media.

"Who are you?"

"I'm Cardinal Spellman," Abbie smiled.

"Where did you get your money?"

"Would you ask *him* that question?" Abbie shrugged.

Abbie fielded a few more questions and then they burned another fiver, yet another photo op. Then we heard sirens in the background. Abbie immediately rushed over to Peter and me.

"C'mon, let's split," he said, and simultaneously stepped into the street and hailed a cab. Within seconds, we were heading back to the East Village. I was shocked that Abbie had left all the hippies to fend for themselves. But inside the cab, Abbie was ecstatic. He was amazed the stockbrokers played their parts so perfectly and scrambled on their hands and knees to grab the money. He laughed about the security guard. But most of all, he couldn't believe the press coverage.

"I can't wait to get home," he bubbled. "I can't wait to see this on the evening news."

* * *

I saw more and more of Abbie that summer. The longer I hung out in the Lower East Side, the more I realized that Abbie was the go-to guy, the mayor of St. Mark's Place. Need a place to crash? Ask Abbie for help. Got burned in a dope deal? Ask Abbie for help. Getting hassled by the cops? Ask Abbie for help. Looking for an interesting demonstration? Ask Abbie. Abbie had an authority about him that stemmed only partly from the fact that he was a good ten years older than the runaways who were pouring into the East Village during that so-called Summer of Love.

So what was the source of Abbie's palpable charisma? Part of it had to do with his fearlessness. Some of it was his incredibly sharp wit. Some was his engaging smile, some his still thick Bostonian accent. Abbie had a way of relating to you that made you feel like you and he were a two-person conspiracy to change the world. But there was no dour quality to Abbie's revolutionary spirit. You knew you weren't dealing with the Trotskyites here. As Jerry Rubin said, if you were going to a demonstration, you knew that Abbie would be the one bringing the ice cream.

After that action at the stock exchange, I knew that Abbie's days as a Lower East Side community organizer were numbered. His talents were too expansive to be contained by St. Mark's Place. Besides, as the war raged on and began dominating the evening news, Abbie and his cohorts had a new full-time job—figuring out ways to end the bloodshed. With the fall demonstration at the Pentagon, and the antiwar protests the following summer at the Democratic convention in Chicago, Abbie's road was leading to larger stages than the band shell at Tompkins Square Park.

But even at these national events, Abbie was the major player. Part of his authority stemmed from his brilliant analysis of how the media worked. Abbie was the father of the electronic sound bite. Want a colorful, humorous twenty-second sound bite from the demonstration? Get Abbie. Abbie was able to engage the reporters covering these events and make them coconspirators just as he did with his constituents on St. Mark's Place. Of course, becoming the de facto spokesperson for the hippie/freak segment of the counterculture also fed his enormous ego.

But it wasn't the media that made Abbie the predominant countercultural star. It was the U.S. government. After the Chicago demonstrations, the Nixon administration anointed Abbie by indicting him and seven of his colleagues for conspiracy to cross state lines in order to foment those "riots" at the Democratic convention. That Chicago courtroom became Abbie's greatest stage.

It was astonishing theater, as you shall see on the following pages. And, by the end of the trial, Abbie was a media superstar. You either loved him or you hated him, but you knew who he was. When he went on *The Merv Griffin Show,* wearing an American-flag shirt, CBS felt compelled to black out Abbie's body when the show aired that night. Censorship only enhanced his legend.

But, as Madonna and countless other celebrities would find out years later, there was the inevitable media backlash. Abbie began to be attacked not only by the mainstream media but by the counterculture itself. The nascent women's movement put him on their Top Ten Enemies List. The attacks, combined with the vacuum everyone in the movement experienced as the war wound down, sent Abbie into a period of introspection.

Like many of his cohorts, Abbie plunged into experimentation in two of the twin pillars of the counterculture—sex and drugs. When the drug experimentation resulted in a cocaine bust, Abbie was able to postpone coming to terms with the massive cultural shift as the sixties became the seventies by going underground.

Abbie ultimately resurfaced into an entirely new culture—the Me Decade. Once again, his environmental work during the eighties mirrored that of many of his fellow movement refugees. Once again, you could trace the remnants of the counterculture by examining Abbie's life.

Abbie never made it into the nineties. He died in the spring of 1989, curled up in the fetal position on the bed in his converted turkey coop in rural Pennsylvania, after ingesting a massive dose of barbiturates and Scotch. And the movement for social change in this country never produced another Abbie. The Berlin Wall fell, the students in China inspired the world with their bravery, the counterculture took over Czechoslovakia; yet these world-shaking events would have resonated far more in this country if we had had an Abbie Hoffman rallying the troops at home. I, for one, would have relished seeing the ultimate Wrestlemania of political debates on the nightly news—Abbie the King of Counterculture vs. Newt the Ripper.

But at least we have the history. Abbie vs. LBJ. Abbie vs. Tricky Dick. Abbie vs. Spiro. And, at the end, Abbie vs. his ex-partner Jerry (Rubin). It's all in these pages. Abbie shone during one of the most amazing eras of American history—making love, fighting war, helping to create a revolution for the hell of it.

* * *

This is not a conventional biography. In documenting Abbie's life and times through an oral history, we arrive at a portrait of Abbie from over two hundred different perspectives. Abbie's friends, Abbie's enemies and people who fell into both of those categories have constructed this narrative. At times, they will complement each other's accounts. At times, they will contradict each other. As in *Rashomon,* you will have to decide whose reality is the realest.

But by tracing Abbie's times through his peers and adversaries, we hope to tell a much bigger story than Abbie's. Read these accounts, then, as the testaments of a wide variety of people who came together under unique circumstances and tried to effect social change. From the perspective of the nineties, these tales might seem surrealistic. But these things actually happened here in America. This is Abbie's story, and it's also the story of these interviewees, human, all too human. But don't forget that through all their glory and foibles, Abbie and the others were all reaching for a dream. Feel free to steal this dream.

Chapter One

REBEL WITHOUT A CAUSE

Suffering from pneumonia, John Hoffman was smuggled into the United States under his mother's coat when his family emigrated here from Kiev, Russia. The family name, Shapoznikoff, was soon changed to Hoffman. They settled in Worcester, Massachusetts. When John was in his twenties, he met Florence Shanberg, a secretary from Clinton, Massachusetts, at a dance at the local synagogue. Two years later, in October of 1934, they were married. Two years after that, on November 30, 1936, their first son, Abbott, was born.

Florence Hoffman *(from* The Jewish Mother's Hall of Fame *by Fred Bernstein)* From the start, Abbie demanded a lot of attention. An awful lot. At three months, Abbott would get on his back and do acrobatics, for the whole family, like he was showing off. Then when Jack was born, Abbott was jealous.

Susan Carey, *friend from Worcester* It was tough for Jack, growing up as Abbie's younger brother. Abbie did bad things, the parents freaked. Abbie did good things, the parents freaked. It was Abbie, Abbie, Abbie.

Florence Hoffman Abbie had asthma. He used to have bad attacks when he was a kid. I didn't know how to bring up children. Now I would know better.

Sidney Schanberg, *Abbie's cousin* Florence remembers that she was "permissive" but I just thought she was no disciplinarian. And Johnny didn't have the energy to do it. He might yell and scream but he was busy with other things. Also, I don't think at heart Johnny was a disciplinarian. Johnny liked a good time.

Jack Hoffman, *Abbie's brother* My father was not an emotional person. He was from that old school, they could never show love, they were too busy working. He was very, very steep and deep in traditional American values, just a little bit overbaked. Whatever the government says is right because they're the government.

John Hoffman was a pharmacist who worked for his uncle Kanef. When Kanef died, he willed his business to his son. He left John $3,000 with the proviso that he remain at the pharmacy and train Kanef's son.

Jack Hoffman Kanef fucked him, so my father started his own medical supply businCss. He was a pill pusher, my father.

Burt Aisenberg, *childhood friend* After the war, John built up Worcester Medical and made quite a business out of it. He was outspoken, blunt, crude. He used the four-letter words. I'll never forget the time in his place of business he had a cutout made of plastic of a woman's vagina, and he said you ever really see what it looked like? And he opened it up. That was John. You loved him or you hated him.

Rabbi Joseph Klein John Hoffman was a very religious man. At the Temple, he often acted as the shammes, the one who was in charge of the daily services.

Haskell Morin, *childhood friend* Abbie's mother was hardly even a mother, she was off doing whatever she was doing. The kids actually grew up themselves.

Jack Hoffman They used to have live cowboy shows, at the Plymouth Theater. The Indians would come out on the stage first. They were dancing around and we were going yeaaaa, and everybody's going boooo, and they were telling us to sit down. We always went against the grain.

Burt Chandler, *childhood friend* The first time I knew that Abbott might have a little different moxie going than the rest of us was, we were out together on Halloween. We were probably eleven, and Abbott's a couple of years younger. Well, while we were blowing peas through peashooters, Abbott quietly took a knife out of his pocket and slashed a convertible top.

Abbie Hoffman *(interviewed by Barry Shapiro)* The first scrap I had with cops centered around Halloween. I was about thirteen and I changed the license plates on an FBI car. The FBI visited my house.

Jack Hoffman So every Friday night he had to stay in the house for like six months. He was under house arrest.

Ron Siff, *childhood friend* Even at ten, Abbie always had an independence. In those days you did what you were told. He was way ahead of his time.

Florence Hoffman Abbie was rambunctious. He wasn't an angel by any means, but he didn't do anything wrong. Wrong in a sense that you would have to go to jail for it.

Jack Hoffman Abbie loved sex. If you want to write about Abbie you gotta talk about sex, and cards. Studying is not on the list of priorities in Abbie's life in the growing-up years, not at all. Politics are not. Abbie was too busy getting laid and playing gin.

We used to sleep in the same bed together, my brother and I, when we were growing up. I don't think I was ten years old, my brother taught me about the glass for when we used to listen to my parents screwing. He showed me how to get laid. We could never afford a cleaning lady, so you'd just take a lady from the poor farm, bring her to your house and give her a white uniform so the neighbors would think we could afford a cleaning lady. Her name was Flo. She couldn't clean, she couldn't do the dishes, she couldn't make the bed. All she used to do was sneak the booze from behind my father's bar. So one day I go down the basement and there's my brother with his big honk; he had a big cock, Abbie. He says, "Come on, I'll show you how to do it right." I was eleven, and he was showing me how to screw her by the numbers.

So then we got this idea, let's get all the boys in. Fifty cents for a hand job, a buck to fuck her. They'd be waiting out in the street to go up there. Remember *Risky Business*? We did that thirty years ago, my brother and I. We were entrepreneur pimps!

Haskell Morin Abbie almost raped a girl. The three of us, we were in Greenhill Park, this was in high school. We were both making out with her, and then he wanted to have sex with her and she said, "No, no," and she's yelling and screaming. I says, "Look, that's it, I don't want to get in trouble." I put a stop to that. But he was forever masturbating. If he'd wake up with an erection, his motto—never waste a good erection.

Jack Hoffman Abbie always protected me. I remember once we were kids on the Cape, and there was a whole gang of guys, ten of 'em, coming down the street at us.

Haskell Morin Abbott was impressed by the Italian hoods that hung out on Shrewsbury Street. He wanted to be like them. He was small but he was wiry and tough.

Jack Hoffman I said, "What're you gonna do, Abbie?" He says, "I'll show you." He walked up to this one guy, hadda be six feet. To me he looked like a giant. All I remember is Abbie going one in the stomach and kneeing him right in the balls. With all these guys around. And they just melted like butter on toast.

Milton Frem, *childhood friend* Suzie Ricker was Abbie's girlfriend, she was his queen. She was a beautiful little kid. But he was rough on her because he was a tough guy. A male chauvinist.

Jack Hoffman One day he came home cut up bad from Suzie Ricker's. A guy from Texas really got him fucking good, whooo! He was knifed up like crazy. I threw a sheet out and I pulled him up to the windows, bleeding. He would hypnotize himself so he'd have no pain. He had this thing about self-hypnosis. He used to keep me up all night long. Four o'clock in the morning he'd wake me up, "Pinch me, pinch me. Are you pinching me?" I said, "Your fucking arm is bleeding, for Christ sakes." He could get to the point where you could actually cut his arm and he'd feel no pain. You could burn his hand too. But that hurt the next day.

How would you like to be our sister, Phyllis, the little girl with two brothers like that? All they want to do is look at her boobs. And take her underwear into the bathroom and masturbate with it. We did it before Portnoy.

The two of us used to have incredible fights. We ended up in the hospital twice. I had my arm broken. I broke his arm once. He had a scar on his leg, I put a knife right in him. And my father was a tough motherfucker, he didn't take shit from anyone. He had a strap that wide, beat the shit out of us. Once he picked the both of us up and just threw us down the fucking stairs.

THE HOFFMAN FAMILY—JOHN, FLORENCE AND CHILDREN, ABBOTT (REAR), JACK AND PHYLLIS. From the archives of Jack Hoffman

Haskell Morin If anybody wanted to have a nice father it was Big John. Whenever we called him Big John he'd smile. The only thing big about him was his belly. He was very permissive. Gave Abbie the car, saw that he had spending money, gave him haircut money. There was a diner downtown, on Chandler Street. If he was hungry, Abbie would go in and have breakfast or lunch, Charlie would feed him and give Big John the bill. Abbie liked his father. He never really said, "I love my father." More "My dad gives me a lot of things, my dad's good to me."

America Hoffman, *Abbie's son* My father used to tell me about how his dad would beat him. He told me that his dad was crazy, his whole family was crazy, and he'd become obsessed with sports, that was his way of getting his aggressions out. He said, "When I was a kid I used to take a handball and hit it against the wall until my hands were soaked red with blood and then I'd come home and I wouldn't let my mother put alcohol on it." I'd just say, "You're nuts."

Haskell Morin He could play basketball till he dropped, he just had so much energy. And yet there were times when he had no energy at all, he would just hang around the house for three days, lie in bed, read.

Milton Frem Abbie's mother always sat in the background and didn't say too much. A bit unstable as far as I'm concerned. You could see by when you walked in the house, the kitchen wasn't kept at all. What belonged in the refrigerator was out on the kitchen table, what should have been on the kitchen table was on the refrigerator. It was scary. Abbie never talked about it. He used to walk in and look at that and shake his head, and we'd go down to the cellar.

Sidney Schanberg I didn't know Florence as a young person. My memory of that whole time was really the vivid memory of her sister Rose because on weekends my uncle Sam would go get Rose at the Worcester State Hospital and take her for a drive. They'd come to our house in Clinton and Rose would occasionally curse or something, and it was weird for a young person ten or eleven to see a person like that. What did I know? I mean, Rose had an operation on her brain, right?

Jack Hoffman A diagnostic letter on my aunt [noted] a psychotic, almost childhood-type behavior. They thought schizophrenic. She could've been manic-depressive though.

* * *

Haskell Morin Abbie used to play cards. One night, I brought a card player out there with a pocketful of money and Abbie knew he could beat this guy. Maybe he won about a hundred dollars. He was a good gambler.

Milton Frem We used to go to the dances at the Beth Israel Synagogue. One evening, I got my father's car, which was a treat. Abbott's father had the exact same car as my father—same color, same everything. We went into the dance, we had a good time and we came out. Abbott got into my father's car and he tried to get the car started and I went out there and I said, "Abbott, you're in the wrong car." He says, "This is my car, get the hell out of here." And he slammed the door on it. It took three of us to get him out of my father's car. We threw him like a piece of steak on the hood of his father's car. He says, "Oh yeah, this isn't my father's car. Geez, I'm sorry about that." And he kind of broke away like nothing happened. But he had gone absolutely hyper, he got spacey, he wouldn't listen to anybody, which was typical. Either his mind was running or his body was running but something was always moving faster than it should have been.

Abbie Hoffman *(interviewed by Barry Shapiro)* I stole cars too, a little joyriding stuff. Clowning in school. Getting kicked out of classes. I remember one incident with a teacher who was a tyrant. There was always a touch of morality. There always is for the clown. I was a middle-class Jewish hood.

Ron Siff I would not describe Abbie as a hood. He just loved to laugh and shocking things made him laugh. He would get a real kick out of driving to school. My mother or father would be driving me to school, and he'd pass us at a high speed, just to get a comment. He had a big grin on his face. Today there's an awful lot of angry kids that drive fast up and down Main Street. Abbie wouldn't drive fast up and down Main Street unless the chief of police was standing there, you understand me. He had a sense of theater.

Herbie Gamberg, *neighbor* There was some truth to seeing Abbie as an apolitical Jewish hood. But on the other hand there were no political avenues at that time for rebellious Jewish kids coming out of privilege. The fifties was much more of an innocent, easy conservatism. Not even conservatism 'cause it wasn't ideologically articulated. It was just an easy acceptance that the world was ours, that regardless of what we did it would all come out all right. So even rebellion was not dangerous for any of us. It was more like a style.

* * *

Jack Hoffman Culturally, Judaism was very important to Abbie. He saw it as a fighting-for-the-underdog type of thing. Listen, there's too many fucking scars on our bodies, as kids growing up as Jews. You couldn't stay at a motel on the Cape if you were Jewish. You'd walk into a restaurant, it was half-empty and they'd tell you it was all filled for reservations. My father once took a whole buffet table and just threw it over because they wouldn't let us eat there.

Stuart Freedman, *childhood friend* The Hoffmans were seen as an average Jewish family but the kids were considered to be a little wild because Abbie was involved in the early fifties with the discovery of rhythm and blues music, and wearing zoot suits, which was basically the beginning of the counterculture movement.

Tony Aaronson, *childhood friend* Abbie had what we used to call a D.A. (duck's ass), a duck-tail kind of thing. He had longer hair when nobody had long hair. He wore those real wide-collar shirts, tuxedo-lapelled jackets, pegged pants and suede shoes. Abbie knew every musician, every rock and roll group. He knew all about sports. Baseball statistics, hockey statistics, anything!

Haskell Morin Abbie would have 45s coming out of his ears which he shoplifted. He never paid for records. He was an avid reader and he would steal paperback books. I didn't get involved, I was afraid of getting caught, but he thought, "Hey, they'll make it up on somebody else."

* * *

Tony Aaronson Abbie did very well in school. He never had to study, he had incredibly retentive powers.

Florence Hoffman Well, what can I tell you, he was brilliant, just brilliant. They expelled him from Classical High. He made the class laugh. Mr. Cravetti, the teacher, said, "It's no wonder half the teachers are in the state hospital." And Abbie said, "What happened to the other half?" And he says, "Hoffman, don't come back unless you come back with your parents." And Abbie said, "It was the right answer, I gave you a good answer." They accepted him right away at Worcester Academy.

Harold "Dutch" Rader I was the senior master at Worcester Academy. Abbie came here in 1953. He was here for two years. His father sent him here because he thought he'd experience a little bit more structured environment.

Ron Siff I had one impression: he was astounding. He was a kid who you never saw open a book and who consistently made honors. His ability to understand and to learn was phenomenal. While we're sitting in our rooms banging stuff in with a hammer, this guy is out bowling. His rep at the academy was that he was a wild man. But at the grading periods, there he was with honors all the time. You couldn't argue with that.

Harold "Dutch" Rader He was a normal kid around here. He got into little troubles but I don't think they amounted to anything. Just kid stuff.

Chapter Two

MR. CIVIL RIGHTS

Abbie Hoffman *(interviewed by Barry Shapiro)* I sort of bumped into college. Some guy that I admired had gone to Brandeis so I went.

Herbie Gamberg I was two years older. So I go off to Brandeis and become an intellectual. I meet New Yorkers and I'm having teachers who are talking about whole centuries and ideas. I come home to the place we all played basketball, and I'm talking rebellion. But not rebellion in any political sense, it's much more individual rebellion against the dullness and stolidity of middle-class Jewish life. Abbie was unread and illiterate. And I was reading Camus and Freud and Kafka and spouting general atheism and just shocking stuff, you know? Abbie is entranced by all this. Abbie's first predisposition was for shock.

FALL 1955

Manny Schreiber I was coming from Elmira, New York. I was given Abbott Howard Hoffman as my roommate. I was sixteen and he was eighteen. I had skipped a year. He had lost a year with his bout with mono somewhere in high school. I think he immediately knew that most people here were rather sheltered, middle-class, largely Jewish, academically oriented, and what he had going for him was knowledge of working-class culture. He knew about the track, knew about gambling, knew about pool halls, knew about street fighting. He was sexually experienced, he knew about girls' clitorises. There was all kinds of esoteric knowledge that he knew about. He certainly was very kind to me, kind of big-brotherly. And he was interested in Brandeis as an intellectual place. He didn't just want to be the oddball identity there, he wanted to make his mark.

Abbie Hoffman *(interviewed by Elli Wohlgelernter)* There was no idea of illicit drugs in the late fifties. You never even heard of marijuana or heroin. Dexedrine was the drug of choice. When you had been goofing off or not going to class or playing basketball and all of a sudden there was the old deadline, word got around that you could stay up for three or four days on end, writing, studying for your exams. There wasn't what you would call dealing, there was more sharing of them. It didn't take me long to figure out on which shelf the Drines were in my father's warehouse. You could take a handful from a five-thousand-pill container, put the cotton back, who would know? It was enough to keep three or four dorms going.

Jeremy Larner, *friend at Brandeis* Brandeis had an unusually political atmosphere in the fifties. As a new school, it took advantage of McCarthy-ism to build a great faculty by hiring teachers who had trouble at other colleges because they were radicals and ex-radicals, including socialists like Irving Howe, Lewis Coser, Bernard Rosenberg and a charismatic Stalinist scholar in the person of Herbert Marcuse.

Herbie Gamberg Marcuse was very inspirational. But we were not really ready for him then. He was an unread guru. Even at Brandeis, there was no clear political Left. But there was a strong lifestyle rebellion.

Esther Kartiganer, *friend at Brandeis* I never took a course with Abe Maslow but of course everybody knew about him. Wonderful, wonderful man. All the young psychology students were in awe of him. They thought you were next to God if you were at the same place that he was at any point.

Timothy Leary, *professor of psychology at Harvard* Abe was tremendously influential in modern psychology because he substituted for the Freudian unconscious, which was filled with animalistic and negative stuff. He said that the unconscious was filled with potential and he also popularized the notion of stages of life, which of course in a sense goes back to Hinduism and Buddhism, that you can go within and you can find peak experiences and enlightenment. Maslow was a very influential transitional person be-

THE YOUNG REBEL, ZOOT-SUITED AND DUCK-ASSED, AT BRANDEIS.
From the archives of Jerry Lieberman

THE 1959 BRANDEIS UNIVERSITY TENNIS TEAM. ABBIE IS AT LEFT. NETWORK TENNIS COMMENTATOR BUD COLLINS, WHO COACHED THE TEAM, IS AT RIGHT. AP/Wide World

tween medical psychiatry and humanist inner-potential, do-it-yourself psychology. The paradox was, as everybody knows, that Abe himself was a deeply depressed person. Abe told me once he never had a peak experience.

Herbie Gamberg I don't think Maslow was a deep thinker, he fits the self-help, self-enhancement specialness that appealed to Abbie.

Jack Hoffman Brandeis had a tremendous influence on Abbie. My father fucking hated it, he used to call it the bastion of communism. They had nice buildings, the teachers are nice, he's eating good, what's wrong with the school? "You don't understand what they're teaching him there."

Manny Schreiber Abbie's mother was very involved with Abbie, wanted to do the readings that he had in some of his Western Civ courses, talked to him about Plato and so on.

Florence Hoffman Parents Day I came. And to sit and listen to Marcuse, he was so brilliant. And Abraham Maslow. As a matter of fact, Abbie, for a date once, brought Maslow's daughter here.

Ellen Maslow Brandeis was a fairly small college. Everyone was a genius. I thought I was retarded. The real stars were much more articulately, brilliantly daring. Abbie was no particular star at Brandeis.

Manny Schreiber Toward the end of that year, Abbie and I needed money, we came up with the idea of selling sub sandwiches. Abbie went into the Italian section of Boston and made a deal where he got some subs up front, and we sold them. We did this during exam week.

Ira Landess The first time I ever saw Abbie was in September or October of 1956, Ridgewood Dorm. This guy was in the quad screaming, "Sub sandwiches! Sub sandwiches!" He struck me as totally different.

Manny Schreiber We made a load of money and almost flunked out of school because people were staying up late studying and we sold as many as we could buy.

Ira Landess From the moment I saw this strange-looking guy selling the sub sandwiches, he was battling an illness. His whole life was manic. My first memory of hooking up with Abbie is at the racetrack at Suffolk Downs where he saw that we both loved playing horses. We'd go to the track pretty often. He needed the action very, very badly, really to stay alive.

Abbie Hoffman *(interviewed by Barry Shapiro)* There was a phase in my life where I gambled a lot. When you gamble for more than you can afford you quickly learn that money's shit. Just a prop in the game.

Ira Landess If you're into any addiction, drugs, gambling, what you are trying to do when you go to the racetrack to get a winner is power yourself out of the depression and jump into elation. That will lead to a mania. Throughout his life, I never knew Abbie when he wasn't gambling big.

Likewise with sex. I'll never forget this. This was in the summer of 1960, Newport Folk Festival. People were camping out all over the place. I remember Odetta was there. We were wandering around in between sleeping bags and Abbie says, "Hang on a second, be with you in a little while." He sees some girl in a sleeping bag, gives her one of his giggles, says, "Can I get in there with you?" and he banged her right there. He did enormous amounts of fucking at Brandeis.

Manny Schreiber He fucked my girlfriend when I was away. Everyone was fucking everyone then but Abbie was very persistent. I could count four women who said he was amazingly persistent to the point of wearing them down, way beyond other people, charming and winsome and persistent way into the night, whereas someone with less energy to do it would have said, "Eh, enough of this, so long." He used to go around just propositioning people, "Do you wanna fuck? Wanna fuck?"

Abbie settled into a relationship with a fellow undergraduate, Sheila Karklin.

Ira Landess Sheila was a sweetie pie at Brandeis. She was very alluring, gorgeous eyes. Sheila was the personification of a bohemian. It was a big thing for Abbie to commit himself to whatever extent he did to just one woman. I guess what anybody would remember in looking back was the tempestuous nature of their relationship. Automatically I think of Sheila storming up the aisle in the Student Union and in a rage, throwing a glass of water at Abbie. Which was just typical in their relationship.

From the *Worcester Daily Gazette,* 4/23/58

NAMED TO DEAN'S LIST

Abbie Hoffman, son of Mr. and Mrs. John Hoffman of 6 Ruth St., has been named to the dean's list at Brandeis University for the last semester.

From the *Worcester Daily Telegram,* 4/28/59

2 CITY STUDENTS CANDIDATES FOR BRANDEIS DEGREE

. . . Hoffman is a psychology major. He is president of the Psychology Club, captain of the tennis team, chairman of the Student Athletic Committee and an editorial board member of the humor magazine.

Ira Landess At Brandeis Abbie was just a guy who fucked around, made money, played pool, got laid, was into scams. And then he went to Berkeley and that's where he really got politicized.

FALL 1959

Abbie Hoffman *(interviewed by Barry Shapiro)* Why graduate school? I'd never been to California. What are you supposed to do—work? You get accepted so you go.

Marty Kenner I was a freshman at Berkeley and I really wanted to drop out and Abbie was always trying to convince me to stay in school, 'cause he was serious about anything he did and he was a good student. But he did a lot of crazy things. Abbie went to the movies once and picked up a couple of fourteen-year-old girls, twin sisters. Abbie also would teach me to shoplift. He took a leather briefcase with a handle and flap over it to Lucky's Market down on Telegraph Avenue. He'd put a steak or two in his briefcase, and then he closed it and locked it and he said, "Listen, if they ask if they can inspect it just say it's locked and I don't have the key, so I can't put anything in it." Then he'd buy a couple of things. But they didn't ask about the briefcase and we took the steaks and went home and ate. Abbie loved the game of it.

But the main impression I have of Abbie was this passion he had for

Lenny Bruce. Also Abbie talked about his girlfriend, Sheila, and he didn't know what to do about that. I talked to him about politics. I was obsessed. I was truly shocked by the U-2 spy plane getting shot down over Russia, and the Cuba missile crisis stuff. I was crazed. I had a lot of passion. It's hard now that everybody knows about the CIA to understand the complete shock. There was this total sense of betrayal and this paranoia about the United States government and what it was doing abroad.

Abbie Hoffman *(from an interview in the* East Village Other, *5/14/69)* The first demonstration I went to was Caryl Chessman's execution in 1960. After having been on Death Row for twelve years, he was finally executed. We were outside San Quentin. Marlon Brando and Shirley MacLaine were there. Very nice picket signs and everybody was very nicely dressed. When it started to rain the warden came out and offered us coffee and doughnuts. You couldn't be pissed off at him. He was a very nice guy. And you really couldn't be pissed at Governor Pat Brown, the leading liberal in California at that time. He came out on the boob tube saying, "I am against capital punishment but in this case my hands are tied." On the way back to Berkeley everybody felt so glum. Nothing could be done.

Marty Kenner The intellectual ferment of Berkeley in '59–'60 was just fantastic. All these red-diaper babies, these former Young Communists. It began the second week we were there with a hunger strike on the steps of the administration building by the son of an air force officer who didn't want to participate in compulsory ROTC. And then in May of that same academic year, there were the HUAC riots.

The House Un-American Activities Committee came to San Francisco to expose union workers suspected of being communists. Public hearings were held in a second-floor chamber of City Hall.

Marshall Efron, *student at Berkeley* A lot of students are really pissed off. These are liberals, not commies or com-symps or subversives. Nothing's going on in the world, this is pre-Vietnam, this is pre-Kennedy. Some friendly people travel with the committee from city to city and they have the same bag of letters they dump on the table. It's all prearranged. And then they have the hostile witnesses who come up, take the Fifth Amendment and try to make a speech, they're gaveled to shut up and they're dragged off by the cops, cited for contempt of Congress. Invitations are sent to special people to attend the hearing, to the members of the Daughters of the American Revolution, the American Legion, the National Rifle Association, whatever. So it's all the same kind of people, people who never had a tan, people who don't know what a natural fiber is, they're more American than thou. If there ever was a fascist bunch, they're all there.

After several days of waiting for the few available seats, the students were finally ordered out.

Marshall Efron The cops say, "You're making a nuisance, disperse." The students didn't disperse. Then the cops came in with clubs and fire hoses and washed the people down the stairs, into the street. All of a sudden the issue changed from the House Un-American Activities Committee to police brutality. The police were goons. Every time the cops arrived in their crash helmets, "Here come the goons, they just sent the goon squad." This is way before they were pigs, they didn't get to be pigs till the middle sixties.

Abbie told me he was arrested. I don't think he was. But he said this was the watershed moment in his life, this radicalized him. This was the one thing that got him started. It was spectacular. I loved it! The water, the fire hoses, the goons. It was like a Costa-Gavras movie, fabulous!

* * *

Abbie Hoffman *(interviewed by Barry Shapiro)* I quit graduate school. I didn't dig it. And I knocked up Sheila. She came out to visit me one Christmas vacation.

Ira Landess When he came back, they got married. He told me it was because the rubber broke. Then he giggled.

JULY 17, 1960

Rabbi Joseph Klein I went to his wedding celebration. Even there he started an argument with me about the meaninglessness of Judaism. Everything that he could possibly say in a negative way about Judaism, he said.

Returning to Worcester, Abbie was in need of employment for the summer. Dick Lazarus, one of his Berkeley professors, wrote his colleague Don Broverman, who was at Clark University, who hired Abbie to help him gather data.

Don Broverman In 1960 I was a new staff psychologist at Worcester State Hospital. I started a research project testing members of the local Lutheran Church. Abbie was given a structured interview, a series of questions [to] ask these husbands and wives. Everything went too smoothly. I always wondered if he fudged the data a little bit.

Bob Baker, *professor of psychology, Clark University* He caused some considerable amount of vexation for the people at the hospital. Some of the people up there started to hear about Abbie identifying himself to people around the city as Dr. Hoffman, Clinical Psychologist.

Jack Hoffman Abbie used to have a softball game with the patients at Worcester State. He used to call me up to play because they didn't have enough players. He had this catatonic schizophrenic playing center field. He had all his patients out there playing softball, running backwards on the bases. You had to see this.

OCTOBER 1961

Don Broverman The following year he took up with another psychologist, a real one, Eli Sturm. They opened up the first art theater in Worcester.

Ron Siff Abbie had two people sometimes in his theater and I was both of them. I'll never forget one night, I was alone in the theater, watching *The Magnificent Seven.* And it was snowing out and at that time there was a trampoline place next door to the theater. I wasn't aware of this. And Abbie said, "Watch this," and he opened up the side door of the theater, walked down to the end of the aisle that was facing the side door, and he started to run like crazy out the door, jumps into the air and into a snowdrift. Of course, he knows the trampoline is there and he comes out of the snowdrift about ten feet, and I'm sitting inside with my eyes wide open.

But he was very discouraged with the theater, the fact that nobody turned out for it.

Bob Solari, *Worcester activist* H. Stuart Hughes was a Harvard professor of European cultural history and he was running for U.S. Senate. That was '62, when Kennedy was running and Cabot Lodge was running. Abbie was one of the main organizers of the campaign in Worcester. We'd go to meetings, and everybody would be talking about Abbie. It was Abbie was organizing this and getting these speakers and getting placards made and so forth.

Hal Gordon, *Worcester activist* Abbie held a meeting for people interested in the Stuart Hughes campaign and I showed up. Nobody else. I wasn't too impressed with Abbie at the time. He seemed like a wild-assed kid. He was a lot younger than I was and not too stable. But he was bright. I got involved with him because I was interested in the movement. Worcester was such a dull place. There was absolutely nothing happening. Abbie was the only one who had the time and the energy to do these things. He was the greatest kicker-offer there ever was. Never finished anything, but he did start a lot of things.

Don Broverman Abbie had some falling-out with Sheila, and decided it was time to leave Worcester. And he and Eli went to New York together to try to open up theaters down there.

FALL 1961

Ira Landess The Baronet and the Coronet were supposed to open up simultaneously but one of them opened up a half year ahead of the other. He was managing one of them. I remember the first movie that played was *The Loneliness of the Long Distance Runner* and there's Abbie in his tux, which is quite a sight to see. Abbie was a total movie freak. He was getting optimistic about where he could go in the Walter Reade Organization. When the second theater opened up he was assigned to manage both of them at no increase in salary. He was totally insulted and felt used. Abbie said "Fuck you" and went back to Worcester.

Florence Hoffman Abbie had to have a job. So John must have arranged a job with a medical company. But he never took much interest in it.

Haskell Morin They had a son, Andy, by then and then they had a daughter, Amy, and they bought a house on Hadwen Road. Abbie had a job as a sales rep with a drug company, Westwood Pharmaceuticals. In the morning he'd go out and talk to a few doctors and the rest of the day, he would just fill in his time sheet and say he was there but he never was there.

Abbie Hoffman *(from an interview in the* East Village Other, *5/14/69)* I had it all down to a science, working four hours a week, stealing like crazy by selling the samples and forging motel receipts. For that they paid me fifteen grand a year and I was mowing the lawn on weekends. But in between all that I devoted the major part of my time to organizing in the ghettos for SNCC. Sort of a schizophrenic, and after a while it got to me. I remember asking my boss, the regional sales manager, "Is this shit any good?" "It won't kill you" was his response. It sort of hit home.

Manny Schreiber He ended up with a lot of Keri lotion. But he was enthused with Father Gilgun.

John Schezinsky, *Worcester activist* Bernie Gilgun was involved with the Catholic Worker movement. Bernie was a great admirer of Martin Luther King and at some point took up his style of oratory. Abbie and him became almost like father and son. Abbie always kept referring to Bernie Gilgun as his rabbi.

Rabbi Joseph Klein While I may have admired the basic idea of trying to do something that was helpful, to blacks especially, I was disturbed that here was a young man, brought up in a Jewish home with a father who was a very positive Jew, who wouldn't lift a finger for anything that was Jewish, but who was breaking his back doing everything that he possibly could in a very loud, raucous way for blacks. Now, certainly I'm not a racist, I'm a life member of the NAACP. But there was a hostility, it seemed to me, toward Judaism.

Dan Dick, *Worcester activist* We had a storefront called the Phoenix started by a group of Catholics in Worcester who were looking for an intellectual and cultural meeting place. We would discuss civil rights, we would discuss birth control. We had a program committee and Abbie got on that very quickly. He would bring speakers—a professor from B.U., Howard Zinn, an economist from Harvard, Samuel Morse, people from New York that we would have no real way of contacting or knowing. He broadened our horizons. We were no longer quite so Worcester-oriented. Within a year Abbie was the program chairman.

Father Bernie Gilgun I met Abbie at the Phoenix. I was talking about housing in Worcester. I was under the impression that things were not as bad here as they were elsewhere. Abbie said he thought what I said was a lot of bullshit. He challenged me, and right away I said, "Show me." He showed me the slums of Worcester, and I became convinced that they were worse than I had been given the impression. I really didn't think that we had a major problem with police brutality but he thought we did and he came to convince me. Part of it was that it was going on across the country. He just knew that it must be here and he went looking for it.

APRIL 1962

D'Army Bailey was a student civil rights leader who was expelled from Southern University in Louisiana. The students from Clark University in Worcester raised money and brought D'Army up North on a scholarship. He soon returned to radical organizing and began the Worcester Student Movement.

D'Army Bailey Abbie came to us because we were the only game in town. We were organizing on the campus to go out and launch demonstrations in the city. Abbie was brash. We used to call him "Crazy." Affectionately. Abbie's philosophy was if you make up something and you tell it with enough sincerity, somebody's gonna believe it.

Burt Chandler Now, take my word for it—while the rest of the United States of America exploded in the sixties, nothing happened in Worcester except for Abbott Hoffman. His name would be in the paper and we would see him and Sheila and it was beginning to dawn on everybody, especially in the Jewish community, whose roots were with Abbott and his parents, that their son was beginning to be a little different from everybody else. The first thing that I recall was somebody told me that Abbott was picketing Wyman-Gordon's. And what for? Because they have no blacks except the elevator operator. I guess that's something we all knew but nobody in Worcester was doing anything about it.

D'Army Bailey Bob Stoddard was the head of the Wyman-Gordon Company and the national secretary of the John Birch Society, and he also owned the *Worcester Telegram and Gazette.* We met with Stoddard, me and Hank Chaiklin and Father Gilgun. We told Stoddard we wanted him to hire some blacks in upper-level jobs; they were all janitors. He said no. So we organized protests to picket the plant. We had a good, strong picket line; we must've had forty, fifty pickets.

Hank Chaiklin, *Worcester activist* When we were picketing, Abbie showed up with some literature he was handing out. He had these stories of discrimination at Wyman-Gordon about people we had never heard of. I remember saying to Abbie on the picket line, "Abbie, where did you learn about this? I've never heard of this." He said, "I made it up." I said, "But,

Abbie, this is horrible, this is not true." And he said, "It doesn't matter, it supports your position."

Since the picket line was blocking delivery trucks, the police decided to arrest some protesters.

D'Army Bailey I didn't want to get out of the picket line, so I beckoned Abbie over to me, but I couldn't get him over to that line. I was trying to tell him to go call the press, because if we were going to get arrested we wanted to have the media. But he seemed real timid about coming over to that picket line.

In his book he wrote that he climbed underneath a truck to block it. And that his father came down and was pleading with him to get out from under it. That's a bit of Hoffman embellishment. What happened was we had made a real tight line. And the truck that had attempted to back in was stopped. The black people had all stopped working and they were cheering, I guess, to see us arrested. So in this moment of drama, the sergeant said, "Look, I don't like this Stoddard son of a bitch either. He's no good to the working people and I don't want to send you people to jail. You've made your point, why don't you all back off so we don't have to arrest you?" And we let the trucks go in. No one was arrested. But it was so out of character that Abbie would not come over to that line. He never evidenced any hesitation about putting his body on the line. But I didn't know about the business relationship between Stoddard and his father.

Hank Chaiklin I remember him mentioning how this was gonna upset his father.

Dan Dick There's all of this male, Jewish, member-of-the-club stuff down at the Temple. I'm sure the rabbi practically excommunicated Abbie from the congregation. I don't think Abbie's father ever got over that sort of stuff.

Abbie Hoffman *(interviewed by Barry Shapiro)* My father would say, "You can't picket this company. They're our best customer." In my head it got very personal in terms of the kinds of decisions you made and the commitments you made with your life. It wasn't like doing it in the big city or doing it in the South. It's more than just the kind of thing of "Oh my parents don't understand what I'm doing." Not only didn't they understand, they could see it, I was down on the fucking corner.

Angela Dorenkamp, *Worcester activist* I guess his father was an assimilationist Jew. He was the head of the businessman's group, the Probus Club, but when Abbie was raising money for things, his father would get money from Probus to donate to some of these causes. So his father didn't approve of his politics but he would never reject Abbie. And his mother, of course, never.

Dan Dick Abbie was pulling us maybe faster than we were willing to go in challenging an institution. Abbie was way out in front of the front line lots of times, and some people were afraid to go out there naked with him. But Abbie was fearless.

Abbie Hoffman *(interviewed by Barry Shapiro)* In Worcester, I had the feeling that if I didn't do it, nobody's gonna. I did a civil rights newspaper where I wrote all the articles under different names so it wouldn't seem like I was doing it all. You got a sense of accomplishment, if I wake up this morning and lick all these stamps and send out this mailing, this is gonna change things right here and people are gonna come out and we're gonna march right here and this community organizing project is gonna happen and we're gonna confront the city council and it did work. I suppose you could go back to the same neighborhood and say this is the same fucking slum, what happened? White people ride on the turnpike, throw their garbage out the window, it lands on the heads of the spades in the ghetto living there. So somebody could develop a cynical attitude. The point was that I didn't at the time.

Father Bernie Gilgun Abbie spurred me. His enthusiasm, his passion for the unpleasant truth, his youth, he was very, very, very sharp. We would be together sometimes a whole evening and I would go home exhausted and go to sleep. A day or two later, I'd get a long letter clarifying [the] ideas of the evening. Just indefatigable. I think unquestionably the movement precept that moved him was loving the poor close-up. Abbie's father and Abbie both envisioned an integrated existence, but Abbie's father wanted to have society in consort with the rich people and the prominent. And Abbie wanted consort with the poor.

Burt Chandler Abbie went through a lot of causes very fast, from the fine arts to the blacks. Then when the blacks caught on, he came to the poor. I remember talking to him one day right around Thanksgiving time and there was an automobile dealer who was running a big newspaper series of ads. "Anybody who's poor comes down to our place, we give 'em a free turkey." Frankly, I thought that was a nice, decent thing to do. Abbie looked at me with a very straight face and said, "It's probably the worst thing that's ever happened to the poverty movement in this area. For one day, the poor are gonna forget they're poor. And that shouldn't happen." He suggested it was being done deliberately by the establishment.

There was a constable named Lenny Miller, a Jewish guy, who knew everybody in town. One day he came in absolutely outraged, and he said, "I had to serve some process on Abbott Hoffman. It's terrible. Everybody you know from the old country that came over here, they tried to better themselves. Where does Abbott live? He's moved back to the East Side! Not only is he back to the East Side but you go into his house, I can't even tell you what the house looked like. The place was a disgrace, I feel so badly for Johnny and his wife." Abbott said he deliberately moved back because he wants his children to be raised so they'll understand the struggle and the poverty. I thought about that for a long time.

Gloria Solari, *Worcester activist* A professor at Clark thought he was a provocateur. He said Abbie's working for the FBI. He was too energetic, he can't be real.

Father Bernie Gilgun Even though Abbie was so adept at keeping everybody together, when the Congress of Racial Equality began in Worcester, Ruby Jarrett, the founder of that, did not trust Abbie. She was convinced that he was a communist. I'm sure she had no idea what a communist was but she knew it was naughty.

Ruby Jarrett was a Chicago-based CORE leader who moved to Worcester with her family in 1964.

Ruby Jarrett I got to Worcester and nothing was happening. I started talking to people and they said, "Well, you got to meet Abbie Hoffman." I say, "Who's that?" They say, "Mr. Civil Rights." I liked Abbie right away. He had something that I didn't have, he had energy. He could go go go go. He had a sense of humor, except he took Abbie very seriously.

He immediately started to discuss ideology. I said, "Abbie, I ain't interested in that stuff. Our needs are very basic. How in the world can these middle-class kids here in Worcester, Massachusetts, understand the need for housing, education, shelter and jobs? His thing was to bring the establishment down and I said, "No, we want to get into the establishment."

Where I know I taught Abbie was when he started jumping on the *Worcester Telegram* because it was owned by one of the founders of the John

Birch Society. I said, "Man, you don't attack the press. Are you crazy! Start a love affair with the press. Don't try to make the press your adversary. Who the hell are you? They don't even want to try to break you, you're not that important." So I showed him what we could do. I said, "In order to deal with the press you've got to tell them the truth." Abbie used to lie. It sounds good—that was his attitude.

So I started calling the press and told them why we were in Worcester. I let them in on every doggone thing that we planned to do and I told them the truth. You have to be scrupulously honest or they're not gonna have anything to do with you. And you can't make it without the press, not in our movement. I said, "You've got this organization and you've got a mimeograph machine. How many leaflets can you turn out? The *Worcester Telegram* is a small paper, but it turns out 100,000 copies a day. You gonna turn out 100,000 copies of leaflets a day that nobody's gonna read anyway? They'll read the newspaper, right? So we've got to make the press our allies." At that time civil rights was big, big news. The people in the press loved us, we were copy, right? I could write a news release, go down to the *Telegram,* drop it on the city desk and they'd print it verbatim. He was astounded. "This is the way you do it, man."

Bob Zellner, *SNCC activist* I went to Huntington College in Montgomery, Alabama. Montgomery in the middle to late fifties was the civil rights hot spot in the United States. When I graduated I heard about a position with SNCC for a campus traveler to go to white campuses in the South. They were looking for a white southerner and there weren't a lot of applicants so I lucked out and got the job.

SNCC, the Student Nonviolent Coordinating Committee, was a loose, grassroots organization working among black people in the South, doing nonviolent actions such as sit-ins against segregated public facilities. By 1963 the emphasis of their work was registering voters.

Howard Zinn, *radical historian, SNCC adviser* What happened in '64 is the call for volunteers from the North. And it's mostly whites, mostly students who come down for the Freedom Summer. Some of the people in SNCC were worried about it. I was at meetings in Mississippi where the thing was being argued and [SNCC leader] Bob Moses enunciated his view in his usual very quiet way but it had a very powerful effect. He thought they should go ahead and do it. And so with the addition of the volunteers, SNCC became this huge group of mostly white people.

Bob Zellner I went full-time on the SNCC staff until 1963. The summer of '63 was brutal and I met a Brandeis student who told me about the graduate school there. I had to have some rest from the movement, so I went to Brandeis. My wife and I were both basically full-time movement people, so it was only natural that Dottie would open a fund-raising office for SNCC in Cambridge which became the main recruiting agency for the Northeast for the summer of '64. Abbie started coming over and he went through Dottie's meat grinder as a volunteer for the summer of '64. Abbie was rejected by Dottie. He demanded to know why and she said, "Well, I just think you're mentally unstable." He was in a complete snit. He said, "You can't keep me out of this." But he was a good soldier and he didn't go South in '64.

JUNE 1964

Howard Zinn While the volunteers were getting ready to go down to Mississippi, a busload of Mississippians came up to Washington, D.C., to plead with the federal government to send federal agents into Mississippi to protect them. They had a jury of citizens at the National Theater in Washington, D.C., Paul Goodman, Robert Coles, Joseph Heller, writers and artists and some actors. There were two kinds of testimony: one, black people testifying about the terror of Mississippi and appealing to the federal government to do something; the other testimony was from constitutional lawyers who testified to the constitutional power of the federal government to do something. All the testimony was transcribed, and delivered immediately to the White House. The federal government was being asked to send federal marshals, plainclothes people, into Mississippi to protect civil rights workers wherever they went. It wouldn't take much, it wouldn't take much at all. And there was no reaction. Not a word. Twelve days later Goodman, Schwerner and Chaney were killed in Philadelphia, Mississippi.

Bob Zellner That summer started out on a horrendous note for all of us because J. Edgar Hoover got on television and made it clear to everybody in the nation, including the Mississippi Klansmen, that the volunteers had no protection. He declared open season on the volunteers before they ever got there, and even though they're not usually as good as we give them credit for, I think the Klan timed it to kill somebody as soon as possible. All these volunteers who had been recruited around the country went to orientation in Oxford, Ohio. When Schwerner, Goodman and Chaney turned up missing during the weekend between the first session and the second session, I started my summer by going down to Nashoba County with Rita Schwerner, Mickey's wife, to see if we could glean any information whatsoever.

Zellner and Rita Schwerner were almost killed themselves in the course of trying to find the missing men. Contacts with the FBI, Governor Johnson of Mississippi, Governor Wallace, Acting Attorney General Katzenbach and even President Johnson were fruitless.

Bob Zellner They didn't find the bodies until sometime in July or August, I think. The murders had a chilling effect on all the volunteers who were down there. It certainly drove home one of the messages that SNCC was making at the orientation sessions all throughout the first week: that you don't go on this trip unless you're ready to die.

Ellen Maslow The SNCC leadership was mostly young black men. I was in absolute awe of them. There was the big bulletin board there about each project and who was getting shot; someone you just had lunch with is now arrested somewhere and everyone's running around trying to get him out of jail.

Ruby Jarrett CORE planned a national demonstration to bring to light the fact that the civil rights workers were being murdered in the South and the FBI wasn't giving them proper protection. So we devised our little plot. In Worcester we had a sit-in at the FBI office. Sheila goes in but Abbie wouldn't because he said he might want to run for political office someday and he didn't want to get arrested.

Bob Zellner That summer, some of the best minds in the country came down and taught in the Freedom Schools. There was tremendous political ferment with the local people organizing what became the Mississippi Freedom Democratic Party. It broke the back of the fear in the black community—that's why *Mississippi Burning* is such a disservice as a movie. If you didn't know anything about the civil rights movement and you looked at that movie, you'd think that the black community was totally ineffective, completely cowered and in terrible shape. The fact is that they were showing tremendous courage and ingenuity in fighting this monster.

Ruby Jarrett At the end of that summer, the CORE chapter went to Atlantic City to the Democratic convention with Abbie. We went for the challenge by the Mississippi Freedom Party.

ABBIE, FIRST WIFE SHEILA AND CHILDREN AMY AND ANDREW IN WORCESTER.
THE FAMILY THAT PROTESTED TOGETHER DIDN'T STAY TOGETHER. *Worcester Telegram*

Abbie Hoffman *(from an interview in the* East Village Other, *5/14/69)* I remember going in 1964 to the Democratic convention in Atlantic City. We were involved with the Mississippi Freedom Democratic Party challenge. All the liberals came out singing. "We Shall Overcome" was number one on the Hit Parade on the boardwalk. They put on all the buttons and gave us money. We were the heroes of the convention. Then Johnson called up from the ranch and said, "Hubie, you get them niggers in the back of the bus and get them to shut up. The kids from the boardwalk you send home to take baths or *else* you don't get to be the vice president." Then they started to twist arms and when you got inside the convention hall all the buttons disappeared and they stopped singing the songs. When you asked what's going on they said, "Well, we are with you, but in this case our hands are tied." Right after Atlantic City, we dropped the facade of working in terms of appealing to the country's conscience. That, at least for me, was the turning point.

* * *

Susan Carey Abbie and Sheila's relationship was not great. They fought a lot. And Sheila was organizing. She was very involved and very active.

Angela Dorenkamp I don't doubt that Abbie may have felt competitive about Sheila because he was competitive about everything. His metaphor was game, playing, winning.

Dan Dick Sheila knew that she was gonna have to cover her bets. She went to the state college at the bottom of the hill to get her teaching degree.

Jack Hoffman She was constantly criticizing him, constantly. She was a real fucking picker-onner. My fucking brother hated her guts. She made his fucking life miserable.

Susan Carey She definitely wasn't a housekeeper. And that was a bone of contention between them. I remember going in their house and seeing boxes of socks because she didn't do the laundry. I think that she totally loved him. But Abbie needed so much attention that I don't think Sheila got a lot of attention.

John Sechinsky I think of Sheila as almost always being with the children. On one level that's what permitted Abbie to pursue his values. I would rarely see Abbie with the family.

Jack Hoffman He just couldn't spend the time with those kids and be on some demonstration or in some fucking jail. I think my brother was a lot like my father too: he had a difficult time showing emotion.

Ruby Jarrett Sheila idolized Abbie. He was her life, he was the one that did the things. Then Sheila read Betty Friedan. *The Feminine Mystique.* She became a raving feminist, almost overnight. I was up at their house once and her and Abbie got into this argument. Now, previously, if Abbie would say something, Sheila would do a "my hero" type thing. "Ssshhh, Abbie's speaking." It was so cute. That night, he told her she didn't know what she was talking about and she said to him, "Abbie, if I listened to you, I wouldn't think I had brains enough to get out of bed in the morning."

Dan Dick Sheila was the one who really introduced women's liberation at the Phoenix. She put together a panel of local people in 1965 and they began to discuss birth control and the right of a woman to the mastery of her own body. It was pretty shocking stuff. Together Abbie and Sheila turned a good part of this city upside down.

* * *

Ron Siff One night Abbie and I took a ride, got a hot dog at Hot Dog Annie's out in Leicester, and we went down to park near the reservoir to talk and he says, "Ron, I'm going down to Mississippi. I don't know what's going to happen to me but I have to do it." This was a result of a lot of conversations we had about what was wrong with the world. He says, "I've got to go down. I can't be quiet anymore." I said, "Boy, I wish I had the courage to do that."

In August of 1965 Abbie left Worcester for a two-week stay in Mississippi.

Ira Landess The main thing we did in 1965 was a Head Start program but we wanted to keep the Freedom School going as well and Abbie came down and taught. He was fabulous, the kids just loved him to death.

Jerome Washington I was working for SNCC in a place just outside of Luxor, Mississippi. We were having a real hard time trying to get people out to register to vote. They were scared. I can understand that. We're only gonna be here for a while and leave and they're gonna stay. Three of us were staying in a little shack that this preacher had. During the day the state troopers and the cops would be harassing us and during the night it would be the Klan. You really couldn't go anyplace. Then we got the word that the Klan were coming.

So we left that shack and got in the chicken coop. We was hiding there when they shotgunned the shack full of holes, then burnt it down. So we got out the chicken coop and walked four miles to Biloxi. [In] Biloxi, this woman put us up in her cellar. We called somebody to come get us 'cause we had to get the hell out of there. Early the next morning we got a call, told us that this crazy white boy is coming down to get you. We were still hanging out at this woman's house, and a guy came and he took us to another place, an old garage. So we get more and more paranoid, like hey, you're gonna take us to an old garage and tell the Klan we're there? So when we got there, instead of staying inside the garage, we went across the road and were laying flat on the ground, watching the garage.

Here comes this car down this road. Swings around, goes past the garage, makes the U-turn, goes right to the front of the garage, the lights on, honks the horn, *bam, bam, bam, bam.* And we said, "What the fuck is going on here?" This guy *is* nuts. He starts looking in the garage, yelling, "Where you guys at? I'm from SNCC." So we came across the road and we ask him, "Who are you?" He says, "It's all right, man. I'm Abbie, I'm Abbie." We get in the car, he hits the gas and *brrrrrrm,* the wheels turn, and he takes off. He starts turning off the highway. He drove all these back roads at night. He drove his ass off, scaring the shit out of us.

My first impression was that they were right—this crazy white boy's coming to get you. And the second impression, here was a guy who was really letting the shit hang out on the line. It wasn't like he was gonna try to play it safe to save his ass. He was there to do a job and he was gonna get us out. I would've done it in a more subtle safe way. When we got to Jackson, the car looked like it had been through the swamps. It had mud and dirt all over it. He said he had learned from moonshiners what roads to take to avoid the police.

Ellen Maslow Down South, Abbie and I had our adventures. We had Fannie Lou Hamer in the car with us. The cops stopped us and she had to hide in the backseat. It was just terrifying. We had a few close calls, Abbie and I. We traveled back and forth many, many times 'cause once we hooked up with Jesse [Morris, SNCC field director], we created the Poor People's Corporation, a statewide network of craft cooperatives of the most brilliant, simple economic design.

Years later one of his black women in Mississippi said, "Oh yeah, I remember you. You were the little girl with those tight jeans on." We were running around down there so oblivious to the people, oblivious to the culture, so caught up in our excitement that we were doing good stuff. With all the good works, what this woman remembered is I was this little twat running around shocking them in these pants.

Ira Landess Abbie came onto the scene in the South when it had its death throes. Yet still there must have been something spiritual about it for him. I had to deal with a certain despondency about how different it was between the first and the second year. The first year wherever you walked, some black would come off the porch and say, "Hi, Freedom." Everybody's name was Freedom. In 1964 when I was bringing a carload of people down to the courthouse to register, out front was a white Caddy. A big, big guy sitting in the Caddy calls me over, announces his name, says, "I'm the head of the Klan around here. Take a look at what I got in my lap." It was a pistol. He says, "I just want to talk with you though. What the hell are you doing down here with all the trouble you got up North?" I don't remember what answer I gave him but I know what I was thinking, which is that something can happen here that can't happen up North right now and this thing that can happen here can change this country forever. In 1965 I'm sitting there thinking, I better go back North, that guy's right. Nothing's happening here that's going to matter anymore.

Letter to the Editor, *Worcester Gazette*, 8/12/65

To the Editor:

Entering Mississippi is a strange experience that affects you as soon as you cross the state line. Immediately you see a huge billboard that says "Welcome to Mississippi—the Hospitality State." Twenty yards down the road you see a second billboard that says "Martin Luther King is a Communist." You know right away they didn't mean you in that welcome . . .

In the mornings I teach at the Freedom School . . . This afternoon I marched with some local maids and civil rights workers. We picketed an inn. Previously the maids struck for higher pay. They earn 39 cents per hour and most are the chief breadwinners in the family. It is the first strike ever to take place in McComb for anything, and was completely the maids' idea. The picketing was tense, with a large crowd watching. There were no incidents.

We are working on a book composed of local Negroes relating their experiences in McComb. The stories are incredible: Lynchings, shootings in broad daylight, total economic bondage, superhuman bravery on the part of those who have protested. You almost feel they are all made up, that these things just never took place. But then you remember the intense hate you could read in the eyes of the whites, and you know it happened—all of it.

ABBOTT HOFFMAN
65 Hadwen Road, Worcester
(702 Wall St., McComb, Miss.)

* * *

Ron Siff Abbie came back from the South a little more directed and more dedicated. He was going to get his point out to the world.

Ruby Jarrett I think I did get it across to Abbie that a black army don't need no white general, right? I said, "This is the civil rights movement. Even though it's an integrated movement, Abbie, there is no way for you to lead black people, it just can't happen." CORE was getting bigger and more publicity and he was no longer Mr. Civil Rights.

From the *Worcester Gazette,* 10/15/65

GOOD EVENING

By Julian F. Grow

The following are Abbott Hoffman's replies to questions about Worcester Friends of the Student Nonviolent Coordinating Committee and its aims:

If the movement has gone so far as it can toward civil rights laws, and that hasn't proven to be enough—what then?

"We're going to have to get into the poverty fight, for if you're talking about Negroes as a race, you're talking about poor people. We are going to insist on a strong voice of and for the poor in the poverty program. And we are going to be more and more involved in the campaign for peace. We are in Viet Nam. Why?"

Hank Chaiklin Worcester was a pretty conservative city, a hostile environment [in which] to oppose the war. People got beat up, stones and eggs and cigarettes were thrown at us when we demonstrated.

Susan Carey Marty and I were experimenting with drugs at that time and we were bored to tears living in Worcester because there were very few people who were really pushing boundaries at all. Then Abbie started to take drugs, and Sheila wasn't. I remember Sheila being angry. So he needed someone to hang out with and we were perfect because we were right at the same place he was. Just starting, and having a lot of fun. I remember seeing him a lot, during the day, so I know that he wasn't working.

Manny Schreiber Ira Landess and my girlfriend Anne and I went up to Worcester to visit with Abbie and to trip together.

Ira Landess Manny brought acid. I had agreed to chaperon them through this trip. I was supposed to stay clean. For most of the time I did, and I was taking notes in one of those little four-ring loose-leafs and Abbie takes it and writes in it too. And he pinches his finger in one of the rings and goes into a psychedelic agony and then writes down in the book, "I got burned on the silver rim of space." Meantime, he's trying to get out and I'm running after him, literally tackling him. He diverts me. I run out and I cannot find him and he comes back in an hour with deli sandwiches for everybody. He said he had gone bowling. That was Abbie's first trip. I remember him curling up in a window thing and talking to God, like a Lenny Bruce thing.

Abbie Hoffman *(interviewed by Elli Wohlgelernter)* I had strong hallucinations that lasted, God, eight, ten hours. Even while all this wild imagery is flying around in my head, in a very nice setting with friends who had experience with the drug, there's something nomadic in me that just doesn't want to sit and meditate for eight hours on all these thoughts that are flying by, and I got out, started roaming the city on my own. I still had enough in me to check my watch and show up at some church and give a speech on civil rights while I'm definitely under the influence.

Ira Landess I don't know what acid did to Abbie but he took a hell of a lot of it.

Susan Carey Around that time Marty and I did this antiwar happening at Clark.

Marty Carey Susan was dressed as a nun, and me and two other friends who came up from New York were dressed as priests, wearing Kiss-type makeup. There were erotic films and bombs and tapes. And then Bernie Gilgun came out at the end and said Jesus Christ was a revolutionary. People were really pissed off 'cause it was psychedelic and X-rated.

Burt Chandler There were four or five of us over my house one night and we got into an argument over the significance of the happening. So I said, "What are we arguing about, let's get Abbie over." He came over with Jan Selby and three or four priests. Must have been ten at night. We're in the recreation room of my house, my two little kids have toy guns all over the place. Abbie comes in, walks down to the recreation room, turns out all the lights, and all of his party exhibited green-glowing Batman rings or some doggone thing. Turns on the lights, sees all the guns, he destroys all my kids' guns 'cause they're instruments of war and one should not have war instruments for little kids. He didn't leave till three in the morning. We had to give him a ride home. Before we saw him again, we were all saying it wasn't quite right, something was wrong there and somebody said it was almost as though Abbie had drugs. So we became aware he had advanced a little further along the line.

* * *

Elaine Edinburgh I was at Classical High School in tenth grade. I went down and volunteered to person the [SNCC] store after school. And there was Abbie Hoffman. He could barely interview me. "What's your name? What afternoons can you work? Fine. Go." He's off raising money, totally manic.

He talked a lot about going to New York for these meetings and this movement was real important and he had to do all this stuff. I'd be really happy if we raised fifty dollars or I got a really big donation but it was brushed off. There was always this quest of more, more, more, more.

Ira Landess Nineteen sixty-six he finally breaks up with Sheila. They were polar opposites. He succeeded in enraging her to the point of frequent physicality, she would have to lash out at him, throw something at him. And he was simultaneously very attached to her and would get very morose about the idea of losing her.

Abbie Hoffman *(interviewed by Barry Shapiro)* I got married because I knocked up a girl. That was the fifties. Find 'em, feel 'em, fuck 'em, forget 'em. The four Fs. You might toy with the idea of an abortion, but then it was pretty scary. So I got married early and had kids early for my peer group. That was a violation of the rules. You don't have kids till you have two feet firmly on the ground, right. And a divorce for me, being Jewish, was frowned on. I had a value system that I was breaking a number of times.

FALL 1966

Bob Weihrauch Abbie came in to visit with me when I returned to Worcester from practicing law in Boston. He tried out certain things on me that he was planning to do. I don't know whether you recall this, during Johnson's great War on Poverty, they were busing people within the city to the poor areas of the city so they could observe poverty. Abbie thought the whole concept was ridiculous and organized a busing of the poor people of Worcester through Westwood Hills and Salisbury Street so they could observe the wealth that existed in the city.

Then Sheila and he came to me together for a divorce. I told them that I couldn't represent both of them. I recommended several people to Sheila and one was Seymour Weinstein. I did know from Abbie that he was jealous of Sheila's success and recognition in SNCC. If she'd been the male, she would've been the leader. I think, with respect to the divorce, the only comment he ever made to me is that he always considered Sheila better qualified to make a living than he was. I have no idea how he reached that conclusion.

From the *Worcester Gazette*, 8/16/66

CITY MAN NAMED SALES HEAD

> Abbott Hoffman, chairman of Worcester Friends of the Student Nonviolent Coordinating Committee, has been appointed national sales director of the Poor People's Corporation in New York City. He will begin his new duties in mid-September. The corporation, created last summer, is composed of 15 worker-owned cooperatives in Mississippi. Hoffman said the co-ops have trained 350 Negroes in a variety of handicrafts and that top priority has been given Negroes who have lost their jobs because they attempted to register to vote.

Gloria Solari Abbie told me Worcester wasn't big enough for him. He says, "You know, Gloria, I'm going on to New York. You watch, I'm going to be into some real big things."

Seymour Weinstein represented Sheila in the divorce case.

Seymour Weinstein She filed at the beginning of October 1966. Abbott had indicated that he no longer wished to remain married to her. She wanted to be sure that he had no more interest in her and we did have a meeting in approximately the third week of September 1966. Abbott was present with his attorney. Abbott at that point was indicating that his job was virtually a volunteer job. In fact, his wife had serious doubts that his pay was as low as he claimed but she also believed that Abbott would never accurately disclose this information, he was [living] out of state, and as a result of that meeting, she did want to move quickly with the divorce.

Abbie and Sheila entered into an agreement that included some alimony, child support, and visitations. The divorce was granted on November 4, 1966

Seymour Weinstein Sheila was the person who introduced him into the movement involving the rights of the poor and of the black people. It was her view at that time that his response was not sincere, that it was an effort at a new career direction and that he felt there was a void there for leadership and an opportunity to exploit the situation. Abbie was a newcomer. She was the radical. She felt one of the reasons that Abbie wanted to leave her was that he was more caught up in this movement. It required him being in New York, and he didn't want her and the family in New York.

Looking back, I would say Sheila and Abbie represented perfect balance. She had a commitment and a seriousness and a devotion to work at things he could get a lot of publicity out of. And she probably would have been very good for him in this movement. And he wanted his freedom. How do you avoid that?

Dan Dick Abbie had a birthday party when he turned thirty, at one of those social clubs. Somebody asked Abbie's father to say a few words and he said, "I don't know my son Abbott all that well, that's why I call him Abbott." That's all he said. This'll give you some idea of what a lot of us thought about Abbie. A doctor's wife was very good with her hands and I had her make a crown of thorns and I put it on his head. I don't know as Abbie understood what we were doing, but number one, we knew that Abbie was a certain special kind of person, and number two, chances are if he continued he might have a similar ending.

Chapter Three

IT'S ALL FREE

Bill Kunstler, *civil rights attorney* I first met Abbie here in New York City when he started Liberty House, because my first wife, Lotte, was working for Ellen Maslow.

Ellen Maslow Abbie started calling me from New York to come and do the store with him. He said his mother gave him money to fix his teeth and he used it to get this storefront on Bleecker Street.

Bill Kunstler The purpose of Liberty House was to sell products made by poor black women in the black areas of Mississippi, who couldn't sell them there.

Ellen Maslow He said, "It's Christmas, I'm selling rocks, garbage, anything." People will buy it 'cause it was the heyday of civil rights.

Terri Priest, *Worcester activist* During the summer of 1966 we raised $900 and I took it to Abbie in New York so he could use it for the Poor People's Co-op. He brought me to his apartment on Avenue A and we had to walk through four or five inches of cut glass along the sidewalk to get there. His apartment was a real pit. When I got back to Worcester, there was a letter waiting.

> *I'm all alone here, alone . . . The other night I couldn't sleep so I watched the streets. A Puerto Rican family came scurrying up the street, a man and a wife with two children, searching the rubbish piles and filling their shopping bags while keeping an eye out for the cops. There is a heroin pusher and the addicts shiver their way to his doorway all night and I can hear the rats in the partitions and a W. C. Fields looking guard says "Macy's don't give nothing away free kid."*

'Cause he used to pick up the discards and bring them to the Poor People's Co-op and give them to people who didn't have furniture and this one night he went to Macy's and they used to put out a lot of old furniture and evidently the police ran him out.

These are the kinds of letters he sent. They scared me, they made me cry, they made me get angry at the people who didn't understand the pain that many of us were going through because of the Vietnam War and the many other inequities we saw.

Ellen Maslow When I was still at Brandeis and he started Liberty House, he was working his ass off. But he was not big on commitment, he was not big on continuity or sensitivity to anyone's feelings. He would just take off like a firefly. We were comrades, we were buddies. But we were never friends. I can't imagine being friends.

Jim Fouratt, *Lower East Side activist* That was a period when whites were being thrown out of the black movement. It had a lot to do with the black women feeling that the white women were there to fuck the black men.

Tom Hayden, *SDS and civil rights leader and antiwar activist* White society had been unable to accommodate black revolt. Black organizations had become legitimately tired of white leadership. Jewish organizations are not run by gentiles, Protestant organizations are not run by Catholics, and yet there was this uproar over the issue that blacks should run black organizations. In plain fact, for like thirty years, whites had been very influential in black organizations, like a neocolonial residue in American history, and to change it took a revolt. A lot of people's feelings were hurt because they had given of their time, lives, their blood, their careers. It was very, very unpleasant. And Abbie was adrift.

Abbie Hoffman *(interviewed by Barry Shapiro)* I took it all personally, I'm doing my schtick. I said, "I know Stokely. What do you mean you don't trust me? Fuck you." I was saying, "What do you mean white people are bad? I'm white and I'm not bad."

From the *Village Voice*, 12/15/66

THE PRESS OF FREEDOM

SNCC: THE DESECRATION OF A DELAYED DREAM

By Abbie Hoffman

> . . . I never really understood what it meant to be in SNCC or out of SNCC because it was more a way of life than a membership thing. Now I'm out and I'm mad. It's the kind of anger one might feel in, say, a love relationship, when after entering honestly you find that your loved one's been balling with someone else, and what's worse, enjoying it . . .
>
> I feel for the other whites in SNCC, especially the white females. I identify with all those Bronx chippies that are getting conned out of their bodies and bread by some dark-skinned sharpie over at the Annex . . .
>
> Frankly, I am interested in fundamental changes in American society, in building a system on love, trust, brotherhood, and all the other beautiful things we sang about. Trust is a sharing thing and as long as Stokely says he doesn't trust white people I personally can't trust him. It doesn't matter how beautiful he thinks I am.

Bob Zellner I said to myself, "If I could get a hold of you, Abbie, I would shake you until your teeth rattled." First of all, he didn't do as much for SNCC as the legend has it, and secondly, if he had been that intimately involved in SNCC, he would have known not to do an article saying how mean it was for SNCC to kick him out.

There was no danger of SNCC "being taken over by white people" for one very simple reason—any white person in SNCC who had any influence or power whatsoever had it precisely because he understood that the leadership was in the hands of very capable black people. I never had any formal positions. You had influence and power in SNCC because of what you did, basically.

So there was no need from that point of view to become an all-black organization, and when that happened, it was the last straw for a lot of people supporting SNCC who were maybe looking for a way out anyway.

Ira Landess I remember having tremendous empathy for what Abbie was writing. Talk about peak experiences, that first year in Mississippi I felt that this was the most important thing I'd ever done in my life. The plan was the next year to take the one thousand people and make them ten thousand people through five states and I still believe to this day that if that ever happened we'd be living in a very different country than the country we're living in now. Abbie steered me onto this book, *The True Believer,* by Eric Hoffer, who said all these movements die from within. That wing of the movement that wanted to move on and have ten thousand volunteers in five states was decimated by the let's-get-the-whites-out-of-here. Stokely Carmichael.

Howard Zinn Abbie called me for advice. He got a reaction from that first article from Ivanhoe Donaldson which really worried him. Ivanhoe Donaldson was one of the poor people in SNCC, a colorful character, an intelligent guy, just wild enough to be threatening. I told him I know Ivanhoe, he's not as bad as he sounds, he's not gonna kill you. But if you'll feel better staying out of things for a while, go ahead.

Susan Carey He hid at our apartment for three days.

Jeremy Larner When the *Voice* piece came out, Abbie caught a lot of flak from the Village Left, especially from those who got their rocks off on Stokely and Rap Brown and their white counterparts, who had no commitment to the process of politics and were a tremendous gift to the Richard Nixons and Ronald Reagans of America.

To me, that *Voice* piece was a real turning point for Abbie. From then on, he seemed to make a point of never criticizing anyone on the Left.

Paul McIsaac, *Lower East Side activist* Stokely told Abbie to sell the store and get into it. The war was reaching that point where it had to be responded to.

Robin Palmer, *antiwar activist, revolutionary communist* There was this real con job that Lyndon Johnson did on the American people, him being in the vanguard of the civil rights movement, better than Kennedy. He gets up in Congress and says, "We shall overcome." No president had ever done that. I was listening to that speech in my car and I stopped at Eighth Avenue and 42nd Street in New York City and I got out and started cheering, "You fucking LBJ, you great motherfucker. I'm proud to be an

American." Within months I would have proudly put a stake in his chest because of Vietnam.

* * *

Ellen Maslow I remember when Anita walked in Liberty House. Abbie sized her up. "Her father owns a fabric factory, we could really get some shit out of this one."

Anita Hoffman, *Abbie's second wife* I had quit a job at the Civil Liberties Union because I felt they wouldn't promote me because of sexism. Liberty House needed volunteers so I signed up. I was pretty straight. But I was getting politicized by reading the *Times* between the lines. I had a master's and I was gonna go for my Ph.D. in psychology but I dropped out because I was upset about the war. I was not a movement person. But Ellen was very sweet. I thought, "Oh God, they'll actually accept me as a volunteer."

So the first day I go, it was this rainy day. I had this little short haircut, I'm wearing a miniskirt. I see the store is empty and there's only this guy, the store's founder, like this is all I need. The door was even locked. It was very romantic. He's sweet, he's hopping around to the cash register, tacking up quilts, doing all these little shopkeepy things as we talk. He mentioned he had a master's degree in psychology too and that he had gone to Brandeis. Then it just melted away, we had something in common. He did toss a little acid to me. There were two main songs that were playing in the background that whole day. I remember "Penny Lane" and it might've been "Lucy in the Sky."

We made a date for that night. Abbie shows up at my apartment dressed in his brown corduroy Levi's. And he's got this little paper bag which contains his food. I learned that's what movement people do. You don't want to impose on your host who's as poor as you, so you bring your own food. I put on the *Revolver* album. I remember him telling me, maybe even as we danced, that Mao wrote poetry and there weren't hungry people in China.

Abbie spent the night there, and the evening with him was so powerful. It was like this was it. I had had sexual experience but this was fireworks. I don't think I knew if I would ever see him again. I wasn't sweating it, it was just like I was coming out of this overwhelming experience. From then on

I guess I saw him every day. What I learned later was that he was spending every night at the home of a different volunteer from Liberty House.

Susan Carey God, he was totally in love. This was the one. First of all, she looked totally different from everybody else. Anita looked like a witch. Anita had real style. She was so dramatic-looking.

Truusje Kushner, *Anita's younger sister* My sister was this very straight girl who'd gone to Goucher College, who had been brilliant and gotten all these great grades and wore circle pins and round collar shirts, McMullen blouses, right? I think he offered her an alternate way to live, that just said "Fuck you" to everything that she didn't want to have to deal with. The two of them were soulmates.

She had to have my parents meet him. So she brought him to the Metropolitan Opera for the evening. My parents had season tickets. Abbie wore this totally crumpled suit, with a white shirt that had not been starched but which was buttoned up and some kind of hideous tie. He wore his hair in a ponytail, which at that time was just like the worst thing that a human being could do—if he was male. My parents took one look at him and my father was heartbroken, because he realized my sister was really in love with this person. My father was a vice-president of a company that had offices on Fifth Avenue that made thread. And he was wonderful, sweet, intellectual, a really good guy. But nonetheless, he was rather appalled by Abbie. I think my mother was equally appalled but ultimately they became terrific friends. Basically their reaction then was "Live with him but don't marry him."

Anita Hoffman When I first met him he really was unconventional. He never did anything because it was expected, including brushing his teeth. So then I stopped brushing my teeth, and then my teeth got fuzzy and I started brushing them again. He probably started brushing at some point, I don't know.

John Eskow, *Lower East Side friend* One of the first conversations I ever had with him, he said he hated hippies. And proof to him of the corrupt nature of what he kept calling hippie capitalism was that the Jefferson Airplane at that time had a radio commercial for Levi's. Abbie said, "Don't they know that the Levi's workers are on strike in North Carolina? They're fucking, they're taking acid. But their brothers and sisters are on strike, so fuck 'em." And he had completely written off the whole hippie world as being a diversion. Literally the next time I saw him, which was about a month later, he was stoned on acid, his hair was up to the ceiling, he was listening to the Grateful Dead.

Anita Hoffman When we were at Liberty House still, Abbie used to see these kids parading through the Village in these costumes or with face paint and he said, "I think there's something there." I can remember him actually saying he wanted to combine the hippie with the political.

Grace Slick, *lead singer, Jefferson Airplane* We were the first, and I think still to this day, the best educated generation in the history of man. Since we had gone to college we had a chance to compare Paris at the turn of the century, say, with what our parents were doing. And what our parents were doing just seemed like nothingness, a ticket to limbo.

Tuli Kupferberg, *beat poet, member of the Fugs* The Lower East Side was a place where anyone young and looking for the artistic life would look for rooms. Allen Ginsberg was there already; I had lived there for over ten years.

Rudi Stern, *artist* The Lower East Side felt like an eternal spring. Everything was fresh, everything felt like the first time. People trusted each other, there was great kindness among people, great sharing, violence felt unknown. Everything was possible. It was a time of collaboration of people, and fusion of ideas and cultures and wonderful experiences with LSD that just seemed to open up more and more channels, and it feels so far away from this moment that it's hard to conceive of it as the same lifetime even though it's only thirty years.

Tim Leary Dozens of sociological, historical vectors were coming together. Mass communications and the mass availability of the drugs, due to jet planes taking the mushrooms up from Mexico and grass and, of course, the synthesis of LSD.

The psilocybin experience you're floating around, like in a glider or a balloon over the world, you look down and see the cities and towns, the stretches of your normal life and you can gently transcend them and you're a changed person. But the full-blown, full-tilt LSD experience just whirled you and accelerated your brain process so that literally hundreds of thousands of neurological realities will be flashing through and it's very, very confusing, particularly when you take it in a situation where people are performing normally. I remember walking around my house and there's my son and daughter watching television and it almost seemed plausible that out of the millions of things going on that I'd be in this temporary structural form called the family that was obviously not gonna last for more than a year or two anyway.

Allen Ginsberg, *beat poet, activist* Acid was one of the main catalysts, the deconditioning agent that got people into another real world, into the flower-power, the psychedelic thing connected with the antiwar movement.

The government had been experimenting with acid from the fifties. But the government had given it to so many people that they all picked up on it and were making their own. When Leary came to New York in 1960 to talk about acid politics, his big question was "Since you've had experience with drugs since the forties or fifties, should we do as Aldous Huxley says and keep it secret and have an hermetic, inner group, or should we democratize?" And I said democratize, otherwise it'll lead to powerheads giving it out and saying, "It's *my* power." So actually, Leary played a tremendous role—not an entirely clean one but not a dishonorable one. Some "professionals" think that Leary spooked the scene and brought too much attention down by attempting to democratize it too fast.

Abbie Hoffman *(interviewed by Barry Shapiro)* Everyone should try acid once, I guess. Did it change my life? Yeah. It's the whole chicken and the egg thing. The whole thing is overcoming all that fear. In other words, the acid taking is more important than the experience itself. The whole secret is to overcome the fear of death. All the rest is easy.

Anita Hoffman The first time Abbie and I took acid was in the Careys' house. Then we walked back through the Lower East Side to my apartment. We passed a tenement building on fire with firemen putting it out. Abbie said, "See, that's part of reality too. It isn't all just flowers and pretty hallucinations."

Because he was tied into social justice and the real world, because he wasn't just a mystic about to fly off, things happened and he responded to the regular world and those became very deep and heavy experiences. We took acid as a sacrament and as a celebration.

John Eskow We would be sitting there in Marty Carey's apartment tripping on acid. Somewhere in the back Moby Grape would be playing, but unlike most people of the era we weren't like saying, "Oh, dig what the bass is doing." Maybe I was, but if I did Abbie was ignoring me because he was talking about Mao and Che and whether violence should be used in the revolution. He could be at the absolute end of the known world, seeing mandalas and hands coming out of the walls, but it never distracted him. His vision and his focus was so intense that he could maintain it in the face of any chemical, political, police action.

Abbie Hoffman *(interviewed by Barry Shapiro)* We consciously played fads and fashion. Let's say I come to New York, I'm down in the Lower East Side. Having developed an understanding of the political process in America, it's very hard to create a revolution, in the classical political sense. But certain things can be used to communicate ideas and then you get into the whole cultural level. So you at once notice this thing, like people growing their hair long. What if I attach political significance to that? Then at the same time you're doing that, it happens. Your reality is made up of myths and that's what it is when you do propaganda.

I'd say letting my hair grow long was a very radical act. That started when I moved to New York. There was no way of going back to my hometown, getting the same job that I had. It was like you had jumped a class barrier. So defining myself as a hippie defined me as a radical. Ideas were always something you could pull out or pull back. For me, moving to New York, letting my hair grow long, meant full-time. It took you a year to grow your hair. No matter how hard I was working in Worcester or New England or the South, it was always part-time. Which I essentially viewed as "liberal," 'cause that was how every liberal I knew was working at it. Changing the world was a hobby. So when I came to New York I met the people who had it as a full-time passion, people that I always felt in communion with. People like Dave Dellinger and other people at the War Resisters League, A. J. Muste, Dorothy Day. I fell in with the wrong crowd when I came here.

Marshall Efron Abbie would sell marijuana from his apartment to people he knew. I thought he was taking a chance. But he was generous. He gave away a lot.

Anita Hoffman If you wanted to have some grass for yourself you'd buy an ounce, you'd sell half to your friends. Everybody was doing that sort of thing. Pot was certainly our recreational thing of choice. We didn't drink. I would say out of a week, we'd smoke maybe four days. But it wasn't a routine. Nothing was ever routine with Abbie.

Howie Glatter, *Lower East Side activist* They had started to have some free rock and roll concerts in the band shell in Tompkins Square Park. It was at one of these concerts that they had the first smoke-in. Dana Beal, who led a group called the Provos, started throwing handfuls of joints in the air, and everybody started scrambling.

Captain Joe Fink, *9th Police Precinct leader* At first we used to make arrests for everybody that smoked a joint. But then it became too prevalent. The success of the hippie movement was based on Mahatma Gandhi's passive resistance techniques. They all sat down in the park, what are you gonna do with them, right?

Art Goldberg, *Lower East Side activist* There was a smoke-in at the *Daily News,* and then we went over to Grand Central Station. First of all, you can make a lot of noise in Grand Central Station 'cause of the marble and we were going, Woo woo! They had those escalators that run between Grand Central and the Pan Am Building, and Abbie orchestrated people smoking joints and passing them back and forth to people going up or down. Then we went back down to the subway station to go back to the Lower East Side and Abbie opened up the exit door saying, "It's free, it's free!" Some transit cop tried to arrest some guy and Abbie arrived and said, "Are you a cop? Let me see your ID." And the cop starts to pull out his ID and we all ran away into the subway. That was a lot of fun.

Paul Krassner, *satirist, publisher of the* Realist You couldn't separate laws against drugs from the war, they were just variations on the process of the humanization. More and more people on the New Left started to do drugs, and more and more hippies started to go to demonstrations. Abbie saw that people who could be organized to go to a smoke-in could be organized to go to an antiwar rally.

Anita Hoffman We found a perfect place on St. Mark's Place. It cost $105 a month, it was in the center of everything, on the ground floor. Abbie got expenses from the job at Liberty House but it wasn't anything dependable. I wanted to make sure we always had enough money to pay the rent. Part of the motivation was I was alone with this guy. I'm not gonna live in a commune with him because I was always seeing women flirting with him. I got a job so that we would have our private nest. That may have been very bourgeois of me, but I know he really needed that respite. I think he was basically monogamous in the sense that he really did believe in love, he really liked having a partner, he liked being married. That's what Sheila said too. She said she never met anybody who wanted to get married as quickly or as much as Abbie.

Randy Wicker I had a head shop at 28 St. Mark's Place. I was selling pipes, posters, psychedelic music, buttons. I had strobe lights, no one had seen posters with black lights. Abbie lived at the very next building. One day, he came in selling beads. He said, "Man, my wife and I, we need money, we're making these beads." And being successful, I was filled with all these good vibes. "Oh yeah, man, let me help you out, I'll buy your beads and sell 'em." So he starts selling me these strings of beads and it seemed to me he sold an awful lot, and I didn't notice that many being sold. Then I found out from one of the hippies. "Hey, he sells you the beads and then he sends his friend in and they steal 'em and then they sell 'em back to you. Man, don't you know what's going on, you're real naive."

Anita Hoffman Maslow's philosophy about self-actualization was really key. During the first year when I met him, it gave him a whole way of being. Maslow talks about a hierarchy of needs, that we need art and we need beauty but we also need food, we need sex, we need sleep. You can't talk about appreciating a great painting if you're starving. So in a society of abundance, which we were in the sixties, you can become an artist or a mystic. You will have these self-actualizing peak experiences, some of which verge on mysticism. But you could also think of those as social ideas, that when a society cures its sick people and feeds its hungry people, then it has room to support the arts and to create beauty and to build a generous, humane and inspiring society that keeps evolving.

Ellen Maslow Oh dear. My father loathed Abbie and Abbie never knew that.

Allen Ginsberg Abbie was an action poet in the sense that some of his political gestures were very similar to inspired "happenings."

Ed Sanders, *beat poet, member of the Fugs* Happenings were these Apollonian stitched-together vignettes conducted in a climate of cool. So they were very much up for grabs, the components of a happening. The happening movement was kicked off by Alfred Jarry, the guy who wrote *Ubu Roi,* by lettering the word "shit" in 1896 and shocking the French . . . causing a riot, basically. And you've got progressions of futurists and then dadaists in Zurich and the surrealists, and you have John Cage and Merce Cunningham and others do Black Mountain College, keeping the happening movement alive through the fifties, and then you have Claes Oldenburg's store in '61, you have Allan Kaprow and Charlotte Moorman in the early–mid-sixties doing that series of happenings. And so the tradition was kept alive from 1896 through 1965 or '66, when it mated with the concept of guerrilla theater, the Chinese concept of direct-action political street theater, and more importantly, the Bread and Puppet Theater and the Living Theater. The Living Theater, with their series of plays and their confrontation with the government, Judith Malina and Julian Beck having those general strikes for peace in '61 or '62, and being driven out of the country. Abbie sucked it all in.

Jean-Jacques Lebel, *artist, French protest leader* I did one in France in 1964. To get in the theater, you had to go through a very thin, long corridor, and in the corridor on both sides there were enormous slabs of red meat. And the only way you could get in was to be completely full of blood, like being born. Then a nun arrived onstage, kneeled and started praying. She got into this very religious state, getting hysterical, her rapport with God getting near. All of a sudden, she tears her headdress off and brings her tits out and starts massaging them. She starts tearing her clothes off. She's got this beautiful body and she's rubbing her crotch, but her back is to the audience, that's extremely important. She grabs a package of carrots and leeks, and she masturbates her asshole, fucks herself with these vegetables and then throws them behind her back to the audience. The audience starts eating these vegetables. And when everybody's completely excited, the whole room's on their feet screaming, she turns around and she was a man, a transsexual. I got busted, of course.

JANUARY 1967

Keith Lampe aka Ponderosa Pine, *Lower East Side activist* My friend in San Francisco Michael Bowen had a dream of a lot of people getting together, and when he woke up he recited it to his wife, Martine, and the two of them decided to make it actually happen. It was called the Great Human Be-In. It was Martine's insight that the be-in should not just be the Haight-Ashbury hippie but a fusion of the Haight hippie and the Berkeley radical. So she went over and got Jerry Rubin.

Jerry Rubin, *Berkeley activist* They brought all the Berkeley radicals into a room, there was Mario Savio, me, Stew Albert, Mike Lerner.

Mike Lerner There was this meeting with the Grateful Dead and the Jefferson Airplane at a house in the Haight and all the walls and the ceiling were covered with these carpets. It was very dark, we're smoking dope and talking. Finally after about an hour and a half, somebody said, "We'll have this band playing, we'll have that band play" and so forth. I said, "Well, who's gonna speak?" They said, "Speaking, man, forget it, what a bummer. This is a gathering of the tribes, we want to communicate." So I said, "Well, the tribe that we come from over there on the East Bay, we communicate with language."

Jerry Rubin The Berkeley radicals kept saying well what are gonna be the demands of this event? And the hippies were all saying no, no, no, just our presence is a demand, we're just gonna *be* there. Finally I got the point, let's go on their trip for a while. But Mike Lerner didn't get the point— "No, no, if you're gonna bring 25,000 people together and you're not gonna make any statement to the American people, this is a waste of time." Finally we all said, Mike, you go write your statement over there and we'll read it at the end.

Allen Ginsberg The afternoon began with Michael McClure, Gary Snyder and myself chanting mantras and then reading poems, then the Grateful Dead played. We had the Diggers [San Francisco–based actors turned activists] giving out food, and the poets were the masters of ceremony. Jerry Rubin got up and tried to make an angry political speech to this crowd of people who were totally zonked on acid, listening to music and poems about ecology, nature and the war in a meditative mood. I think he was booed.

Jerry Rubin I gave Mike Lerner what he wanted. No one heard it though. Just went out into the air.

Allen Ginsberg The idea of the levitation of the Pentagon came out of that be-in. And Woodstock and Altamont. It was the original mass gathering. The early evening came, people went home. And then the police made a sweep down Haight Street, busting everybody with grass and acid. Within two weeks the place was flooded with amphetamine and heroin. The police took revenge, busted all the nonviolent drugs and opened the floodgates, either deliberately or not. Some veteran came from Vietnam with two gallon jugs of heroin which he gave to the Diggers. So they all got strung out, including [Digger leader] Emmett Grogan. Emmett always thought the CIA did that.

Jim Fouratt I organized the first be-in in New York in Central Park after they'd had one in San Francisco. Ours was on Easter Sunday.

Bob Fass, *WBAI radio personality* I had been up all night the night before on the radio. And then we went there and saw the sunrise in Central Park. Then slowly the park began to fill like a bathtub, brimming, going out the spout. There was Ginsberg with the finger cymbals. He led a march all the way up from downtown and people had trailed in behind them, like the Pied Piper.

Stew Albert Jerry had been to Cuba and he saw the power of these giant rallies that Castro had. So Jerry and others had this sense that we can really have a massive teach-in.

MAY 21, 1965

Jerry Rubin The teach-in went thirty-six hours, that's where I met Paul Krassner. Krassner spoke. Phil Ochs folk-sang. Isaac Deutscher flew from Europe and at 1:00 A.M. had ten thousand Berkeley students standing as he said, "I am a communist."

Stew Albert There was also a thing of getting on the tracks and stopping the recruiting train. Jerry believed in big marches, radicalization through confrontation. People used to say he thinks if you get hit over the head with a club you become a revolutionary.

Jerry Rubin When I was in Berkeley we formed a Vietnam Day Committee whose purpose was to create theatrical, disruptive events to make Vietnam an issue in people's lives. We did the marches. There was the march on the Oakland Army Terminal that was stopped by the police. Then the second march was attacked by the Hell's Angels, and then the third march Allen Ginsberg came; if you want to see the birth of Yippie, he came out and he gave a speech about how to march again with the Hell's Angels attacking.

From "How to Make a March/Spectacle" by Allen Ginsberg

> We have to use our imagination. A spectacle can be made, an unmistakable statement OUTSIDE the war psychology which is leading nowhere. Such statement would be heard around the world with relief.
>
> The following are specific suggestions for organizing march and turning marchers on to their roles in the Demonstration.

- Masses of flowers—a visual spectacle—especially concentrated in the front lines. Can be used to set up barricades, to present to Hell's Angels, Police, politicians, and press & spectators whenever needed.
- Marchers should bring CROSSES, to be held up in front in case of violence; like in the movies dealing with Dracula.
- Marchers should bring harmonicas, flutes, recorders, guitars, banjos & violins. Bongos and tambourines.
- Marchers should bring certain children's toys which can be used for distracting attackers: such as sparklers, toy rubber swords, especially the little whirling carbon wheels which make red-white-blue sparkles.
- In case of threat of attack marchers could intone en masse the following mantras

  The Lord's Prayer
  Three Blind Mice (sung)
  OM (AUM) long breath in unison
  Star-Spangled Banner
  Mary Had a Little Lamb (spoken in unison)

OTHER MORE GRANDIOSE POSSIBILITIES:

- Small floats or replicas in front:

  Christ with sacred heart and cross
  Buddha in Meditation
  Thoreau Behind Bars
  Dixieland Band Float dressed as Hitler Stalin Mussolini Napoleon & Caesar

Allen Ginsberg Then [Bob] Dylan came to town. Dylan sent a message to Rubin and his cohorts and offered to join the demonstration and help out, providing the demonstrators would meet up on Nob Hill, right in the middle of San Francisco, carrying signs with pictures of oranges, lemons, avocados, artichokes, and be silent. The Vietnam Mobilization Committee didn't react to it. They didn't realize that Dylan was giving them a way that provided both entertainment, meditation, spiritual upgrading and antiwar feeling.

We had a second march, which had floats and chants and mantras. And that was picked up in New York in '66 and '67 by Keith Lampe and the Vietnam Veterans of America who organized a Yellow Submarine march to change the tone of the march from impotent protest and anger to humor, theater, communication. Realizing that the whole point was, what were the images broadcast of our behavior?

Bob Fass The best antiwar demonstration ever, took place in Grand Central Station. Some people from Woodstock asked me if I wanted to take part in a demonstration against the war. I said yeah, you want me to announce it on my radio show? They said no, no, it's just you and about sixteen other people. They were architects and artists who had measured Grand Central Station. And they had bought weather balloons, filled them with helium and put them in enormous cardboard boxes with a specially designed catch. You just had to pull a string and the box would fly open. There were banners attached to the balloons that said War, Peace, Vietnam, Kill, Money, Wall Street. And there was a silken bag filled with forty dollar bills, which was practically the whole cost of this thing. The bills were stamped on one side, "You're a dollar richer, but if instead this were napalm, you'd be dead." And at five o'clock, everybody arrived, put the boxes down. And we pulled the cords on the boxes and the balloons flew up to the vault trailing these leaflets. And some of the string was attached to the bag, so that as people pulled, the dollar bills poured down. It was like five o'clock, Grand Central Station. Everything stops!

Jim Fouratt There was a march in New York to support the boys in Vietnam organized by the superpatriots. We decided that we wanted to be in the march too, because we wanted to bring the boys home; it was very logical. We were about thirty people. We had banners "Bring the Boys Home," "Stop the War."

Anita Hoffman That was a right-wing demonstration in favor of the war through the German neighborhood. We were the Flower Brigade. Abbie gave instructions which he had learned in the civil rights movement about how to protect yourself, which is basically to just lie on the floor in a fetal position. Those right-wing working-class people who lived in those tenement buildings pelted us with rotten eggs and fruit and they ran and lunged after us. I was scared. But I think Abbie enjoyed it.

Jim Fouratt I remember being beaten up right around St. Patrick's and they tarred and feathered a couple of people. When they started to really attack us the cops cut them off.

From *Win* Magazine, 6/16/67

LOVE AND HATE ON FIFTH AVENUE

By Abbie Hoffman

> They grab our American flags and rip them up . . . "Get those bearded creeps!" (No one had a beard.) "Cowards! Go back to the Village!" Cops appear out of nowhere. We are marched back to Second Avenue and get a police escort to St. Marks Place. The Flower Brigade lost its first battle, but watch out, America . . .

Jim Fouratt I don't remember the cops escorting us back to the Lower East Side. I think we dispersed. More like running for our lives.

Marshall Efron This was the beginning of the summer of flower and hipness or whatever they call it. So there were a lot of these kids with long hair that were gooned out on acid, bad complexions, looking terrible. They didn't know what they were doing, chewing gum, picking their noses, looking at the sun, burning their retinas, peeing on themselves.

Captain Joe Fink I was assigned to the 9th Precinct as captain in 1964. We had a white population that was split between Ukrainians, Poles, the middle European countries, an Italian section, a Jewish section. And then we had the blacks and the Puerto Ricans moving in over a period of time until they took over whole neighborhoods. Troubles started when the hippies who came from middle-class backgrounds, subsidized by their parents, were taking some of the living space that the crowded minorities needed.

Howie Glatter I was involved in the Memorial Day bust in 1967 in Tompkins Square Park. People were picnicking and everybody was out there, the Puerto Ricans and the hippies and the blacks and the conga drum players. And the cops got one of the parkies to sign a complaint that the hippies were picnicking on the grass. No one had ever paid any attention to those Keep Off the Grass signs. So I'm trying to reason with this cop when they decided okay, that's it, and the nightsticks started flailing. They started dragging people away, beating people up.

Captain Joe Fink The Tactical Patrol Force was sent down and that's when the whole fracas busted wide open. They tried to get in touch with me but I was off that day.

Marty Carey This was the first chance for Abbie to apply his new cultural skills. A switchboard was set up, a bail fund, free food in the park like the Diggers did in San Francisco. And the crash pads were set up.

Jim Fouratt We used to have these community councils. We'd all sit around like American Indians, and this drove Abbie nuts because there would be a consensus model. They were going around, you can't say anything until it comes around again, right? He would just be impatient and go crazy and people would be very upset with him and tell him to shut up.

I had started the Communications Company. If someone got busted or if there was an action, it was a way of getting information out on the street immediately. My first real betrayal by Abbie was around then. He stole my Gestetner mimeograph machine. He was gonna do a better job and it was the people's right to do this. He liberated it from me.

Marty Carey The runaways didn't know what they were getting in for when they came. And Abbie took care of them. He knew that they were gonna get arrested, he knew that they would need a bail fund, they'd need a community switchboard.

Jim Fouratt I was the head of the Jade Companions, which was basically a bail fund, and Abbie stole all the money, made a drug deal, people got busted and took all the money that was in our community bail fund to bail out this drug deal, the wrong people, not our people. I was really pissed, yet who do you complain to?

Susan Carey What Abbie understood, better than anybody almost, was distribution of labor. He was like Huckleberry Finn that way. He had an exceptionally charismatic personality. He drew people to him because he looked like he was having fun. He never ordered anybody, he totally charmed them and things got done.

Andy Kent, *Lower East Side activist* I don't think Abbie was an opportunist, I don't think he was an exploiter. Long before he was a media figure he was out there doing altruistic things. Everything he's done has been directed either to motivating people, getting media attention or embarrassing the powers-that-be. I think of him really as a performance artist with an agenda. He had a hell of a lot of fun. A lot of radicals were very angry, with no sense of humor, they followed Marxist polemics to a letter, they had this whole notion of political correctness. Abbie was above all that.

Jeff Nightbyrd, *SDS leader* In that period before he was famous, Abbie manifested lots and lots of hope. A crash pad either could be tawdry or something beautiful. With Abbie it was "Fuck, this isn't a crash pad, this is a new world being born."

Kate Coleman Abbie was a good community organizer. He was out of doors all the time, he was athletic, he had a real grace about him in the streets. I can remember Abbie being confrontational. But he was mostly cute about it.

John Eskow I remember one Saturday morning meeting in 1967. The Motherfuckers [a left-wing street gang] were there, the Panthers were there, a militant gay group was there and a very tiny, two-man organization called the League of Militant Poets. Abbie was running this bizarre giant meeting according to Robert's Rules of Order, and one of the League of Militant Poets guys kept interrupting him and saying, "Who the fuck elected you, man?" Finally Abbie said, "What organization you representing, man?" And the guy said, "The League of Militant Poets." Abbie said, "How many people are there in your organization?" And the guy said, "Two now, but soon there'll be many more." And Abbie said, "What do you do, have your meetings in a phone booth?" The guy started cursing at Abbie, and the meeting threatened to turn to complete anarchy, and finally Abbie said, "Let's go outside. Fuck you." And Abbie took the guy in the hallway and they punched each other around for a while, and then came back inside and the guy shut up. Abbie was the Vince Lombardi of leftism in that way. He gave the hippie a sort of street dignity. So did the Diggers.

Danny Schecter, *Lower East Side activist* Abbie was very inspired by Emmett Grogan and the Diggers in San Francisco. What this community had going for it was the Digger notion that things should be free.

Peter Coyote, *actor, Digger cofounder* The sixties were awash in political ideologies. And what always seems to get lost in political ideologies is the individual. Individuals are always getting stood up against the wall and killed in the name of some cause or another, on the Left or the Right. I think that one of the things that artists always speak for is the uniqueness of the individual. And it's no accident that much of the Digger energy came out of the San Francisco Mime Troupe. And that much of what we did was based on this idea of personal autonomy and personal authenticity. So you didn't follow Emmett Grogan because he was your leader, you did something that Emmett wanted to do because it was an interesting, compelling and fascinating thing to do. And if you came up with something equally compelling and fascinating, people would follow you. You could right now start living the way that you wanted to live, if you were inventive enough and fearless enough and committed enough.

Peter Berg, *actor, Digger cofounder* We were doing what I had called guerrilla theater, preparing a play in advance and dropping it down into the middle of demonstrations. Eventually I decided that theater should go even further than that, so when the Diggers began we acted out a lifestyle that was different from what was around at the time, exemplary and progressive.

Peter Coyote We were light-years ahead of the Living Theater. When the Living Theater came to the Straight Theater [in San Francisco] and tried to perform *Paradise Now,* it was like you were driving into a small town and all of a sudden you find Marlon Brando's pumping the gas and Oscar Homolka is writing the tickets. We had taken it off the stage. We were not trying to represent it in art, we were trying to live it. To come up with improvisatory, imaginative moments, moment after moment after moment for the rest of your life, it's exhausting. It killed a lot of us. So the whole point was to get rid of the stage and get rid of the proscenium arch, get rid of everything that calls it art. Because that was a buffer. If you tell people, "Oh, you're gonna go to a happening," they're safe. They leave and they say, "I went to a happening." But if you're just sitting on the bus next to somebody who starts taking off their clothes and playing "Melancholy Baby" on the trumpet and giving away condoms, what are you gonna say about it? Except describe what happened. And when you describe what happened, you invariably transmit the message of the event.

Peter Berg A book titled *Thespis,* about ancient Egyptian theater, used the phrase "created the conditions described." And that became for me a goal of theatrical exposition, "Create the condition you describe."

Peter Coyote Billy Murcott was a friend of Emmett's from New York, a cabdriver, a strange, hermetic little guy who made wall charts of historical forces and movements. And Billy started to put out these handouts, Digger Papers.

LEADERS

Beware of leaders, heroes, organizers. Watch that stuff. Beware of Structure-freaks. They do not understand. We know the system doesn't work because

SOME OF THE DIGGERS ON THE STEPS OF SAN FRANCISCO'S CITY HALL MOMENTS AFTER CHARGES OF CREATING A PUBLIC NUISANCE WERE DROPPED. FROM LEFT: LA MORTADELLA, EMMETT GROGAN, SLIM MINNAUX, PETER BERG AND BUTCHER BROOKS.
Bob Campbell from *The Summer of Love* by Gene Anthony, Last Gasp Books

we're living in the ruins . . . Any man who wants to lead you is the man. Think: Why would anyone want to lead me? Think: Why should I pay for his trip? Think: LBJ is our leader—and you know where that's at. Watch out for cats who want to play the systems games, 'cause you can't beat the System at its own games, and you know that. Why should we trade one Establishment for another?

FUCK LEADERS

Peter Berg I think it's Billy Murcott's phrase, the Diggers. He'd been reading a book about the utopian anarchists and came upon this phrase naively.

Peter Coyote Somewhere around Cromwell's time, Gerrard Winstanley was the leader of a group of people who began to try to graze their animals again on the commons. As I remember, the king of England needed the commons to raise sheep to feed the woolen mills that were growing up in the Industrial Revolution. And they took away the common lands and the people decided it was theirs, didn't belong to the king or the nation or anything, and they were just butchered. They were called the Diggers because every morning they would be digging graves.

Peter Berg At any rate, it was the same time as the Fillmore District was going up in flames. That night, in fact, Billy and Emmett had been on a rooftop watching the blacks burn the Fillmore District during a riot. They thought that these were revolutionary times and young white people didn't have a revolutionary purpose. They wanted one but they didn't know what it would be. Billy gave me something that he had written, titled "The Diggers," and the next day I was out of the Mime Troupe and with them.

Peter Coyote We were all left-wingers, very analytical, very result-oriented. But at a certain point, you realize that it's the culture itself that's the enemy. Everybody is operating on those premises. And it's the cultural premises of identifying with your job, of private property, of living in a culture where the unimpeded demands of capital have full sway. That's the problem. And so imagining your way out of it was the task. And then acting out that imagination was the way to prove that it was possible. That started here.

Peter Berg One of the first Digger actions was to feed people in the Panhandle of Golden Gate Park in the Haight.

Peter Coyote The free food was a theatrical event, it's just that there was no stage. All of this began because the Haight-Ashbury was attracting national media attention, and the powers-that-be in San Francisco were just burning the kids. The kids were bringing the tourists in, but they were just fodder. And Emmett and Billy and some people felt like this is bullshit, let's just feed 'em.

John Garabedian, New York Post *reporter* There was one man, above all else, who Abbie Hoffman and Jerry Rubin and lesser lights sought to emulate, and that was Emmett Grogan. This was the only man that I was unable ever to interview successfully in this period of the sixties. I chased him around San Francisco and I finally met up with him, after several weeks of trying. I made a few notes as we were talking. He immediately took my notes and tore 'em up. "What we're about is what we do. If you want to understand what we do and the notion of Free, you have to hang out with us." I hung out with him and his pal Peter Berg, for a day, anyway. We went out to a tomato farmer's fields north of San Francisco in the back of an old pickup truck. Had amphetamines to get going and then marijuana to keep us going. We were, in effect, stealing tomatoes out of this guy's farm to use for the Digger free food, to prove there is such a thing as a free lunch. This was a crew of very hardworking guys, I mean they got up at dawn and did this shit.

Peter Berg Emmett was certainly a romantic character about it. Emmett got arrested for stealing a side of beef out of a truck.

Peter Coyote Emmett and a bunch of the women went out to the produce market, early in the morning. They'd stop by the Farmer's Market and the Italians and the Asians would give them surplus stuff. And then it would be cooked into a big, hearty stew and brought out to the Panhandle in these twenty-five-gallon milk cans.

Peter Berg John Cage had said put a frame around anything and it's art. So as soon as I got involved I said let's put a frame around it. And so we got a twelve-by-twelve-foot frame of wood, painted it psychedelic orange and put it in front of the people being fed in the Panhandle. There are two roads by the Panhandle that are very heavy with commuter traffic in the morning and evening. So people were driving by looking at this, a Renoir of hippies in tie-dyed headdresses, eating out of twenty-five-gallon milk cans, in a frame. It really was an extraordinary thing to see.

Peter Coyote The kids would show up with their tin cups, and they had to walk through a six-foot-by-six-foot yellow square, called the Free Frame of Reference, and they'd get their food. And then they'd be given a little two-inch-by-two-inch yellow square to wear around their neck, and that was the portable Free Frame of Reference. But you didn't have to do anything. Show up and you were handed a key to your own liberation, if you were hip enough to use it.

Country Joe McDonald, *singer, activist* I remember being in an apartment in the Haight. There were two groups—the women were in the kitchen and then there were all these men, Diggers, and Emmett was in there with them, doing some heavy discussion about the revolution. I was in the kitchen with the women and they were all going "Fuck that revolution shit, who the hell's gonna wash dishes tonight. I'm so sick of this crap. What's with these fucking guys?"

Peter Coyote Abbie was fun to be around. Abbie liked to party. He was eternally ebullient. The Diggers were sometimes so fucking heavy, involved in serious, analytical rap. Hard to go to a Digger party and get people dancing.

Superjoel, *LSD dealer* I'll tell you something about Emmett. I was working for somebody who manufactured LSD. Emmett would come into the pad I would use in the Haight to distribute the L to the dealers, and try to strong-arm me for the free store. That wasn't the way we operated, strong-arming hippies. And let's talk turkey here. Emmett had a heroin habit the entire time. He fed that heroin habit off of what he was stealing in the name of the people. So fuck him!

Peter Coyote Abbie was blown away by the free store, which was basically Berg's invention.

Peter Berg An actor named Kent Minault and myself went downtown, wore sports coats and told the owner we wanted to open a boutique in the Haight-Ashbury and we rented this spot. I called the free store the Trip Without a Ticket. We got the money from some hip merchants that were terrified of us.

TRIP WITHOUT A TICKET
Free store / property of the possessed

The Diggers are hip to property. Everything is free, do your own thing. Human beings are the means of exchange. Food, machines, clothing, materials, shelter and props are simply there. Stuff. A perfect dispenser would be an open Automat on the street. Locks are time-consuming. Combinations are clocks. So a store of goods or clinic or restaurant that is free becomes a social art form. Ticketless theater. Out of money and control.

Diggers assume free stores to liberate human nature. First free the space, goods and services. Let theories of economics follow social facts. Once a free store is assumed, human wanting and giving, needing and taking become wide open to improvisation.

A sign: If someone asks to See the Manager
Tell him He's the Manager.

Someone asked how much a book cost. How much did he think it was worth? 75 cents. The money was taken and held out for anyone. "Who wants 75 cents?" A girl who had just walked in came over and took it.

A basket labeled Free Money.

No owner, no Manager, no employees and no cash register.

. . . The question of a free store is simply: What would you have?

Peter Coyote Many, many times soldiers came in in uniform and would take clothes off the racks and leave their uniform on the rack and just walk out and disappear into the street.

Peter Berg One time reporters from the *Saturday Evening Post* and *Time* magazine showed up at the same time and one of them asked me who was the manager of the free store. So I said, "It's that man over there," pointing to the other reporter. So I saw one reporter being cozy with the other one for five or ten minutes, trying to warm him up to be interviewed, before finding out that he was just another reporter.

Peter Coyote People were always trying to test how real you were about Free. So they would give you money and they'd expect you to say thanks a lot. What they didn't expect you to do was call up Huey Newton and say I got $1,000 here, do you want it? The only people you could really take money from were brothers or sisters who wouldn't use it as a status play against you. Abbie learned all that stuff from out here. All that stuff.

Peter Berg I remember the first time we used donations as theater. Somebody would say, Well, what do you mean everything is free? And we'd just pull out a dollar bill, light a match and set it on fire and hold it out for a photo.

Peter Coyote All the big free parties with the Grateful Dead and the rock bands playing in the Haight-Ashbury were all thrown by the Diggers. And it's not an accident that there was never any violence at these events. They were planned that way by being included in a frame of reference, like the solstice or the equinox, that made everyone equal. There were fabulous events, all promulgated by somebody having a vision. Truckfuls of naked belly dancers going down Montgomery Street at five in the afternoon with black conga players, with bottles of wine and dope and inviting people to climb on. You know? The invitation was there, if you had the courage to snatch it.

JUNE 1967

Keith Lampe aka Ponderosa Pine Students for a Democratic Society was having a big national meeting at a summer camp in Denton, Michigan. My friend Bob Ockene [a Lower East Side activist/theorist] thought that those SDS guys should be doing psychedelics and letting their hair grow, they're too straight, they're culturally rigid. So he arranged for a few of us from the East Coast and a few Diggers from the West Coast to go.

Peter Berg As a good New Lefter at the Mime Troupe a few years before, I had read the Port Huron Statement. I'm one of the three people in the universe to have read it through. So when this meeting to reevaluate SDS came up I said, "Let's go." They said, "Why?" And I said, "Because we're gonna turn these guys on."

Tom Hayden A lot of the original SDS people felt bypassed by history. Intellectuals were no longer leading, we had to have some new manifesto or program or organization. It was back to the drawing board. So the Diggers showed up as the opposite of this hyperrational tendency. Their viewpoint was that no meetings, no plans, no talk was necessary, that chaos was splendid. And they came in dressed like Indians and started doing guerrilla theater.

Peter Berg I talked about media being more dominant than reality and that the way to retake the media was to create alternative realities. And that the hippies had been media-ized in San Francisco, and that the Diggers

THE DIGGERS' "1% FREE" POSTER. DESIGNED BY PETER BERG AND TAKEN FROM AN OLD CHINESE TONG PHOTO, THIS POSTER WAS INTERPRETED BY SOME HAIGHT-ASHBURY MERCHANTS AS AN ATTEMPT BY THE DIGGERS TO SHAKE THEM DOWN. *The Realist*

were connecting the image of hippies to Diggers, [who] were going to be socially conscious. I saw this one guy there in a combat army-surplus coat absolutely starry-eyed. And this guy said, "My name's Abbie Hoffman." I asked him what he was into and he said he'd been with SNCC and he had been waiting for a message about the way to go and that we had given it to him. Hoffman was just wonder-struck. It turned out that he had been a guilty white boy up to that point. I guess, in all fairness, he had wanted something else. We were saying it's not enough to just try to change the racial thing or the war thing, you've got to change the basis of the society from being exploitative and in a radical way, not in a do-gooder surface way.

Paul Krassner Later we were being driven to the airport by one of the locals. This guy's doing us a favor and the Diggers are calling him an asshole to his face. So they were not exactly Ms. Manners.

Peter Berg I have always suspected that at that moment, Tom Hayden decided to go legit and to let the crazies be because these guys are too far out. Some of the audience were pale. Billy Fritsch was on his knees chasing women around saying, "Come on, fuck me. I don't want to get romantic or nothing, would somebody just please fuck me?" That put off some of these women who probably taught second grade.

Todd Gitlin, *SDS leader* The conference was blown. Abbie seemed to me out of control and jubilant about the destruction that he was wreaking. I thought he in his way understood that what was taking place was a collision of two cultures. And his guys had come out on top.

Jim Fouratt I remember Emmett taking me over in the corner and telling me not to trust Abbie Hoffman, he's out for himself. It shocked me. And then I thought it was just this rivalry between them. Emmett wanted everyone to call themselves Emmett Grogan. Abbie, pissed, says, "Let's all call ourselves Abbie Hoffman. What's the matter, he's afraid of being Jewish?"

John Eskow I would hear Abbie talking about Emmett like Marilyn Monroe talking about Jayne Mansfield. It was like a competing-blondes thing. They were the two stars.

Ellen Maslow Later on we started a second Liberty House on the Lower East Side. And Abbie decided he was a Digger. He never told me I am a Digger now so my belief system has changed. He just started taking things off the walls and giving them away. I was so horrified that he would do this to the black people in Mississippi that I said, "Get out of here. I will do the store without you, thank you, go be a Digger and go fuck yourself." We knew the people who were starving to death, who needed this. And he's a Digger now? I could vomit. He wasn't ripping off AT&T.

Jeff Jones, *SDS leader* We were living in total poverty on the Lower East Side. Abbie was the first person I ever knew who had a color TV. I was both appalled and impressed.

Peter Berg I think Abbie was in the audience at the Alan Burke TV show that I did in New York. Burke was an early antagonist-type interviewer. The way he used his guests was he played to the fact that they wanted to be on television. He said, "Now, why do you want to be famous?" Then he would cut their knees out from under them. So I never talked to the guy. They put me on, I sat down, looked at the audience and said, "I'm really glad to be here because this whole thing is a bad film. Television is a control media." Burke's on the side, I'm talking away from him and I look at him and say, "Will you please shut up so I can say what I want?" He didn't know what to do, this had never happened to him before. I kept talking about how the media's in control of your lives and it's telling you what's going on. Actually you should be telling the media what's going on and break yourself loose from this society and media framework.

When a hostile audience member defended Burke and the American way, Berg asked one of his cohorts to "show the woman what we believe in." The Digger took out a pie and pushed it into the woman's face.

Peter Berg Burke was totally flustered. He said something like, "I don't know what's going on, is there anything you want to say to the people?" I said, "Yes, I'd like to say something to people watching this, you're watching a little box and we're in a little box as well," and I looked at the cameraman and said, "Will you pan the microphones and whatever?" He pans the superstructure, lights and cameras and I said, "Look at this box. The only way to get out of this is to walk away. I'm going to walk out of this box, I'm going to ask you to turn off your box. The way you do it is, you get up." And I got up. Burke at this point was pissed. Wordless, speechless. Didn't believe it. And I went over and as I walked through a door that said Exit, I said, "See, it says Exit, you can exit. You can control American media yourself. And now I'm gonna open it and I ask you to turn off your set." I opened the door and I walked out of the studio. I think Abbie was there. I remember Krassner was because we went to his place afterwards. He loved it, it was like, "Jesus Christ, you can bring these suckers to their knees."

Lynn Freeman House, *Lower East Side activist* Abbie and I had gone to Boston to be on a television talk show to talk about acid, the dropouts, the street scene. We spent the next day sightseeing and talking about Emmett Grogan, who had been in New York recently and had called a meeting of local activists in my place. What was most impressive to us was the fact that Emmett had made this character and then given the name away. That had blown both of us away. That you could invent a character for yourself that really didn't have a whole lot to do with your own persona, and then use it. And then discard it. So during that afternoon is the first time I'd ever heard Abbie talk about using himself that way.

My impression twenty-five years later is that he overestimated his own capabilities and underestimated the power of the media, television in particular. And that he was not able, ultimately, to keep himself clear of the image he had created, which is not to fault him. He was brave enough to try it and it took him a long, long way, but Emmett didn't get away with it either. In my mind it had a lot to do with killing both of them.

Jim Fouratt When Abbie got married in Central Park he saw it as a media event. Why else do you get married in Central Park and call up *Life* magazine? This was a combination of using the mystique of a be-in in Central Park and a wedding. He thought a lot about those things, what would work. He was like a Flo Ziegfeld.

Anita Hoffman Our wedding picture was in *Time* magazine. But it just said "a hippie couple." That's what was so nice about it. We planned a celebration for the community, not to get in the media. Abbie may have been more savvy that the media would show up, but it would be like getting publicity for this alternative way of life. I was afraid my father would have a heart attack. That's why I put on the dark glasses.

Jim Fouratt Lynn House, and Anita certainly, and Wavy Gravy and Bob Fass and a lot of other people saw it as a ritual of much more meaning. Anita wanted a public acknowledgment of this relationship. She needed people to know no matter who he was fucking, no matter what he said, that she was his wife.

Lynn Freeman House We developed a little ceremony, all it amounted to was throwing the I Ching and taking the reading that came as the ceremony. That's courage. As a matter of fact, the reading that came up was Conflict and we went ahead with it. We had all stayed up all night using STP, a very strong psychedelic. It was a lovely little thing except for the fact that Abbie had let all the reporters in New York know about it, which was a stoned surprise to me. At one point I remember looking up from my psychedelic daze and there was this phalanx of cameras and notebooks and microphones. I remember saying to myself, "Never again."

Truusje Kushner Afterwards, Anita says to me, "Oh, God, would you call mother?" I said, "Are you out of your fucking mind!" Ultimately, there was an actual rabbi wedding, which took place at the restaurant there in Central Park, Tavern-on-the-Green!

Captain Joe Fink The mayor at the time, John Lindsay, was a liberal guy and he had people like Sid Davidoff and Barry Gottehrer who were his assistants for Community Affairs. They're the ones who put Abbie on the payroll. The whole atmosphere was live and let live.

Sid Davidoff Fink was an outcast as cops go. The command never understood him. Somebody smoking marijuana on the street corner, you're supposed to arrest him. And here you had this cop who followed the mayor's party line, which was very liberal. The East Village was a wacky neighborhood. You had the Hell's Angels on one corner, you had Abbie Hoffman on the other. Two in the morning, Abbie'd walk out in the middle of Second Avenue, he'd stop traffic making speeches.

I decided to put Teddy Mastroianni in that neighborhood to watch Abbie. Teddy was a former deputy sheriff out of Suffolk County, active in Young Republican politics, and a bouncer in a bar. He's the most unlikely guy that you would put in the East Village, that's why I did it. He was just a very tough, street-oriented guy, worked well with the unions. I had to have somebody who Abbie couldn't co-opt but who was likable yet tough. So Abbie would go out on St. Mark's Place and they would call Teddy and Teddy would call me and I'd come down there and we'd begin to negotiate, "What's wrong with him tonight?" We'd get him off the street corner. He used to love bringing us down.

Teddy Mastroianni The cops identified thirteen problem areas in the city and one of them was the Lower East Side. In '67 there were some kids with long hair fighting some Puerto Ricans and blacks. At that time, nobody knew what hippies were.

Barry Gottehrer The Lower East Side then was the most complex area of all.

Ted Mastroianni I think at one point I gave Barry a list of sixty organized groups we had in the Lower East Side. This was the most organized disorganized community in the city.

Barry Gottehrer It was the one area where an Abbie could flourish, where a white could suddenly stimulate the action, come to the forefront. By then we had already begun to raise money from the private sector. We'd identify off police and youth agency lists the people that the Youth Board and the police thought had leadership abilities in each of the thirteen neighborhoods. Then for a period of twelve weeks every summer we'd hire eight to ten people in each of the thirteen neighborhoods. I think they each got about $75 to $100 a week.

Teddy Mastroianni Barry asked me to identify people that we could have as urban action task force advisers so I got Linda Cusamano and I got Pee Wee Feliciano and then I tried to get the hippies. Well, this was the antithesis of what the hippies believed in. They didn't want any organization, they didn't want any money. I'd met this guy Abbie Hoffman. He had apparently just taken a couple doses of LSD and he was talking to me pretty coherently so I sort of sold him on the idea. I was on a street corner, I said, "Why don't we make the deal now? I want you to help us keep this city well organized." He said, "I don't want the city to be organized. I want to fuck it up." So I said, "Could you talk to Barry Gottehrer?" That's when Barry first met him, I put him on the phone and by that time the drugs were taking effect. He says, "Who is this?" Barry says, "Barry Gottehrer." Abbie says, "Well, I'm here swinging around the universe and today I think I'm going to be a black and tomorrow I think I might be Hispanic and did you ever read Kafka's *Metamorphosis*? I can see my hands already growing and I'll take the city, yes." Finally I get on the phone and Barry says, "Who the fuck is this guy? Who do you have there? What's going on?" I said, "Barry, I'm sorry, I think this guy is key." Barry says, "I don't know what the hell he's talking about." I says, "I don't either but I think he's key."

Jim Fouratt We were paid to go out and talk to people, essentially. I think from the city's point of view they probably thought we were gonna keep a lid on. From our point of view we just took their money. None of us had money. We saw it as a way to organize with some sort of semilegitimacy.

Teddy Mastroianni Abbie wouldn't have his picture taken with the task force. The boxer Joe Louis was the honorary chair and he was photographed with Joe Fink, me and the other members but Abbie would not take a photograph because he said his soul would be stolen by the camera like in the Indian movies.

Barry Gottehrer Probably the only time Abbie wouldn't be photographed.

Teddy Mastroianni One night Abbie invited me to his house and I was absolutely bowled over because I remember it being so neat. White bookcases with hundreds of books. It looked like an upper-middle-class house and this is in the Lower East Side slums. He was talking to me about how he wanted to reconstruct the city and break down institutions. He said he was so angry that he wanted to make a parody of the system. He said, "We're going to have sideshows." Then he'd start laughing.

Shortly after he gets on the task force, the environment is now becoming an issue and Abbie calls me up and says he wants to plant a tree and I call Barry up and I say, "How do we buy a tree?" Barry says, "How the hell do I know, go to the parks department and ask them." Then Barry gave me the money and I gave the money to Abbie and we have an area where he's going to plant it, right? He goes out and buys about fifteen trees and he has these vans, they would pull up, the doors would open, they'd throw tons of dirt out into the middle of the goddamn street, put a tree in and plant it in the middle of the street and zoom away. He had these trees all over the Lower East Side and the cops are going crazy.

Susan Carey Joe Fink and Abbie really had quite a relationship. Fink used to call up Anita to make sure Abbie was okay after his busts. He really loved Abbie.

Captain Joe Fink He was full of fun, he was laughing all the time. And every once in a while he'd have some serious thoughts and come in and complain about specific injustices. He evinced the idea that he was in it to provide democracy and freedom and a healthy atmosphere for these kids. I've never seen any evidence that Abbie was doing it for self-aggrandizement. Abbie lived modestly in a little apartment on St. Mark's Place. He had his philosophy, but he recognized that he couldn't run roughshod and do everything that he wanted all the time. So we had a way of life delineated where he could do his thing and I had to do my thing, see?

Andy Kent The thing to do on a Friday or Saturday night in the East Village was to go out and bait the cops. Back when the TPF [Tactical Patrol Force] was around, that was heavy-duty shit. Joe Fink spoiled it for everybody 'cause he sensitized his cops. So you would have Joe leading this group of helmeted, billy-clubbed cops who you knew you could piss on their shoes and they wouldn't hit you. I remember one night when Joe and Abbie had a tug-of-war on the corner of St. Mark's and Second Avenue. Abbie had a group of people and Joe and his cops tried to break up this demonstration. Abbie said, "Joe, this is my corner, get off my corner." Joe had to save face by arresting Abbie and Abbie had to save face by resisting. They took him down to the precinct and of course everybody marched down to the precinct and by the time they got there they were giving Abbie a desk appearance ticket and cutting him loose. This kind of stuff was a weekly ritual.

* * *

Paul McIsaac The Motherfuckers had their own weird combination of an attempt to bring together street cultural politics and serious New Left thinking through Tom Neumann, whose father-in-law was Marcuse. Neumann was black clothes, black beard, heavy karate, "kill the motherfuckers," "NLF's [National Liberation Front] gonna win." Saw himself aligned with SDS, certainly saw they were organizing the youth. And the Lower East Side was the center of that work. Their leader, Ben Morea, was a little more mixed-bag, a little more larceny in him, a little more real street. And most of the other Motherfuckers were politicized biker culture.

Tom Neumann The Motherfuckers would organize demonstrations around police harassment of hippies and busts and then those demonstrations would lead to more busts and then we'd have more demonstrations. We were into the Lower East Side as dangerous and we were gonna be real defenders of the people. The system was violent, it was going to try and crush people. All that stuff that Abbie was doing was *fun* but at some point it wasn't gonna work and so our whole ethos was very different from Abbie's. We would go and have demonstrations at the 9th Precinct and we'd throw rocks and they'd call out the Tactical Patrol Force and we would have fights all over the Lower East Side. We were into creating a liberated space.

Stew Albert The Motherfuckers were into a cult of the lower depths, guys living on the Bowery. They were gonna be the revolutionary class. The scuzzier, the more lumpen you were, the more the Motherfuckers wanted to organize you or throw in with you. I used to say the Motherfuckers believed in creating socialism in one garbage can. They were the opposite of us. They had a very narrow sense of certain classes. We were very expansive.

Paul McIsaac Eventually they pulled the TPF out of the Lower East Side, and I think that had to do with Abbie's ability to negotiate with Fink. The politic at the time is we have no leaders, we'll meet you, four hundred of us. There were times that he worked things out with Fink that if the Motherfuckers had known it, he might've been in personal danger. Abbie was not afraid to walk on the razor.

Anita Hoffman CBS was going to give Paul Krassner money to tape an acid trip. There's like nothing to see! Just people in a room, since everything that's going on is in your head! CBS changed its mind at the last minute and Paul had the acid, so we did it. We were in our apartment tripping. Somebody knocked on our door and told us some black kids were busted for smoking pot in Tompkins Square Park. I didn't want to go out. But Abbie was totally into it.

Paul Krassner We went to the 9th Precinct. Abbie wanted to get busted to show solidarity between the hippies and the ethnic groups. But they wouldn't arrest him.

Ted Mastroianni I was out on Long Island and I get a call from the mayor himself. He said, "You have to get down to the Lower East Side, the hippies have just surrounded the police station and they said they were going to burn it down." So I drove in and there's Abbie sitting down in the middle of the street with all the people. He said, "I want to be arrested because I'm a nigger. You're arresting my black brothers. Arrest me." I sat down with Abbie and said, "Can you come in and talk with Joe Fink?"

Captain Joe Fink Abbie came running in. Abbie used to run into the station house all the time, he was frenetic sometimes in his enthusiasm to get things done and to be everything to everybody. There was some sort of a dialogue and I walked Abbie to the door and said, "Anita, take him home, there's nothing for him to do here. We can't cancel arrests." And Abbie went out, then came back, and he wouldn't go.

Teddy Mastroianni Joe Fink was a great man but he had a big ego. His precinct was good in football and basketball and he prided himself on all these Police Athletic Awards. He had them in these glass cases and Abbie looks at 'em and he says, "I want to be arrested." Joe says, "There's no way I'm going to arrest you because you just want to be arrested to create a riot." So Abbie says, "I'm going to force you to arrest me," and he runs right into the cases and he starts kicking the glass out and smashing the wings off the trophies and Fink says, "You goddamn bastard, now you've had it." Not because he was breaking the law, because he was breaking the trophies.

Joe Fink Abbie says, "Now I've done something, you have to arrest me," and we did.

Teddy Mastroianni Abbie's jumping on these big police desks and he's jumping off going "Na, Na!" and he runs out and the cops try to get him and they can't. So Joe says, "I'm going to arrest him." I go out into the neighborhood trying to look for Abbie and he's laying out for three or four days and finally he calls me up. He says he's going to voluntarily give himself up on Avenue A and Seventh Street because he doesn't want to get beat up by the cops. He wants to be arrested in public. So he let the word out and a huge crowd gathered and Joe Fink and I and the paddy wagons are there.

Abbie said he'd show up at exactly nine o'clock. Comes nine o'clock Joe Fink says, "Are you sure he promised you?" I said, "Joe, he said that he would be arrested because he's sorry that he damaged your trophies." Nine, 9:15, 9:20, 9:30 a van pulls up and a guy goes "Beep, beep." "We have Abbie Hoffman in the back." We had about forty cops, so all the cops come forward and Joe said, "No violence, guys, he's going to give himself up." The van opens up and about seven guys come running out who look exactly like Abbie Hoffman with the big Afro and they run into the crowd and the goddamn cops are chasing all of them! They're grabbing them and they're all wigs and they're wrestling them to the ground and pulling these wigs off and they say, "I'm not Abbie," and then all of a sudden from the other side of the street, you hear, "Yoohoo, yoohoo! Here I am." And Fink says, "That son of a bitch, get him!" and Abbie disappears again and we never did arrest him. It just got forgotten.

Joe Fink He came running into my office a day later and he threw five dollars on my desk and he said this pays for the glass.

Peter Coyote Abbie had to get arrested to build his authenticity. But there's a certain point at which media events just stop being significant. See, Emmett had an uncanny sense of what a workingman street guy's reality was, what the reality was of people who did not have a lot of slack in their lives. And he embodied that in his life and this kind of quasi-legal, always walking-on-the-edge persona that he created. Abbie couldn't quite do that. So he took Emmett's insight and he added to it the sense of fun that is only the province of people who have slack and fat and money to burn, and somebody they can drop a dime to and call in a pinch. Emmett had a kind of contempt for Abbie because Abbie was turning his insight into a game, into a joke. Also, Emmett's ideology demanded a kind of secrecy and a furtiveness, so Emmett was completely ubiquitous and famous but he was never in the media. Abbie didn't have those restraints. Abbie could get all this attention and credit that I think Emmett was hungry for.

Anita Hoffman Abbie was provocative. We'd go to the store, the security guard recognizes him, and at any time he could end up being arrested. And he was, half the time in those early years. Then I'd be on the phone, bailing him out, it was a drag. But I was always faithfully there, doing it.

Jim Fouratt He hurt her, he embarrassed her, she rescued him, she took care of him. If he said carry this bomb to that place and detonate it, she'd complain, "Abbie, I don't want to do it" as she would be putting it into her purse; "Abbie, I don't want to do it" as she'd be putting on her jacket; "Abbie, I don't want to do it" as she would cross the street; "Abbie, I don't want to do it." And he would finally say, "You don't have to pull the fucker" as she was there ready to do it.

Paul McIsaac My wife and Anita were close, because we lived two blocks from him. I would go over and I wouldn't expect to even see him, I was going over to see Anita, and I would back into his personal space. Which was black depression. Not "I feel bad, I'm sort of bummed out." Black depression.

Anita Hoffman Abbie had loads of energy. Mostly the manic was helpful to him. I don't think I ever saw him depressed. The closest thing to depression was when he was sick. I used to love it when he was sick, because he would slow down, I had him all to myself. And then he was like a normal person. It was like a natural day, you cook a meal, you lie around, you read, you fuck. But the only times he was ever like that was when he was sick. And so I used to have this kind of guilty pleasure. And then I even enjoyed playing Jewish mother and making chicken soup.

John Eskow One time Abbie and Marty Carey and I were tripping in Marty Carey's apartment, and the talk came to martyrdom. This was very early on, late '67, when everything was still very much kind of Jefferson Airplane, and soap bubbles glistening and rays of sunlight and all that, and Abbie said, "They'll kill me. I know that I'm gonna be backed up against a wall one day with a gun in my mouth. I know my brains are gonna be against the wall. There's no question about it." Maybe it took acid for him to say it in such a casual way, that he expected to be killed. I was really shocked. When did we start signing up for shooting in alleyways?

Teddy Mastroianni Abbie used to talk to me about getting the poor people food, jobs, better housing. But he just believed that the system was so corrupt that you couldn't even modify it, you had to destroy it. I said, "Well, what are you gonna create?" He said, "We'll have to create a whole new system." I said, "Like what? What are you gonna do?" He said, "We need to teach people how to get free food." I said, "That's a welfare state. You can't live in a welfare state, who's going to pay taxes?" Then he would almost reach the point of some understanding and then he'd go off, "We shouldn't have any taxes, we shouldn't have any government, we should have free food." He wrote that manual ["Fuck the System"] and he tried to clean up the crash pads, and he was trying to keep people healthy. He was actually cooperating, he had the kids going down there when Barry started a program of TB vaccinations. So there was a real decency about him. But he was taking so many goddamn drugs that he would just reach the point of this very profound statement and then he couldn't really put it all together. He told me once that one day when he was tripping, he saw the vision and he tried to capture the vision of what this new model would be. But he could never capture it. He kept on taking LSD and he said, "I hope my brain doesn't get eroded before I see the vision again." How do you deal with a guy like that?

Barry Gottehrer As part of the problem of the police and FBI telling us that we were going to have a terrible influx of youths, we had a discus-

THE COVER OF "FUCK THE SYSTEM," A STREET SURVIVAL GUIDE THAT ABBIE PRODUCED USING MONEY FROM THE MAYOR'S OFFICE IN NEW YORK.

sion of what was the best way to try to deal with the kids. I don't know whose idea it was, either Abbie's or Ted's or mine, but we decided to print a book that would tell kids where to go with an overdose, where to go if they had no place to stay. So Abbie and I worked out a deal where he would write it. I didn't want to have anything to do with it. I would pay for it surreptitiously. The feeling was that if it was our booklet, it would compromise him and also clearly would compromise people reading the book.

From "Fuck the System"

FREE FOOD

> Check the Yellow Pages for Catering Services. You can visit them on a Saturday, Sunday afternoon, or Monday morning. They always have stuff left over. Invest 10 cents in one of the Jewish Dailies and check out the addresses of the local synagogues and their schedule of bar mitzvahs, weddings and testimonial dinners. Show up at the back of the place about three hours after it is scheduled to start. There is always left-over food. Tell them you're a college student and want to bring some back for your fraternity brothers. Jews dig the college bullshit. If you want the food served to you out front you naturally have to disguise yourself to look straight. Remarks such as "I'm Marvin's brother," or—learning the bride's name from the paper—"Gee, Dorothy looks marvelous" are great. Lines like "Betty doesn't look pregnant" are frowned upon.

Barry Gottehrer I had cops saying to me, "Could you believe the shit these people are printing and distributing?" And here we were paying for it.

Dennis Dalyrimple, *Lower East Side activist* At that point, Abbie was very much enamored with the Diggers credo. He opened a free store. I brought some old clothes down.

Marshall Efron You could walk in and take anything, no money needed, everything was donated or stolen. So guys would come in with filthy clothing and take off their clothing and put on the filthy clothing that was in the Digger store and walk out and leave their filthy clothing for somebody else to come and take.

Sal Gianetta, *friend from the Lower East Side* Ab had said one night that this free store sucks, we don't have a loss leader. We need a big thing to attract people. So we sat around talking about it. And this guy Angel's father was a contractor and Angel ripped off his father's truck. Angel was only about sixteen. So we had this truck and we had these green chino cloth uniforms in the back. The jacket I had, said "Fred." There were all these goddamn American names, Fred and George and John in yellow-thread handwriting. There was four of us. And there was two hats! Ab took one, he was gonna kill if he didn't wear a hat.

Ab said if you went in there like you owned the goddamn place, you owned it. Klein's was a department store on Union Square and it opened at nine o'clock. They had all the TVs, all these huge fucking wood cabinet gloss shit, and there must've been like four back and six across. We pulled up to the store and Ab had an invoice thing. We walked in and Ab stood there looking and going "No, no." And the manager came out, he said, "Yes?" Abbie says we had this order from headquarters and there was a TV here that wasn't working well. The manager says he didn't know anything about it. Ab starts reading the number off the back of one of the TVs. He said "409078." The manager went behind and looked—409078. Of course, Ab was reading it off the goddamn television. Ab said, "That's okay, we'll get the hell out of your way before customers come in." And then he told the manager to grab the door. Angel blew it. Angel started laughing like a motherfucker and Ab turned to me and he says, "Poor kid, we've gotta get him to a doctor as soon as we finish this." And the manager's standing there shaking his head up and down. He held the door, we lifted the goddamn television, opened the sliding door and put it in the van. And then Abs went back in and gave the manager a receipt. I swear to Christ. We were yelling at him from the truck, "Come on, come on." He went back in the store and wrote up the thing and he gave the manager the fucking receipt.

The TV was a big mother, an Admiral with all kinds of buttons and dials. We put it in the window of the free store. And people would come in and they wouldn't look at the television. We had some decent stuff by then, sets of dishes and radios and we had a deal where all the clothing was being cleaned and hung on hangers. But for three months not one person asked about the TV. So we made up a big sign and put it on the television: "Everything is free." But no one ever asked for the fucking television! They were psychologically blind to it.

One day, this guy walks in the store. There's something very odd about this guy. And he says, "Is the TV free?" And the minute he opened his mouth we knew he was a cop. He has this list of stolen shit and he looked at the TV and he said, "We understand there's a TV here that's from

S. Klein." "Jeez, man, I don't know, people bring us stuff." Goodbye television. The cop came in, he was gonna arrest everybody. But by the time he left, he and Ab were like brothers, they were gonna go out and have a drink. After it was all straightened out and they walked out with the television, he came back in and he smiled and said, "Oh, I forgot to give you your receipt." That took all the pain out of losing it.

* * *

Stew Albert Jerry Rubin had a reputation for turning out people at the antiwar demonstrations on the West Coast. Then when he ran for mayor of Berkeley he got a pretty good vote. So that's how Dave Dellinger came to call on him. These *alte cockers* in the national Mobilization Against the War said, "Well, he's a youth leader." They needed somebody to come in there and turn out the young people. There were differences of opinion as to what radicals should be doing. It wasn't universal that it should be working against the war. Some people said no, we should build bases of power in the poor black and white neighborhoods. There's a big depression coming, massive unemployment, and we should get in on the ground floor. Of course what was coming was the greatest period of prosperity in capitalism's history. So they were a little off the mark there on their analysis. But Jerry and I had our eye on the antiwar movement. The Trotskyists and the Communist Party all had their front groups in the antiwar movement. Dave Dellinger was looking to bring in something that would counterbalance this. So Dave invited Jerry to come out East and organize and Jerry asked him if I could come too and he said yeah.

AUGUST 1967

Jerry Rubin When I arrived in New York, I ran into Keith Lampe. Keith was the first person to mention Abbie's name to me. He said, "Abbie's a Digger. He believes it's more important to burn dollar bills than draft cards." I said I want to meet him, I like that statement. Abbie was already intending to do the stock exchange two days after I arrived, so Abbie just took me.

Jim Fouratt It was my idea. But Abbie, like everything else, appropriated it as his. We decided to focus on who really ran the war and who the war really affects. We said American soldiers were dying but the people on the stock exchange on Wall Street were untouched by the war. Then we gathered up real money. We went to some people who'd made money off of our community and demanded they give us some. Dope dealers. Liberals, hippies. I was in charge of getting money from the hippies and Abbie was in charge of getting money from the others. Abbie's big thing was he wanted to make sure that the money was in dollar bills so that it would look like we had a lot more and that the stockbrokers would be bending over to pick up fucking dollar bills.

Jerry Brandt I owned the Electric Circus, this club on St. Mark's Place. You know how he conned me? First he asked me for a thousand singles. I said, "That's a little heavy. How about if I give you a hundred?" He says "Okay, if you autograph 'em, I guarantee you in life you'll get one back." You want to know something? I got two back.

Jerry Rubin We arrived at the stock exchange, busy noonday, and Abbie stuffed our pockets with cash.

Stew Albert We started throwing dollar bills. Well, this was extraordinary. It brought the floor to a halt and the brokers down there, these millionaires, they're running for the money. I couldn't believe it.

Superjoel Then the television crews showed up outside. Stew and Jerry burned the five-dollar bill.

Stew Albert That event got incredible coverage all over the world. And what'd it cost, a couple of hundred bucks? The media asked me if I lived in a commune with all these people. I said I don't even know them.

George DiCaprio, *Lower East Side activist* I remember people talking about it. It came back to the street within ten minutes after it happened.

Superjoel It went network. We were elated. That was beyond our wildest dream.

FROM *SANDY LESBURY'S WORLD,* WOR RADIO

Sandy Lesbury: I'm just a little confused. Some of you went down to the stock exchange and tore up money and threw it down?

Abbie Hoffman: Threw out real money. I was coming up here in a cab and the driver says, "Didn't I just see your picture in the *Daily News*?" It was a picture of me burning a five-dollar bill in front of the stock

ABBIE AND JERRY RUBIN'S FIRST PHOTO OP TOGETHER—BURNING MONEY AT THE NEW YORK STOCK EXCHANGE. AP/Wide World

THE FREE MEN AND WOMEN OF THE HAIGHT-ASHBURY IN SAN FRANCISCO MOURNING THE DEATH OF THE MEDIA-IMAGE HIPPIE. Archive Photos

exchange. We started talking about that and he says, "Yeah, you're right, money doesn't mean anything." So I ducked out of the cab and didn't pay and he starts yelling. I said, "You just said money didn't mean anything. We take people for their word. Let's see how well you believe that." That cabdriver's still out there in front of this building yelling for his money.

I watched every news report about what we did at the stock exchange. Now, we threw out at least six or seven hundred dollars. Jim and I had a hundred dollars in singles that we showed the TV cameras that we were going to throw out. Now, on one report I heard that we threw out monopoly money. On another report I heard that we threw out fake money. Another report I heard that it was all torn up. Another report I heard that we threw out at the most twenty or thirty dollars. Now, what the hell happened down there? There's no source out there for checking reality. The only reality is in your head.

John Eskow I think Abbie was a genius who's never been equaled in his understanding of TV and sound bites. We would watch the nightly news together and he would say, "You gotta look at the news. See, like at 7:26, after they've done all the heavy stuff, they gotta have a sign-off piece, something cute and weird and wacky and whimsical. So I know we can't get on at 7:03. That's Johnson's time. But we could get on at 7:26." And that was how he conceived of the stunt at the stock exchange. He knew enough about surrealism to know that surrealism would play well at 7:26 on the nightly news. And that it could be dismissed with a chuckle by the commentator. But the kids would never remember what the commentator's sardonic put-down encapsulation of it was, but they would always remember the vivid image of the bills cascading down the stock exchange. Nobody was that hip to the media at that time. He was millions of miles ahead of everybody else.

Jerry Rubin Now that's taken for granted—the abortion people do it, the antiabortion people, everyone's doing it. Reagan perfected what we did. Wouldn't you say? Little one-sentence stories that go Bop! and Pow!

Michael Rossman, *antiwar activist at U.C. Berkeley* The stock exchange drop was perfect because it had a kind of elegant and caricaturational simplicity to delight the mind of a fourth grader, but that did not keep it from being profound theater because it exhibited exactly what it purported to exhibit. Look how crazy these people are about money, look what they will do to each other for the sake of these little pieces of paper, look what they will do to themselves and the dignity they assume as professionals in this sacred chamber of money, when you give them a chance to grab in a socially unlicensed way, for trivial bits of this stuff. For all the simplicity and casualness and naturalness of it, it was a peak moment of his life as a social artist.

Michael O'Donoghue, *satirist* A few weeks later they had to put up glass barriers to keep people from throwing money to the stockbrokers. Do Not Feed the Animals!

Barry Gottehrer It came out that Abbie was on our payroll. I had never met Abbie. I relied on Teddy. I assume Abbie gave out an interview and said he worked for us. So the *Daily News* calls the press office the next day and said Abbie was on our payroll. I get the mayor screaming at me, "What is this program? What are you running here?" I called Teddy and said, "What the hell is this asshole doing? Get him up to my office."

Teddy Mastroianni Barry said, "Did you organize that trip to Wall Street?" I said, "Are you crazy? What Wall Street trip?" So I run to the neighborhood and I find Abbie. I get him up to Barry's office and I'm screaming at him and Barry's screaming at him and he looks at Barry, looks at me and he jumped up on Barry's desk and screamed, "You're trying to compromise me!"

Barry Gottehrer Abbie said, "What you're looking for is an Uncle Tom hippie," at which point I started laughing. I just thought it was hysterical.

Teddy Mastroianni Then he ran out of the office. After that he wouldn't be on the payroll anymore. He said that he'd help me but he didn't want to be compromised by capitalist money. He said, "You're trying to buy my soul." But I still remained friends with him.

* * *

After the symbolic assault on Wall Street, Sheila Hoffman sent a letter to her lawyer, along with a photo of Abbie in front of the stock exchange. She said she felt "slightly tormented" since she had only $16.17 in her bank account and her next welfare check was already earmarked for rent. She said she sent the picture to her lawyer "to give you [Weinstein] some indication of Abbie's involvement with his image, with his antiestablishment but pro-people and certainly pro the poor. I feel that if I were clever enough I could use it to convince him that he'd better pay me or suffer the consequences of publicity of how he's allowing his own children to live on welfare."

Seymour Weinstein He had a long record of nonpayment of his $72.50 a week. And the medical bills. And he didn't visit the children regularly and there were long periods she didn't hear from him.

In those days it certainly was unusual in a Jewish divorce to have the mother go on welfare, if there was any real ability in the father to pay.

Jim Fouratt Sheila used to call him all the time about money. Anita had to work and I remember being present when there was a fight about why does Sheila get everything and I don't get anything?

Abbie had failed at his marriage and with his children and that never left him. He hated Sheila. Sheila represented everything Abbie didn't want to be. Abbie did not want to be an ordinary guy.

Stew Albert Sometimes he could be very relaxed and just talk about everything. But then he'd go on binges of need-to-know. Sometimes you'd be surprised that someone who had been so open at one point was then kind of need-to-knowing you. But when you say open, what are your standards? By 1990s, touchy-feely culture, he wasn't open. But if you mean by garment manufacturers' standards, I'm sure he was more open than Stalin. I'm sure he was more open than Meyer Lansky.

Jerry Rubin I fell in love with Abbie because he had magnetism, electricity, humor, a he-was-on-this-earth-to-have-fun quality. I kept saying "God, if I could make Abbie political, he would put America totally off balance." But he was probably more political than he let on. He would say, "I don't care about the political demands, I want to know who's bringing the ice cream to the demonstrations." But that was good because he's making the point that if people don't have fun they're not gonna do it. He didn't seem very angry either, he seemed more like a guy who had just gone into show business.

Susan Carey There was a big parade in San Francisco, "Death of Hippie," and then we did it in New York and went on the David Susskind TV show. Marty and Abbie organized this thing that when David Susskind said the word "hippie" they were gonna release a duck. And the duck shat, and Susskind freaked out.

Jerry Rubin On the Susskind show Abbie made up all these stories about the hippies. "We have all these institutions and we feed thousands of people and we do this and we do this . . ." Abbie would say anything if it achieved the goal of promoting the hippie myth and promoting the myth of Abbie. I didn't like that part of Abbie, 'cause you can get caught on that.

From an Unattributed Article by Abbie Hoffman in the Open Press, *Street Handout of New York Provo,* 9/7/67

PROVOCATION AT CON EDISON:
HIPPIE-LEFTIST-ANARCHISTS FREAK CON ED EXECUTIVES

> At 4:30 sharp 50 people made it to Con Edison's offices on 14th and Irving Place—carrying soot, wearing Con Ed smokestacks, bearing soot-stained flowers. A banner read: "Breathe at your own risk." Their object: to return some soot, ugliness, and sulfur dioxide to the executives responsible for the dirt in our air . . .
>
> Con Edison executives were just leaving their building at 4:30; they paid no attention at first. But when the soot and dirt began to fly they gathered in the doorway, and a fat, flower-battered manager screamed for some employee to shut the door . . . A smokebomb "whooshed" on the soot-covered sidewalk, and another was carefully dropped into a "Dig we must" enclosure. The executives yelled; they thought something was about to explode. At this point it was over; everybody split. Photographers and TV caught it, but the Man was late. Timing was success.

Stew Albert Jerry and I became increasingly alienated from the Mobe. Jerry was hanging out with Abbie and smoking dope, and the hard nuts-and-bolts work of being the project director of the upcoming antiwar demonstration became very unappealing. The Mobe people started complaining that he wasn't doing enough work, and he started getting attacked. Then we put out an issue of a newsletter, the *Mobilizer,* and Keith Lampe wrote a proto-Yippie piece called "On Making a Perfect Mess," and the newsletter was suppressed. I remember the guy from the Department Store

Workers Union said, "This article calls for looting department stores; I can't go to my members with this newsletter."

Jerry Rubin When I came to New York the Mobe was planning to march on Congress, not on the Pentagon. I told Dave Dellinger that's a big mistake because the Pentagon would be seen as the enemy, whereas the Congress is kind of neutral. So that weekend we all flew to Washington to scout out the Pentagon and we all became convinced. Then I became closer and closer to Abbie. It was my idea to confront the Pentagon. It was Abbie's to do the whole exorcism. I didn't even know what exorcism was.

Allen Ginsberg It was Gary Snyder [the poet] who conceived the notion of the levitation of the Pentagon.

Jerry Rubin Dave Dellinger's big mistake was inviting me to come to New York. They were trying to have an orderly, peaceful, middle-class protest and I brought in Abbie. It was a perfect partnership because Abbie added the theater, the humor, the sparkle, and I added the purpose. I took the Abbie windup doll, I wound him up and pointed him toward the Pentagon.

Bill Zimmerman, *antiwar activist* Abbie really played a seminal role in the development of American political opposition because of what he did with getting our message into the mass media. Everyone now looks back on the late sixties and attributes a lot of the development of the antiwar movement to the fact that the war was on television. We found ways to get the establishment to deliver our message into everybody's home through the use of television.

But as the same story began to be repeated endlessly, one demonstration after another, the interest of the media waned. And in '67, Abbie and others began to figure out how to execute something that came to be called guerrilla media. Visual images and dramatic confrontations like the raining of money down on the stock market or the Pentagon exorcism became wildly interesting from a news standpoint. That began to tell the kids in America that there wasn't just a movement against the war, there was a different way of looking at the world, there was an ability to call things absurd that they could understand and relate to and that disengaged them from the reward structure that controlled them and kept them from opposing the war. It was critical to the development of the movement that you could sacrifice your career, you could sacrifice material wealth, you could sacrifice stability and have more fun!

Jim Fouratt The Pentagon action showed the real brilliance of Abbie, to be able to take the hippie element and weld it with the hard-line political reality. It did a lot of things. It acknowledged where the war was being fought, where it had to be stopped, the physical space. The Pentagon was a mythic thing. Most people didn't know what the Pentagon looked like. And then you bring in Allen Ginsberg, and you bring in American Indians, and you bring in shamans, and you burn yarrow around the whole fucking place. You think Abbie believed in a lot of that stuff? I don't think so. But he's smart. Anything that would disrupt the mind-set of Middle Americans, anything that attacked their value system, Abbie thought was good.

Anita Hoffman [After] the stock exchange thing happened, and the *New York Post* had this big picture of Abbie, their writer John Garabedian was assigned to cover us.

OCTOBER 1967

John Garabedian The whole Lace thing was probably *the* most bizarre story I ever covered. It was the week before the march on the Pentagon. I was at my desk in the city room and there was a message to call Hoffman. When I called him back, he let me know that hippie chemists had invented a new wonder drug which combined the best properties of LSD with a drug called DMSO, a legitimate skin-penetrating agent used to treat certain kinds of arthritis. And therefore on the day of the march to the Pentagon—which, by the way, by magic was going to be levitated—hippie chicks would fill squirt guns full of this love potion, which consisted of LSD and DMSO, and squirt them on the soldiers or anyone else of an evil or warlike frame of mind, thereby causing them to want to stop making war and immediately make love. Abbie was having a live demonstration of the product that evening at seven o'clock in his apartment. And he would guarantee that reporters would see people really make love. When I went to his apartment there was a guy from the *New York Daily News,* someone from either UPI or AP and me. Oddly enough, Hoffman himself did not show up there that evening. There was only his wife, Anita, who introduced the participants in this drama, [then] three hippie couples came in.

Anita Hoffman We used water guns to spray the Lace. We had Shapiro's Disappearo, a novelty item which was a red liquid that disappeared when you sprayed it on. Half of me couldn't believe this was actually happening in my own living room. I just shyly snuck away and I waited it out.

John Garabedian Each of the girls took a squirt gun, which probably was full of nothing but water, and squirted it on the males. They then proceeded with ecstasy and immediately swept them over onto the mattresses. These three couples got undressed and after a little foreplay, all three of them were screwing. This was one of the more colorful and I might say aromatic events that I ever observed.

Teddy Mastroianni I was at the precinct talking to some cops and Abbie comes in. He has his bottle of Lace and he says, "If I spray this stuff on any one of you guys, you're going to fuck each other." The lieutenant is behind his desk, and the sergeant was doing his paperwork. The sergeant, one of those big, hairy muscular guys, had short sleeves. So Abbie jumps up on a desk and sprays the sergeant. And the sergeant says, "Get out of here!" And Abbie says you're going to fuck the lieutenant and the sergeant says, "Nooooo, noooo!" They chased Abbie out of the precinct. The sergeant was really convinced that he was going to fuck the lieutenant.

Marty Carey We got the idea we're gonna exorcise the Pentagon, which meant that we're going to hold hands, circle the Pentagon and chant. Traditional ritual. Abbie and I decided we have to figure out how many people it takes to circle the Pentagon. So we went down by train. We get to the parking lot of the Pentagon and we put all of these leaflets on the windshield wipers of the cars there. Then we go to one side and we hold hands one, two, and then we switch and alternate. We were just starting to count when some security people come out and arrest us and bring us inside the Pentagon, which was pretty eerie. There's big huge hallways and messengers are roller-skating down them. They take us down to this little room and this black security guy says we were arrested. So Abbie says, "What's the charge?" "Littering." The guard starts to ask us what we're doing here and I tell him that we were a theater group from New York and we were gonna exorcise the Pentagon, and explain the whole thing. Then Abbie starts talking to this black guard. "How can you be black and work for these guys?" Now I'm scared shitless. Finally they say they're gonna let us go but Abbie doesn't want to be let go. Because if we're not let go then somebody can say they're arrested for littering and then it gets publicity. I just said, "Let's get out of here." So they let us go.

Jerry Rubin We actually negotiated to what extent we could disrupt the Pentagon. That was the craziest thing about it. Lyndon Johnson's government, the General Services Administration negotiated—you can step here, you can't step there, you can do it here, you can stop there, don't do this.

Daniel Ellsberg, *Pentagon researcher, antiwar activist* I was both inside and outside because I was working on the Pentagon Papers then in a room next to McNamara's office. We were working with the files on Vietnam. I'd spent two years in Vietnam and I'd come back in June of '67 and started work on this in the fall. I'd come back very anxious to see the war end.

While I was in Vietnam, I wasn't seeing any newspapers at all, so I didn't have a very vivid notion of the movement but I was very anxious to support anybody who was trying to get the war ended. Levitating the Pentagon struck me as a great idea because removing deference from any of these institutions is very important, and this is of course the kind of thing that Abbie understood instinctively. So they have a press conference, and they're talking about their plans, in a very straight and measured and reserved way. And when it gets to be Abbie's turn to speak, he says, "We're gonna raise the building six feet in the air." I think that really changed the terms. In the Pentagon it became, "Can he really do that? Six feet!"

Sal Gianetta The two meetings I knew of, one in New York and one in Washington, were probably the best examples of Ab's brilliance. There were some Washington representatives and there were two military representatives. It started out that no way in the world was there gonna be any kind of activity anywhere around the Pentagon, which was the fucking basilica of Peter of the United States, no fucking way. Right away Ab says, "Fuck you, we'll levitate the fucking thing high enough you won't be able to get in. Then what're you gonna do with your fucking Pentagon?" They actually responded. That was the first inkling he had that he might be able to suck them into this. After that the levitation became *the* cause célèbre.

At the other meeting I was at Ab threw the levitation on the table, right for openers. Ab was adamant that the fucking building was gonna go up twenty-two feet—because somebody had told him except for fire ladders, you can't get a ladder that's twenty-two feet. So he was willing to negotiate. If the fucking building went up twenty-two feet the foundations were gonna crack, so there was discussion about foundations and cracks, it was fucking unbelievable. That meeting was two and a half hours or so and probably 20 percent of that meeting was devoted to this fucking serious talk about levitating the Pentagon. This is our military, right? I swear to you, Ab came down from twenty-two feet to three feet, the military agreed to three feet and they sealed it with a handshake. That's how Ab was, he could capture you in that fucking bizarreness. Oh, it was joyful!

Art Goldberg The Mobilization had lined up hundreds of buses to get the people to Washington. Abbie demanded tickets for people from the Lower East Side, so they gave him two hundred. Pretty soon, people were redeeming the tickets, getting their money back. It was Abbie's fund-raising scam for the levitation event.

Anita Hoffman The Pentagon was my favorite demonstration, the perfect flower-power, hippie event. I was wearing the Sgt. Pepper jacket. And we had Mr. and Mrs. America paper Uncle Sam hats. I see the Careys. They got a blanket spread, they're smoking grass, they're having a picnic, singing songs, playing guitar, having a great time. I'm with Abbie, we gotta fucking confront the troops. He's got me by the hand and he's not going where the crowds are going. He's going where they put up these temporary fences and they have these soldiers way out in these fields where if you got beat up nobody would ever know, there's no media or anything. He has me running across fields, jumping barricades. I was shitting inside, but I'm putting up this good front. I thought of the Careys with such jealous hatred. Why can't we be hippies, why can't we just be like them?

It had all moods. The Spocks and the MacDonalds were there, and Norman Mailer. As it became darker it got scarier and scarier. That's where the famous picture of Superjoel putting the flower in the gun was taken.

Superjoel I was between Abbie and Dr. Spock. We're walking up on the grounds of the Pentagon. And on top of this pile of trash there's this bunch of flowers, daisies, right. I grabbed them. I saw these soldiers, and they're all standing there and they were my age. So I just took the flowers and one by one, boom, boom, boom, put 'em in the gun barrels. 'Cause we had done this flower-power crap in Berkeley already. Then that guy Rosenthal, who took the Iwo Jima picture, took that famous picture of me.

Ed Sanders I had gone to Harry Smith, my friend, and asked him what really happens at an exorcism. Since I knew Indo-European languages, I learned this Hittite exorcism ritual. I actually put together a decent exorcism. Our group, the Fugs, were playing the Ambassador Theater in D.C. We had a $2,000 gig, so we had a lot of cash. I needed a cow, so I rented a cow, which I was gonna paint like the Egyptian goddess Hathor. But the cow got stopped by the police. Tuli and I rented a good sound system and a flatbed truck, and we had the Fugs and all the Diggers, and we had this big poster with a *novus ordo seclorum,* with the eyeball on top of the pyramid. My idea was just to get to the Pentagon. But Abbie viewed this flatbed truck with the poster with the back of the dollar bill on it and the sound system and "Out, demons, out" to be the vanguard of the main Mobe march. So he jumped up on the wagon and wanted us to slow down and cut off and become the head of this march. I didn't see it like that at all. I just wanted to get across the bridge without getting arrested and get to the Pentagon early, before they shut things down. Basically I just told the driver to get the hell over there. We got as close as we could get. We tried to get where we felt that the marchers were gonna go by. There was some sort of right-wing nut there on top of a cherry picker, waving a Bible, who kept trying to back toward us, so I had to do this counterspell. I knew he was superstitious, so I raved at him. Then we did the exorcism chant, "Out, demons, out."

Allen Ginsberg The levitation of the Pentagon was a happening that demystified the authority of the military. Its authority had been unquestioned and unchallenged until then. But once that notion was circulated in the air and once the kid put his flower in the barrel of the kid looking just like himself but tense and nervous, the authority of the Pentagon was psychologically dissolved.

Ed Sanders Kenneth Anger was underneath the flatbed truck. He had a pentagram made from Popsicle sticks. It looked like he was burning a pentagon with a tarot card or a picture of the devil and he was making snake sounds at whoever should try to come near. He told me that he had been inside the Pentagon weeks ago to bury something. He viewed the thing we were doing above him as the exoteric thing and he was doing the esoteric, serious, zero-bullshit exorcism. Then Tuli was arrested.

Tuli Kupferberg We managed to sit down in the driveway for thirty seconds. I saw kids climbing up ropes, really trying to get in. When I was being arraigned, there were people there with three-piece suits getting arrested, professional people. You could see Middle America was now against the war and that was amazing to me and I think McNamara and those "Pentagon intellectuals" must have noticed that too.

John Eskow Part of the action, under the heading of the whole exorcism thing, was supposed to be all these couples making love. Abbie took it upon himself to be a kind of matchmaker, grabbing people and saying,

"No, you're with her, and he should be with her and get that other guy out of there, and lie down now. Come on, do it!" There weren't really very many people making love—it was too scary for that. I remember arriving on the lawn with this young woman, and Abbie, on the microphone in the distance, saying that all these couples were gonna make love and then I was tapped on the shoulder by an extremely polite Washington policeman, and he said, "Excuse me, but I have to ask you, are you planning to consummate this?" I said, "Yeah, why?" And he said, "Because if you do consummate, I'm going to have to arrest you." Then Ed Sanders was chanting the ritual invocations and I was up and the passion was over and I wasn't arrested for consummating, and suddenly we were all moving towards the Pentagon itself. There were always those moments in these demonstrations where suddenly, as if from some underlying rhythm, what was a kind of gentle movement of people became a surge. It would just turn from a kind of cultural carnival to a terrifying nightmare. I remember getting the first whiff of tear gas and groping for the hand of the girl that I was with and both of us just being too blinded and overwhelmed by both the tear gas and the cops and the people running away from the Pentagon now to even hold on to each other. Just getting swept up in a real stampede.

Michael O'Donoghue Back then, I had what was called a Vietcong flag rule of marching. I'd always look for the Vietcong flags because those are the people I wanted to march with. They didn't stop for red lights.

Robin Palmer When people started marching from the bridge, there was a race to get to the Pentagon. There were all these different currents going, it was more or less chaos. We got to the Pentagon first and they had these stanchions all the way around, at least in the parking lot closest to the bridge where everyone was walking across. So we went charging across with our Vietcong flags. We used to put them on these cardboard garment tubes because the cops would not let you put a flag on a stick at a demonstration, that was against the law.

The government had recruited marshals from all over the country; they had the marshals lined up on the other side of these stanchions with a rope running from stanchion to stanchion to stanchion. And it was only a few feet high. The marshals were not terribly imposing. They looked like rent-a-cops. So all these people catch up to me and Sharon but when they saw the stanchions, they just stopped cold. I said, "Why don't we just charge 'em? There's just a thin line of marshals. Let's at least bang on the door if

THE PROTEST AT THE PENTAGON, 1967. DESPITE THE LOWER EAST SIDE CONTINGENT'S MOST VALIANT EFFORTS, THE BUILDING WASN'T LEVITATED. Archive Photos

nothing else." I'm trying to organize people to do it and they say, "This is as far as we go." Somebody had a bowie knife and I chopped the rope and then I charged with the cardboard tube and the flag and I started pounding the nearest marshal on the head with the Vietcong flag and the tube and that was supposed to get people to charge up the steps but they didn't do it and the cops started beating the shit out of me. I was probably the first bust. They took me in and then immediately released me so I went back to the demonstration and got arrested again. Dr. Spock bailed me out.

Jeff Jones Some people actually got inside the door and were beaten back out.

Tom Neumann Ben Morea and the Motherfuckers were the only ones who actually managed to get into the Pentagon. They were in the corridors having pitched battle with the security guards while everybody else was out levitating the Pentagon.

Bill Zimmerman Abbie and his people got all the press, but they didn't represent everybody that was out there. There were religious groups and labor leaders, all kinds of people. There had been demonstrations and Fifth Avenue Parade Committee actions that involved people in as large a number as came to the Pentagon but the Pentagon was the first time that such a massive number of people had experience in civil disobedience. It was a mind-blowing event to confront massive numbers of police, backed up by uniformed armed military. And we overran them. They were shoulder-to-shoulder, billy clubs, bayonets, but people started getting through. We didn't know up until that point that we had physical power. We thought we had moral power, but we began to see that with sufficient numbers we had a kind of physical power.

Michael O'Donoghue There was a lovely little thought process I went through, which is let's see, there's machine guns, they're pointed at the enemy, and they're pointed at me! Wheeeew! I guess I am the enemy. I got teargassed pretty badly that fucking time, and because I had hay fever, I was near dying. Then I went to the medical hut that the government had set up and the nice old nurses fixed me up. I said this is a pretty hot little government.

Jeff Jones Years later I heard that McNamara's standing up there looking out and he said, "We've lost the war in Vietnam." We had no idea at that point in time.

Daniel Ellsberg I was personally irritated that this thing was being held on a Saturday, instead of a weekday, that they were demonstrating in front of what I knew was an essentially empty building. In those days, it was easy on a weekday to get inside the Pentagon without a pass. Hundreds and maybe thousands of people could have infiltrated the building and then sat down, taped posters on walls, raised hell nonviolently. I think they could have stopped business for a while. But on a weekend the place was shut tight.

Then I saw people trying to go in through the doors, which by this time, of course, were guarded. They'd imported marshals from the South, the kind that they'd seen do such good work in Birmingham. Real redneck tough guys. They were beating some of the demonstrators on the ground and when you see that, it's amazing how quickly that evokes violent feelings in people watching it. I felt that. Up till that moment I would have said the mood was picniclike.

So after watching that for a while, I decided to go inside and see what was happening. The halls were deserted and I went up to our office and then decided that I could get a better look at what was happening from McNamara's office, which was next door, so I went through the door, and after a minute, I realized that McNamara was actually in there. McNamara had his back to me and he was looking out the window. Well, the natural thing would be to get out since I did not have an informal relationship with him. But on the other hand, I did know him and had written speeches for him. So I decided to just go over to the window and take a look. So he was at one window and I was at another, we were looking down at this thing. Neither of us said anything. He just stood there. I've told people that I wanted to see the expression on his face when they succeeded in levitating the building. But that didn't happen. My own actual feeling was, looking down on them, it was too much of a football-rally kind of crowd. I was afraid that it wasn't having the impact on McNamara that I wanted it to have. I knew, by the way, at that time, that he wanted the war to end and so I assumed that he had a basic sympathy, at least with the goals.

Bill Zimmerman There were maybe 200,000 people. The troops from the 82nd Airborne had surrounded the building with fixed bayonets. And presumably unloaded rifles. Everybody sat down in front of them. As it got dark and cold on Saturday night, people started leaving. A die-hard group of about 600 or 700 people spent the whole night sitting out there.

Jeff Jones Later that night, they started arresting people and taking them away and the arrests were quite brutal and sudden and then things would quiet down again. As the situation stabilized, somebody set up a microphone to serve as a command post on the protest side and Abbie took over that role. The revolutionary emcee.

Stew Albert We had some kind of permit and at the end of the permit period, Sunday night, they made a sweep and arrested everybody.

Anita Hoffman It was peaceful. The men and women were separated. Abbie and I gave our names as Mr. and Mrs. Digger.

Stew Albert They put us in this big van, shut the door, and we drove off. It was real dark in the van and Abbie freaked out. He started trying to kick at the door to break it open. But that didn't succeed, and we wound up in some kind of barracks situation.

Wolfe Lowenthal, *antiwar activist* I think I got hit once or twice, then they just dragged me off and put me in a bus and took me to the compound. I fell in love with Abbie in that compound. Such an up spirit. I remember at one point Abbie put this sheet over his head as if he's a Ku Klux Klan guy and he goes up to the front of the bars and says, "Hey, let me out of here. I'm in here with all these Jews and commies."

Stew Albert When bail was made for him, the cop came in and just shouted "Digger!" And Abbie went out.

Jerry Rubin It was the perfect theatrical event. My goal was for the whole world to hear that the youth of America are opposed to the American war machine and they must stop. Total success. As a matter of fact, probably because of that event Johnson saw his power slipping and decided not to run again.

Robin Palmer We drove back with Abbie and Anita. He was thrilled. He had insisted that they had levitated the Pentagon. Hadn't I seen it? But I began to appreciate Abbie's style and politics. Revolution for the hell of it? I instinctively understood what he meant. On the other hand I was straighter, more orthodox. I considered drugs to be counterrevolutionary. I hadn't opened all my pores the same way Abbie did. I was, in Tom Neumann's words, a well-intentioned politico in Abbie's eyes and Abbie was a crazed nut in my eyes and we resolved a lot of that during that trip back from Washington. I got the impression that Abbie was a cultural revolutionary and he thought more domestically than Sharon and I did. Abbie was definitely not a Marxist-Leninist. Later it was the other way around. But then Abbie would say, "Communist Party, no way. No dope. It's a crime to be homosexual. What are they talking about?"

Jerry Rubin After the Pentagon, we had the "War Is Over" march in New York. That was all Phil Ochs. Brilliant theater. Phil based it on that famous World War II poster of the guy kissing the girl [in Times Square]. Phil said, "Let's just declare it over. The war is over."

Steve Tappis, *SDS member, antiwar activist* We were running down Fifth Avenue saying, "The war is over!" And people were saying, "Is it really, is it really?" Everybody was so happy. I still don't understand why we did it.

Wolfe Lowenthal There was a demonstration against Secretary of State Dean Rusk in front of the Hilton Hotel in New York. We were throwing blood, stopping limousines, a lot of mobile tactics. It was fun!

Anita Hoffman I remember cops on horses galloping along sidewalks and people running in fear. A guy wearing a brown leather jacket tackled Abbie and tussled him to the ground, then showed his badge. So that was yet another arrest for Abbie.

Abbie Hoffman *(interviewed by Barry Shapiro)* It was on TV that night, it was incredible-looking, they chased me around the streets, cops, I'm fighting them, close-ups, wow. Okay, they took me to the 17th Precinct, handcuffs on, and they beat me up. I came to be interviewed by a national CBS reporter. So I put a Band-Aid on my forehead with a little red under it. There was nothing wrong with my forehead. There was no comment made about it or nothing, you just saw this thing going on in the street, all the fighting and I'm describing what happened in the police station and describing where our politics are at, it's very dramatic, but the Band-Aid is totally fake. Now is that a lie? He didn't say, "Is your forehead okay?" I don't know what I would have said. I would have said, "Oh, it's nothing." Which it is. A priest that I used to work with in the civil rights movement called me up after seeing it in Massachusetts and said, "The Band-Aid was fake." He knew.

Bob Ockene had spent the day of the Pentagon demonstration inside the Pentagon, thanks to Sy Hersh of the New York Times. *After the event, Ockene compared notes with his colleague Keith Lampe.*

Keith Lampe aka Ponderosa Pine I was in agreement with everything Ockene was saying. He said, "Okay, the biggest scandal of this whole occasion was that the short-hair–nonpsychedelic–New Left, Tom Hayden and Rennie Davis crowd controlled all of the rhetoric, split when the marshals arrived, and the freaks and hippies took the skull bash and the jail time. Therefore from now on, there has to be some kind of loose media representation of the freaks and hippies if they're gonna do the skull bash and the jail time, and it should be egalitarian and nonhierarchical. It should have a sense of humor to help overcome the increasing paranoia from police pressure." He named the characteristics that this group should have. And so the two of us each phoned about eight people, including Ed Sanders, Allen Ginsberg, Abbie Hoffman, Jerry Rubin, Paul Krassner, Kate Coleman. And out of that meeting we formed Yippie.

Paul Krassner In December of '67 I went to Florida with Abbie and Anita. We needed a vacation.

Anita Hoffman This was at Ramrod Key. Our landlady had a lagoon with dolphins, so we would play with the dolphins. I guess we took acid a few times. This was the first time we ever really played and we were outside of the Lower East Side. Just plain hedonism. No pressures, no slum, no movement, no nothing, just us. It was amazing.

Paul Krassner Abbie and I were discussing violence in the revolution. I had been to Cuba and even though I was not violent I could understand how people, at a certain point, had no choice. They were abstract philosophical discussions, Abbie didn't even have a weapon. But he thought that violence was necessary, that justice was more important than peace. I'm emphasizing that this was philosophical exploration because Abbie's weapons were his wit and his imagination, even though he was a street fighter by nature. By then there had been a vague plan in the movement of going to Chicago for the Democratic convention. It was almost a given that there were gonna be organized demonstrations there. But because of the Pentagon and other demonstrations where there had been music and dance, there had been talk of some kind of a music festival, a Festival of Life. So we were discussing that in Florida, a lot. I called Dick Gregory in Chicago and Jerry in New York. In fact, we came back early, in time to celebrate New Year's in New York.

Jerry Rubin Let them have the credit, but I'm gonna tell you how I remember it just for the hell of it. I'm sitting in my New York apartment and I read that the convention's gonna be in Chicago and I say to myself that's it, that's the next big party, Chicago. I call them and I said to them, "Hey, we gotta go to Chicago." I think they said they were on acid at the time when I reached them. They cut the trip short because they got so excited about it. And that's when we all sat down in a room and laid out this whole plan to take over America through the Yippies.

Paul Krassner So if the conception was in the Keys, the birth took place at Abbie and Anita's apartment on the afternoon of December 31st, 1967. Not the nighttime as many of the legends have it. I brought Carol Shebar. Martin and Susan Carey were there. Ed Sanders was there. Jerry was there. Danny Schechter was there. Everybody was stoned but not on acid. Colombian marijuana. We were making plans. Although I invented the name, it was just a label for a phenomenon that already existed. I knew that the mythologizing process needs a name. Zeus! Something! So I went into the other room, and went through the alphabet, to see what name would be appropriate to demonstrate the radicalization of hippies. I'm going through, ippie, bippie, dippie, hippie, I'm ready to give up, wippie, yippie. Yippie! It was so perfect I stopped there and didn't even get to zippie!

So I sat there, up in Abbie's loft bed. Yippie! That's perfect! Then I'm working backwards. Okay. It was acronym time. I thought what could the words be? Youth, it was a youth movement, no question about that. I, international, it was an international movement, too, it was not just happening in America. And P, P, P, P. Party! It was so perfect, it was like a religious epiphany for me. "Listen to this! Listen to this! I got a name! We can call ourselves the Yippies!" After a little discussion they realized how appropriate it would be, because yippie is a shout of joy, it had all the elements. By the time the meeting was over we were the Yippies, the Youth International Party.

Abbie was angry at me for taking credit. He wanted the mythology to be that it was a community effort. I couldn't deny what was an epiphany for me in order to be politically correct.

Teddy Mastroianni I had asked Abbie why he named his group Yippie and he said that he was walking across the street and there was an old lady who looked like she hadn't had sex for a long time and he grabbed her by the ass and she turned around and she said "Yippie!" and he said he knew then that was the name of his organization.

Jerry Rubin The following week Ray Mungo and Marshall Bloom who ran the Liberation News Service sent out our news release all around the country.

AN ANNOUNCEMENT: YOUTH INTERNATIONAL PARTY (OR YIP!) IS BORN

> Join us in Chicago in August for an international festival of youth music and theater. Rise up and abandon the creeping meatball! Come all you rebels, youth spirits, rock minstrels, truth seekers, peacock freaks, poets, barricade jumpers, dancers, lovers and artists. It is summer. It is the last week in August and the NATIONAL DEATH PARTY meets to bless Johnson. We are there! There are 500,000 of us dancing in the streets, throbbing with amplifiers and harmony. We are making love in the parks. We are reading, singing, laughing, printing newspapers, groping and making a mock convention and celebrating the birth of FREE AMERICA in our own time . . . Everything will be free. Bring blankets, tents, draft cards, body paint, Mrs. Leary's cow, food to share, music, eager skin and happiness. The threats of LBJ, Major Daley and J. Edgar Freako will not stop us . . . The life of the American spirit is being torn asunder by the forces of violence, decay and the napalm, cancer fiend. We demand the politics of ecstasy. We are the delicate spoors of the new fierceness that will change America. We will create our own reality. And we will not accept the false theater of the Death Convention. We will be in Chicago. Begin preparations now! Chicago is yours! Do it!

Jerry Rubin The *New York Post* picked it up, big story on page five. So we knew we had a hot thing. Then it was just planning towards Chicago, creating a big theatrical event.

Abe Peck, *writer,* Chicago Seed Someone once said the revolution ended the first time that Abbie was on *Cavett* and they broke for commercial. I'm not sure if it's all Abbie, some of it's Jerry and some of it's Krassner, but this is how the thinking goes. The evidence is that in every large city and frankly in every small town where we're speaking, there are these new kinds of people, these freaks. They're not in one place, they're everywhere. And because we care about changing this country and also because we see that they're the ones with the energy, how can we reach these people? We're not organized, we don't have the reputation, we're a fringe group. We're like the vegetarians or the Santa Claus Party. How do we get publicity? And so because Abbie and Jerry and Paul are clever they began to really engage in this kind of media battleground of essentially forcing their way to media attention.

Anita Hoffman That whole fall-winter, we hung out with Jerry and [his girlfriend] Nancy a lot. We'd get together with them in their apartment and play around with ideas, or go to the movies.

Jerry Rubin I didn't get along with Anita at that time because she saw me as injecting Abbie into danger, taking him away from her family life and putting him in the streets. Of course, I was hard to get along with at the time too, I'm not saying that I was exactly a picnic.

Stew Albert When they first met, Jerry idolized Abbie. But Jerry would always fall for these charismatic male figures like other guys would fall for a woman. And Abbie wanted to work with Jerry. There's something you have to remember about Jerry at this point. Although this is very hard to believe, in Berkeley Jerry was a behind-the-scenes guy. Jerry was not a good speaker. I think Abbie had a sense that he'd be out front, doing the speaking, and Jerry'd be making it happen. Abbie'd be like Fidel Castro, Jerry'd be like Lenin. Jerry couldn't buy it and then Abbie thought that Jerry was invading his turf.

Anita Hoffman Jerry understood power. Abbie was an artist. He was very existential, in the moment, going with it, I don't really think he cared about power.

Jerry Rubin I was more angry, I was a much more single-minded, obsessively purposeful political person to my core. I don't know if I want this quoted today, we're now in the nineties, I'm blending in here, but I was for the overthrow of capitalism, the destruction of white culture, who knows what. I had in my mind it would all be one big rainbow family. We're gonna take the money away from all the rich, share it among everybody, transform society and have one big peaceful world. That was my goal. When I first came to New York, Abbie took me on Bob Fass's radio show and showed me how to speak like a hippie as opposed to a Berkeley political radical. I was modeling Abbie, just hearing how he talked. I'm an ex-journalist. I was a reporter from 1955 to 1962 for the *Cincinnati Post.* I covered the Reds, I interviewed Fabian, Jack Kennedy, Pat Boone. So I understood media. I knew opposites make stories. I have a journalist's soul. I knew that if I was gonna wear a Revolutionary War uniform to HUAC in 1966 that would be a national story. Reporters are lazy, right? They're just gonna pick up on this, even electronic media. I wasn't an electronic media journalist but like Abbie I was there for the birth of television. But despite that, we were probably more into print media. Print in a way is just as powerful because that story about burning money at the stock exchange was the feature story in every paper in the country. With TV it just hits and it's gone! But the newspaper hangs around and then it comes out a week later in *Newsweek*. You get a second hit.

Stew Albert Jerry had been writing these big articles about Yippie for the underground press. And so pictures of Jerry as Mr. Yippie were appearing all over the country, and this was pissing Abbie off.

Jerry Rubin Abbie was very entertaining but I'd say when does the entertainment end and the serious discussion begin? I saw all American youth waiting to be organized, from working class to hippie to children of the rich. We had this whole idea, we were gonna take the children away from the establishment, channel the working-class anger into politics, politicize the hippies. It'd totally isolate the government.

Stew Albert It almost seemed that a lot of what went on was acid by-products, you know? You can't overestimate the effect of acid on the scene. People really were in a surrealistic, absurd sort of way and Yippie was definitely a political manifestation of it. You combined politics with acid and grass and doing wild stunts and it was a marvelous way to live! Yippie was a blending of decadence and idealism. We appealed to idealism. But we also appealed to fucking off, decadence, taking dope and getting laid and doing weird drawings on your body, the stuff that's usually identified with the decline of civilization. And yet we somehow got it all packaged into some kind of romantic, idealist, revolutionary mode.

Marshall Efron Yippie was part of the design to disrupt the Democratic Party and get the antiwar message across. Had nothing to do with anything else. It wasn't free love. All of it was designed to say we're in a war that's bullshit. The generals are lying to us, the politicians are lying to us. Dow was manufacturing napalm and we were defoliating the forests and you read in these scuzzy magazines that Vietnamese babies are being born with two heads or nineteen fingers, their nose is growing out of their asshole and the government didn't care. No, Agent Orange is good for you, and there are no people in those jungles anyway, because we cleared all the good people out. We're just fighting to protect democracy in Southeast Asia. So it was Abbie and Jerry and the other freaks, who were taking acid and smoking dope and looking wild and being the worst thing that could happen to your daughter, facing off against enraged hard-hatted Americans with sideburns saying, "We're fighting communism, we're on God's side." The American public was docilely accepting what its so-called leaders were giving them. And then there were these acid freaks, reading porno comic books, who were saying, "This is not true." So it was a topsy-turvy, upside-down world.

Kate Coleman All our Yippie meetings were open. Did anyone tell you about the time that the cops came? There were these black guys who came in dashikis with straight black pants and black shiny shoes and tape recorders. And none of us could throw them out because they were black, we didn't want to offend them.

Ed Sanders The Motherfuckers were disruptive at those meetings. Ben Morea stood up and said I had Swiss bank accounts. I felt so humiliated to have to stand up and say, "I do not now nor have I ever had any Swiss bank accounts." I had trouble paying my rent. I had turned my bookstore over to the community and they'd wrecked it and given away all the books.

John Fisk, *Lower East Side activist* At one meeting Abbie and Jerry announced that they were gonna give themselves a salary of fifty dollars a week. I took a little bit of offense at that, particularly because Rubin was independently wealthy at the time.

Jim Fouratt I was probably the only one at those public meetings who would speak up against the way an action was being planned. Abbie didn't like people being critical of him in public. He didn't know how to behave around it. He knew how to behave if it was a cop or someone on the other side.

Jeff Nightbyrd The SDS line on Yippie was that it was egotistical and self-centered, not serious, wasn't gonna build a revolution. I had mixed feelings about Abbie then because he and Jerry were doing really smart media stunts but not building organization. So where does this wind up, some cult figure, a political Lenny Bruce? Abbie, being a very instinctual person, hadn't really thought it out.

Sid Davidoff I remember Abbie in two different ways. One is [as] a rogue, funny, interesting, bright, one of the great con artists that we had in New York, and I think he thought that he was that himself. He didn't take himself too seriously. Because of that, the other Abbie is a very dangerous one. Because Abbie did not follow through. He would bring a crowd down to City Hall, sit on the grass, we'd begin talking, he'd make a demand, I'd make a counterdemand and then he'd disappear. You can't really deal with a leaderless mob and we often found ourselves with just that. Grand Central Station was probably the best example.

Jacques Levy, *stage director and writer* The idea was to go to Grand Central Station and have this thing called a Yip-In. And then a few weeks later there was going to be Easter Sunday in Central Park, which was going to be the Yip-Out, and these were the two events that were going to attract people to go on to Chicago. All of us were throwing in ideas about what to do in Grand Central Station. Can we get in early and decorate the place before the rush hour? Can we get all the guys from Madison Avenue to miss their train? Can we turn Grand Central Station into a picnic area?

Ed Sanders Keith Lampe thought we should celebrate the end of winter. The rock stations ran ads saying, "Let's have a groovy Yip-In at Grand Central tonight."

Jim Fouratt Abbie would play with the rhetoric of hippies, the rhetoric of a be-in. But Abbie was not a hippie. Ever. He was never a pacifist, he never claimed to be, he never lived his life that way.

Bob Fass Grand Central was a beautiful place. Nice big vaulted ceiling. I'm at WBAI, playing all the train songs. People are calling up and saying how great it is, people are coming with flowers and the police seemed to be having a good time themselves.

Jacques Levy Sid Davidoff and Barry Gottehrer were trying to be cooperative. But they did not want us to go in and take over Grand Central Station. They warned Abbie that there were going to be police there.

Teddy Mastroianni Barry was concerned that the kids might get hurt. They were thirteen, fourteen, much younger than before. The police chief, Sandy Garelik, was given orders not to arrest any kids and not to have any altercations.

Jacques Levy The place began to fill up until finally there must have been three thousand people there, much more than anybody expected. And more and more cops were coming in too. Somebody had a guitar, other people were dancing around, some people brought food and drinks, some were smoking dope. Crowds were coming off trains and getting

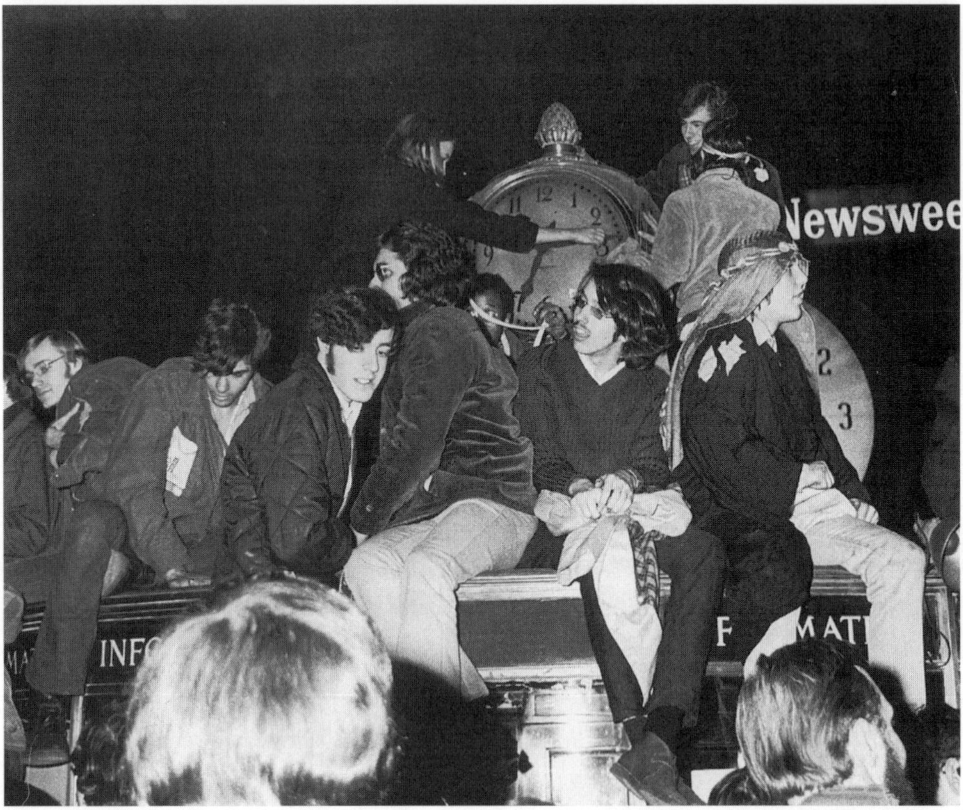

THE YIPPIE BE-IN AT GRAND CENTRAL. THREE THOUSAND HIPPIES DESCENDED ON THE TERMINAL, AND THEN THE POLICE DESCENDED ON THEM WHEN TWO OF THE UP AGAINST THE WALL MOTHERFUCKERS RIPPED THE HANDS OFF THE TERMINAL'S CLOCK SHORTLY AFTER THIS PHOTO WAS TAKEN. UPI/Corbis-Bettmann

stuck, they couldn't get out and there was a lot of jostling. But in general, the feeling was festive. But the cops were getting nervous. At one point the cops began to urge people to leave. When they wouldn't leave they began to poke at them with sticks and move them back, and form those lines that became standard stuff after this. But what was going on was a much more New York–oriented kind of thing, they'd push them, and the streetwise kids would run up the stairs, out the door, and come in from another entrance. This thing must have been going on for maybe an hour, and that's when a couple of guys from the Up Against the Wall Motherfuckers climbed up on the clock in the middle of Grand Central Station, and started to shout stuff like "Time is meaningless." To me this was a wonderful surrealist moment, getting up there not saying we rule the world, but shouting out intellectual slogans like "Let's abolish time, all time, all place." It was very funny. But as happens in a lot of these things, you get to a certain edge and if nobody stops you, you push a little further. One of them started to take the hands off the clock.

Teddy Mastroianni Three cops went up after the guys and they started using really excessive force. Then one of the cops said "wedge" and we saw these cops just hitting the goddamn kids. This reporter for the *Village Voice* got thrown through a plate-glass door. Then some cop got a shopping cart that's used to carry luggage and he hit this kid, broke his leg and we tried to stop him and the cops started swinging at us. I remember pulling out my badge saying "Mayor's Office" and the cop said, "Stick it up your ass."

Barry Gottehrer With blacks there was prejudice but there was also some fear. There was no fear of these white kids. It ended up being the worst police riot I've seen.

Sid Davidoff I can remember arguing with Garelik that we could handle this, we'll negotiate with the leadership, and Abbie at one point was no place to be found. And there was nobody to talk to.

Jay Levin, New York Post *reporter* I was covering the Yip-In for the *New York Post.* There were politics behind the Yip-In that they hadn't counted on because that asshole Garelik was positioning himself for a mayoral run. He was a wheeling, dealing, sneaky fuckup. He had the liberals thinking he was the good cop, right? But he couldn't afford to lose the line police or the establishment people. So he ordered this unprovoked attack by the cops and went and hid. I remember finding him hiding in a phone booth. I opened the door and I said, "What are you doing in the phone booth? Your guys are out there beating heads." "I don't see anybody beating anybody up." I said, "This is bullshit, you gotta stop this." He says, "I'm on a very important call."

Sandy Garelik Taking the hands off the clock, that's a symbolic act, yes. But how do you describe it to police officers who were tremendously outnumbered? What you had really was an assault on police officers, in a way. They're pushed out of the way, they lost control. There wasn't anybody that you could negotiate with. It just blew, the lines broke.

Sid Davidoff I got whipped that day. One of our guys went to the hospital. The horses can't tell the difference between a Mayor's Office guy and a Yippie, right?

Anita Hoffman The horror was that the only way to leave was through a gauntlet of police, and they were gunning for Abbie.

Abbie Hoffman *(from the ACLU report to the mayor)* As we were leaving Grand Central Station, going up the ramp to 42nd Street, a policeman entering Grand Central clubbed me in the back. The blow knocked the wind out of me and I blanked out for a few seconds. When I came to, I was picked up and pushed through the glass doors.

Anita Hoffman We took Abbie right to Bellevue.

Ed Sanders That was the beginning of the death of Yippie.

Jerry Rubin I don't remember. What was the idea there, to have a party all night? I was sorry somebody was hurt. But Keith Lampe was the moving force in the Yip-In. I didn't take responsibility for that one, that's his.

Keith Lampe aka Ponderosa Pine It hadn't occurred to me that too many people would show up and the police would get nervous. Abbie got his head smashed in. Some musician had a bad hand injury, his hand was ripped up when it got smashed through a revolving door. I was really worried about that. I dreamed about it all night.

Barry Gottehrer I think we all failed. We allowed it to happen. We didn't stop the cops.

Jim Fouratt I don't think Abbie anticipated a bloodbath. But the power establishment had had it with him. He wasn't playing according to their rules. He wasn't about to disrupt a major transportation center. This was not planting a tree on St. Mark's Place. This was where the people who live in Connecticut pass through every day.

From that point on, Abbie understood that bloodshed was a part of the scenario. That's why he was ruthless about Chicago, that's what the Yip-In taught him. That it was worth it as long as we get the press.

Jacques Levy I spoke to Abbie the next day. The feeling was that the cops had overreacted, but look at all the people that came out. There were more people than we thought who were really serious about this. So he was looking forward to the next event, the Central Park Yip-Out.

The Yip-Out was a relatively uneventful gathering of hippies. Abbie dressed as the Easter Bunny.

Sid Davidoff We cleared the park of uniforms. Somehow Lindsay was willing to suffer the image of letting people smoke marijuana in public rather than having to crack their heads. I think it was a big movement for government to recognize that beating up kids, whether they take showers or not or look dirty or not or wear bras or not, is not the answer to the problem.

* * *

Tim Leary There was a serious disagreement between me and Abbie and Jerry because I had been in Chicago that spring, and I had a press conference down in Lincoln Park where they had a zoo and they had some cows, and I had myself photographed with the cows. I had a lantern and I said, "We're gonna burn Chicago down like my great-grandmother, Mrs. O'Leary. Johnson will not land at that airport 'cause I'll have fifty thousand kids on the landing field."

Keith Lampe aka Ponderosa Pine We might have agreed but Leary didn't check it out, he just went to the networks all by himself with that quote inflammatory statement. It just gave the police an excuse, it was like saying we're going to put acid in the water supply.

MARCH 1968

Marshall Efron President Johnson couldn't appear anywhere without being booed. I remember the night that Johnson went on the air and said he wasn't gonna run for president. Abbie thought that he'd brought down Johnson.

Tim Leary I thought, "Wow, we toppled the fucking dictator." I was shocked when, like a locomotive in motion, the whole group wanted to go and have a demonstration anyway! That was one of the great moments of revolutionary suicide. You don't go into the middle of a scorpion's nest. Particularly when it was simply a question of whether it was going to be Kennedy or McCarthy. We were gonna have a youth president, a hippie president.

Chapter Four

CHICAGO, CHICAGO, THAT TODDLIN' TOWN

Ed Sanders From January till April of 1968, it seemed like Chicago was gonna be great. Abbie was lining up this Festival of Life. He always seemed to organize very intelligent, high-powered people, people who already had careers going and were overworked, and force those people to do more work in social action. To get Judy Collins, we were reaching out to all kinds of people. But after the Yip-In at Grand Central and the blood carnage, there was a kind of a crimp, and then somebody insulted Judy Collins and musicians began to get turned off by the thing.

Al Kooper, *musician* I played at a Yippie benefit to finance the Chicago thing at the Electric Circus. I'm very apolitical, but I was moved to do this because the political climate in this country was fucked up. So the gig comes and I have this fabulous Fender Telecaster guitar and somebody rips it off. I said to Abbie, "Hey, my fucking guitar got ripped off from the dressing room." He said, "Fuck you, so what!" That put the capper on my political career. Needless to say, I didn't go to Chicago. I was sitting shivah for my guitar.

Anita Hoffman After the Yip-In, they went to Chicago to negotiate.

In Grogan's "memoir" Ringolevio, *he recounts how he learned that Abbie was compiling a book allegedly based on the Digger papers that Emmett had given*

Abbie previously. Emmett went to Abbie's apartment only to find out from Anita that Abbie was out of town. Just then the phone rang and it was Abbie. Emmett asked Abbie to return the papers. When Abbie claimed not to have them anymore, Emmett threatened Abbie that if he printed or paraphrased any of the Digger papers he would have to answer to the Diggers.

From *Ringolevio* by Emmett Grogan

> Hoffman came back with the words to the effect that it was all "free," wasn't it? So how could he or anyone else steal "free"? . . .
>
> Emmett asked Abbot [*sic*] whether everything he had was really "free." . . . Abbot replied that it was all "free," that Emmett could take anything he wanted.
>
> Emmett hung up and walked to the front room where Abbot Hoffman's wife, Anita, was sitting . . . and talked with Anita for a while, before he took what he had to take, to show Abbot Hoffman how something "free" could be stolen and how it felt to have it taken.

FEBRUARY 1968

Abe Peck I'm a New York freak who's living in Chicago. I was an avid reader of the *Realist* and read this ad that Paul Krassner had put in saying, "I'm burning out in New York and I'm thinking of relocating the *Realist* to a farm." So in the true spirit of the time I immediately volunteered this guy's farm, without asking of course. Instead of getting Paul on the farm, I got Jerry Rubin in my living room telling me about this great party they were gonna have in Chicago in August '68. A big-time freak comes to my house and says, "Hey, wanna be the Yippies' man in Chicago?" I hate the war, I don't want a straight society, what's not to like? You mean I get to write for the underground press and hang out with hip people and maybe not go home alone? That doesn't sound too bad. So the first piece I wrote for the *Seed* was about this groovy festival that's gonna be in Chicago. At the same time, we had started feeling a lot of police pressure. Our first meeting of the Chicago Yippies was raided, we had twenty-five people busted because someone had a couple of joints with them. There was obviously an informer in that meeting.

Jim Fouratt The Yippies presented a letter to Mayor Daley with a list of demands, wrapped in a *Playboy* centerfold, because that was the big Chicago industry. When it was not responded to we went ahead and planned the Chicago action. And it became increasingly clear that it wasn't gonna be a festival. We had no real commitments from any real performers.

Peter Coyote These guys all knew there were not gonna be any rock bands, and no park permits, and no nothing. This was a piece of chicanery that they were playing on the backs of kids from all over the United States to come and get their fucking heads cracked.

Mike Rossman was a Berkeley radical who was asked by Jerry Rubin to help coordinate the Yippie protest.

Mike Rossman There had come to be by then a severe and profound division between the leadership echelons of what came to be seen as distinct wings of protest, the political and the hip. But both wings were projecting irresponsible lies through the media. The contradictions involved in the Yippie call were deeper than the contradictions involved in the Mobe call because for one, the political projection was to resist the warmakers, which is an activity that you kind of expect to get bloodied at. Whereas having an affirmative festival of life as a protest to the war was deeply contradictory, unless one understood that an affirmative festival of life included getting beat over the head.

Jim Fouratt Allen Ginsberg and I had agreed that Chicago was wrong. It was just not fair to the young people to manipulate them in this way. Then Allen told me that he'd had a nightmare. It was in Chicago and it was a bloody sea, and he was like Moses—he walked through and he separated it. He told me that he had to go to Chicago because he knew unless he went it would be a massacre.

Allen Ginsberg Jerry came over to see me and I said, "Listen, I don't want to do this unless it's really gonna be pacifist. On this occasion are you interested in violence or not?" He said no, absolutely not, that would be the wrong thing for this occasion. But I think he was lying to me, by hindsight.

Jim Fouratt The breaking point with Abbie was when I announced that I was not going to support the Festival of Life. Abbie told the press that I was a homosexual, that I was in love with him, and that is the reason there was a break. I can't tell you how it hurt me. This was before the gay liberation movement, and I was humiliated. How do you tell someone, a straight journalist, yes, I love Abbie but no, that wasn't our relationship. What do I do? Do I denounce him? I basically supported him. I never forgave Abbie for that and he never apologized to me for it. He said, "What was I gonna do? We had to get people to Chicago."

APRIL 1968

Abe Peck Martin Luther King is killed, there's riots all over Chicago. I wrote an open letter to Daley. Before it ran in the *Seed,* the April 27th peace march here was wiped out. It was probably the least violent march in the history of demonstrations, all suburban dentists for peace, little old ladies against the war, and it was just crushed. Then on May 2nd, we have twenty-six people arrested at a benefit at the Electric Theater. Police march in and declare a fire law violation; they threw fourteen hundred people out.

Dr. Eugene Schoenfeld I was writing a column for the underground press at the time as Dr. Hip. That's why I volunteered to do the medical planning for the demonstrations. I went to New York to meet the Yippies. Abbie was there and Jerry and John Gerassi. They were talking about how they were going to move right into the police lines, and that's when I said, "If you do that, people will get killed." And Abbie said, "Well, maybe a few people will be killed in Chicago but it will save thousands of lives in Vietnam." They told me what they wanted to do was to have Nixon elected; [then] things would become so bad that the revolution would take place and then the forces of good would take over, right? When I heard this, I said, "I'm backing out of this."

Jerry Rubin Gene's crazy. We didn't believe that. What we wanted was to have Walter Cronkite on national TV say it's a police state. That was our goal. It ended there. I wanted the inherent violence of America to be exposed. I felt America was a violent country, but the violence was being done to invisible people, browns, blacks. So I wanted the violence to be on TV, prime time, nonstop, boom! Smack right in your face. My plan in Chicago was we want good to be facing evil, we want young white kids beaten up by the cops.

Stew Albert We wanted to punish the Democrats. Look, the Democrats had given us this war. Now, of course that would mean that Nixon would get elected. I'll tell you the truth, we didn't care between Hubert Humphrey and Nixon.

Jerry Rubin Hayden met me and Abbie and he said people are gonna die in Chicago, we're gonna have to go underground, we'll have to form armed units. I thought this guy's nuts. I said, "Tom, why don't you just come to the Lower East Side, hang out with me and Abbie, we'll form a youth culture alliance, we'll create a whole alternative to America." He said, "This is serious, fascism is coming." I never felt fascism was coming, that's where Gene Schoenfeld's wrong. I thought that when push came to shove, the liberals would win.

From FBI Memorandum

U.S. Government Memorandum

TO: Mr. W. C. SULLIVAN DATE: 5/9/68
FROM: C. D. BRENNAN
SUBJECT: COUNTERINTELLIGENCE PROGRAM
INTERNAL SECURITY
DISRUPTION OF THE NEW LEFT

Our nation is undergoing an era of disruption and violence caused to a large extent by various individuals generally connected with the New Left. Some of these activists urge revolution in America and call for the defeat of the United States in Vietnam. They continually and falsely allege police brutality and do not hesitate to utilize unlawful acts to further their so-called causes. The New Left has on many occasions viciously and scurrilously attacked the Director and the Bureau in an attempt to hamper our investigation of it and to drive us off the college campuses. With this in mind, it is our recommendation that a new Counterintelligence Program be designed to neutralize the New Left and the Key Activists. The Key Activists are those individuals who are the moving forces behind the New Left and on whom we have intensified our investigations.

The purpose of this program is to expose, disrupt and otherwise neutralize the activities of this group and persons connected with it. It is hoped that with this new program their violent and illegal activities may be reduced if not curtailed.

Jeff Nightbyrd We started our underground paper *Rat* in '68. And very quickly I was involved in the May takeover at Columbia University.

There were certain allegations against Columbia: one, that they were taking all this black [occupied] housing and operating like slumlords; two, that they were seizing the blacks' park to make a gymnasium and swimming pool that the blacks couldn't go to; three, that they were intimately involved with the defense industry in doing war research; and four, that the structure of the university was operating in collusion with the "military-industrial complex" and not giving people education, but schooling them for running the empire. In the course of the night in [university president] Grayson Kirk's office, I and about two other people went through all his files. We printed the documents in the *Rat* proving the allegations that everybody was making and which the *New York Times* wouldn't touch.

Michael O'Donoghue The first time I was really taken with Abbie was at Fairweather Hall. This was when it was still called the Free University, and to get in, you had to go through a window and off a ledge. Oh, it was great excitement. There was an SDS meeting and French Maoists were attending this event. Abbie got up to speak and rather than stand behind the podium Abbie was walking on the desk. He had an electric yo-yo. He was making some point about destroying the state and he smashed the yo-yo against the wall, where it flew into pieces. Anyway, the French Maoists began giving him shit about some sort of revolutionary line that he wasn't being particularly true to. And he replied, "Shut up, you fucking commies! Come down here and say that." And just threatened to kick their ass. "Ohhhhh, what would Jean-Paul Sartre say about this?"

Sid Davidoff The establishment at Columbia truly believed that if we bring the police in, it's the end, they'll clean it up, the next day school would start. Never anticipating what would happen.

Sandy Garelik Well, the police went into Hamilton Hall and objects come flying down from the fifth floor.

Barry Gottehrer The kids who got hit and beat up the most at Columbia was the white kids with the long hair, the Abbie Hoffmans. Because these guys hit the cops the hardest emotionally.

Sid Davidoff The kids thought the cops were gonna throw tear gas in and the police thought that the kids had Molotov cocktails ready to throw out. You had seven busloads of TPF, which were the storm troopers in those days, former motorcycle cops, seeing these girls with the long hair and no bras, and these guys unshaven. If we had held them in that bus much longer, they would've hit *us*. As it was, my resignation was called for by the police for interfering, so it was a very tough day.

From FBI Memorandum

U.S. Government Memorandum

TO: Director, FBI DATE: 5/27/68
FROM: SAC, Newark
SUBJECT: COUNTERINTELLIGENCE PROGRAM
INTERNAL SECURITY
DISRUPTION OF THE NEW LEFT

Re Bureau letter to Albany, 5/10/68
It is believed that in attempting to expose, disrupt, and otherwise neutralize the activities of the "new left" by counterintelligence methods, the Bureau is faced with a rather unique task. Because, first, the "new left" is difficult to actually define; and second, of the complete disregard by "new left" members for moral and social laws and social amenities.

It is believed that the nonconformism in dress and speech, neglect of personal cleanliness, use of obscenities (printed and uttered), publicized sexual promiscuity, experimenting with and the use of drugs, filthy clothes, shaggy hair, wearing of sandals, beads, and unusual jewelry tend to negate any attempt to hold these people up to ridicule. The American press has been doing this with no apparent effect or curtailment of "new left" activities. These individuals are apparently getting strength and more brazen in their attempts to destroy American society, as noted in the takeover recently at Columbia University, New York City, and other universities in the U.S.

It is believed, therefore, that they must be destroyed or neutralized from the inside. Neutralize them in the same manner they are trying to destroy and neutralize the U.S.

Stew Albert By the spring, Chicago was on the verge of being called off. With Kennedy and McCarthy in the campaign, all the energy would be with them and no one would be much interested in the protest demonstration. Then Tom Hayden asked us not to call off the Yippie demonstration. Tom and Rennie [Davis] were working with the latest incarnation of the National Mobilization. Hayden said if you call it off, the media will interpret it that the Chicago demonstration as a whole had been called off. It would sabotage them. So we were going back and forth.

Jerry Rubin I don't think we ever wavered. Why would we not go? That's like saying you're not going to Broadway.

Stew Albert I was at Jerry and Nancy's and it was the middle of the night and the phone rings. It's Tom Hayden and he tells Jerry to turn on the television, Bobby Kennedy's just been shot.

Early that morning, we had a major Yippie meeting. It was a strange morning. Abbie was up. I'm very reluctant to say that, 'cause it makes him seem so horrible and he wasn't, it was just that how would Bobby Kennedy have felt if he heard Abbie had been shot? These people had put in a lot of time planning this event; Bobby Kennedy's entrance into the primaries had screwed all their energies, and now he was out and they were back up to doing what they had been doing. So they were happy about that. It wasn't so much that Bobby was dead, it was that he was politically out of the way.

Ed Sanders Rubin calls me up and says, "Did you hear the good news?" I said, "What good news?" I'd been crying, I was very upset. He says, "Now we can go to Chicago." So then it kicked forward. But events killed the Festival of Life. The abdication of Johnson, the assassination of King, the assassination of Robert Kennedy, the rise of Humphrey, Mayor Daley, violence, the CIA, the military intelligence operations going on, the war, everything convulsed and wrecked it. Plus, the Yippies themselves wrecked it. By trying to create Cuba on the Hudson. Or not having a thought-out program. We used to call Rubin "Pizza Street" 'cause we always felt he wanted this giant disgorgement of jugular veins in the streets.

Jack Newfield, *journalist* The Left became fratricidal, it turned in on itself and began to disintegrate. Bobby Kennedy and Martin King were the two mass leaders in the country, with a real following among liberals, students, poor people. And once they were both murdered, the leaders became maniacs.

* * *

Rennie Davis, *SDS leader* The war was the unifying issue. As much as I could identify with and work to end oppression or discrimination in the United States, Vietnam demanded our united effort. It was so horrible, and so hidden from us. Saturation bombing of villages took shape in buildings behind the college gymnasiums where we played basketball. It was just not comprehended that grants to university professors doing research would lead to cluster antipersonnel weapons. The war ignited a passion in me, a passion that Abbie had also. I came out of a fairly conservative family, I wanted to see the values of America redeemed, not destroyed. I wanted to see our generation save the country.

Larry Sloman, *journalist* I ran into Abbie a lot on St. Mark's Place those months before Chicago and it was always "You coming to Chicago, man? It's gonna be incredible, we're gonna blow some minds." He was doing everything but selling bus tickets.

Abe Peck June, no permit. And at this point, the New York Yippies are thinking of pulling out. We were not told that. Then Jerry's unfortunate statement, Sirhan Sirhan is a Yippie. Abbie called Kennedy's assassination the fastest recount in history.

The thing that got it for me was Abbie and Jerry were in the office and there's a moment of flipness from Abbie. They were doing the schedule for the convention week, which of course turned out to be impossible to schedule. And on the Wednesday, Abbie penciled in a riot. He was talking about twenty to thirty killed, six thousand wounded. Was that a prediction, a caution, a desire, an obituary, gallows humor?

So Chicago Yip decided to pull our permit application, we felt that this was untruth in packaging. Then I wrote this piece in the *Seed:* "If you're coming to Chicago be sure to wear some armor in your hair." I said we had a right to permits but at the same time if you're coming you ought to be aware that it's gonna be a potentially heavy scene. You can imagine the response to that. We had this huge meeting at the *Seed* office, Hayden showed up and the police were outside in their brown Chevys. Jerry was roaring about safety in numbers and Abbie was quite eloquent, he made comparisons to what the civil rights workers had faced in the South. He said when you bite the tail of the tiger you just don't let go.

Eventually a compromise was hammered out. Most of the original Chicago organizers kept their names off the new permit application. And everyone agreed to advise those who wanted a festival, purely a festival, not to come to Chicago.

John Schultz, *professor of journalism in Chicago* Chicago Mayor Daley was a very political animal, he could play the spectrum back and forth. So the FBI material that's coming into Daley and the army intelligence material is really reinforcing his basic get-tough conservative position. The FBI came in, they talked with the ninety-five commanders of the police department and the report of April 19th is a summary of what was said by them. It starts out saying that the New Left is a conglomeration of peace groups, civil rights groups, antiwar groups, this and that, and is not an arm of the Communist Party. So far pretty accurate. The next sentence is "But it will be penetrated and used by the communists at whatever opportunity." By the end of the first paragraph, everything this report called communist has dominance over anything that was said accurately in the very first sentence. By the end of the first page of this report, all Daley has heard is disruption, fomented by communists. "That's what I believed all the time. This is what's going to come down, I'm going to take a very tough stand against it." He's always disposed to do that in any case.

Although subsequent intelligence gave no support to Daley's fears, he acted on the earliest reports.

Paul Krassner Abbie and I negotiated with the mayor's assistant David Stahl. At one point Stahl asked me, "What do you guys plan to do in Chicago?" I said, "Have you seen *Wild in the Streets*?," the film where teenagers took over the government and put acid in the water supply. He said, "No, we've seen *The Battle of Algiers." Battle of Algiers* is guerrillas blowing up ice cream parlors. So what was gonna happen in Chicago was a clash between our mythology and their mythology.

Lee Weiner, *radical professor of sociology* Why didn't they give us a fucking permit? Because Daley was the mayor and he didn't want to give a fucking permit. He didn't like fucking bad Jews. Hey, if it was my city I wouldn't have given us the permit either.

Barry Gottehrer I remember having a conversation with the deputy mayor from Chicago. My recommendation was to give them the park and let them do whatever the hell they want to do and say you can't go beyond this. I didn't really believe that anything would happen. They couldn't even disrupt the Lower East Side. But the Chicago authorities really believed they would be able to do these things. I remember Abbie saying, "Barry, they really believe it when we tell 'em that we're going to put LSD in the water." I said, "Can you poison the water with LSD?" He said, "No, it won't work." When Abbie met with Stahl, at one point Abbie even offered to call everything off. "You give me $100,000 and we won't put LSD in the water."

John Schultz They pretended to take the Yippie threats seriously. You've heard about the LSD threat. Well, on July 20th the city received a letter from the Department of Narcotics that tells them it's impossible, it can't be done. The amount that would be required would be enormous and the chlorine would neutralize the acid. So the city had the Yippies stuck on the quiver, and they just kept pushing it. Abbie said that sometime in July, he and Rubin told David Stahl, "Look, this is impossible, this can't be done, you can't go on reacting like this." And Stahl very blithely told him, "Well, that's what our scientists say too, but maybe your scientists are more advanced than ours." Abbie thought that was pretty funny.

John Eskow Around this time, I was back living with my parents for a little while. The phone rang in my parents' little suburban kitchen and my father picked it up in his bathrobe, and his face went ashen and he held the phone out to me and said, "It's Abbie Hoffman." It was as though Mao Tse-tung had called and said, "Hello, can I speak to John, please?" My father just kept repeating "Abbie Hoffman wants to talk to you," like it was so bizarre. This was the nightmare call of any suburban parent at that point. Abbie Hoffman was coming into their kitchen with the Pop-Tarts!

Abbie Hoffman *(interviewed by the Walker Commission)* It was decided at that point, after that Chicago [permit] meeting, that I would stay on in Chicago and that I would essentially begin full-time organizing—twenty-four hours a day. I think I slept no more than three hours each night for a twenty-day period. But I was very stoned on it all and I really dug it.

Report to Chicago Police Department Intelligence Division

> *Re Youth International Party*
> *also known as Y.I.P., Yippies*
>
> The accompanying leaflets and pamphlet distributed by the Youth International Party should give a general idea of the activities to be engaged in by this organization. There are no set rules on what participating persons should or will do. Keith Lampe encourages everyone to attend and just do what you want to. This is referred to as "Doing your own thing."
>
> From prior demonstrations it can be expected that the participants will engage in:

Yippie!
CHICAGO AUG 25-30
SPREE — WOWEE — ARLO GUTHRIE — COLOR — GIGGLE — STREET — PLEASURE — HAPPENING — DANCING — JOY —
THE POLITICS OF ECSTASY — COUNTRY JOE AND THE FISH — BLANKETS — POETRY — SLAPSTICK — VENCEREMOS —
LIGHTS — CHALLENGE — YES — ALLEN GINSBURG — FREE — TRIBES — EXPERIENCE — ZIG-ZAG — SKULLDIGGERY —
COPSEATFLOWERS — SYMBOLS — PIPES — NOW — ABANDON THE CREEPING MEATBALL — TIMOTHY LEARY — JOY —
FLESH THEATRE — WARLOCKS — GUITARS — BELLS — HUGH ROMNEY — PEACOCK FEATHERS — PAUL KRASSNER — OM
— INNER SPACE — HELL NO WE WON'T GO — LIPS — CHERRY PIE — LIBERTY — LSD — STREAMERS — MACBIRD — VOTE
FOR ME — SUN — TURN ON — PETER MAX — PHIL OCHS — CANDLES — DRAFT BEER — MANTRAS — JOIN — GALA
MORE — DIGGERS — ROCK MUSIC — UNITED STATES OF AMERICA BAND — ENERGY — MRS. LEARY'S COW — BLOOM
— JIM FOURATT — NO CENSORSHIP — BEAUTY — KISS — NIRVANA — FLASH — SHIRLEY CLARKE — BEADS — BIRDS
— GO — BEWARE LOCAL POLICE ARMED AND CONSIDERED DANGEROUS — FOOD — GAMES — DICK GREGORY — HUG —
TENTS — LOVE — CARAVAN — WONDERFUL — FUGS — SKYDIVING — BLACKS — FREE CITY — IDEAS — TOUCH — HI!
— END ALL SYSTEMS — BARBARA DANE — BONNIE AND CLYDE — HOPE — TRIP — DRUMS — SWEET — DRAGONS —
PURPLE — PIN THE TAIL ON THE DONKEY — PANHANDLERS — PLAN NOW — SMILE — HARI KRISHNA — TAPIOCA —
LET'S GROK — TAMBOURINES — PAUL WILLIAMS — RALLYS — NAKED — CHICKEN LITTLE — CARNIVAL — BUSES —
MONKEY — COLOR — BROTHERS — MICROBOPPERS — TOGETHER — STEVE MILLER'S BLUES BAND — VISIONS — NOW
— FREE — EXPLOSION — JOHN WILCOCK — END WAR — SPIRIT — PLAY — COMMUNITY — JUDY COLLINS — FANTASY
— REALITY — ALTERNATIVE — THE WALRUS — BREAD AND PUPPET THEATRE — SWIMMING — MASKS — HUZZA — NEWS
— DELIGHT — BUTEO KINO — NORMAN MAILER — GEODESIC DOMES — MEDIA — WASHINGTON FREE THEATRE — GURUS
— BANCROFT T. HOGG — FLOWERS — PAGEANT PLAYERS — SISTERS — POT — MARVIN GARSON — SINGING — FREAK OUT
— STARS — GRASS — MORE — PETER WALKER — MONKEY WARFARE — RUNAWAYS — RICHARD GOLDSTEIN — MYTH —
CHILD — BOOB — BUBBLE GUM — WATER — CHEER — GUERRILLA THEATRE — TED BERRIGAN — SMELLS — LOVERS —
WHITE LIGHTNING — FULL ENEMPLOYMENT — SPARKLE — ALIVE — GROW — MORE — JERRY RUBIN — KITES — TUNE IN
— BOB FASS — LIGHTS — CARNIVAL — EQUALITY — HELL'S ANGELS — END PAY TOILETS — SWAMIS — LAUGHTER
FREE TV — BREAKOUT — NOW — KEITH LAMPE — BALLOONS — TOE FREAKS — BRING — JACQUES LEVY — FANFARE
— FESTIVAL — TRUCKS — ABBIE HOFFMAN — WHISTLES — MINNEAPOLIS PLAYERS — COSTUMES — NEWSREELS —
UNDERGROUND NEWSPAPERS — MINSTRELS — BELLY BUTTONS — MAGIC — DO — SKIN — FREE YOGURT — VITALITY —
RASCALS — SHARON KREBS — FREE AMERICA — WARMTH — FLY TRANSLOVE AIRWAYS — RESISTANCE — FROLIC — DIG
— BLOWOUT — HUG — IRA EINHORN — CIDER — BREEZE — ZODIAC — SPYS — HOG FARM — LIFE STYLE — MOCK
CONVENTION — BIRDS — ALAN KATZMAN — MOON — DROP OUT — MOUTH — REBORN — REVOLUTION — LEN CHANDLER
— THE EGGMAN — SHELLS — INDIANS — LIBERATION NEWS SERVICE — THONK — MIDDLE EARTH — END PRISONS — UP
— SPEED — PAN — FREE — POETRY — JAZZ — STRENGTH — RICHARD SCHECHNER — PEPPERMINT — EXCITEMENT —
PLANETS — OPEN — GATHERING — SLAPSTICK — KEEP THE MAN UPTIGHT — CHOOSE — STREET — MAKE LOVE NOT
WAR — TROUBADOR — BARRICADE JUMPERS — ART — PETER GESSNER — BALL FOREVER — BORN — HAPPINESS — BOO
— BARBARA GARSON — INCENSE — LIFE — TWIRL — WITCHES — DENNIS GASTON — LEGEND — LIBERATION — FREE —
EAGER — PROVO — EXALTATION — HEAVEN — MIMES — MIMICS — BONK — WING — NONSENSE — ABE PEKOLICK —
BUBBLES — WINGS — GODS — DOLPHINS — STP — BURST — HEART TRANSPLANT FOR LBJ — MOVIES — BANNERS —
POPCORN — MELLOW — BREAST — NIRUMA — FUNNY — BOO HOOS — THIGH — COME — HEAD — EXPLOSION — MAU-MAU
— CLOUD — FLAME — MYSTERY — PULSE — WREN — EUCALYPTUS — SURPRISE — FLUTES — BREAD — KIWIS — SONG
— GREGORY CORSO — SMOKE — HOPSKOTCH — MARBLES — TEEPEES — KALEIDOSCOPE — STU ALBERT — ZANY —
DOGS — HAIR — SATIN — TREES — LAKES — LYSERGIC ACID CRYPTO-ETHELENE — COMMUNION — DIZZY — BLOOM —
BREATHLESS — STREAM — CONFETTI — RHYME — HARMONY — MIKE ROSSMAN — FONDLE — ROMP — FROLIC — HUG
— LEGEND — DRAMA — MYTH — REVELRY — FERIA — HIP — DELIGHT — IMPLOSION — DAY GLO — BUNKO — OPEN —
BE — ELECTRICITY — DISCOVERY — FILMS — SHARING — BANANAS — LEAFLETS — BLESSINGS — EXHILARATION —
DRUMS — THE MAN IS UPTIGHT — GOSSIMER — POSITIVE — RICE — FEATHERS — ALICE'S RESTAURANT — CANDY —
DATES — EXORCISM — ED SANDERS — SLEEP — FLY — HARMONY — EARTH — BLINK — WINK — KISS — PEACE — SEE
— DROP OUT — SOUL — DO YOUR THING — BURST — TULI KUPFERBERG — COME — TASTE — GROOVE — ACT-OUT —
DO-IN — SWING — FLOAT — HUM — SKYLARK — BELLY BUTTONS — BEAT ARMY — JOSEPH PAPP — CELEBRATE — YES
— SKETCH — RHYME — WALTER BOWART — CHALLENGE — ROMP — BELIEVE — WEAVE — PEE — GIGGLE — VIBRATE —
PAINT — CHANT — BILLY THE KID — MEDITATE — JINGLE — TANGO — CHARLIE BROWN — HURRAY — EMANCIPATE —
BLOOD, SWEAT AND TEARS — BRAIDS — STEW — CREATE — DEBATE — CANDLES — LOVERS — CYMBALS — VIOLINS —
LOLLIPOPS — GYRATE — JUBILATION — HOOKAHS — REBELS — GODDESSES — ELATION — FAITH — RADIOS — HOLY —
PHANTASMAGORIC — RABBITS — JU JUBES — PLUMES — HONEYSUCKLE — HOURIS — PARTICIPATE — GRAFFITI —
PASSION — WIZARDS — PEANUT BUTTER — LEPRECHAUNS — MIRTH — SWEAT — LINKS — PICNIC — MIMEOGRAPH —
JUVENILE EXHIBITIONISM — MARIONETTES — NATURAL — NAIADS — MOBILE — PHOENIX — LOAVES — LEVITATE —
PERFORM — LEAVES — MAGIC — MUTANTS — ANIMALS — OLIVES — BASEBALL — ELLEN SANDLER — OUTDOOR — ANTIC
— PETE SEEGER — AIR — FEEL — SYNCHRONICITY — TICKLE — SERENADE — SUMMER — INTERPLANETARY NATIONALISM
— BALMY — SUPER — PANTOMIME — MORE — CHESTER ANDERSON — AMERICAN EXPEDITIONARY FORCE — SNATCH —
UTOPIA — PUPPY — BEES — PEACEPIPES — QUICKSILVER — INDEPENDENCE — STRANGE — INTERGALACTIC — EROS —
GET HIGH WITH A LITTLE HELP — WAVES — DANDELIONS — GROUP IMAGE — CIRCUS — TAROT DELPHI — WARPAINT —
HALOES — TOUR — RICHIE HAVENS — CONTACT — DREAM — BERRIES — GINGER — WHIZ — LICORICE — SPACESHIP
JANIS IAN — PING PONG — LOTUS BLOSSOMS — SHALOM — PIE — SPAGHETTI — GARDEN — CUCKOO — WHISPER —
ZAP — DANDY — IMAGE — PEACE EYE — DROP OUT DON'T CUP OUT — ENGAGE — TRUST — WINDMILL — ELASTIC —
FIRM — MUSHROOM — CUSHION — SIP — JIMI HENDRIX EXPERIENCE — TAKE OFF — RING — QUIXOTIC — DECLARE —
GARGLE — FACE — PEACH — MARTIN JEZER — PEPPERMINT — INTERNATIONAL — VIVID — COMMUNITY — DANCING
★★ YOUTH INTERNATIONAL PARTY — 32 UNION SQUARE, ROOM 607, NEW YORK, N.Y. 10003 — (212) 982-5090 ★★

THE FAMOUS YIPPIE CHICAGO DEMONSTRATIONS RECRUITMENT POSTER. ABBIE AND JERRY HAD A FALLING OUT OVER THE SPELLING OF "YIPPIE."

From the archives of Tuli Kupferberg

a) Flying helium-filled balloons.
b) Long dancing Conga lines.
c) Musical instruments, in particular guitars.
d) Folk singing.
e) Flying pigeons.
f) Climbing trees and monuments.
g) Outlandish clothing; Keith Lampe usually wears an old-time police uniform.
h) Still and movie picture taking.
i) Incense burning.
j) Painting each other with Day-Glo paint.
k) Possible marijuana smoking.
l) Burning U.S. currency
m) Petty thievery.
n) Defacing public property.

Allen Ginsberg I went to Chicago about a week or two early and talked with Rennie Davis and Tom Hayden and said, "Listen, this is going all wrong." For one thing, Wolfe Lowenthal was training everybody in some kind of Japanese snake-dancing karate to defend themselves from the police. I said it was the wrong signal. And Davis and Hayden said no, they're sure the police are going to attack and the kids have to be taught to defend themselves. Years later Lowenthal agreed, he should have been teaching t'ai chi.

Wolfe Lowenthal Boy, I remember Allen lecturing me about the snake dancing. That was borrowed from Japanese students, where they'd form lines. It's supposed to be a very effective maneuver in dealing with police. I don't know how it works. They'd shout something fierce. I can't remember the exact words, we were all so stoned.

Steve Tappis This was a secret weapon—Chicago police could not defeat Japanese snake dancing. If you dance around and kind of zigzag they'll never get you.

Allen Ginsberg One of Mayor Daley's assistants said something very mysterious that I never understood till later. He kept saying, "You guys are all wrong. There's a secret plan to end the war soon and you guys don't realize that the people in the White House are on your side." Of course, nobody gave them any credibility, but it was during that time that Johnson was trying to end the war for Humphrey and calling on South Vietnam

President Thieu to make a compromise and accept the Vietcong on the peace table so that they could end the war in time for the election. That would've been better than what happened actually, the Vietcong winning all by itself and fucking everybody up. At that time Nixon got Madame Chennault to telephone Thieu and tell him not to compromise with Johnson, hang on and don't help him win the election and when we win we'll win the war for you. So that locks in what was going on behind the scenes, when the Left was trying to attack Humphrey in a kind of vicious way and was chortling that it lost the election for him. Enormous mistake, paid for by the blood of the Vietnamese.

Stew Albert Jerry got to Chicago maybe a day or two before us. When I got there he said, "Thank God you're here, Stew, you gotta help me. We gotta work together here as a team and counterbalance Abbie." Jerry then offered to back all my political positions in turn for my support.

Jerry Rubin When Abbie got to Chicago his manic self completely took over. Press conferences every hour. Me, me, me, me. He went mad. No planning, no strategizing, each man for himself with the media. I think it was Abbie's goal to eliminate me from history that week and steal the show. It was a shock. I don't think it's even a rational thing. With all the media descending on Chicago, with a year and a half of buildup, he just became totally manic. Not sleeping, talking a mile a minute, supercreative.

Abbie Hoffman (*from the film* Conventions: The Land Around Us) There'll be a hundred thousand people in this park. There'll be bikers over there. There'll be speed freaks over there. There'll be flower children over there. Veterans over there. Women over there, blacks over there. We will develop a community, the thing that's totally lacking in American society. This is called the Festival of Life and life just is. It's not based on success and failure. You do what you can and the way it comes out, that's groovy. That's the kind of society that we envision, where people share things and you don't need money. Where you have the machines do the work for the people. A free society, that's really what it amounts to. Our culture is based on trust. I can go out on Second Avenue and eat my whole breakfast walking down the street. Somebody comes up and says have a bite of this, man, have a bite of this, have a bite of that and I'll try it. I'm not afraid of them. Somebody puts something in my mouth, says you're gonna really groove on this, I'll try it. Try anything. We're prepared to enter mystery. What we're all about is chaos.

Keith Lampe I had to play referee between Abbie and Jerry. It reminded me of the theory of the Adlerian power drive, they were both around five seven, short males. I would decide how many minutes each person would get during the news conferences.

Stew Albert Abbie and Jerry didn't really speak to each other in Chicago. It was over the pig.

Anita Hoffman One bright morning we're driving out into the flat country on the outskirts of Chicago and we go to a livestock auction. And we bought a pink pig; I think it was fifty dollars. Jerry and Stew thought the pig was too small. It wasn't small, it was a decent size, but too friendly-looking.

Jerry Rubin I got the idea from Marvin Garson, he says, "Let's run a pig for president." So we ran a pig that whole year, Pigasus. But Abbie got this little cute pig and I had my whole critique against Abbie at that time: All he cares about is a laugh. All he cares about is having a good time. All he cares about is his name. He cares nothing about the issues.

Anita Hoffman They eventually got another one which had a black spot on it or something.

Stew Albert We kept Pigasus in the backyard someplace in Chicago, and then we brought him downtown to the Picasso statue. We started singing "The Star-Spangled Banner" and we were all arrested. Abbie was not there. This is an indication of the degree of the split. This was a big media event, *Time* magazine and so forth, and Abbie had excluded himself, he didn't think we could pull it off.

Wolfe Lowenthal I remember being in that paddy wagon with the pig. I thought he was gonna bite me.

Dennis Dalyrimple The pig was on my lap most of the time. It didn't shit, thank God, and somewhere along the line they stopped and took the pig to the ASPCA, then they took us to the Cook County jail.

Stew Albert When we were in jail a cop came and said, "I have bad news for you boys, the pig squealed." That was the best cop joke I ever heard. The pig squealed.

Wolfe Lowenthal It looked like the Yippies were gonna split up. Abbie was the flower, Jerry was the clenched fist. We were putting Abbie down as a Cutefier, whereas we were the Horrifiers.

Country Joe McDonald A week before the convention started we played at the Kinetic Playground. Jerry and Abbie showed up to discuss our playing at the Festival of Life but Jerry and Abbie weren't speaking to each other. I told Abbie we weren't going to play. He was just stunned. It was assumed that we would get into the let's-get-our-ass-kicked mode to save the world because Jerry and Abbie think it's fun and it makes a political statement. Immediately after that little discussion, I left and walked into the hotel lobby and this Vietnam vet sees us. I was in the elevator and he said, "I fought in Vietnam for creeps like you." And he punched me in the nose. Broke my nose. I looked down and there was blood pouring all over my favorite psychedelic shirt and then the elevator doors closed and I went upstairs and we left Chicago.

Rennie Davis My police tails started following me two weeks before the convention. They introduced themselves and explained the rules of the game, making serious threats of physical harm if I tried to evade them. I was tailed every day for approximately four years after that, everywhere I went, anywhere in the world. The only place that I was free of them was when I went into Hanoi and the government couldn't follow me in.

John Zitek I was a supervising Chicago police sergeant assigned to the Intelligence Division, responsible for surveillance. Not necessarily covert, many times overt. Most of the time, I had Abbie. We worked in pairs, sometimes four. Abbie and Jerry were intelligent, hyperactive, half the time fucking doped up, self-centered. These guys were scared shitless. Rubin way more, I know that for a fact. Hoffman loved to walk his nuts off, then stop on the porch and sit down. You take a break, he'd disappear. We'd go crazy following the son of a bitch.

Art Goldberg Jerry was upset by being tailed, which was understandable. Abbie, on the other hand, got very friendly with them and told them everything as if he had nothing to hide.

CHICAGO POLICE DEPARTMENT

Intelligence Division Surveillance Report 22 Aug. 1968 Investigators 378-364-342-486

TIME 0500 TO 0900

OBSERVATION

. . . RO's [reporting officers] took Hoffman for a cup of coffee and during the conversation he stated that he has had a falling out with Jerry Rubin that almost resulted in a fist fight . . . Hoffman also stated that an individual has flown in from France and has set up a lab for the production of hallucinatory drugs which are being put into candy. He stated that he "took a trip" on this candy in Lincoln Park on Wednesday.

Hoffman stated that the real day of trouble will be Wednesday 28 Aug. 68 when they will march on the amphitheater without a permit. He states they now have about 3,000 out of town people housed in "crash pads" but that these will close Sunday, 25 Aug. when the people will be informed to move into Lincoln Park.

. . . Hoffman further stated that after Wednesday night the Yippie movement will be over, stating that he expects about 5,000 persons to be arrested during their demonstrations.

John Zitek He would try to buy us coffee, sweet roll. We wouldn't accept. He was saying back off, cool off, this isn't all that bad, he was giving you that message. And we would like to give him a message back, listen, you little prick, we're out here twelve fucking hours a day because of you. He became a pain in the ass, a thorn that you would like to just pick out.

Stew Albert The thing that brought about the final break between Abbie and Jerry was definitely precipitated by Jerry. We had this meeting and I was there and my girlfriend, Judy, and Jerry and his girlfriend, Nancy, and Abbie and Anita and Paul Krassner. Jerry had written up a statement which he said he was gonna give out as a leaflet in the park, which was a total attack on Abbie. So he reads the statement to Abbie. It's the most vicious, insulting, maybe it's even brilliant, you know? Everything that you could possibly see as a dark side or negative side, he just pours it out. Anita absolutely goes into a rage.

Jerry Rubin I felt Abbie was trying to exclude me from that week, trying to dominate the media. I was saying you're not the story here, Abbie. The story is the war, the story is the confrontation of cultures, the story is young kids. I said I didn't do all this so that Abbie Hoffman could steal the stage and become the issue. I was coming out of ego too, hey, give me a little piece here.

Stew Albert Abbie once told me that if I wasn't sitting by Jerry's side he would've jumped him.

Jerry Rubin Stew would've killed Abbie. But by my challenging him like that Abbie became, even though he won't admit it, more political and a touch more sensitive and aware. And he then went out to show how political he was. So it probably had a good effect but we didn't talk the rest of the week. Quite a conspiracy.

Stew Albert I don't believe Jerry ever had any intention of actually giving this thing out. But Abbie went home and wrote up an eighteen-point political program which he distributed in the park as the Yippie program.

From Revolution Towards a Free Society: Yippie!

By A. Yippie

This is a personal statement. There are no spokesmen for the Yippies . . . We are all our own leaders . . . We demand a society built along the alternative community in Lincoln Park, a society based on humanitarian cooperation and equality, a society which allows and promotes the creativity present in all people and especially our youth.

1. An immediate end to the War in Vietnam and a restructuring of our foreign policy which totally eliminates aspects of military, economic, and cultural imperialism . . . and the abolition of the military draft.
2. Immediate freedom for Huey Newton of the Black Panthers and all other black people . . .
3. The legalization of marihuana and all other psychedelic drugs. The freeing of all prisoners currently in prison on narcotics charges . . .
5. A judicial system which works towards the abolition of all laws related to crimes without victims.
6. The total disarmament of all the people beginning with the police. This includes not only guns, but such brutal devices as tear gas, MACE, electric prods, blackjacks, billy clubs and the like.
7. The Abolition of Money. The abolition of pay housing, pay media, pay transportation, pay food, pay education, pay clothing, pay medical help, and pay toilets.
8. A society which works toward and actively promotes the concept of

"full-unemployment." . . . Adoption of the concept "Let the Machines do it."

9. A conservation program . . . committed to the elimination of pollution from our air and water . . .
12. A restructured educational system which provides the student power to determine his course of study and allows for student participation in over-all policy planning . . .
13. The open and free use of the media. A program which actively supports and promotes cable television as a method of increasing the selection of channels available to the viewer.
14. An end to all censorship . . .
15. We believe that people should fuck all the time, anytime, whomever they wish. This is not a program demand but a simple recognition of the reality around us.
16. A political system which is more . . . responsive to the needs of all the people regardless of age, sex or race. Perhaps a national referendum system conducted via television or a telephone voting system. Perhaps a decentralization of power . . . with many varied tribal groups . . .
17. A program that encourages and promotes the arts. However, we feel that if the Free Society we envision were to be fought for and achieved . . . we would have a society in which every man would be an artist . . .

It is for these reasons that we have come to Chicago [and] many of us may die here . . . Political Pigs, your days are numbered. We are the Second American Revolution. We shall win. Yippie!

CHICAGO POLICE DEPARTMENT

During the next week the eyes of the nation and the world will be on our city and our department . . . the finest police organization in existence. We have been tested on many occasions and have met these tests with distinction. This time we will do even better. It will be by our actions that the rest of the world will judge Chicago and to some degree our nation itself. We must continue to be constantly mindful of the welfare of others, never act officiously, and never permit personal feelings, prejudices, or animosities to influence our decisions or our actions. I have every confidence that all members of the Department will reflect credit on the City of Chicago in the highest traditions of the Chicago Police Department.
James B. Conlisk, Jr.
Superintendent

Keith Lampe aka Ponderosa Pine The police killed this teenager, half American Indian down from the upper Midwest, and called him a Yippie. It was like throwing a dead body on your doorstep as a warning. The Democratic convention had not yet begun but already had its first martyr.

John Schultz Apparently Dean Johnson was a native North American, I guess of the Sioux tribe, but pretty much a hippie. There was an altercation of some sort on Wells Street, the police asked to see what he had in his flight bag, whatever it was they were after, drugs or what, I don't know. Now, I'm reporting very conflicting and contradictory testimony. But even the guys with him say he did pull a gun out of his flight bag. The police say they were fired at and then they fired back and I believe at some point they say that Johnson was running away.

David Lewis Stein *(from his book* Living the Revolution*)* Abbie looked stunned. The CBS man had left; this was no media freak show. He stomped around the *Seed* office muttering: "We've got to stop them killing our people."

John Schultz Anytime I saw Abbie for the rest of convention week, he was leading people out of confrontation, not into it.

Ron Kaufman, *civil rights and antiwar activist* I went to Lincoln Park the week before the convention and that's when I met Abbie. I had an apartment and I had a car. Abbie needed a place to stay, he needed transportation, so I was told that I was gonna be Abbie's bodyguard. So he moved in immediately to my place, and Anita moved in a few days later.

Keith Lampe Ron Kaufman had a Ph.D. from Stanford. He had so little ego he was willing to run out for the sandwiches and coffee with his Ph.D.

Stew Albert Jerry and I were equals. Abbie had sycophants, and he also had people who worked with him, but not as equals. Ron Kaufman, Brad Fox. They were people who had a task-oriented relationship to Abbie. He always had to prove he was more than everybody else.

Jacques Levy I was very hopeful when I got to Chicago. I got there late at night and I went to a courtyard of a church because I knew a lot of people who were staying there. There was a fire going in the middle, little groups sitting around, talking and sharing food. I had the impression that it

ABBIE STROLLS THROUGH LINCOLN PARK WITH HIS "BODYGUARD," RON KAUFMAN, DURING THE YIPPIE PROTESTS AT THE 1968 DEMOCRATIC CONVENTION IN CHICAGO.
UPI/Corbis-Bettmann

must have been like the night before the fight at Valley Forge. Abbie was very excited, he said this is gonna be great, lots of people are coming.

Jerry Rubin At the last minute everybody decided not to go to Chicago. Mass cold feet all across America. I was very disappointed.

Tom Hayden I felt relieved that we had enough people to make a fight of it. The specter of violence was limiting the numbers who were gonna come to a couple of thousand.

Abe Peck There were ten thousand people in town. At least five thousand people were locals from the suburbs and the city.

Sal Gianetta Everybody was absolutely flabbergasted at the number of kids that showed up for the convention. The numbers weren't low. No, no, no! All the numbers that were passed out and everything, 100,000 people coming to march, none of us believed it. If 200 people came we were gonna be excited. Two hundred people, there isn't a lot of responsibility. But 6,000. I don't want 6,000 kids, I don't want the responsibility, I can't watch them.

John Schultz In the first two days, Abbie, Jerry and the Mobilization marshals were all advocating, "Get out of the park, go to the streets, don't confront people in the park." On the first night, Saturday night, Ginsberg was largely responsible for avoiding a confrontation. He led them out of the park Om-ing and through the streets of Old Town.

Sal Gianetta Abbie had a charisma when he spoke that I've never seen commented on. They said he roused people but there was something else. He was too spastic. Too many fucking ideas. Too much that he wanted to do. Plus he was totally out of his mind with the mood swings and with the fear and with the adrenaline and everything else, he was cuckoo. But so was everybody else.

SATURDAY, AUGUST 24, 1968

Jacques Levy By the first night I realize it's heavy. There was tear gas, there was an escalation way beyond what anybody had seen prior to this. Abbie was obviously aware that it was serious, and he felt a real responsibility. He didn't know how to control it now.

John Schultz The leaders were failed, discredited, actually being disparaged by the folks who were left in the park. It was rather ironical to me that those seven white guys would later be indicted for something that they actually tried to stop!

From the *Berkeley Barb*

PREDICTIONS FOR YIPPIE ACTIVITIES

By Ed Sanders

Poetry readings, mass meditation, fly casting exhibitions, demagogic Yippie political arousal speeches, rock music and song concerts will be held on a precise time table . . . a dawn ass washing ceremony with tens of thousands participating will occur each morning at 5 A.M. as Yippie revelers and protesters prepare for the 7 A.M. volley ball tournaments . . . universal syrup day will be held on Wednesday when a movie will be shown at Soldier's Field in which Hubert Humphrey confesses to Allen Ginsberg his secret approval of anal intercourse . . . filth will be worshipped . . . there will be public fornication whenever and where ever there is an aroused appendage and a willing aperture . . . 230 rebel cocksmen under secret vow are on 24 hour alert to get into the pants of the daughters and wives and kept women of the convention delegates.

From the *Chicago American*, 8/25/68

JACK MABLEY COLUMN

Here's why an army of 20,000 police and soldiers is needed in Chicago this week. Every one of the following acts of sabotage had been threatened by black or white militants.

. . . Militants have said they will put agents into hotel or restaurant kitchens where food is prepared for delegates and put drugs or poison in the food.

The water supply has been threatened, either by sabotage at pumping stations or dumping drugs in the lake near intake pipes.

A mass stall-in of old jalopies on the expressways at a given time would stop traffic.

. . . Yippies said they would paint cars as independent taxicabs and take delegates away from the city. Yippies' girls would work as hookers and try to attract delegates and put LSD in their drinks.

. . . Threats to the Amphitheater include gas in the air conditioning system, shelling it with mortar from several miles away, storming it with a mob, cutting the power and phone lines.

These are just some of the threats. Making them public does not increase the hazard because every one of these has been printed or mimeographed and has been circulated among militants.

How many other sophisticated schemes of sabotage exist may only be imagined.

Jacques Levy There was no one central organizing thing going on in Lincoln Park. It was like these be-ins. This group playing catch, and this group doing Indian dancing, and this group doing yoga, and this group over here sitting around and eating a picnic, and this one making beads. Someone gets up once in a while and starts to make a speech and a group gathers around.

FROM CHICAGO POLICE DEPARTMENT FILES

INTELLIGENCE DIVISION BIS 25 AUG 1968
TO T. Lyons, Director CONFIDENTIAL
FROM W. Schmid, Legal Adviser
SUBJ Hoffman organizational meeting in Lincoln Park this date

At the 113th Intelligence Group quarters, 2231 Howard, Evanston, I viewed the videotape of HOFFMAN discussing plans for the forthcoming week for YIPPIES. The SUBJECT stated that commencing at noon this instant, the group needed $500 for the purchase of supplies, including blankets and 10,000 frankfurters, and "if someone can steal $500" this can be accomplished. He suggested that a lot of things are loose and can be taken. "You're a revolutionist not a thief," and "we're just redistributing" the property of property owners. He suggests one could live free by stealing, "you just steal loaves of bread." He stated on Tuesday a seminar would be held advising participants how to live free, and booklets would be distributed entitled, "Fuck the system" (sic).

The SUBJECT made all of his statements in a general fashion and it is my opinion that the SUBJECT would be acquitted of any charges; however, cause may lie for the issuance of an arrest *warrant,* causing the SUBJECT to post bail, or in alternative, await trial. This would be a policy decision, and it is my conclusion, based upon the Appalachian and related cases, that *no* (NO) liability for false arrest would accrue if prosecution was initiated in this instance. Asst. State's Atty. Bob Boyle stated there is a chance a conviction might result, and would seek non-Army witnesses.

Also present was Special Agent Richard N———, US Army Mil. Intell., who was thanked for his cooperation.

Jerry Rubin Sunday was the Festival of Life and the rock bands didn't show up. Only the MC5 showed.

Keith Lampe aka Ponderosa Pine The Festival of Life lasted about thirty minutes because of police terrorism. Somebody from the MC5 came and said, "We're so broke, we can't afford to have our sound system trashed and if we play, they're gonna do it." The cops surrounded us, they were beating their billy sticks against the trees or whatever they could do to scare us. Also, Sanders and I had been given some kind of honey, I don't know whether by a secret policeman or what, that had some kind of weird psychedelic stuff in it, but not the kind of stuff that we were familiar with, and it was hard for us to maintain.

Ed Sanders Abbie was conducting the honey guy around. He was introducing him as Jim Morrison. He'd say, "Hold out your tongue." And they'd spatule on a gob of this stuff. I took mine just before the MC5 went on. I got the plug in, [then] I remember being escorted back to my hotel by my two plainclothes guys because Lincoln Park [had] turned into green froth. I didn't see the hotel through the froth.

Honeyman aka Jim Morrison, *counterculture chemist* There was a great myth that floated around in the pot circles about this thing called Sacred Honey. The idea was supposedly when the bees would pollinate the plants, their honey was a real high.

The Honeyman made a pilgrimage to Lebanon to investigate the Sacred Honey, a concept that amused the residents of Baalbek. He did pick up many recipes to cook with cannabis along with a few suitcases full of hash. Back in Rome, he met a fat old lady from Hollywood who had a famous recipe for hash brownies. She taught him how to render the butter and create sacred ghee. Ultimately, he created his incredibly potent hash oil, ruby red in color. When seventy drops of this oil were added to one pound of honey, Honeyman had the most potent cannabis-based product he'd ever encountered. He smuggled the oil back into the States in Italian wine bottles and ran into Abbie on the streets of the Lower East Side.

Honeyman aka Jim Morrison "Hey, man, I brought this bottle of stuff and we're gonna get everybody high in Chicago," I told Abbie, and he said "Great!" I had never met him before that. So we went to Chicago and somebody gave us their loft, and we set up a lab. It was a matter of taking this little bottle and turning it into cases of honey. We had a production line of very stoned-out people.

The word passed out very quickly that there's this honey, that it's free, but it's one spoon and watch out! Abbie and others were trusted with the honey. They would decide whether somebody looked like they could handle it. There was a point where there were a lot of very stoned people in Chicago. It added to the anarcho nature of the event, because many leaders were in the grass, looking up at the sky, while folks were just doing what they had to do. In fact there is at least one article in an underground paper at the time that thought it was a CIA/FBI conspiracy to immobilize the movement. There were a few politicos who made the drastic mistake of having some of the honey because suddenly they were unable to operate on quite the same level. From my particular politics, and I know Abbie shared them as well, we committed an act of Yippie terrorism on their heads. It did immobilize a number of people, but probably for the good.

Stew Albert I took some and I couldn't make it home. I collapsed on the steps of my house that I was staying at, being followed by cops. Do you think it was a CIA thing? This is one of the things that made me suspicious. In the FBI files they knew that this honey was coming in. They knew who was gonna be distributing it, they knew Abbie was involved. They didn't bust them for it. They let it happen. So I think—what is that about? I'll tell you, if the government didn't do it, they should have. Because it just put a lot of people out of commission.

Tom Hayden The honey was our side? It wasn't a policeman?

John Schultz Some of the SDS told me that they were very angry at Abbie when they saw him in the park passing the honey out. People were often looking for the Yippie leaders and in fact they were somewhere stoned out of their heads! That again turns over the scene to the younger, more aggressive kids. From Thursday, August 22nd, on, you had more and more of these greaser types coming into the park.

Bob Zmuda I was brought up on the Northwest Side of Chicago, blue-collar area. I was a greaser. We didn't like these filthy hippies from San Francisco and New York. Then stapled on every telephone pole in the neighborhood was a one-shot thing that said, "Come to Lincoln Park for the Love-In. Grass. Free love." I was maybe eighteen years old, so I probably was the fastest-radicalized person you could ever see. We go down to Lincoln Park and it was just like the one sheet implied. People handing out flowers, great girls, some of them taking their tops off. And it's the first time ever I got stoned in my life. I got sharkskin pants on, got my dago tee on, got my Cuban heels on. And I'm going, this is fucking fantastic! And then, like about 10:30, a cop car goes through the park and says, "The park is closing. If you stay in the park you'll be arrested." Everybody's laughing, what is this shit? There's this weird guy with a beard, Allen Ginsberg, chanting. I'm chanting, I'm stoned. Now people are throwing things at the cop car, the cop leaves. Then some more come. "You people have to disperse, you'll be arrested." I got uncles that are Chicago cops, never in a million years would I ever think that in Chicago would a cop ever give me a hard time. I'm making out with this beautiful girl, having the greatest time. Well, eleven o'clock, Chicago's finest went in and just started chopping at everybody. I'd never been teargassed in my life. They wedged you so you had to leave the park. I ran by a fucking cop and this guy takes a billy club and hits me in the fucking back full force. I couldn't believe it. The next day I went back to my buddy's and we got cycle helmets. We weren't gonna take this shit.

Spain Rodrigues, *cartoonist,* East Village Other The action was really kicked off by locals. They just started dragging cars out into the street and digging up the concrete and throwing everything they had. The cops were in retreat. The Yippies didn't look much of a threat but once the locals got into it, man, it was really a battle.

Stew Albert The leaders were quickly rendered impotent. That's a very important point to make. We had no impact on the actual course of events in Chicago. We just went with the flow. And the flow was more and more confrontational and violent.

John Schultz The cops on the three-wheelers were riding toward people, causing them to stampede.

Jacques Levy Clearing the park went on for hours and hours. They were clubbing people and there was blood. In the evening it got worse. It was dark, searchlights were going on in the park, and there was smoky mist all over the place. The scary part of it was that you were gonna get trampled on, caught underneath. And then there were a lot of kids running around trashing things. Just random smashing car windows.

Art Goldberg Right before they pushed us out of Lincoln Park, Hayden was trying to teach people how to snake dance, which obviously wasn't going to work worth a shit. Then we could see the Daley dozers and the gas things and all the cops lined up on the lake side of Lincoln Park. It was just about completely dark, and finally a group of people gathered around Abbie. "What should we do?" Abbie said, "I don't know, maybe we can figure something out here." I was amazed. I would have thought that they had a plan.

John Schultz The marshals were arguing that they should get out of the park and this fourteen-year-old boy just took this meeting over by leaping up and yelling, "Fuck the marshals! Bullshit!" He made it impossible for the group to agree on anything whatsoever. When the police line came up, the demonstrators who were on the grass stood up as if the occasion demanded that you rise to it! For a moment they just faced each other rather calmly. Then the police attack and they move the people up. As soon as the police slow down and the contact is broken, there are these guys who start saying, "Back, back," back into the confrontation. Then the police charged and attacked again and on it goes for the whole night. They attacked with clubs—there were very strict orders not to use lethal force unless a cop's life was in danger. They used a little gas that night. They had used bombs, the canisters, but not the full-scale hosing. That was done from trucks the next day and next night.

Art Goldberg And then there was mayhem in the streets of Old Town.

John Schultz On Sunday night, after the big confrontation began in Lincoln Park, I was coming up Clark Street. There was a stoop of a building where some steps came down. Right at the top of them there were Hayden, John Froines, Rubin, I think Davis was there, I'm not sure if Abbie was there. They were just standing looking out on the streets. They had no idea what was going on. I asked Froines what he thought about it and he said, "Beautiful, beautiful." But they were commenting like people who are watching an electrical storm, they had no idea how this thing had come about.

There was another confrontation in the park Monday night, again in a very improvised way.

Jacques Levy At one point a whole bunch of people put up barricades. They were a mixture of horses and whatever else they could find, chairs and crap from all over the place. Then the cops knocked it down, coming for them.

Michael Shamberg, *TVTV cofounder* Abbie was walking along these makeshift barricades, rallying people's spirits. He had this really cute girl with him and he was making out with her.

Paul Krassner Anita saw them, and she was upset because they were holding hands. I was very touched by that because it's as if fucking is just getting off, but holding hands is serious, it's romantic.

John Zitek One girl during one of the walks, she started fucking some guy in broad daylight, right off the street a little bit. We popped her. She was scared shitless. She was telling us that Abbie told her to do that. She'd be like a decoy so we would arrest her. He wanted us off his ass. He had a ton of puss, always a different broad. It amazed me that he would trust that many broads if he was that big a person. Maybe one of those broads wasn't quite loyal to him, maybe she was more loyal to the police than to him. I don't know if he ever thought about that. I'm just saying that hypothetically, of course. I would never even think of doing nothing like that.

Jerome Washington The first person bashed in the head Sunday at the park was Stew Albert. And it was obviously done by an undercover agent because the uniformed cops were across from us, and Stew got hit from the back.

Stew Albert They were brilliant in setting us up. They really had an understanding of Jerry. First some cops approached Jerry and said, "We'd like to talk to you on the side." They said, "We don't like what you're up to, but we're cops, and we've heard there's a plan to kill you, so be on your guard." Jerry says, "I need a bodyguard." Now, there's this guy Bob Pierson. Pierson infiltrated the bikers and then he offered himself as the bodyguard. So for a few days we were constantly in the company of this Chicago policeman, Big Bob Pierson, the biker. In retrospect, he was a little too good to be believed. Why should he have this fealty to Jerry? Why should he say he'd be willing to die for Jerry? It's nonsense.

Jerry Rubin He was handed to me by the inner core of people in charge of self-defense. They said, "Here's a biker from Chicago, he's well accepted by the biking community, he's gonna stay by you this entire week and protect you from people who might attack you." Sounds good to me.

Stew Albert Pierson did only one thing that was of a provocateur's nature. I had been instrumental in getting Bobby Seale to come to town. I went out to the airport on Tuesday to get Bobby. I called Jerry up to tell him that Bobby's here and to ask him where we should go. Suddenly Pierson was saying there should be a march and Bobby should lead it. I said, "No way, that's not gonna happen." So then Pierson said "Okay, we'll just have a rally and Bobby'll speak." That's what we did. And Bobby was indicted for that speech.

John Schultz The sequence of action at several points showed the police taking the initiative. The police who were chosen for Lincoln Park and Grant Park were taken deliberately from what are called the tactical units, and the tactical units were specifically policemen who were generally bigger and known to be what they call proactive, not just to be ready for trouble but even to cause trouble.

Sal Gianetta Chicago had a momentum of its own. And this is the part that absolutely gives me chills, the momentum came from the young kids. Not us fucking guys. We were arguing and fighting about it all. If we had marched on the third night it would've changed things, and the National Guard would've fired, and they would have killed us. And once they shot and killed one, two, three people, we won. It would've collapsed everything. But we didn't have the fucking guts to do it. I certainly didn't and neither did Ab and neither did Jerry. The kids were conscious of it and they wanted to do it. Some of the kids that we had sleeping at the church, I remember little Randy. Little Randy verbalized it—"So some of us will die," he would say, "but we'll win." He got that shit from us, that's what scared us.

John Schultz The conventional leadership were totally fragmented. When they had the Tuesday morning press conference, Abbie was furious at the Mobe people for still advocating nonviolence in the face of these police attacks in which whoever showed the slightest glimmer of passive resistance was beaten worse than people who were actively resisting the police. So he came to the press conference carrying a tree branch. Dellinger and Davis got very distressed.

John Sack, *journalist* Jean Genet, William Burroughs, Terry Southern and I were there for *Esquire* magazine. I was with the Chicago police, doing an article from their point of view. I was wandering around Lincoln Park. Sitting under this tree, there was this man who I immediately figured had to be Abbie Hoffman because he was wonderful and funny. He had a group of about thirty or forty people gathered around him.

TUESDAY AFTERNOON, AUGUST 27, 1968

David Lewis Stein *(from his book* Living the Revolution*)* Abbie talked for over an hour. He had a sore throat and sipped a codeine solution from a brown bottle while he talked.

John Sack Abbie was telling the kids what to do when the Chicago police attacked, which they did that night.

Abbie Hoffman *(from his speech in Lincoln Park, from Stein's* Living the Revolution*)*

> *Theater can be used as an offensive and defensive weapon, like blood. We had a demonstration in New York. We had seven gallons of blood in little plastic bags. You know, if you convince 'em you're crazy enough, they won't hurt ya. Cop goes to hit you, right, you have a bag of blood in your hand. He lifts his stick up, you take your bag of blood and go whack over your own head. All this blood pours out, see. Fuckin' cop standin'. Now, that says a whole lot more than a picket sign that says end the war . . .*

John Zitek Hoffman and Rubin didn't lead 'em. What they did was instigate, rile 'em up, aggravate the situation, holler over the loudspeakers. We had informants among those people, let's face it. The informants were not planned on, these were kids that were given a break after they were arrested.

They had boxes of old ceramic tile stashed behind trees in Lincoln Park to throw at the police that night. Helmet or no helmet, you got hit in the balls with that damn thing. They were fakers, with their bullshit blood, and they run out to the street where the stupid reporters were, and I'll say it into this damn thing, and tell them that they were hit over the head and they had bullshit cow's blood and they banged themselves up.

Jeff Kamen *(broadcasting for WCFL)*

> *Late last night and early this morning, the Chicago Police Department sent 700 men, lobbed tear-gas grenades into a mob of some 1,500 Yippies and their sympathizers in the southeastern end of Lincoln Park. And there were confrontations on the street. More than 2,500 young people ran wild in the streets. They didn't break up any property. Some youths did try to turn over cars and were unsuccessful in that. Some heads were cracked by police, some newsmen were injured by policemen. It may be another rough day and an even rougher night between the Yippies and the police and some of the people put in between—the newsmen.*

Paul Sills, *founder of* Second City On Tuesday night we stood and watched the ministers go in.

Carol Sills We went with them in the morning to the cop station in the park. We protested about the nonsense that had gone on before and on Sunday night. The ministers announced that they were going to go into the park that night with a cross at curfew time. Commander Braasch said, "Why, that would be an act of civil disobedience."

Allen Ginsberg In order to provide the kids refuge and protection, a group of priests went to the park and held a religious ceremony and set up a cross. The police actually teargassed the floodlit cross and drove the priests and the kids out of the park that night.

Sal Gianetta Hayden was running around in four hundred different disguises. Abbie said to Hayden, "I'm gonna get a disguise too, I'm gonna disguise myself as a manic-depressive." It's one of those thoughts that runs through your head but a year and a half later all of a sudden you say, "Holy shit!"

Ab worked real, real, real hard to organize this, real hard! He was noticeably depressed in Chicago. Maybe 20 percent of his depression was his responsibility for those kids getting banged. It was brutal. Those fucking pig national guards were going after fourteen-year-old kids, whapping them on the fucking head. It was killing him. It was only sometime in the seventies that I started to realize that Abbie's mood swings were obvious in Chicago. But it was clouded because there was an obvious reason for his depression: the beatings.

Tom Hayden I don't know whether Abbie was on drugs a lot in Chicago. But he seemed to me really, really explosive, paranoid, fatalistic, almost to a point of being immobilized. At this point he had become so symbolic to the police that he couldn't lead anything, he couldn't go to a restaurant, he couldn't do anything. He was shut down.

Anita Hoffman We were sitting in this luncheonette having breakfast, and in walked the cops. Abbie had put "FUCK" on his forehead in preparation for the day's activities, the rationale being that with that on his forehead the press will not photograph him and he'll be anonymous and he can do whatever he wants.

Paul Krassner That was an idea that he had gotten from Lenny Bruce. Lenny had done it with toilet paper spelling out the words and

Abbie did it with lipstick. I think he made the mistake of tipping his hat to the cops. I remember Abbie saying, "It's the duty of a revolutionist to finish his breakfast." I have the feeling that they somehow let him finish eating breakfast.

John Zitek I saw him get busted, yeah. I wasn't surprised. No, I think it was time for him to get busted, get him out of the picture. He wanted to get busted. How fast did the word go out? Call it being a martyr, my leader was busted, I'm gonna do worse.

Rennie Davis After the wipeout with the cross at ten o'clock on Tuesday night, that was the end of Lincoln Park for me. I wanted to move our determined presence in front of the convention delegates. So the decision was made to empty out the park and reassemble in front of the Hilton Hotel.

The city granted a permit. It was their public relations strategy to say "Yes, we did grant a permit" and it was clear it had been part of their strategy all along, but it was done at the eleventh hour so we couldn't have out-of-town people come in. And so on Wednesday afternoon, at the band shell, which was in Grant Park many miles from the convention, a rally occurred. We had our marshals out in force because there were mothers there with babies.

Paul Krassner Pierson helped pull the flag down on Wednesday in Grant Park. That set off the riot. It was as if it were a signal to his fellow cops. I'm under the impression that he was throwing rocks at his fellow officers too.

John Sack To take the flag down was a very pro-American and patriotic act, it doesn't show disrespect for the flag, it shows great respect to the flag to say that the city of Chicago does not deserve to have the American flag flown over it.

Rennie Davis When the kid pulled down the flag at half mast and the police came in and pulled him out for arrest, we instantaneously threw up a marshal line and locked arms. I was standing in front of the line with a bullhorn, trying to communicate to the police we have the situation totally secured and the best thing would be for them to withdraw. And then the command was given to charge us with blue helmets and swinging batons. There were policemen literally chanting "Kill Davis" as I was being attacked. I was the first one to be hit. The first strike brought me to the ground, opening my skull. That was where I got my thirteen stitches. But it was the battering of my back on the ground that was really the killing experience. I felt like they wanted to kill me. Fortunately, I was able to crawl under a chain fence and escape.

John Sack We were teargassed and there was a girl crying to her boyfriend, "They can't do this, this is my world."

Wolfe Lowenthal I got hit at the big thing at Grant Park. It was a fucking killer of a shot. I was just not right for the next couple of years. I was waking up every night in cold sweats. I think it made me a little bit punchy. Then I and so many other people started going in the direction of the ultra Left and the violence. We were, in a sense, indulging how hurt we'd been by Chicago.

Rennie Davis I crawled under the chain fence and had two seconds to stand up and fall into the crowd before going unconscious. I was then taken by our medics to one of the county hospitals. There was an all-points alert in the city to find me and arrest me. So while I was at the hospital, the police conducted a room-by-room search. I was on a table with a sheet over me, being moved from room to room. To this day I'm amazed that no one in the hospital administration turned me in.

Tom Hayden The crowd responded according to our plans. One-half got in line with Dave to get arrested and everybody else scattered. They were told get to the Hilton by any way you can. It involved running along Lakeshore Drive endlessly, just running, trying to see if there was a way to cross one of those bridges. The only way into the hotel area and into the city is across narrow bridges that are spaced out by hundreds of yards. At each bridge there's a tank and a jeep and barbed wire and machine guns. So you keep running and you keep thinking the next bridge we'll beat 'em, and you get to the next bridge and same thing, they're there. And you're gonna run out of bridges soon and then you think you're gonna be encircled and arrested in Lake Michigan. Finally, we got to a bridge that was not yet sealed off. About a thousand people ran over this bridge. On the other side of the bridge we're finally on Michigan Avenue.

Allen Ginsberg Burroughs said, "I see no good can come of this." But he was willing to march with Dellinger. Genet, Burroughs, Terry Southern and myself were set up on the front line of the big march and got caught in the tear gas all together.

David Lewis Stein *(from his book* Living the Revolution*)* We got into the park safely. Much cheering. We were like reinforcements arriving on a battlefield. We stopped by a bench to join a crowd listening to a transistor radio. The roll call was still being taken. Pennsylvania put Humphrey over the top. We surged toward the front of the park. For a moment, it felt as if we were all going together in one last, suicidal assault on the Hilton. But the National Guard had already marched onto Michigan Avenue and taken positions facing us. From inside the park it looked like they had bayonets out. Someone on the bullhorn said, "Sit down, sit down, please sit down." The crowd spread out and began to sprawl on the grass. Keith and I found Abbie. He had just gotten out of jail and had come straight to Grant Park.

"They took me to four different stations. They worked me over in a couple of them," Abbie said. "This cop says to me, 'You see this gold bullet? I'm saving it for you, kid.' I told him, 'I'm not scared. I got a silver bullet. I'm the Lone Ranger.' "

Rennie Davis Later I was back out on a trash can in front of the Hilton with my pressure Band-Aid wrapped around my head, looking like a returning war veteran denouncing the war. That picture of defiance in injury became a photograph sent around the world. In fact, when I went to Vietnam to bring prisoners of war out of Hanoi in '69 I arrived on one of the major anniversaries of the Geneva convention and all the ambassadors were gathered in this great hall, and Pham Van Dong, the prime minister of Vietnam, walked off the stage, down into the audience right up to me and said, "How's your head?"

John Schultz Rennie was shocked [by] all the wounded people in the Mobe center. He had to go up and speak to the reporters and he said to Don Rose, the press coordinator for the Mobe, "What can I say?" And Rose, fishing back somewhere from a civil rights experience in the South, said, "Tell them they can't get away with it, tell them the whole world is watching." And that's exactly what he did.

Robin Palmer Every Vietcong flag you see in any pictures of Chicago were personally made by me and Sharon Krebs. That's why I was on the indictment. They knew that, mostly because of George Demmerle, the informant who spent some time with me in Chicago. There was a lot of planned trashing in Chicago. We were making a revolution. Chicagoans were good Germans. I remember going out trashing with George; we took a big chunk of cement and put it in the back window of a Cadillac. I got busted for throwing rocks at police cars. Two or three o'clock in the morning they took me to prison and there was Jerry. They had just picked him up. They dismissed my charges because I asked Demmerle to testify.

Jerry Rubin Wednesday was the greatest. Everybody marched down to the Hilton and that was the night that the cops started chasing me through the streets. They put me in jail and Pierson showed up in a nice blue suit, short hair slicked down. At first I didn't recognize him. He said, "You're in trouble. You're gonna be arrested for treason." I was just stunned. His great success was when I was in that park and the kids and police started fighting. I threw my sweater and screamed something from the back of the crowd and he was able to say that I had caused a riot. For throwing a sweater I got sixty days in jail.

Tom Hayden I could see the Hilton Hotel up ahead, all lit up. You're running along this dark street, like a moth to a flame. And so the final confrontation, where they're on the street being beaten up and chanting, "The whole world is watching," was entirely spontaneous.

Bob Zmuda That's when they did the old police wedge. They pushed the crowd from the back, to make it look as if the crowd was attacking the police. A guy went right through the plate glass. They crushed everybody against it.

Jeff Nightbyrd The Hilton bar was right there. A guy had combat boots on, kicked the window, broke it, and everybody went storming through the plate-glass window into the bar. Here came the cops chasing them through the bar, so people tried to sit down at tables, acting like they were customers.

Tom Hayden Everybody's hands and face were cut, their hair was full of glass and there was no place to hide. So you got beat up and then dragged through revolving doors. I don't know if you've done that but the human body is not designed to be pulled through a revolving door.

Joe LoGuidice, *Chicago gallery owner* I went through the window, backwards, and the people in the bar started beating the shit out of me. I wasn't hurt, but I was bleeding. I was part of the McGovern group on the seventeenth floor. They had gotten a couple of doctors up there and they were treating head wounds so I was trying to get upstairs. I finally got off the elevator and there was this guy pushing this fucking ice machine down the hallway. It was Abbie! He says, "Give me a hand with this." So we

THE WHOLE WORLD WAS WATCHING AS THE CHICAGO POLICE VENTED THEIR FRUSTRATION ON THE ANTIWAR DEMONSTRATORS AT THE DEMOCRATIC CONVENTION.

From the archives of Jerry Lieberman

pushed it to this window in the front, and we looked out and the whole scene's going on down there. Abbie's fucking bagging ice cubes and dropping ice cubes on the cops. You couldn't miss them, there was this rectangle of blue helmets, all packed in. The ice cubes were lethal, you could hear it when they hit one of the helmets. I saw one cop get hit and just go down. It was like getting hit with a coconut. When they figured out where it was coming from, they came up and tore the fucking place to pieces.

Robin Palmer Chicago was when I decided to become what I thought was a communist because this was Pig America. The citadel of democracy was now behaving like Nazi Germany. In those days I thought communism was good. I oversimplified it. An enemy of your enemy is your friend.

From the *New York Times Magazine,* 9/15/68

THE BATTLE OF CHICAGO: FROM THE YIPPIES' SIDE

By Tom Buckley

. . . Other Yippies say that Hoffman, to a greater extent than they, has "integrated acid into his daily life." People who have known him for a long time say that it has permanently affected his mind. One called him a "dangerous paranoid-schizophrenic." Hoffman acknowledges that he may indeed be crazy by the unimaginative and outdated standards of present-day medicine. It doesn't worry him, for he regards schizophrenics—like acidheads, users of LSD—as daring, inadequately understood voyagers into the veiled regions of their own minds.

He is unquestionably eloquent and, within the context of his unorthodox but by no means absurd system of thought, generally rational. Yet even a well-disposed listener senses a certain lack of balance.

On the last day of the convention, for example, several thousand demonstrators, turned back by the police and the National Guard (supported by an armored personnel carrier), withdrew to the equestrian statue of Maj. Gen. John A. Logan, a Civil War commander, which stands on a small rise at the south end of Grant Park.

Deputy Superintendent John Rochford of the Chicago Police attempted to reason with the protesters . . . one of David Dellinger's assistants was counseling caution to the crowd. "I don't see any point in any more bloodshed," he said, and then handed over the microphone to Rochford.

"Sometimes the law is not what I'd like," he began. "When you move in concert and without proper permission . . ." His voice was drowned out by boos. "Let him have his words," someone in the crowd shouted. "Oh, hell," said another voice, "we've heard that song." But the protesters remained quiet . . .

Then Abbie Hoffman had the microphone. "We've got one of the head cops with us," he said insinuatingly. "They won't touch us as long as we've got the head cop . . ."

Abbie Hoffman *(as reported in the* Village Voice, *9/12/68)* So I calls out through the bullhorn, "I wanna talk to the head cop, send over your head cop." And then this very impressive looking cat, a police commander or something, comes over to talk. So I says, "Let's grab this cat and tell the other cops that unless they let the march through, we're gonna snuff their head cop." It would have been so beautiful, man. But nobody would listen to me, so I said what the fuck and I just laid down in front of a fucking tank and laughed.

John Schultz Abbie laid down on his belly, on his face and his hands, his elbows on the pavement, in front of an armored personnel carrier. It was no tank, it was an armored personnel carrier. And it wasn't moving. It was more like a photo opportunity. General Dunn had made sure that the machine gun had no ammunition. But it's an excellent picture of him.

Paul Krassner Thursday night we were in the street and some car came by, without stopping for me. Then it had to stop 'cause of the crowd and so I kicked the tire of the car. That was my level of violence. I could always say, "Well, I was thinking of buying it." Just then I hear this voice behind me, Don Johnson, the senior correspondent for *Newsweek*. He said, "You better get off the street, the cops are looking to bust you." I knew Abbie and Jerry had already been busted, so Anita and I got a cab. I was on the floor of the cab because I didn't want my tails to see me. Then we picked up Abbie. I think we got a midnight flight from Chicago to New York.

Wolfe Lowenthal The plane started taxiing away, and it stopped on the runway. It was like a bad dream. These fucking cops get on the plane and go right up to us. It was some last-minute hassling, then they got off. Just a psychological thing, just one more. Abbie was very quiet. I don't think he said five words on the way back. Not like him at all.

Jack Newfield Even though some of the people who came were assholes, I think the police were 80 percent to blame. They were programmed to do this out of political calculation. Humphrey was twenty points behind Nixon at that point, the Wallace constituency was strong and I think some evil smart people figured, "How do we get the Wallace people? We'll beat the shit out of all these commie, faggot kids." Daley and Johnson and those guys understood that Middle America, white workers, hated the movement. Humphrey began to go up in the polls, afterward.

Mike Rossman Walter Cronkite broke on live camera and said, "The children, my God, look what they're doing to the children," right? But what no one understood at that time is now visible twenty years down the line. That was the psychic instant when America stopped caring for its children. You will recall that the young had been much in favor, up to that point; we had been through a decade of slavish admiration of their styles and their fads. The young had become the cultural leaders, partly 'cause we were interesting but more 'cause we were still loved and adored, even when we stepped out there, somewhat. But when we stepped out there too far, the cultural reaction changed very deeply. I sit here twenty-three years downstream as one who has been a teacher of young children for almost all the time since, and I reflect on this. America doesn't care for its children. And the instance that symbolizes when the culture stopped caring is when it looked at the children in Chicago and just beat them over the head in the public street, in front of the whole world, in a rank gesture of refusal to compromise with the life of the future.

Ed Sanders There is a view that we prolonged the war and helped get Nixon in and that we did not recognize how extremely conservative the white American middle class is in terms of how it will forgive a Nazi if it has a perfect lawn. There is some truth to it. Maybe the war would've ended in '71 and maybe Nixon would've been defeated, maybe Hubert Humphrey would've squeaked in and continued the lumbering Democratic social machine and maybe we would have national health care by now. But a lot of us felt "Jesus, it's so corrupt."

Allen Ginsberg I felt that Rubin was manipulating me and others. After Chicago, Ed Sanders said something that really brought me up sharp. He said, "I will never again compromise and make a political alliance with people who have violence in their hearts."

Jim Fouratt Chicago was, in fact, a bloodbath. It was very few people and it looked like a billion people on television and it played in history as an epic moment. So I guess Abbie was right and I was wrong. Chicago was exactly what he always wanted it to be, a media event. When the police invaded Eugene McCarthy's headquarters and beat the shit out of those kids, Abbie thought that that was terrific, that was radicalization. At that point how could you criticize Chicago? Look what it did. It brought the government down.

Jerry Rubin Abbie and I didn't talk for about a month. Then finally he came over and we argued. He said, "Well, let me just tell you something. My spelling of Yippie won out. So I was right." I was spelling it "Yippee." And he was spelling it "Yippie." But since everybody got what they wanted out of Chicago, it was natural that we'd start getting along again.

Larry Sloman I ran into Abbie on Second Avenue a few days after the convention. I was both feeling guilty that I chickened out of going to Chicago and feeling kind of angry that a lot of innocent kids got their heads bashed in. But Abbie was just ebullient. "You shoulda been there, man, we exposed them," he said. "We exposed them."

Chapter Five

HOFFMAN V. HOFFMAN

Tom Hayden I didn't plan to see Abbie or Jerry again. The Yippies were too anarchistic but I wasn't fit for the antiwar groups either 'cause they were overbureaucratic for me. I didn't know where I fit and I didn't want to be on the national scene; so I went to Berkeley.

Andy Kent Abbie was better known after Chicago and I think that was a double-edged sword. Now he was a target for the police.

In September, Abbie made plans to return to Chicago to stand trial for decorating his forehead with the F-word. But first he needed a lawyer. After consulting with Kunstler, Abbie met with Gerry Lefcourt. Lefcourt was a fresh-out-of-law-school activist lawyer who had been working as a Legal Aid lawyer defending indigent clients. Appalled at the lack of resources that Legal Aid provided the lawyers, Lefcourt organized a union. He was promptly fired.

Abbie was blunt with Lefcourt. "I have no money. I wouldn't pay even if I did. There's one law for the rich and another for the poor and I'm out to fuck that system. You keep me on the street."

SEPTEMBER 17, 1968

The first day of their partnership was, to say the least, eventful. They flew to Chicago together but, because he had inadvertently missed a court appearance, Abbie was immediately arrested at the airport and charged with skipping bail. He was searched and the police found a pocketknife. After Abbie appeared for the obscenity charge (where the bail-jumping charges were dropped), he was arrested again by Chicago police on charges of carrying a concealed weapon.

After some quick legal maneuvering, Lefcourt managed to get Abbie out on bail. They were relaxing on the local precinct steps when two FBI agents in trench coats appeared and arrested Abbie for "crimes aboard an aircraft"—the penknife again. After spending the night in jail, Abbie and Lefcourt finally caught an early morning flight back to New York. They were about to take off when five men boarded the plane and surrounded the pair. Abbie recognized four of the men as Chicago Intelligence officers. The fifth man identified himself as a U.S. marshal. He handed Abbie a piece of paper that began, "Greetings: You are hereby commanded to appear before the House Un-American Activities Committee . . ."

Jerry Rubin I was first subpoenaed to HUAC in 1966. HUAC was the instrument [meant] to smash the antiwar movement, but everybody wanted to get a subpoena. It's just totally the opposite of the way it was in the fifties. HUAC became a means to our end. We were the Katzenjammer Kids looking to shock America. So when I got a subpoena I started to ask myself what I should do. I was sitting with Ron Davis of the Mime Troupe. And Ron said I should wear an American Revolutionary War hat. Then I thought, "What's a hat? That won't get noticed. I'll get the whole uniform." So I went to a Berkeley costume store and got myself a Revolutionary War uniform. The first national theatrical thing, totally pre-Yippie. There was a picture of me in *Newsweek, Time,* every newspaper in the country. It threw HUAC off balance and I was arrested.

The newest round of hearings was to convene on October 1, 1968. Along with Abbie and Jerry Rubin, the Committee had subpoenaed less flamboyant New Left leaders including Dave Dellinger, Rennie Davis, Tom Hayden and other Mobe officials. The HUAC members wanted to demonstrate alleged links between the antiwar movement and international communism. For the Mobe leaders, it would be a forum to make yet another presentation of their case against the war. But Abbie and Jerry (who had reconciled back in New York after Chicago) had another plan. Abbie told the Liberation News Service that they were going to "get crazy . . . 'cause that's the only way we're gonna beat them. So fucking crazy that they can't understand it at ALL."

Jerry Rubin I was dressed as a world revolutionary. Beret, buttons, rifle, barechested. I got Vietcong pants from Bernadine Dohrn, straight from the Vietcong.

After the opening speeches, the Yippie contingent began disrupting the hearings. Jerry's girlfriend Nancy Kurshan, Anita Hoffman and Sharon Krebs were dressed like witches, complete with brooms, and they began sweeping the floors, burning incense and moaning. Rubin turned his toy M-16 plastic rifle on the committee members. Abbie raised his hand, asked permission to go to the bathroom, reached the hall door and screamed "BULLSHIT" at the top of his lungs. But that was only for openers. Abbie had a surprise up (and on) his sleeves for the second day of hearings.

Randy Wicker It actually was made in France and it looked like somebody had cut up an American flag and sewn this thing into a shirt. They were selling it in a boutique in the Village. In those days they cost twenty-five dollars apiece. So I bought one and my lover at the time bought one too. We took 'em home and put them in the closet because I was going on radio and TV. One thing I want to make clear. When I make these complaints about Abbie Hoffman, I really am morally and ethically offended. It isn't because I wasn't given an extra line of print, because, believe me, I had a lot of publicity. I was the only homosexual activist who'd go on TV and radio. Anyway, Abbie was always floating in and out of my store. I showed him the shirt and I said, "Boy, when they call me down to Washington, I'm gonna march in with this shirt on." And Abbie asked me if he could borrow it.

Abbie was intent on appropriating the ultimate symbol of our country. He was also willing to show some other colors too. The morning before the second day of the hearings, Anita dutifully painted a Vietcong flag on Abbie's bare back. He then donned the borrowed flag shirt, intending to appear before the committee and disrobe, revealing the NLF flag on his back. But Abbie's street-theater script was superseded by the improvisation of the D.C. police.

On the sidewalk outside the Cannon Office building, Abbie and his retinue were stopped by policemen who were enraged by his flag shirt. A melee ensued and Abbie's shirt was literally ripped off his back.

Anita Hoffman The shirt was in shreds and he was in his bare chest. Naturally, they're always more violent than they should be, clubs, everything. I was arrested for trying to protect him. I was then locked up in this padded cell through to the next day because Gerry Lefcourt was unable to locate me in the prison system.

The first flag-desecration statute, Volume 18, United States Code, Sections 700 and 711, which protected Old Glory from "defacing and defiling," had recently

ABBIE LITERALLY HAD THE FLAG SHIRT RIPPED OFF HIS BACK OUTSIDE THE HUAC HEARINGS IN WASHINGTON IN 1968. AP/Wide World

been enacted. Abbie was the first person arrested under this law and faced a year in prison and a $1,000 fine. Meanwhile, the hearings went on in his absence.

Paul Krassner Outside the Capitol building, Brad Fox was letting the air out of the tire of the police car. He was hesitant at first, and Jerry saw him and Jerry said, "Do it," which would be the title of Jerry's book. The subtitle should have been "Do It Instead of Me."

Jerry Rubin HUAC was great. I was called a few months later and came as Santa Claus, the only communist. He wears red and gives everything away for free.

From the *National Observer,* 10/7/68

AS YIPPIES BAIT SYSTEM "IT'S ALL A MYTH, MAN"

The Militant "Movement," Without Real Members, Scores With Press Agentry

By Daniel Greene

The rifle, propped against the kitchen wall, is the first thing the stranger notices when the door at the end of the dingy hallway is opened. It stands out, presumably, as a blunt affirmation of everything one hears about the notorious occupant of this three-room pad on Manhattan's squalid Lower East Side.

Still, when Abbie Hoffman, anarchist and Yippie agitator, suddenly grabbed the gun after a few moments of banter, raised it to his shoulder, and aimed it at me, my professional composure wavered. He squeezed the trigger: "Click!" went the unloaded gun. And Abbie the revolutionary collapsed onto his gaudy couch in a paroxysm of laughter.

"It's all myth, man. Yippie's a myth. The pig's a myth. I'm a myth. Whoever heard of a commie-terrorist-anarchist with a color television?" My shaggy host gleefully manipulated the images on his expensive new plaything with a remote-control box in his hand. It was evening-news time, and on almost every channel the "myth" was being perpetuated in pictures of raucous student demonstrations and irate public figures decrying the outrages of youth. "Once a myth starts," Abbie mused, "nothing can stop it."

Abbie went to trial for the flag desecration charge. Lefcourt argued that Abbie was innocent on First Amendment grounds, that wearing the flag was protected symbolic speech. The judge disagreed, convicted Abbie and sentenced him to a thirty-day jail term. Lefcourt appealed.

From the Flag Shirt Trial Transcript

The Court: The Court finds him guilty. Do you want to say anything before sentencing?

Mr. Hoffman: I regret that I have but one shirt to give for my country.

After the national protest leaders left Chicago, there was spirited debate as to who was responsible for the bloodletting. Some liberal elements blamed the police and Mayor Daley. In an attempt to defend itself, the Daley administration prepared a white paper called "Strategy of Confrontation," which laid out their side of the story.

SEPTEMBER 10, 1968

John Schultz Daley's report gave an extremely biased view in favor of the police and showed them reacting solely to demonstrator provocation and managed to leave out incredible hunks of information that would have reflected not so well upon the city administration and the Chicago police.

John Gerassi, *radical professor, antiwar activist* The Yippies called a press conference. They would give a total and complete answer to Mayor Daley in sixty seconds. All the press was there. Jerry and Nancy and Anita were at this table, and there's an empty seat. There's this huge ashtray on the table. At the appointed moment, the cameras begin to roll as Jerry lights a cigarette—and he was not a smoker—and says, "Ladies and gentlemen, our answer to Mayor Daley." At that moment, Abbie walks in with the report, Jerry puts down the match, still lit, to the paper, which immediately catches fire, and Abbie puts the report into the ashtray.

John Schultz By that time the Chicago Democratic Party was split, and there was considerable discussion about forming a third party. This discussion was felt by many important Democrats to be particularly dangerous to the fate of the party. So by the middle of September an investigation got under way that eventually resulted in a book published in the latter part of November called *Rights in Conflict.* This Walker Commission put seventy or eighty investigators on the street, young lawyers, businesspeople, establishment people, most of whom wanted to arrive at some sort of accurate portrayal of what had happened during convention week.

The head of the investigation was Daniel Walker, who had ambitions to be governor of Illinois. And the lawyer Victor DiGracia, his friend and right-hand man, was later campaign manager for Walker in his successful gubernatorial bid. So they put together a book which sought in a far more sophisticated way to shift the blame from government authorities down to the street. They called it a police riot, but cast the evidence in such a way as to show that the "police riot" was caused by the provocation of the demonstrators. They created hybrid facts. For instance, they say in the Walker Report that at a crucial point in this final confrontation on Sunday night, August the 25th, that the police were blinded by strobe lights and then pelted with rocks and then they burst loose, angry, and attacked the demonstrators. I was right at that point of confrontation and first of all, in the raw files, there are two reports by police officers of having been blinded by strobe lights and both of them had occurred at different times in different places. So they took those two reports and put them into a time and place where it did not belong. So the Walker Report carries this peculiar manipulation of fact from beginning to end. And the reporters who had been present on the streets were aware that this was a travesty, and they did a major set of articles in the *Chicago Journalism Review,* taking issue with the report and with its police-riot interpretation.

From Abbie Hoffman Interview with the Walker Commission

WC: Do you know of anyone that participated in activities in one way or another in Chicago during convention week who espouses the violent overthrow of the government?

AH: Me. I espoused the overthrow by any means necessary. I'd like to see it be done with bubble gum but I'm having some doubts.

WC: Any specific things that haven't been covered that happened that may not have been publicized, that may be within your special knowledge about events that took place during convention week in Chicago?

AH: Well, it was just the $10,000 loan that we got from Spiro Agnew that didn't receive much publicity.

WC: Could you tell us about that?

AH: Well, it was on August 17, I met with him on 7th St. and Avenue B at 4:30 A.M. and he gave us a brown paper bag with $10,000 worth of small bills.

John Schultz Mayor Daley, oddly enough, praised the Walker Report when it first came out on December the 1st, and then he ran from the room, not allowing reporters to ask him any questions. Daley wanted to heal the wounds in the Democratic Party as badly as Walker. Three days after Daley accepted the report, he had taken in that time serious criticism, particularly from the conservatives in his party, and he came back and stood shoulder-to-shoulder with Police Commissioner Conlisk and supported the police against the Walker Report.

But *Rights in Conflict* was actually, on its own terms, fairly successful in bringing out this largely false understanding of what happened during convention week. Even demonstrators such as Hayden and Dellinger and Abbie reacted as if they were being thrown a bone. Even if they wanted to say the police riot was instigated from above, they were stuck with this very successful myth of a police riot rather than a police offensive, or rather than a police riot that would not have happened without the encouragement from above. So, what stuck, to the point of rewriting history, was a notion of individual policemen going berserk in the streets because they were incited by provocative, nasty-talking, missile-throwing demonstrators.

John Zitek Where did the former Governor Walker just get out of? He got out of prison. Being a fucking crook. There's your answer. Walker Report! I was pissed off. I thought it was totally bullshit. Sure there were some police that were out of line, but on the whole, it's definitely a bum rap. Everybody said the police overreacted. Police reacted. I certainly wasn't throwing tile at nobody. I put my helmet on when they were throwing and did we go after 'em? You're fucking right. We tried to club the piss out of 'em. First cocksucker you catch throwing that shit at you, guy or broad. And the part about that bullshit blood thing was their best gimmick for the foreign press—by foreign, I mean outside of the city of Chicago.

Marshall Efron Mayor Daley made this movie *What Trees Do They Plant?* An hour-long film showing the provocation that the Chicago police had to absorb before they overreacted to the crowds. It was put on stations all across America. The ACLU went to court and under the Fairness Doctrine, it was determined that the organizations that were attacked in the Mayor Daley film were allowed equal time on the air. The Yippies said we have fifteen minutes, we'll make our own film. When I heard they were making a movie, I said to Abbie, "I'll do a commercial for Yippie helmets." I had a police nightstick and I hit a melon, hit an egg, hit a tomato. They all splattered. Then there was this human head, Bob Fass, wearing the official Yippie helmet, and I hit him in the head and he was smiling.

Ron Kaufman *Revolution for the Hell of It* was written just a few days after the convention, and is probably a pretty good reflection of what Abbie's mood was, which was not depressed by any means.

From the *New York Times,* 1/10/69

BOOKS OF THE TIMES

By Christopher Lehmann-Haupt

"Revolution for the Hell of It," by FREE, at least makes a show of being an anti-book, by scrambling together revolutionary incantations, narrative flashbacks, an auto-interview, favorite quotations, reproduced documents, photos, visual jokes, and autobiographical notes. But it's really very linear and coherent, and surprisingly fun . . .

From *Time* magazine, 12/20/68

SOUL ON ACID
REVOLUTION FOR THE HELL OF IT BY "FREE"

"Free," the author of this disjointed but somehow engaging non-book, is in reality Abbie Hoffman, 32, the wire-haired cofounder of the yippie movement. A self-described "nice Jewish boy from The Bronx" who attended Brandeis and Berkeley, then worked in Mississippi for S.N.C.C. before dropping into hippiedom, Hoffman has now produced a slender, acid-infused account of the rise of the nonviolent yippies.

Letter to the Editor of *Time* Magazine, 1/1/69

Ends and Means

Sir:

Your article about the yippies and Mr. Hoffman's book was grossly misleading. You claim that they are nonviolent. In view of their actions in Chicago, doesn't that seem a misjudgment? I have read Hoffman's book, and he never disavows the use of violence. He brags about hitting a cop with a bottle and threatening to kill the deputy superintendent of police if the yippies were not allowed to march to the amphitheater. He and the yippies seem willing to use any means necessary to further their revolutionary aims, including violence. Wake up.

Pat McNeil
The Bronx, N.Y.

Anita Hoffman That letter to *Time* magazine was really written by Abbie.

Peter Berg What Abbie did seemed self-aggrandizing. Part of our thoroughgoing fucking of the media was to be anonymous. The media couldn't handle that. They'd say, "Is he the spokesman?" when there isn't one. In 1968 I was living in a collective household. Hoffman knocks on my bedroom door, opens the door and says, "Peetah, it's Abbie. I bet ya think I stole everything from you!" I woke up and said, "Abbie Hoffman?" "Yeah!" I said, "I don't think you stole anything, I think I gave away a good tool to an idiot." That was the last thing we ever said to each other.

Paul Krassner Abbie did a lot of anonymous stuff, but he used his celebrity as a tool. So in that sense it was transcending the ego. You're just using it 'cause you know that a reporter will talk to you sooner than he'll talk to some unknown person.

Jeff Nightbyrd I was with Abbie one day on the Lower East Side and somebody came up real mad because Abbie had used his idea and got a bunch of publicity. This guy says, "You stole my idea. I told you that two months ago and you used it." Abbie looked at him and said, "Ideas don't mean anything. I have lots of ideas every day. It's what you do with them."

* * *

That spring, police raided Abbie's office on Fifth Street and claimed to find a shopping bag filled with three loaded revolvers and a quantity of heroin.

Jerry Rubin I wouldn't call any of those busts after Chicago repression. It was more Abbie being the consummate rebel and breaking every rule. Except maybe the thing where they planted guns and heroin. Who did that? The local police, the FBI? On what level was that happening?

The gun and drug charges were eventually dropped but the harassment continued. A month later, Abbie was in court on his earlier Columbia University bust when he inadvertently got caught up in a demonstration in support of some New York Black Panthers who were on trial in the same courthouse. Abbie was pulled out of a phone booth in the courthouse and beaten by local police.

"J.P." I joined the New York City police force in '63. I infiltrated these demonstrations. I got educated by guys like Abbie Hoffman. He was the leader that brought all the other people down. We used to call them cockroaches. I wished I could bust Abbie more than a murderer.

Abbie tried to defend himself against the police officers and was charged with felonious assault. Enraged, he called Gerry Lefcourt, who set up a meeting with Mayor Lindsay's aide Barry Gottehrer where he threatened to campaign for Lindsay's re-election if these latest charges weren't dropped.

Jerry Rubin After the convention, there was the postpartum let-down. But the government came through with a nice project: the indictments.

John Schultz The first major effect of convention week upon radical recruitment was very positive. Hoover didn't even wait for the end of convention week to give instructions for agents to begin assembling evidence concerning possible civil rights law violations, specifically the antiriot statute. So the conspiracy trial was the big nationally focused centerpiece for this campaign against radical dissent.

Around this time, an antiliberal group, the Crazies, formed. Periodically, Robin Palmer and his girlfriend, Sharon Krebs, would infiltrate a public event, get naked and present a pig's head on a platter to a liberal who was not sufficiently against the war.

Ramsey Clark, *former U.S. attorney general* The grand jury in Chicago had indicted eight police officers before I left the government January 20, '69. I had sent out two teams to Chicago because I didn't think the U.S. attorney there, Foran, could be relied upon. One was from the Civil Rights Division. And we also sent out the team from the Criminal Division. Some of these civil rights cases they came up with were incredible. One took place up in Lincoln Park. We had film footage of a kid, early teens, driving a bike down the road and you see a barricade by a bridge. You see the kid coming along, all of a sudden a couple of police officers come charging over and one of them hits him off the bike, sends him sprawling across the street, and the policeman goes back, picks up the bike and throws it in the water. And then the next thing you see is an angry police officer coming right at the camera and then you see the sky and then darkness. That's a civil rights violation. We finally had eight police officers indicted for civil rights violations, excessive use of force, beating up demonstrators or whatever.

But we had no evidence that I felt warranted submitting things to the grand jury on criminal acts by the demonstrators. I don't believe that I even saw an investigative report on Bobby Seale. I don't remember even knowing that Bobby Seale had been there. But I will always believe that there were eight demonstrators indicted because we had indicted eight police.

I was shocked by the indictments to begin with because I didn't know what the Nixon administration had discovered that we didn't. We'd already had a lot of shocking things. I think it was [Richard] Kleindeinst who asked an associate of mine to talk to me about rounding up a few hundred people before the inauguration and then letting them out after, so they couldn't cause trouble during the inauguration. I couldn't believe that anybody would urge you to do that.

While Ramsey Clark refused to press a conspiracy charge against the Chicago demonstrators, Nixon's incoming Attorney General, John Mitchell, was more than eager to pursue a show trial. On March 20, 1969, less than three months into the new administration, the long-awaited indictments against eight of the Chicago protesters were handed down.

John Schultz The eight are obviously carefully chosen. We have Dellinger representing the older Mobilization, Rennie Davis and Tom Hayden representing the younger people of SDS, Jerry and Abbie for the Yippies. John Froines and Lee Weiner were chosen partly because they represented academia and partly [because] the jury would need to have something to negotiate and Froines and Weiner would be the ones they could let go. Seale was tacked onto it because they were very interested in isolating the Black Panther Party.

UNITED STATES DISTRICT COURT
SOUTHERN DISTRICT OF ILLINOIS
EASTERN DIVISION

United States of America
-vs-
David T. Dellinger,
Rennard C. Davis,
Thomas E. Hayden,
Abbott H. Hoffman,
Jerry C. Rubin,
Lee Weiner,
John R. Froines and
Bobby G. Seale

The SEPTEMBER 1968 GRAND JURY charges:

1. Beginning on or about April 12, 1968, and continuing through on or about August 30, 1968, in the Northern District of Illinois, Eastern Division, and elsewhere, DAVID T. DELLINGER, RENNARD C.

DAVIS, THOMAS E. HAYDEN, ABBOTT H. HOFFMAN, JERRY C. RUBIN, LEE WEINER, JOHN R. FROINES and BOBBY G. SEALE, defendants herein, unlawfully, willfully and knowingly did combine, conspire, confederate and agree together with WOLFE B. LOWENTHAL, STEWART B. ALBERT, SIDNEY M. PECK, KATHIE BOUDIN, SARA C. BROWN, CORINA F. FALES, BENJAMIN RADFORD, BRADFORD FOX, THOMAS W. NEUMANN, CRAIG SHIMABUKURO, BO TAYLOR and DAVID A. BAKER, being co-conspirators not named as defendants here, and with divers other persons, some known and others unknown to the Grand Jury, to commit offenses against the United States, that is:

a. to travel in interstate commerce and use the facilities of interstate commerce with the intent to incite, organize, promote, encourage, participate in, and carry on a riot, and to commit acts of violence in furtherance of a riot, and to aid and abet persons in inciting, participating in, and carrying on a riot, and during the course of such travel, and use, and thereafter, to perform overt acts for the purposes of inciting, organizing, promoting, encouraging, participating in, and carrying on a riot, and committing acts of violence in furtherance of a riot, and aiding and abetting persons in inciting, participating in, and carrying on a riot, and committing acts of violence in furtherance of a riot, in violation of Section 2101 of Title 18, United States Code.

Jerry Rubin The day we were indicted we had a champagne and grass party. We were thrilled.

Tom Hayden I thought it's like a bad dream revisited. I had a life in Berkeley where I was living with a woman and with new friends. The trial came as the long arm of the law literally reaching out and bringing me back to a world that I didn't particularly want to be in.

Jeff Nightbyrd Abbie pulled me aside at that party and said, "Here's how I see it. Our only chance is to transform the trial into a theater which exposes the whole justice system for what it is. Tom wants to make legal arguments, I want to mock, belittle the court. You wouldn't believe this judge, Hoffman, we've got the perfect guy." But he was the only one who was arguing for this among the defendants. So he says, "I'm going to act crazy. When the cameras turn on, Jerry won't be able to stay away. So now if both of us start disrupting the legitimacy of the courtroom, then they're gonna bring in police. They're racists, they're gonna go after Bobby Seale. That's gonna bring Dave Dellinger over. Rennie Davis, who is eminently sensible, is going to then try to be spokesperson for this. The way I see it, if

I confront them with life theater versus death theater, everybody's gonna come along, even though there's only one of me arguing this position." He called the dialectics of the trial months before it took place. Everybody but Hayden took Abbie's course.

Jerry Rubin We saw the vision. The courtroom would become a theater, good and evil, reduced to a cartoon. The judge would be evil. He'd represent parental authority, university authority, state authority, the United States government, the troops in Vietnam, the Pentagon. We would be seen as underdogs, as American revolutionaries, David versus Goliath. The media would be the window to the world. Having a drama of good and evil set in the middle of the country would absolutely make protest hip. The plan was to steal the youth away from the rich, to actually subvert the government by taking away their kids.

Len Weinglass When Tom got indicted he asked me to come in to represent him. Gerry Lefcourt was in for Abbie. And through a process of meetings, it was decided that Bill Kunstler and myself and Charles Garry would represent the eight. Gerry dropped out to do the Panther 21, who were arrested in the meantime. The pretrial period from March to September was relatively harmonious.

Mayer Vishner, *antiwar activist* I'm producing a benefit for the Emergency Civil Liberties Committee at the Fillmore in May of '69 with Country Joe. Abbie is supposed to do a bit. Backstage, everything's frantic and crazy, and Anita comes in with this guy. He's wearing a suit and a tie, greased-back hair, incredibly nondescript. It was time for the show to start and I go "Where's Abbie?" Anita starts to giggle and she looks at this guy and he looks at her and I look at him again and it's Abbie. He looked like a nerd. And he's got an attaché case. When it's Abbie's turn to go on, Krassner says, "Ladies and gentlemen, please welcome Sirhan Sirhan." Out goes this guy whom no one can recognize and he's talking about how he used to be a drug salesman and how he realized that there were moral ambiguities to his job.

Wolfe Lowenthal As he talks he starts taking off his clothes. He had tied up his hair so tight that you didn't see it. He opened it up and the hair came out, and the fucking place exploded, man! People were jumping on their seats.

Mayer Vishner Before anybody realizes what's hit them, he's stark raving naked, he's yelling "Free!" and jumping in the air.

Paul Krassner Oh, that was beautiful. He showed how he had started trying to work totally within the system, working for a political candidate in Massachusetts. And then he did voter registration work in the South. Voter registration work is certainly within the system but going with SNCC to the South in those times was outside the system. He ended up naked when he was totally outside the system.

From an Interview in the *East Village Other*, 5/14/69

Jaakov Kohn: What do you foresee as the future tactic of the movement?

Abbie Hoffman: Sabotage. Today I don't think I'd sit in a building . . . The movement is bound to become more violent. In order to have a revolutionary attitude you have to be willing to use all the means necessary. I'm not preaching violence, I'm just saying that people should check out their resources and use whatever they got . . .

Peter Berg In 1969 things started to unravel. There were police in the Haight every day, coming in by van and paddy wagons, they'd check everybody's ID, heroin was all over the place. So I designed an event called Free City.

For three months, the Diggers occupied the steps of City Hall, giving out free food, hosting poetry readings, defiling civic consciousness. Exhausted, the Diggers ended their activities.

Peter Berg We told everybody, "This is our last celebration, we can't continue." Well, people would say, "You've led us to the garden but we can't get in."

Peter Coyote It was a daunting task we set out to do. It killed us. In the first place, we have introjected the culture that we're trying to change. We're a product of it. So every time you would come up against a form or a limit, you didn't know whether it was legitimate or something you'd been taught. So you'd have to break through to see what would happen. And the way that you would fuel your imagination to go through, unfortunately, was drugs.

Lynn Freeman House In the beginning, there was nothing you couldn't do. And then you find out what it cost. There was some smack. Emmett was in and out of it a lot. I got strung out on methedrine for a few months. It was over, partly because of human frailty but there was an historical element to it, a wave that swept the world, then receded. I don't know why it rose or why it receded. I know I certainly am still trying to figure it all out.

Jean-Jacques Lebel Coming from Europe and having studied revolutionary movements and having been in the revolution in 1968, I knew that this sex, rock and roll and drugs wasn't gonna get nowhere. Except more Madison Avenue, more television and more hype. I tried to tell Abbie that having music in Woodstock wasn't gonna get us anywhere.

Ed Sanders Abbie wanted to shape the Woodstock Festival. He kept talking about [the promoters] like they were of intense use to him. He was very much involved in getting money out of them.

AUGUST 1969

Jeff Nightbyrd The promoters really didn't seem like they knew what was going on so we went up to the site in Bethel. There were some Hog Farm people already there. They were trying to set up their kitchen and they had two fifty-pound bags of brown rice. It was as if you have a vision of the whole Ethiopian famine and somebody comes in with a box of Clark bars.

So we demanded that the promoters give us $65,000. We were going to have free bus rides from the Lower East Side, free food, medical services, acid freak-out tents. They started calling us rip-off pirates and decided that they wouldn't give us any money. And Abbie started getting red in the face, screaming, "Fuck you guys, I'm going to jail anyway, we're gonna have everybody sit in, you're not gonna have a Woodstock. We're gonna close down your headquarters. You think Columbia was something, wait till we shut you down." Oh, fuck, it was a good rap. So they go back in, talk it over, come back out again and give us the bread. We set up a bank account and portioned out the money.

While Woodstock was an artistic success, the huge turnout (nearly 600,000 people), a massive rainstorm and forces of exploitation turned it into a commercial failure with minimal political emphasis. Survival supplies were being sold by scalpers, and nude mudsliding became an impromptu group activity. In the face of a natural disaster, Abbie almost single-handedly coordinated the medical unit.

Jeff Nightbyrd Governor Rockefeller declared it a state disaster, and this National Guard colonel comes in a helicopter. He's walking around trying to figure out who to report to. And we're joking around, "Well, Abbie Hoffman's running everything, he's over in the medical tent." "Is that who I report to?" "Yes." So the colonel takes our little Woodstock map and figures out where the medical area B was and goes over there, clicks his heels and throws this big salute. "Mr. Hoffman, Colonel So-and-So reporting, sir."

Richie Havens, *musician* You actually don't see Woodstock in the movie. It's taken me twenty years to realize that. Because what really happened there could probably never be documented.

Jeff Nightbyrd They were shooting the movie. I shoot the camera crew the finger, so the cameraman stopped filming. Abbie swears at me, "Dammit, Jeff, you ruined my chance to be in the movie, damn you." I'm saying, "But, Abbie, they're ripping us off." He's saying, "You're a revolutionary fool."

Richie Havens There was a definitely commercial attitude to that concert. Those guys said wow, you mean Monterey Pop had that many people at it, free? Maybe we can make real money here. But Abbie had to get hit in the head with a guitar so that we can understand what was going on there.

Jean-Jacques Lebel Abbie and I wanted to make a declaration for John Sinclair.

Ken Kelley, *White Panther activist* John Sinclair was a schoolteacher and poet from just outside of Flint, Michigan. He started this thing called the Artist's Workshop on Plum Street, Detroit's very much diminutive equivalent of the Haight. And he'd been one of the first guys to get busted for pot in Detroit two years before.

Along with Pun Plamodon, Sinclair started the White Panthers, Ann Arbor's version of a fusion of the Black Panthers and the Yippies.

HUNDREDS OF THOUSANDS OF FREE SPIRITS DESCENDED ON MAX YASGUR'S FARM FOR THE ORIGINAL WOODSTOCK FESTIVAL IN 1969. ABBIE DEEMED THE THRONG "WOODSTOCK NATION" IN HIS SUBSEQUENT BOOK. Archive Photos

Ken Kelley John had just been convicted for selling to an undercover narc who begged him for it. John didn't even have it, but just to get the narc off his back he went out and got what we used to call lemonade, really weak dope. Boom, second time conviction, judge sentenced him to nine and a half to ten years in jail, [the] maximum. They took him to the slam immediately. And then began the struggle to get him out, which was intense.

Paul Krassner Abbie was trying to be responsible and raise consciousness. But apparently Peter Townshend thought that it was somebody from the audience taking the stage.

Jean-Jacques Lebel We had been backstage discussing this for a long time with the Who and their managers. They were in it to make money, man, they didn't give a shit about John Sinclair or anybody else. But Abbie's exuberant discourse made them feel guilty, and while they were tuning up nothing was happening anyway. And they said all right, you have exactly three minutes to read your political message about John Sinclair while we are tuning up.

The idea was that Abbie would make this statement and I would say it in French and in Italian later to make it very international. But the problem is that Abbie took too much acid.

Country Joe McDonald I'm on the side of the stage watching the show and there was a pause and they're gonna go into another number and boom! there's Abbie talking very loudly into the microphone. He said, "How can you people sit out there having so much fun when John Sinclair's rotting in prison for possession of two joints?" I don't think that Peter even noticed him at first. Everybody was just kind of like "Huh?" Then Pete looked over at Abbie and Abbie didn't even see Pete at all.

So Peter came up and just tapped the end of his guitar on Abbie's cheek. It was just a tap, I don't know if it hurt him, but Abbie was stunned. I think they made eye contact and it was like "Whaa?" And then there was like this hushed moment. And then Abbie just fled.

He jumped down into the press pit, and then over the fence and through the crowd, *pffttt pfftt,* like a Bugs Bunny cartoon. And then the Who started playing and I remember saying to somebody, "What happened? Was that real or what, you know?" I remember thinking, "Geez, I should go talk to Abbie." It was obvious that he had been embarrassed. He just didn't understand it's not really too cool to like jump up in the middle of somebody's set and give a commercial.

Danny Fields, *record company executive* We laughed about that. Townshend said, "I really didn't know what I was doing. Who was this person?" I said, "You know, he's famous and we sort of like him." And Peter went, "Oooh, I didn't mean to beat up someone famous that we all liked. I didn't know, I thought it was a nut. I'm not myself up there."

Faye Schreibman, *Yippie* I went back to the city with Abbie and Ron Kaufman. He sat in the back and he didn't say a word, he was just bummed out. It was a very long ride.

From *The Bob Fass Show,* WBAI, 8/19/69

Caller: We got so much pleasure from giving the peace sign up at Woodstock.

Abbie Hoffman: I don't get pleasure from giving the peace sign anymore because I'm not into peace and music. I'm into war and music. I don't think that pays as well, tell you the truth. What would have happened if they had some statements that said things like "Power to the People" or "We're going forth from here and crush American culture" or "Kill the American dinosaur" or "What you kids really ought to do when you go home is kill your parents"?

Caller: What? Kill our parents?

Abbie Hoffman: Well, that's an image, huh? If it's a new emerging culture it's out to kill the old culture and what about the people who are running that culture and what about the government that runs it? Well, then they might get themselves in conspiracy charges.

Caller: That's what you're doing. War and music. I'm not quite up to that yet, I don't think. Personally, I'm a little bit attached to my parents because they're really pretty cool so I couldn't do anything like kill them.

From Abbie Hoffman interview with Barry Shapiro

Abbie Hoffman: I have to escape into poetic license.

Barry Shapiro: Did that bother you? That you had to talk a certain way to get a point across? Like you say "Kill your parents."

Abbie Hoffman: I'd get caught up in the rhetoric too. It's a problem when you have to exaggerate it for the media to get a point across, but you have to do it. The "kill your parents" thing for me was personally resolved when my parents went through that heart attack phase [Abbie's father had had a heart attack during the Battle of Chicago and was hospitalized for twenty-nine days], so you kind of feel that well, it's sort of done, so you can go beyond that. Did I want to kill my parents? No. It's hard to sort out your original feelings after you go through so much psychology. But definitely there was strong competition with my father. I'm very aware of it.

Alex Ducane, *friend of Johanna Lawrenson* Johanna Lawrenson and I met Abbie together in 1969. At the time, Johanna was living with Johnny Kidd [a pseudonym], who knew Abbie. Johnny was primarily a pot dealer, but he also dealt coke. Johanna was with him for about a year because she was totally broke and she had nobody to pay her phone bill. He was from Florida, he's short and squat.

The Woodstock festival had just finished. So Johnny said to the two of us, "I'm gonna take you downtown to meet Abbie." Johnny was always going on about all the famous people he knew. And Abbie was very famous, it was like his heyday. So we went for an hour or two. Just the four of us, Anita wasn't there. Abbie was reasonably aggressive and unpleasant. He didn't come on to Johanna. But he was really nasty to me and I didn't understand why. I was sitting with my hand in front of my mouth, which I tend to do. And he kept attacking me, saying, "Do you always sit with your hand in front of your mouth?" But he kept on and on and on about it. And that was that. The evening wasn't particularly interesting.

Chris Cerf, *editor, son of Bennett* Abbie came to Random House to see Jason Epstein. He had the idea of doing a book about Woodstock, but he also frankly needed money 'cause the trial was on. Jason called me in and said, "Would you like to edit this book?" I loved Abbie's sense of humor; I loved the idea of being a coconspirator. Especially, for me, I wanted to identify more with the sixties than with being the boss's son.

Abbie wrote a lot of the book in my office. One day I wasn't there but Abbie was and he was smoking a joint, lying on the floor, with his shirt off as usual, with pads in front of him, writing. My dad was showing an old friend of his around Random House and was just coming to the office to say, "Here's where my son works." My dad was apparently just opening his mouth to say, "That's not my son," and Abbie looked up and said, "Hi, Pop!"

In a few weeks, Abbie had completed the book. He called it Woodstock Nation.

Abbie Hoffman *(interviewed by Barry Shapiro)* That was no fucking Nation, that was a music festival. What was the Nation? I created that concept in my head. I looked out, I'm on acid, I see it all as an army of young people, we're gonna take on the pig empire. But the reality of the situation is most of these kids, they're not revolutionaries ready to go to the barricades. So you use the fashion. You're treading a tightrope here, trying to use the culture to change political reality.

Ken Kelley *Woodstock Nation* blew John's mind. There was a lot of admiration for Abbie for that. Bingo! suddenly youth was a class. Sinclair was incarcerated, reading Lenin and Engels and Marx and Kant and Mao. He not only read it, he took copious notes, he'd send back instructions.

Jeff Jones I moved out to San Francisco for six months, in January of 1969. During those six months we formed the Weatherman organization. The Progressive Labor Party was turning SDS into these rigid opposing factions of Marxist-Leninist cadre and we had these differences of opinion the way revolutionaries do—whether workers or minorities would lead the revolution.

The summer of '69, we get to Chicago and we take over SDS. We won all three offices and we threw the Progressive Labor Party out at the urging of the Panthers. So now we had control of the national office. We had a very intricate and complicated evolving political ideology—that the Third World revolution was the force that was going to change the world and we, the white kids of privilege at the counterrevolutionary center, [had] special responsibilities and also special possibilities. If we could be successful at the center, we could be part of an international revolution.

So out of that we created the Weatherman ideology. Our tactics grew out of Chicago and the Pentagon demonstration. We felt we had been most successful at exposing the system through militant—violence came later—militant confrontation in the streets.

Todd Gitlin The politics coming out of their mouths was absolutely senseless. They apparently believed that the world was on the brink of a great gunfight in the great OK Corral and that on the side of good was the collective revolutionary might in the Third World, which either discredited or needed, or illogically both, the white mother country revolutionaries. And that America as a whole was hopelessly retrograde, but if you kicked the shit out of it, then you would be doing your bit for the triumph of the great searing revolution that would purge the world of its sins. Everything was teetering on the edge of this vast transformation. Their talk was loaded up with a lot of other mumbo jumbo about classes and white youth and so on, but all that was an excuse for the rage and the hijinks and the fun and the gang quality of what they were doing. It was James Dean, Charles Starkweather, Richard Speck, Charles Manson, whoop-de-do. Insofar as I was part of the old guard of SDS, it was like watching some of your cousins and nephews go berserk, and in the name of redeeming the family, you feel helpless and you feel at the same time implicated.

Allen Ginsberg The Weathermen said that they also had to eliminate the bourgeois organization of the SDS, of which they were the head, so they deliberately destabilized SDS. That's why there is no student movement in America. When I talked to Rudd a few years ago, he said, "We must've been lunatics."

Jeff Jones In Marxist-Leninist theory you have to have an agent of change, right? We looked at ourselves and we still believed that young white people could also be revolutionaries. Therefore, based on our own experiences, it must be the youth. And what is the most oppressive thing for youth but schools, which are nothing more than jails? That's what led to the strategy of trying to encourage students to just trash their schools and leave. We were just trying to expose the system. I don't think we ever thought we would be able to close down all of the schools in the country or anything like that.

John Gerassi The idea is you barricade yourself in a working-class school and talk to everybody. Any teacher that tries to stop you from talking to the kids, you throw him out, and then you fight your way out through the cops that have by then encircled the school. The idea being that working-class kids will not be impressed by your theory, but when they see you fighting your way out through the police cordons, then they'll say, "Oh boy." Then you disperse. Whoever can get through, fine, and at the next corner, there's somebody going to be there waiting for you. If you're not being followed he'll say 16 Park Street, which is where the safe house is. When you get [there] you have an orgy and you take LSD. Why? To celebrate? No. Because you're gonna be so hyper that you're gonna freak out and somebody is gonna be there from the Weather Bureau to tape-record it. That way they'll catch any police agent. Well, it's true. Weather did not get infiltrated. But . . . Their theory was you ought to be able to make love to whoever you love. Now you love your comrades, male and female. So you gotta be able to make love to both. So what do you do? You have to force yourself to be lesbian or homosexual? That was nonsense. Abbie couldn't stand them.

JUNE TO DECEMBER 1969

Jeff Jones What I look back on with horror was the group dynamic. It was cultlike. People were driven to certain beliefs and certain ways of being that really broke down the individual in a very destructive way. It took a lot of people a long time to recover. In the self-criticism sessions, you would sit anywhere from a couple of hours to a couple of days talking about a person's political weakness or why they're a racist or sexist or homophobic and then analyzing the impact this has on a person's politics. This wasn't done with drugs. The trips were after. Then there was the sexual experimentation which was to smash monogamy and all sexual roles. The valid dynamic in all of this is that many women, maybe even most women, maybe even all women, were in oppressive relationships so there was a natural reason to break up whatever relationship they were in to settle the score.

Robin Palmer This was war. And in war you didn't have time for marriage. Everything was dialectical. If you were a thesis and she was an antithesis, then you will synthesize in bed and then your antagonisms will be resolved and you will be better members of the Weather Underground. It was probably just an excuse for everyone to fuck everybody.

Allen Ginsberg The Left radicals were thinking LSD is a distraction, until they started taking it and getting extremist and starting apocalyptic revolutions overnight.

* * *

Robin Palmer The reason I didn't go to the trial was because I began to do bombings in New York City. Dynamite. The defense of the Chicago conspirators was that we were innocently having guerrilla theater, we were protesting the war but it was basically a nonviolent thing from our side even though we had every right to be violent; it was really the police who were violent. I didn't want to undercut that political posture of Jerry and Abbie. So I stayed away and was bombing here in New York City. Bombed all kinds of buildings in 1969. Sam Melville and Jane Alpert and I and others, about eight of us, we got together and said, "None of this democratic process is working. The communists are right, Che's right, Castro's right, not only right for Cuba and Vietnam, they're right for the United States. We're bullshitting if we're not gonna do the same thing."

We had a tight-knit collective. I'd say about 80 percent cultural communists to well-intentioned political communists like myself and Sharon Krebs and then there were about 15, 20 percent cops, if not out-and-out cops. There was George Demmerle to be specific, who was our spiritual leader who was all the time informing, and our photographer Lou Saltzberg, who was also informing. We didn't know they were informing. The cops had even theorized that maybe this Crazie group was connected to the bombings but they dismissed it saying no they're just too ridiculous for anybody to take seriously but in fact we were the bombers, me and Sharon. We were using Crazie as a cover, we were saying we're into taking off our clothes. We wouldn't dream of doing a bombing.

We started the bombing at the same time the Chicago trial was gearing up. Sam Melville was an anarchist in a lot of ways, he was not a collective-type person. He'd been the prime mover in all this, and he and me and one other person went and actually stuck up an explo out in the Bronx. We tied up a night watchman and made off with a box of dynamite and some detonating caps. But then, as a collective, we sat around and couldn't make up our minds what the targets would be and just the right communiqué to go with each target. Sam's real name was Sam Grossman and sometime in his life he changed his name to Melville after reading *Moby-Dick,* which he claimed was the only book he ever read. We called him Ahab because he was that kind of possessed person.

While the collective squabbled over a target and a communiqué to the press, Melville acted on his own and planted two bombs—one at the United Fruit Company pier and another at the Marine Midland Bank.

Robin Palmer The Marine Midland bombing really backfired on Sam, because although he called in a warning, they didn't believe him and the night watchman did not tell people in the building. Some female night workers got scratched up bad. Sam really got scared then. We trashed him at the next meeting of the collective. Sam made us a promise that he would never do anything on his own. But he recruited George Demmerle on his own at Woodstock after we'd already done about four or five bombings.

We finally did eight altogether. We did the Federal Building across from Foley Square. We would take turns. We got dressed up straight. We'd go in with the sticks in a briefcase and a clock and the detonating caps. Almost always we left the bomb in bathrooms. That seemed to be the place we could find nooks and crannies. Nobody was ever injured. The closest thing was the Marine Midland. The other ones were General Motors, Rockefeller Center. We did the draft board at Whitehall Street. I put the one in the courthouse in 100 Centre Street. So that's what we were doing and we didn't want to jeopardize the politics of Chicago and the conspiracy trial by being prominent out there.

Wolfe Lowenthal I was one of the unindicted coconspirators, the minister of defense for the Yippie party. There was no party, I had no troops. I started getting a very real sense that I was living a complete myth, I had absolutely nothing to back it up. If I was gonna continue, I'd probably get killed. I was terrified. I was waking up every night drenched in sweat, drenched, every night! Okay, I got two choices. I can either continue to play out the myth of Wolfe Lowenthal, or I can actually try to become what the myth represents. That was the choice I made. So when they asked me to come to Chicago, I said no! It was very hard for me to say. I got a little part-time job and spent the next five years studying t'ai chi. And I healed.

Letter from John Hoffman to Abbie Hoffman (from *Soon to Be a Major Motion Picture*)

September 22, 1969

Dear Abbott,

On this, the eve of your coming trial, I hope and pray that you conduct yourself in a respectable manner. For, after all, the courts of our land are still our way of justice, and when they lose their respect, what have we left? After all is said and done, this is still a God given land and as one who has lived through two atrocities of man's inhumanity to man, this country has exemplified itself in more ways than one. Please stop to realize that your manners and conduct in the court room will both act for and against you. I am not trying to be a preacher, but just trying to give you a little advice. As a parent we still love you and wish you the best.

Dad

Stew Albert There's a file where J. Edgar Hoover lays out that he wanted a show trial; he used that term. The purpose was to destroy the New Left. On the other hand, Jerry and Abbie's strategy was the exact reverse of Hoover. To use it as a show trial, but from their point of view. See, both people had the sense of theater.

Roger Lowenstein, *attorney* We had a great actor in Judge Julius Hoffman. People were always saying to Abbie, "Are you related to Julius Hoffman?" So he'd say, "Yeah, he's my illegitimate father."

Jerry Rubin I was upset with the judge because of his name. It gave Abbie the total edge. You couldn't have planned that better if a playwright had written it. Oh, the judge was great, a total Yippie judge. Whatever we planned for him, he outdid it.

Bill Kunstler In many ways the judge was not the villain of the piece. We thought he was. But long after the trial we listened to a recording on his secretary's Dictaphone. Before the trial he had been visited by FBI agents and one of these agents said, "They're gonna take over your court. You'll show em, won't you, Judge?" He says, "I'll show 'em a fair trial . . . ," real vindictive. They poisoned him against the defendants. But he was a rather urbane guy and I think he also had a sense of humor to some degree.

John Schultz Judge Hoffman actually had a very liberal set of decisions behind him. In 1960 he ruled in favor of *Big Table* magazine, which had published portions of Burroughs' *Naked Lunch* and Kerouac and Ginsberg and several of the beat writers whose work had been impounded by the post office on a censorship charge and he gave a very literate ruling too. He had also ruled in favor of black students who had brought a desegregation case.

Stew Albert You know the story about Jerry and Abbie exchanging rings? They swore to each other that this time they weren't gonna fight, that they had to stick together against Tom Hayden. Tom wanted a very straight legal defense. The thing is to win the trial and get on with the revolution.

Jerry Rubin I don't think Tom had any understanding or appreciation for Abbie's strategy, his whole personality. Abbie came more from the heart. Tom veered between guns and backdoor politics. Where you either do shit on the streets or make a deal with the Kennedys behind closed doors. Abbie was more into we're gonna laugh the establishment out of power. Tom was also saying to us there's no need to disrupt the courtroom because before the trial is over, the Weathermen are gonna blow up the courtroom. Which was kind of a far-left argument for doing nothing.

Bill Kunstler When they were charged with conspiracy, Abbie said, "Conspiracy? We can't even agree on lunch."

Tom Hayden Apparently there was an early Abbie who was an antiwar activist, Stewart Hughes supporter, civil rights worker. That I agreed with. But that was no longer there when I met him. I was more political, I didn't think that the counterculture was that much of a superior culture. It's just a foggy recollection of a lot of madras sheets and mescaline and bodies and concerts and some rallies. To me this wasn't an alternative lifestyle. I didn't live it, and it could very well be for the very simple reason that I never took acid, so the doors were never opened. However, that doesn't mean that I didn't admire certain things about this Abbie too. I admired his passion, his courage, his very emotional desire to be recognized as an American who was doing something for the good of his country.

Lee Weiner It was dope-taking, longhaired Jews against these straight-assed goyish guys. I remember Ab and I once were screaming at Lenny Weinglass to make a motion in the court in Yiddish. It was a Jewish morality play. The major lawyers were Jewish, the key people on the jury were Jewish, the judge is Jewish, a lot of us defendants were Jewish. But ultimately we had to put on every possible defense 'cause we couldn't decide on one. So we had about eight trials there. First we got a nice, coherent-type defense, Tom Hayden. Then we put on an ideological defense, thank you, Rennie. Then we put on the cultural freak show, thank you, Abbie. Then we put on a hysterical freak show, thank you, Jerry. Then we went into the civil rights thing—oh, my God, thanks, David. Jesus, give me a break.

Tom Hayden Charles Garry [attorney for the Black Panthers in San Francisco] was the agreed-upon counsel. Sort of. The Panthers had such power in the process, virtually a veto, and Bobby Seale wanted Garry. None of us knew Charles Garry.

Stew Albert If you weren't from the West Coast, it's hard for you to understand the attraction to the Black Panthers. Our movement owed a lot to the civil rights movement in terms of morality and tactics. And then SNCC becomes a black nationalist organization. Whites feel bad that they don't have a relationship with blacks. Now the Panthers come along. They're militant as hell, they have a definite base of support in the black community, especially in the Bay Area, and among a variety of social classes. And then they say we'll make alliances with white people. That was an offer you couldn't refuse.

On top of that, they certainly met the charismatic macho requirements for leadership in those days. Eldridge Cleaver had a best-seller, *Soul on Ice,* ex-con intellectual, powerful speaker. Bobby Seale, an extraordinary speaker, witty, had been a stand-up comic. Huey Newton was enigmatic, mystical, extremely handsome and very brave with an extraordinary reputation as a street fighter and an intellectual. Kathleen Cleaver, only the most beautiful woman in America. Huey Newton used to write essays about the meaning of Bob Dylan. They were just very appealing.

Jean-Jacques Lebel I thought the Panthers were in bad faith. Jean Genet, an absolutely overt homosexual, said what he loved in the Black Panthers was the macho, dick, Leninist, power thing. Most of these Park Avenue radical chic people were into the same love affair with the mythical, macho image, but never admitted it. It was just a sexual thing, in fact, rationalized into a political thing.

Art Goldberg Charlie [Garry] had to have a gallbladder operation and Hoffman wouldn't grant a six-week postponement. Of course, Hoffman didn't want Garry in the courtroom.

Lee Weiner There was no defendant, except for Bobby Seale, who was too upset that Charlie Garry got too sick to be on the trial. We wanted to run our trial. If Garry did show up, there was no question there would've been enormous conflict.

Charles Garry Would I have had a different strategy as chief counsel? Abbie Hoffman answers that better than I can. He was very happy that I wasn't in the case and he gave his reasons that had I been in the case we would have won the case at the trial and that I would have been a strict disciplinarian. And they would not have been able to expose the system.

Ken Kelley We used to have this Michigan saying, "horny as a three-peckered goat." Bill [Kunstler] was that. But what was great about Bill is, he always said the right thing and, again, on the drop of a dime, he could just launch into all the historical antecedents and give a great speech. He was funny and fun and all of a sudden, he'd rediscovered his youth. He was clearly on the last legs of his marriage and he loved us because, hey, whoopee, drugs, girls, this wonderful hippie commune. I think it was known that Lenny did all the legal-precedent work. But Bill was a great mouthpiece. He and Lenny were an incredible team.

Michael O'Donoghue I was doing a thing with some *Harvard Lampoon* people, George Trow and Chris Cerf to help raise funds for the Chicago 8. We did a souvenir program in the form of a baseball program that was sold outside the courtroom. We called it a souvenir pogrom. You know, you can't tell the players without a pogrom.

Bill Kunstler The prosecutors were Thomas Foran and Richard Schultz. Two assholes. They were so cocksure that they couldn't lose that case, never in a million years. Foran had a lot riding on it. He was going to get the senatorial nomination that Adlai Stevenson got.

Len Weinglass Schultz was a needling nitpicker who could really get under your skin. Foran was just a careerist. A Daley appointee. He ran for governor after the case was over. It's totally shocking that in the second largest U.S. Attorney's Office in the country, the U.S. attorney plus the chief of the Criminal Division were tied up for five months trying a case that involved a demonstration in the streets. I met with people on that staff

"GET YOUR 'OFFICIAL CHICAGO CONSPIRACY PROGRAM' HERE!!!" ABBIE ENLISTED SOME *NATIONAL LAMPOON* STAFFERS TO PRODUCE A SATIRICAL "POGROM" FOR THE CHICAGO 7 CONSPIRACY TRIAL. Domesday Books

at night at predetermined places and they would tell me the whole staff was falling apart and there's a lot of internal dissent because of the energy going into this ridiculous thing.

The other lawyers were arrested on the first day. We informed [Judge] Hoffman that Bobby Seale's lawyer was in the hospital, and Hoffman looked back through the records and he said four other lawyers entered appearances in this case for pretrial motions. And since you claim Bobby Seale doesn't have a lawyer, I'm going to insist that they be here to defend Bobby Seale, unless he drops his claim to not having a lawyer. Bobby wouldn't drop his claim and so Hoffman ordered the marshals to arrest these four lawyers and bring them in. Michael Tigar was teaching a seminar at UCLA Law School called Repression and the Law, and they had him put a notice up on the door of his classroom that the class was canceled because the professor was arrested by federal marshals. Lefcourt was brought in, [Michael] Kennedy was brought in and Dennis Roberts was the fourth. The judge lined them up in front of him and he said, "I'm directing you all to defend Bobby Seale." They refused, he held them in contempt and put them all in custody.

When he denied them bail we contacted the Seventh Circuit Court of Appeals. They said, "What! You don't need papers, come right up here." We went up, no papers, no briefs, no motions. They freed the four of them. You could see that this wasn't going to be a trial. It was total confusion.

Lee Weiner Our sophisticated jury selection. Nelson. That was the bum. The fucking Democratic Party registers everybody on skid row. That's how he ended up in a jury pool. And we were all for him. Here's us asshole, neo-comms saying, "Let's take this homeless fucking person, let's have the government feed him four fucking meals a day and put him in the greatest place he ever lived in his whole life, and he'll vote for us 'cause he's an underclass person." Jesus, what fucking analysis!

Len Weinglass Professor Walz [of Northwestern University] watched the jury selection, met with the defendants and Bill and me after the jury was selected on day one and said the rest of this case is just an exercise. No convictions will stand up. Abbie said, "You mean this one doesn't count?" Walz said no. Abbie had a wild glint in his eye, jumped up and down, and said, "Let's go for it."

Jerry Rubin Abbie's true genius came out in the Chicago trial. He charmed the judge, he charmed the jury, he charmed everybody. They're introducing all the defendants. Hayden gives the jury the clenched fist. Abbie blows a kiss to the jury. That's the perfect Abbie act, right? Always lateral thinking, a little off balance, you know? I forgot what I did. How do you top that?

John Schultz In a pretrial ruling in August of 1969, Judge Hoffman had ruled that the substance of the crime was a state of mind. That's a very important ruling because the defendants were being brought to trial for their intent, not for their actual actions during convention week. It became very much an issue throughout the trial, what did intent mean? The judge, of course, was notoriously supportive of the prosecution.

Bill Kunstler One time I said I'm from New York and Lenny's from New Jersey. Judge Hoffman said, "I used to practice in New York myself." Abbie piped up and said, "That must've been when the British had it."

DAYS OF RAGE, OCTOBER 8–11, 1969

Jeff Jones We wanted to repeat Chicago at the opening of the conspiracy trial, so we put all of our energy into that. Tom and Dave Dellinger were trying to tone us down, put the brakes on what we were organizing.

Stew Albert Initially I thought Weatherman was just a crazy cult thing. When I got out to Chicago for the trial, some of the Weatherpeople, Bernadine Dohrn and Billy Ayers and Jeff Jones, were around. Bernadine was an extremely attractive, appealing, intelligent woman, an amazing, irresistible personality in every way. Jeff Jones was a friend of mine from the West Coast. So after talking with them they seemed a little more comprehensible to me. But I had a real disagreement with their idea of having a demonstration and attacking the police. You'd lose a lot of support if you clearly started the fight and then boasted about it.

Allen Ginsberg Mark Rudd told me that the Weathermen were all paranoid and they thought that America was ready for a revolution and if they started a fire as in the prairie, the whole prairie would go up ablaze. The blacks would rise, the hippies would rise, the women would rise, the workers would rise. So they thought that they had to ignite the spark by attacking the police in Chicago.

Stew Albert The Weathermen had their demonstration in the park. I saw an FBI file that indicated that if the Weathermen decided they were going to sleep in the park, Daley was gonna let 'em do it. They didn't want a repeat of the last thing. He would let the Weathermen sleep in the park but not the Yippies. Daley had learned his lesson: stop listening to J. Edgar Hoover.

John Schultz Hayden gave a speech and was catcalled off the stage and Bernadine Dohrn took over, and she let him have it but good.

Tom Hayden If you didn't go along with them you were less than a man and less than a revolutionary. The situation contributed to it because, after all, what are you supposed to do? Get a tweed jacket and become a professor and write occasional articles for the *Nation?*

Looking back, I would not have spoken if I thought they were carrying weapons and simply gonna trash a lot of cars. I was a thinking man's violent revolutionary, too repressed to believe in the logic of chaos.

Jeff Jones I consider that the most frightening night of my life. We had a much smaller number of people than we had hoped for—there were five or six hundred of us and our goal was to march somewhat destructively from the park to Judge Hoffman's house on the Gold Coast. We didn't have much planned. As we were marching, I began to hear the sound of breaking glass and car windows being smashed and I realized this is it, it's started. We went four, five, six blocks and there's a wall of cops waiting for us and there's nothing to do but charge the line.

The inevitable confrontation with the police resulted in the beatings and arrests of the protesters.

Jeff Jones The trashing may not have been my personal intent but I don't want to be hypocritical about it, our slogan was "Bring the War Home," right? We felt that it couldn't be business as usual in the United States while the war was still going on.

Ron Kaufman Abbie wanted to go with them. I said, "You're on trial, you're responsible for a hell of a lot more than these people running amuck in the neighborhood here." I literally grabbed him by the arm and stuffed him into a cab.

Abbie Hoffman *(interviewed by Barry Shapiro)* When the scene started I put a cowboy hat on and a kerchief. We're running down the streets and

Kaufman's dragging me away from the battle. I'm throwing my rocks, having a good time, really getting stoned, just running around. I saw a cop aiming his car at a demonstrator and raced the motor and hit him going forty. I said, that kid's dead. Broke both his legs. Now they want me. A trophy. They knew I was there. So we snuck into the Second City. I used to hang around there. I made friends with Peter Boyle 'cause I wanted them to come to Lincoln Park during '68. They said, "How about doing a number?" So I dressed as the judge, the audience don't even know, and I did a whole improvisation thing with me playing Judge Hoffman, then I got snuck out at the end. That was my alibi.

Jerry Rubin To just attack people, to me that's the movement at its lowest point. I don't think anybody liked that. It's true Abbie never publicly criticized it but he was scared to because these people would guilt-trip us.

Roger Lowenstein It was the stupidest fucking demonstration ever. And there's Tom Hayden, out of our apartment, while a defendant in the trial, on the phone, directing his minions as these young, white middle-class SDS kids run all over Chicago, breaking windows. Abbie knew it was pointless and stupid. But he stayed out of it. So Abbie's lying on the couch, his eyes half-open, just listening to what's going on. I remember Abbie, without opening his eyes, yelling out, "Hey, Tom. Tom!" Tom's on the phone, "Hold on a second. Yeah, Abbie?" Abbie says, "You know, before you became the father of SDS, you might've considered using a rubber."

From the Transcripts of the Chicago Conspiracy Trial

OCTOBER 20, 1969

The Court: Mr. Clerk, the motion of the defendant Bobby Seale to appear pro se will be denied as will his motion for release on bail. Will you bring in the jury.

Mr. Seale: I would like to say, Judge, that you denied my motion to defend myself and you know this jury is prejudiced against me.

The Court: I will ask you to sit down.

Mr. Seale: I should be allowed to speak so I can defend myself.

The Marshal: Be quiet.

Mr. Seale: Don't tell me to shut up, I got a right to speak. I need to speak to defend myself.

The Court: Mr. Seale, I must admonish you that any outburst such as you have just indulged in will be appropriately dealt with at the right time during this trial and I must order you not to do it again.

Bill Kunstler I realized with the putting of our lawyers in jail, we were into something strange. But I didn't realize how strange until Bobby was bound and gagged. See, Bobby was smart. I said to Bobby you've made your point, I'll represent you from now on. You don't have Garry here. He said no, I don't want to ever have any other lawyer. I didn't think so at the time, but it was very good legal advice. Say fuck everybody, you want Garry, and stand up every minute. It was really very proper. I've learned from that.

Charles Garry I knew that unless Bobby took self-action, the railroading would be continuing. We forced the situation that gagged Seale. We expected the gagging and shackling long before it happened.

From the Transcripts of the Chicago Conspiracy Trial

OCTOBER 28, 1969

Mr. Seale: Hey did you see me make a speech in Lincoln Park, Mr. William Frapolly?

The Court: Mr. Marshal, will you ask that man to be quiet.

Mr. Seale: Do you know a Robert Pierson? A lying agent?

The Court: You needn't answer any of those questions. I must admonish the defendant and his counsel—

Mr.Seale: Counsel ain't got nothing to do with it. I'm my own counsel.

The Court: You are not doing very well for yourself.

Mr. Seale: Yes, that's because you violated my constitutional rights, Judge Hoffman. Sixty-eight thousand black men died in the Civil War for that right. That law was made for me to have my constitutional rights.

The Court: I am warning you that the Court has a right to gag you. I don't want to do that. Under the law you may be gagged and chained to your chair.

Mr. Seale: Gagged? I am being railroaded already.

OCTOBER 29, 1969

Mr. Seale: You have George Washington and Benjamin Franklin sitting in a picture behind you, and they was slave owners. You are acting in the same manner, denying me my constitutional rights to cross-examine this witness.

The Court: Well, I have been called a racist, a fascist—he has pointed to the picture of George Washington behind me and called him a slave owner—

Mr. Seale: They were slave owners. Look at history.

The Court: As though I had anything to do with that.

Mr. Kunstler: We all share a common guilt, Your Honor.

The Court: Bring in the jury, please.

Mr. Seale: What about Section 1982, Title 42 of the Code where it says the black man cannot be discriminated against in my legal defense?

The Court: Mr. Seale, you do know what is going to happen to you—

Mr. Seale: I have a right to defend myself.

The Court: We will take a recess. Take that defendant into the room in there and deal with him as he should be dealt with in this circumstance.

OCTOBER 30, 1969

The Court: Mr. Seale, I order you to refrain from making those noises.

Mr. Davis: Ladies and gentlemen of the jury, he was being tortured while you were out of this room by these marshals. It is terrible what is happening.

Rennie Davis That was really the most intense time of the trial. You'd actually see blood coming out of the mouth of Bobby, because they had spent two hours trying to push gauze, against his resistance, into his mouth before wrapping his mouth and head. And the shackles were so tight, he was losing the circulation in his arms.

Tom Hayden I thought I had seen everything. I had been in the South, I had been beaten up, battered and dragged around and had my head split open, suffered far more physical violence than this. But this was uniquely disturbing. In retrospect I think it brought up some historic terror and feelings that are in us having to do with slavery and chains. I don't think we knew what to do. There was emphasis from Garry and Bobby that we shouldn't do anything. Garry thought it should be a naked confrontation between one black defendant and the white system of prosecution, not only for the drama of it but in order to lay the basis for an appeal of the court's process and to be able to say that it was essentially unprovoked and unnecessary.

On the other hand, Jerry and Abbie wanted to disrupt and we were also under pressure from Bernadine Dohrn and the Weather Underground to destroy the courtroom. Jerry and Abbie I think wanted to disrupt simply because it was moral and it would add to the drama and maybe bring the trial somehow to a halt. I think the Weather Underground had a different agenda. They were just forming and they had an interest in the symbology of white defendants permitting violence on behalf of a black.

I had the most legalistic view, the belief that we would win either by getting a hung jury or getting the victory on appeal. But we had to lay the foundation for that. Then there were simply human factors. You just couldn't sit there, it's impossible. It's very difficult to know what really happened. I just remember people on their feet, crying out, and bedlam.

Len Weinglass We had a meeting. It was decided that either we couldn't proceed with the trial because of what was happening to Bobby, or everyone ought to show up in court chained and gagged. Bobby said, "You don't understand the moment correctly. I am the only black man here and I as a black man am being chained and gagged. If you all are chained and gagged then it's a different statement, it's the movement that's chained and gagged. But I represent the movement for black liberation and it's important that the focus be that I'm chained and gagged. And if you stop the trial that will also be the news. Trial is stopped, you all will be arrested. It's important that the case go on but that I symbolically be the only one chained and gagged. That's got to be the message."

From the Transcripts of the Chicago Conspiracy Trial

OCTOBER 30, 1969

Mr. Hoffman: You may as well kill him if you are going to gag him. It seems that way, doesn't it?

The Court: You are not permitted to address the Court, Mr. Hoffman. You have a lawyer.

Mr. Hoffman: This isn't a court. This is a neon oven.

Len Weinglass I felt like I had been run over by a truck. They kept putting the gag deeper into Bobby's mouth because he could speak through it. They brought him out at one point and he tried to speak, and his eyes were rolling up into his head. They had to stop the court and pull him out and tear the gags off him so he could catch his breath. He had one hand free, that's when he started to write and he couldn't even finish 'cause he dropped the pencil.

We went home after court, around five o'clock, and I just fell asleep and I slept through the whole evening and night. And we went in the next day and we told the judge we couldn't go on. We asked for permission to fly to California to meet with Garry. I flew with Hayden and with Rubin. We met with Garry's people and they said, "It's impossible, Garry can't come." We brought back a medical certificate from his doctor that he couldn't come. And faced with that, the judge backed down and said the trial can't go on this way, severed Bobby and sentenced him for contempt.

Todd Gitlin Maybe it's true Abbie invented sound bites. I think Abbie was something of a media genius. He understood the intrinsic staginess of television at a time when television didn't quite know what it was yet. There was a symbiotic relation between television producers looking for gaudy shows and these showmen who were looking to electrify America. The theory was that, this was Abbie's line, kids were runaway slaves. Sound the word and they'll leave the plantation.

Tom Hayden It really wasn't until violence and confrontation and Stokely Carmichael and the more militant SDS that the media got interested in who these people were. Everybody was very competitive and you always felt enveloped in tension as opposed to the good vibes that everybody would profess.

Todd Gitlin Abbie and Jerry seemed to have walked directly in from central casting. Call up the freaks, get out the clowns. It was dangerous in a sense that it put a lot of power for setting the tone of a large and diffuse political movement into two people's hands. And nobody had ever chosen them to do that. And they abused that power. Their ambition was to become clichés. But there was a further irony about the media that they didn't get, namely a revolutionary cliché is a cliché. It's not an act of

THE CHICAGO 7 POSE WITH THE EIGHTH CHICAGOAN'S WIFE AND SON. FROM LEFT: JERRY RUBIN, DAVE DELLINGER, LEE WEINER, JOHN FROINES, BOBBY SEALE'S SON, TOM HAYDEN, RENNIE DAVIS, MRS. SEALE, BILL KUNSTLER, LENNY WEINGLASS, ABBIE HOFFMAN.
New York Times Co./Archive Photos

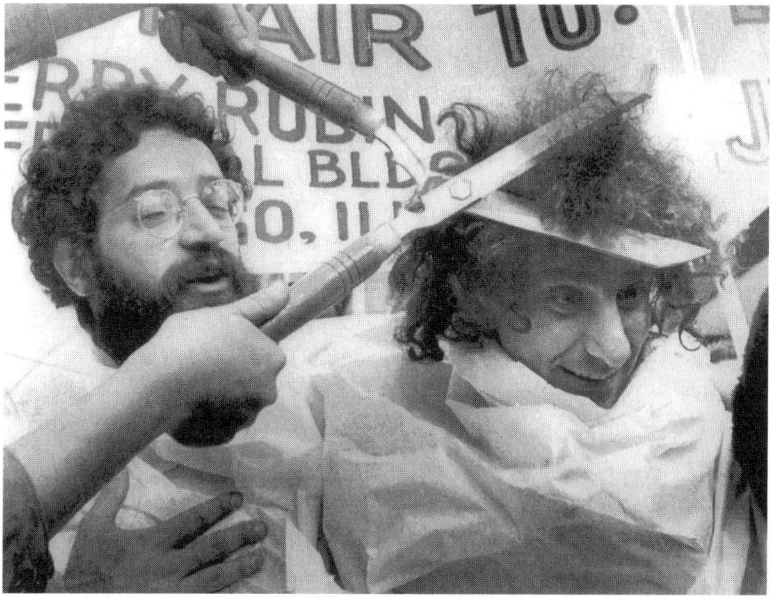

CHICAGO COCONSPIRATORS LEE WEINER AND ABBIE HOFFMAN VOLUNTEER THEIR LOCKS IN A DRIVE TO RAISE HAIR FOR CODEFENDANT JERRY RUBIN, WHOSE LONG HAIR WAS SHORN WHILE IN JAIL. UPI/Corbis-Bettmann

liberation to be a media phenomenon, it's in fact an act of submission unless you know where to draw the line.

Roger Lowenstein It was Abbie's idea to make a special motion to have Fidel Castro admitted as cocounsel. Castro's a lawyer, bring him in. Everybody loved this idea.

Norman Mailer, *novelist* There was one of Abbie and my disagreements. I think the media's poison. I think when you work through the media what it does is it leeches out your radicalism. That happened to Jerry. He ended up loving the media more than his radicalism and so he was just fascinated with ways to keep it going.

Jerry Rubin It was seven minutes on national TV every night. All three channels. We'd run back to watch it. Are you kidding? We wouldn't miss it.

Len Weinglass There would be a prosecution witness on the stand and Abbie would say to me, "Is this witness hurting us?" I would say, "Yes." He'd say, "I'll make this witness disappear." I said, "How're you gonna make this witness disappear?" He said, "By clapping my hand." And he would stand up and clap his hands and pandemonium would break out. That night, all that was on the tube was Abbie stood up and clapped his hands. He'd say to me, "See, the witness disappeared."

Jerry Rubin There was no decorum at all at our defense table. We put our feet on the desk, we ate candy.

Bill Kunstler Jerry had been in Santa Rita prison and they had shaved him absolutely bald so he wore a wig throughout the whole trial. And the judge was as bald as a coot. So Abbie had put out a circular asking everybody to send hair for Jerry and Julius. Every morning the marshal would give us twenty or thirty envelopes filled with hair. Pubic, underarm, head hair, leg hair, anything you can think of, people sent in. One day I opened one of the envelopes, and out came, on the table, an ounce or so of very good-smelling grass. Abbie grabbed a section of the *Chicago Tribune* and put it over the grass. It stayed on the table all day under the paper. Our table looked like a shit heap anyway.

At the end of the day Abbie said, "Let's get that out of here, why should we let the marshals have that?" I said, "How are you gonna get it out of here, there's FBI agents, marshals, the judge's bailiffs, court officers? Leave that here and then the sweepers will get it." Abbie said, "No, no. Why give them an ounce of grass?" So I made my first, last and only marijuana motion to the judge. I said, "One matter, Your Honor, before we leave tonight. There was delivered to our table courtesy of your marshal this morning, a supply of cannabis which as you know is a controlled substance under the federal and state laws. And I would like Your Honor's permission to dispose of it." He said, "You're a very intrepid lawyer, Mr. Kunstler. I know that you will be able to dispose of it." I said, "Your Honor, I can give you assurance it will be burned tonight." So then we wrapped it up in the *Chicago Tribune* and we took it out of the building. I was shaking like a leaf, it was only the first month or so into the trial and I hadn't yet shed all this middle-class lawyer business.

Len Weinglass The judge grew up with a fellow named Weinruss and every time he went to say my name, he'd slip and say Weinruss. Abbie wrote out a cue card and held it up. At one point the judge got very angry and tried to say my name and got it wrong and called me Weingrass and Abbie said, "Weingrass, boy I've gotta try that combination."

Stew Albert The defendants all did a lot of speaking, on the road. The FBI was always hoping that something would happen on these speeches so that they could [revoke] their bail.

Robin Palmer At demonstrations Abbie and Jerry would say, "A lot of people in the movement say it should be nonviolent. Bullshit, we support the bombings. I'll show you how we support them. *Boom boom boom.*" They'd get the crowd to chant right along. We loved Abbie and Jerry. It's like that Robert Frost poem "A Tuft of Flowers," "Men work together from the heart, whether they work together or apart." I looked at them the way Robert Frost looked at his neighbor cutting grass.

Lee Weiner We had spoken at the University of Illinois. God, we were both stoned out of our minds. We hadn't the slightest fucking idea what we talked about. We had to get back to the trial by nine in the morning. And some lunatic had a plane. So we got these big bags of money—quarters, dollars, dimes. We got on this tiny plane, the guy says just don't smoke 'cause it'll affect me! We had all the change out on the floor and we're splitting up the money, going one for the conspiracy, one for Abbie, one for Lee, one for the conspiracy, one for Ab, one for Lee. We're blowing so much smoke you can't believe. All of a sudden the whole damn plane goes *whoooom!* and Abbie and I and the change get slammed against the side of the plane. I'm convinced we're dead men. Abbie was only concerned that the neatly divided piles were getting all fucked up.

Ken Kelley I tried to stay away from the conspiracy office. At one point, the staff made everybody sit and they said, "Listen, chumps, you gotta start treating us with a little respect."

Faye Schreibman We called ourselves the Yippie slaves. We just sat in this little room doing mostly shitwork. I was very discouraged because the defense represented every issue except for the women's movement. They said, "If you don't like it you should work someplace else." I said, "That's what AT&T told me." Abbie hardly ever conversed with me. So we just took any shit we could and stuffed his mailbox. I put a screwdriver in. He felt bad, because he lost us. We left. The Yippie slaves left.

Abbie Hoffman *(interviewed by Barry Shapiro)* The trial turned Anita off. The gap between us became too great. It wasn't any equality thing. Jerry and Nancy broke up after that. Tom too. Rennie. Women's consciousness, when they start to get a sense of what their identity is, then they have to be involved in a kind of competition with the mate, it's a tough catch-up.

Faye Schreibman Whenever Abbie wanted me to do something he crushed me against the wall and whispered in my ear what he wanted to do. The sexual pressure made me very uncomfortable. Just talk to me like a person.

During the trial, there was a huge antiwar demonstration in Washington.

Ron Kaufman Abbie and Jerry wanted to fly overnight to stand on the steps of the Justice Department wearing boxing gloves, at a press conference demanding Mitchell to come out and fight fair. My role was to go buy boxing gloves, get the airline tickets and send them and their boxing gloves to Washington overnight.

Abbie Hoffman *(interviewed by Barry Shapiro)* We were banging on the door, that's pretty violent imagery even though it's clowny.

NOVEMBER 1969

Wavy Gravy, *Hog Farm leader, antiwar activist* I remember that demonstration. Pete Seeger singing "Give Peace a Chance." And then Mitch Miller gets onstage and says, "Everybody make a sea of Vs." And he goes, "All we are saying . . ." Abbie comes over to me and says, "They got Norman Luboff in the wings." I said, "Middle America has taken over the peace movement. We can retire." And they let loose these doves and one of them shit on my third eye.

G. Gordon Liddy, *security adviser, Nixon White House staff* I had some business over at the Department of Justice. At the major corridor intersections I found the 82nd Airborne Division in full battle dress, manning automatic weapons because the threat had been that the mob was gonna come in and shut the government down by trashing the records of the Department of Justice. And they were under orders that if these people got through the GSA building guards, they were to be machine-gunned in the halls of the Department of Justice.

Faye Schreibman I saw Abbie being threatened at the trial. I saw an FBI agent smash him up against the wall right outside the courtroom and say, "We'll wait till the cameras aren't on you, we'll wait out the years. We'll get you. We'll get you."

Len Weinglass The government rested its case on December 3, the day that Fred Hampton, the chairman of the Black Panther Party in Chicago, was killed. There was then the discussion that in light of that fact, should we even proceed? It seemed like maybe the trial was becoming a postscript.

Jerry Rubin I wanted the trial to go on for a year and a half. But I had to fight people like Dave Dellinger who wanted to put up no defense at all. Hayden wanted no defense and he almost won. And then who testified? Rennie and Abbie.

Abbie Hoffman *(interviewed by Abe Peck)* Hayden said, "How can I go before the jury? I'm a cold-blooded strategist." And Jerry and Tom in a sense came from that same kind of set, "Fifty dead—well, you can't make the omelet without breaking the eggs." Somebody's got to have that kind of attitude, but it isn't me and it wasn't Rennie. So we could go before a jury pure of heart saying we're innocent. They were guilty and they knew it.

Len Weinglass Hayden worked hard putting together a lot of witnesses. It was decided that Rennie would sum up the politics of the war and that Abbie would sum up the politics of the counterculture. And we would end with Ralph Abernathy on the issue of race and poverty.

John Schultz So the defense mounted a case that was fairly patched together and that made almost no attempt to deal with what actually happened convention week. But it was, in some ways, fairly powerful.

Bill Kunstler We put on about sixty people and they were wonderful.

Allen Ginsberg My point was to prove that they had invited me there to try and keep the peace, so therefore there was some element on their part of trying to keep it peaceful. The prosecution, in order to attack my character, had brought up these supposedly dirty poems. I thought, "Oh great, now I can read and explain my poems." I'm good at that.

Len Weinglass Abbie had to be prepared to answer for everything he'd ever written, we saw that because of what they did to Ginsberg. They made disparaging innuendos about his homosexuality. I said to Abbie, "Look, we've got to have answers for them." Abbie looked up at me and said, "When I finish testifying they're not gonna say send this man to prison, the jury's gonna say send this boy to camp."

From the Transcripts of the Chicago Conspiracy Trial

DECEMBER 23, 1969

Mr. Weinglass: Will you please identify yourself for the record?

The Witness: My name is Abbie. I am an orphan of America.

Mr. Schultz: Your Honor, may the record show it is the defendant Hoffman who has taken the stand?

The Court: Oh, yes. It may so indicate.

The Witness: Well, it is not really my last name.

Mr. Weinglass: Abbie, what is your last name?

The Witness: My slave name is Hoffman. My real name is Shapoznikoff. I can't spell it.

Mr. Weinglass: Where do you reside?

The Witness: I live in Woodstock Nation.

Mr. Weinglass: Will you tell the Court and jury where it is?

The Witness: Yes. It is a nation of alienated young people. We carry it around with us as a state of mind in the same way as the Sioux Indians carried the Sioux Nation around with them. It is a nation dedicated to cooperation versus competition, to the idea that people should have better means of exchange than property or money, that there should be some other basis for human interaction. It is a nation dedicated to—

The Court: Just where is it, that is all.

The Witness: It is in my mind and in the minds of my brothers and sisters. It does not consist of property or material, but, rather, of ideas and certain values. We believe in a society—

The Court: No, we want the place of residence, if he has one, place of doing business, if you have a business. Nothing about philosophy or India, sir. Just where do you live, if you have a place to live. Now you said Woodstock. In what state is Woodstock?

The Witness: It is in the state of mind, in the mind of myself and my brothers and sisters. It is a conspiracy. Presently, the nation is held captive, in the penitentiaries and the institutions of a decaying system.

Mr. Weinglass: Can you tell the Court and the jury what is your present occupation?

The Witness: I am a cultural revolutionary. Well, I am really a defendant—full time.

Len Weinglass During his testimony, Abbie got Yippie pneumonia from overwork. Dr. Quentin Young examined Abbie and ordered him immediately hospitalized. He was coughing up blood. He was in the hospital for three or four days.

Abbie Hoffman *(interviewed by Barry Shapiro)* I did not like my testimony. That's why I decided to get pneumonia right in the middle. I said, "Fuck it, this isn't working, I'm going in the hospital." I went into the hospital, spitting blood. Neat trick, you learn how to do that shit.

Jack Hoffman Abbie used that asthma whenever he didn't like a situation. They told me he's gonna die, so I went out. He got me in the room, he says, "What do you want, steak or lobster? Or the blond nurse with the big tits?" He ended up screwing the nurse.

From the *Chicago Sun Times*, 12/30/69

ABBIE (TOOT!) TRIPS WITH SANTA

Abbie Hoffman rolled his wheelchair into a press conference at Michael Reese Hospital and made the following announcements:

That he and Santa Claus had spent Christmas Eve getting high on hashish.

That the Conspiracy Seven trial, in which Hoffman is a defendant, would probably last until 1984.

Hoffman chirped "Toot-toot!" as a nurse wheeled him into a lounge crowded with newsmen, cameras and lights.

"I want to thank the people of Chicago for sending me all those cards, candy and flowers," Hoffman said. "If the food is this good in prison, I'll consider changing my plea."

John Schultz The high drama of Abbie's testimony came in Richard Schultz's cross-examination. It was very obvious from the beginning that Schultz had read just about every word of Abbie Hoffman that he could get hold of.

Tom Hayden Years later, I spoke to Schultz, off the record, for my book. He thought that Abbie was doing everything he did for money. Schultz just despised him.

From the Transcripts of the Chicago Conspiracy Trial

DECEMBER 30, 1969

Mr. Schultz: Did you see some people urinate on the Pentagon, Mr. Hoffman?

The Witness: On the Pentagon itself?

Mr. Schultz: Or at the Pentagon?

The Witness: There were over 100,000 people. People have that biological habit, you know.

Mr. Schultz: Did you symbolically urinate on the Pentagon, Mr. Hoffman?

The Witness: I didn't get that close. Pee on the walls of the Pentagon? You are getting to be out of sight, actually. You think there is a law against it?

Mr. Schultz: Did you ever state that a sense of integration possesses you and comes from pissing on the Pentagon?

The Witness: I said from combining political attitudes with biological necessity, there is a sense of integration, yes.

Mr. Schultz: You had a good time at the Pentagon, didn't you, Mr. Hoffman?

The Witness: Yes I did. I'm having a good time now too. I feel that biological necessity now. Could I be excused for a slight recess?

The Court: Ladies and gentlemen of the jury, we will take a brief recess.

Jerry Rubin Abbie's testimony at the trial was pure genius.

Lee Weiner We thought Abbie was spectacular. Even Tom loved Abbie's testimony.

From the Transcripts of the Chicago Conspiracy Trial

DECEMBER 30, 1969

Mr. Schultz: Do you recall having coffee with—

The Witness: I don't drink coffee. It is one of the drugs I refrain from using.

Mr. Schultz: Now at that time, then, you wrote, did you not, that you dismissed the thought of attempting to take over a building right across the street from police headquarters? Isn't that right, Mr. Hoffman?

The Witness: Did you ask me if I had the thoughts or if I wrote I had the thoughts? There is a difference.

Mr. Schultz: It is a convenient difference, isn't it, Mr. Hoffman?

The Witness: I don't know what you mean by that, Mr. Schultz. I have never been on trial for my thoughts before.

Mr. Schultz: Mr. Hoffman, you were in Chicago, Illinois, on Thursday, August 29, 1968, were you not?

Mr. Weinglass: Your Honor, that question is proof of the fact that there was no testimony offered on direct examination on that. I think that another objection is appropriate.

The Court: I overrule your objection.

The Witness: I consider that an unfair ruling and I am not going to answer. I can't answer.

The Court: I direct you to answer.

The Witness: Well, I take the Fifth Amendment then.
The Court: I order you to answer the question, sir. You are required under law.
The Witness: I just get yes or no, huh? Yes, I was there. All my years on the witness stand, I never heard anything like that ruling.

Abbie Hoffman *(interviewed by Barry Shapiro)* I always choked on the word "yippie" after the Chicago demonstration. The trial forced us to work with old imagery. Another problem with a trial like that was that you have to justify a state of mind that you had at a different time. In other words, I was justifying idiotic speeches saying, "Let's go, it's our turn, let's take the streets." Didn't mean shit, by then. By the time the trial came I believed that we should blow up all the buildings in the country, everything, every military structure, shoot the generals, kill the president. I believed during the trial that I was guilty in the sense that I believed in starting riots. I didn't in Chicago but I did during the trial because of that experience in Chicago.

NEW YEAR'S EVE 1970

Len Weinglass I had moved in with Abbie and Anita. Here I am with one of the national leaders of Yippie, New Year's Eve; I thought it was gonna be wild and crazy. Abbie prepared a gourmet dinner, roast duck, and Abbie and Anita and I sat down and had this tremendous dinner, champagne and wine, and then we all fell asleep at 10:30.

Ken Kelley Abbie was on LSD a lot during the trial. LSD was like cornflakes to him in the morning.

Stew Albert At the conspiracy trial a couple of times at parties, Abbie did some wild stuff. I saw him strip to his underwear at one party. I think maybe he might have tried to assist a woman or two doing that, let's put it that way. A little out of control.

John Schultz The defense called Mayor Daley as a witness. Kunstler gave him a direct examination and tried quickly to get Daley declared a hostile witness. Judge Hoffman said he had answered as a gentleman. Came time for the noon recess. After lunch, the trial was a little bit delayed, and Mayor Daley came in, sat down on the witness stand, folded his hands in front of him and waited. There were just a few people milling around. Abbie came in and saw the mayor in the witness stand. He walked to the end of the defense table closest to the bench and turned around and looked at Daley, then walked back to the far end of the defense table and then suddenly turned around, faced the mayor, slapped his hips like for six-shooters and said, "To hell with this law stuff, why don't you and I settle this here, right now!" The mayor laughed! He really enjoyed it.

Paul Krassner Abbie said he wanted me to make the judge have a heart attack on the stand, I think that was my assignment. He said, "Look, you can only hurt us. But since your name has come up so much in previous testimony as being at this meeting and saying this and saying that, the lawyers felt it was necessary to have you." The night before the trial he was giving me all these things I had to memorize, facts and dates and places to corroborate what had already been testified to. The next day, they were passing around hash at the lunch table before I was supposed to testify. I didn't take any hash because I was afraid I'd get dry mouth on the stand. So I said, "I'll take this instead." And I took out this Owsley white lightning, three hundred mics, and Abbie said, "Acid? I don't think that's a good idea." It was like I was disobeying him. And Jerry said, "I think you should do it." Once again advertising his book.

Jerry Rubin I egged Paul on. I was surprised that Abbie got so angry at that. But Paul got a little disoriented on the stand.

Paul Krassner I took acid because I thought I would throw up in court. I figured that would be my theatrical statement about the injustice of the trial. And they'd get me out of there and I wouldn't have to give all those names and dates and places.

Bill Kunstler I said, "He doesn't look right to me," but Abbie and Jerry said he never looks right and so I put him on.

Paul Krassner At one point they were asking me where this meeting took place. I couldn't think of the word "Chicago." I'm saying "this city right here, this city that we're in now." Abbie was mouthing the word "Chicago."

Bill Kunstler I would say, "Now, did you come to Chicago in the summer, August of 1968, for the Democratic National Convention?" And he'd answer a totally different question. I asked five or six questions, the judge didn't seem to know the difference and I'm sure the jury didn't either. But Abbie and Jerry said, "You better get him off." Finally he gave some crazy answer and I said, with the greatest satisfaction, like he just said the thing that won the case for us, "Thank you, Mr. Krassner!"

Len Weinglass We were hurt more than legally. We were hurt in terms of credibility. For years Abbie was really pissed at Paul. So was I.

Then when Judge Hoffman wouldn't allow Reverend Abernathy to testify, that was a big blow. Abernathy flew in and he was a few minutes late so he couldn't testify. We had put on our war witnesses, we had put on our counterculture witnesses. Now we were moving into the race area, and he completely cut us off. That's why Bill took his heaviest hit and contempt, on that.

From the Transcripts of the Chicago Conspiracy Trial

FEBRUARY 2, 1970

Mr. Kunstler: I have sat here for four and a half months and watched the objections denied and sustained by Your Honor, and I know that this is not a fair trial. I know it in my heart. If I have to lose my license to practice law and if I have to go to jail, I can't think of a better cause to go to jail for and to lose my license for than to tell Your Honor that you are doing a disservice to the law . . . I am going to turn back to my seat with the realization that everything I have learned throughout my life had turned to naught, that there is no meaning in this court, and there is no law in this court—

Voice: Right on.

Mr. Kunstler: —and these men are going to jail by virtue of a legal lynching. And that Your Honor is wholly responsible for that.

John Schultz Toward the end of the trial, Commander Riordan had said that he saw Dellinger leading a group of people flying Vietcong flags out of the park into the confrontation at Michigan/Balboa, with that intent and that purpose, and so forth. Dellinger just got up and said, "Oh bullshit!" This caused utter consternation not only through the courtroom but through the press of the United States because they didn't know how to put this word on the front page. The *New York Times* finally called it a barnyard epithet.

That afternoon, the judge revoked Dellinger's bail and the defense attorneys felt that he put Dellinger in jail not because of the bullshit remark but because of a speech Dellinger had made just a few days before at Marquette University in Milwaukee, in which Dellinger had been very critical of the judge. So the question for the defense was how they were going to react. Jerry and Abbie felt that at this point the trial should just be completely disrupted, that the defendants should go in, do whatever violent performance numbers they were going to do and just bring the trial to a complete halt.

From the Transcripts of the Chicago Conspiracy Trial

FEBRUARY 4, 1970

Mr. Kunstler: Your Honor's action is completely and utterly vindictive. There is no authority that says because a defendant blurts out a word in court—

The Court: This isn't the first word, and I won't argue this.

Mr. Davis: This court is bullshit.

The Court: There he is saying the same words again.

Mr. Davis: No, I say it.

Mr. Schultz: It was the defendant Davis who made the last remark.

Mr. Rubin: Everything in this court is bullshit. Take us, too. Show us what a big man you are.

Mr. Hoffman: You are a disgrace to the Jews. You would have served Hitler better. Dig it.

The Court: Clear the courtroom, Mr. Marshal.

Female Voice: You little prick.

Mr. Rubin: You are a fascist.

FEBRUARY 5, 1970

The Court: I have beseeched you and Mr. Kunstler throughout this trial, beginning with the Seale episode, to try and get your clients to behave in the courtroom. At no time did you lift a finger or speak a word to either Mr. Dellinger or any of them. I have been patient for nearly five and a half months.

Mr. Hoffman: Your idea of justice is the only obscenity in the room. You schtunk. Schande vor de goyim, huh?

The Court: Mr. Marshal, will you ask the defendant Hoffman to—

Mr. Hoffman: Tell him to stick it up his bowling ball. How is your war stock doing, Julie? You don't have any power. They didn't have any power in the Third Reich either.

Mr. Rubin: You are the laughingstock of the world, Julius Hoffman. Every kid in the world hates you. You are synonymous with Adolf Hitler. Julius Hoffman equals Adolf Hitler.

John Schultz Abbie and Jerry started making whatever kind of remarks they could come up with. Abbie got off his remark, *Schande* for the goyim, shame because Judge Hoffman being a Jew was an agent of the oppressor. At first Judge Hoffman started to react very strongly, in his typical highly emotional way. And then apparently he had finally been advised that his highly charged remarks were often inciting trouble and so he just went quiet. The whole courtroom sat there absolutely silently, while Jerry and Abbie went on with their verbal attacks upon the system. Abbie began to experience an almost tearful feeling of impotence and his voice welled up. Without the response, nothing was happening. The theater was now being created by the other side.

Jerry Rubin The judge's robes. That was actually Abbie and I sitting down and consciously saying, what are all the things we can do to drive this judge crazy? Hey, there's no rule that says how defendants have to dress in a courtroom. So we got black robes and came in the next day and Julius went crazy. He would not continue the trial unless we took off our black robes. Of course, he used to always blame Kunstler. "Another one of your brilliant ideas, Mr. Kunstler? Take the robes off." So when we took the robes off Abbie was dressed as a Chicago policeman underneath it. That was awesome. That's the essence of Abbie—that he goes one step beyond and doesn't tell me, right? He stayed up an hour later, right?

Len Weinglass Abbie wanted Groucho Marx to testify as the last witness, an expert witness in the area of American humor, because they were playing some of Abbie's lines like they were serious. The chief of police's name was [pronounced] Roquefort, and Abbie said at a meeting attended by a lot of people, with the chief there, "Let's snatch the big cheese." They played that to the jury like a kidnap attempt. And Abbie's other schticks,

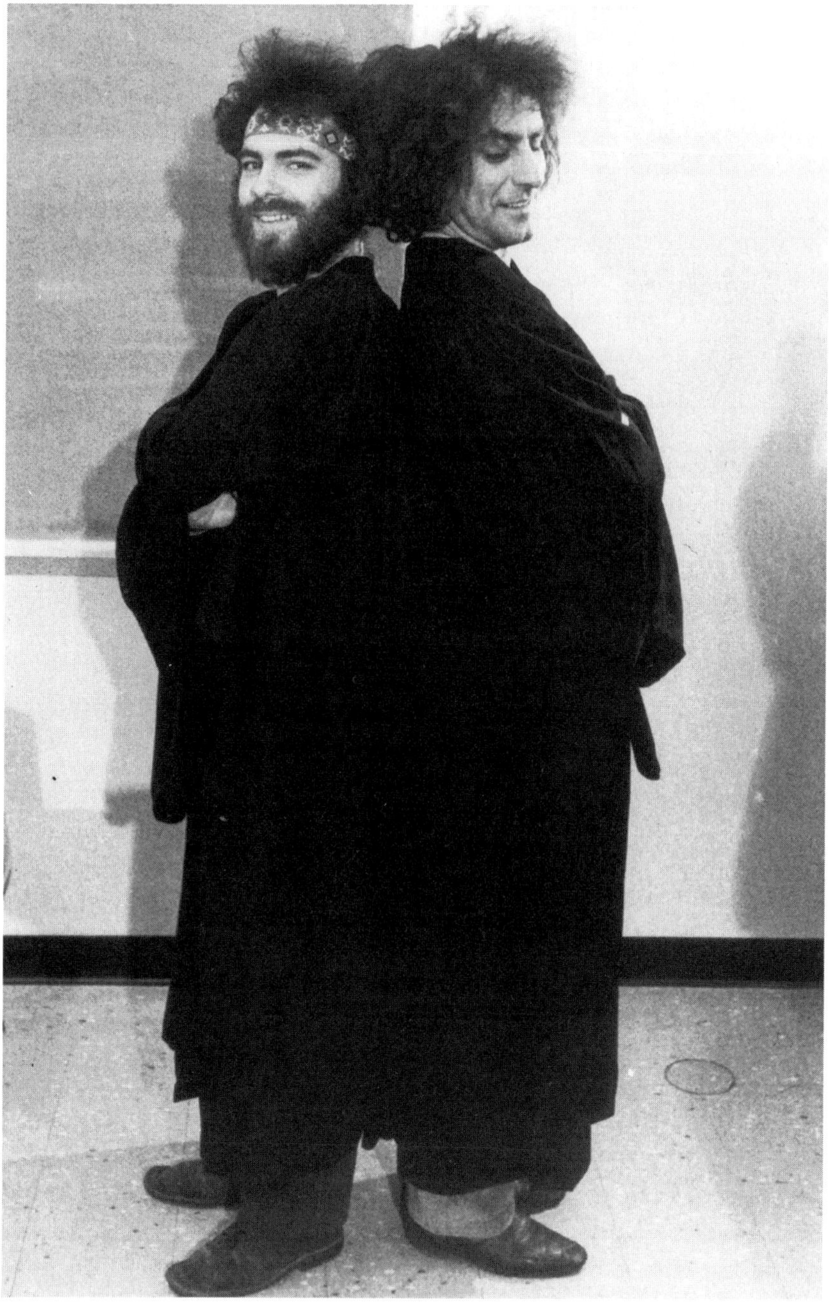

ABBIE AND JERRY CAUSED A DISRUPTION AT THEIR CONSPIRACY TRIAL BY DRESSING UP IN JUDGE'S ROBES. WHEN FORCED BY JUDGE HOFFMAN TO REMOVE THEM, ABBIE WAS WEARING A CHICAGO POLICE SHIRT UNDER HIS ROBE. AP/Wide World

we'll walk on water, the Yippie navy will come ashore, all of that stuff was played to the jury as if this guy was really into fomenting civil strife.

So Abbie said what we need is someone to come in and say this is all in the vein of American humor, the put-on. He said Groucho would be the only one to explain this to a jury. So we called Groucho and he said, "Hey, I hear the judge you got up there is crazy. This guy is gonna put me in jail, right?" I said, "We haven't lost any of our witnesses but he has threatened them. Groucho said, "Well, I'm too old to become a homosexual." But he said, "I think I can come out there and I'd like to do it. But let me call you back tomorrow." So he calls me back the next day and he says, "Well, you've gotta talk to my lawyer and my agent. They're raising some questions about this." I said to Abbie, "Oh, we're in big trouble now. They're gonna lean on him not to do it." Sure enough, they turned Groucho around. But Abbie wanted to end with Marx.

From the Closing Argument for the Government by Thomas Foran

FEBRUARY 13, 1970

> There are millions of kids who resent authority, want to fix things up. You feel a terrible frustration of a terribly difficult war that maybe as a young kid you are going to have to serve in . . . There is another thing about a kid, you have an attraction to evil. Evil is exciting and interesting. It is a knowledge of kids like that that these sophisticated, educated psychology majors know about. They know how to draw the kids together and use them to accomplish their purposes. They corrupt those kids. They are sophisticated and they are smart and they are well-educated. And they are as evil as they can be.

John Schultz The jurors later told me that they didn't buy that Abbie was evil or part of an evil conspiracy.

Len Weinglass Abbie knew that every time he spoke up in court there was a risk of contempt charges. I told him the cap was six months for each citation. So Abbie would say something, he'd sit down, he'd turn to me and he'd say, "Did I get a six-pack?"

From the *New York Daily News*

SENTENCE 4 OF CHICAGO 7 FOR CONTEMPT

COURT EXPLODES AFTER CASE GOES TO JURY

Chicago, Feb. 14 (Combined Services)

The 100-day trial of the Chicago Seven went to the jury today and the judge immediately sentenced four defendants to lengthy terms for contempt. A screaming, sobbing melee broke out after Federal Judge Julius J. Hoffman, citing "intolerable disruptions" and "anarchy" sentenced David Dellinger, 54—described by the prosecution as "chief architect" of the riots—to 29 months and 16 days in prison on 32 counts of contempt.

CONTEMPT SENTENCES ASSESSED BY JUDGE HOFFMAN

Bobby Seale—four years
David Dellinger—two years, five months, sixteen days
Rennie Davis—two years, one month, nineteen days
Tom Hayden—one year, two months, thirteen days
Abbie Hoffman—eight months
Jerry Rubin—two years, twenty-three days
Lee Weiner—two months, eighteen days
John Froines—six months, fifteen days
William Kunstler—four years, thirteen days
Leonard Weinglass—one year, seven months, twenty-eight days

Len Weinglass I think Judge Hoffman liked Abbie. There were times during the trial when there would be things happening that weren't terribly exciting and I would look up, and Hoffman would be sitting there staring at Abbie with a look on his face like what's happening to my country? He tried to figure it out. Abbie did get the lightest contempt sentence. Dave challenged his authority. Abbie played around.

From the *New York Daily News*

5 OF CHI 7 GUILTY OF TRAVEL FOR RIOT

BUT ALL ARE CLEARED ON PLOT CHARGES

Chicago, Feb. 18 (UPI)

A Federal Court jury found all the defendants in the tumultuous trial of the Chicago Seven innocent today of conspiring to incite riots during the 1968 Democratic National Convention but convicted Dave Dellinger, Abbie Hoffman, Jerry Rubin, Tom Hayden and Rennie Davis of crossing state lines with intent to incite riots.

Tom Hayden I think that the jury drew a commonsense conclusion that we were guilty of something, but didn't want us put away for life. So like typical Americans they split the difference.

From the *New York Daily News,* February 20

CHI 5 ARE SLAPPED WITH 2 OTHER 5S

JUDGE HOFFMAN GIVES THEM MAXIMUM PRISON TERMS

Rennie Davis We already had a heavy contempt of court sentence. Now five years on top of that, the maximum sentence for the substantive charge. We didn't know if we were ever coming out. The judge had us. We all stood up, made our talks, and they were fiery and everything but the defiance and the humor was gone.

John Schultz Just before he was to be sentenced, Abbie put his arms around himself. He looked like he was shivering, like for the first time he really was aware of something just god-awful serious was happening to him.

FEBRUARY 20, 1970

ABBIE HOFFMAN ADDRESS TO COURT IN RESPONSE TO SENTENCE

Mr. Foran says that we are unpatriotic. I suppose I am not patriotic: But he says we are un-American. I don't feel un-American. I feel very American. I said it is not that the Yippies hate America. It is that they feel that the American dream has been betrayed. I know those guys up on the wall . . . Thomas Jefferson called for a revolution every ten years. Thomas Jefferson had an agrarian reform program that made Mao Tse-tung look like a liberal . . . Washington grew pot. He called it hemp. He probably was a pot head. Abraham Lincoln. In 1861 Abraham Lincoln in his inaugural address said, and I quote, "When the people shall grow weary of their constitutional right to amend the government, they shall exert their revolutionary right to dismember and overthrow that government." If Abraham Lincoln had given that speech in Lincoln Park, he would be on trial right here in this courtroom, because that was an inciteful speech. That is a speech intended to create a riot. I don't even know what a riot is. I thought a riot was fun. Riot means you laugh, ha, ha. I didn't want to be that serious. I was supposed to be funny . . . Well, we said it was like Alice in Wonderland coming in, now I feel like Alice in *1984*, because I have lived through the winter of injustice in this trial. And it's fitting that if you went to the South and fought for voter registration and got arrested and beaten eleven or twelve times on those dusty roads for no bread, it's only fitting that you be arrested and tried under a civil rights act . . .

From the Transcripts of the Chicago Conspiracy Trial

FEBRUARY 20, 1970

The Court: The defendant Abbott H. Hoffman will be committed to the custody of the Attorney General of the United States for imprisonment for a term of five years. Further a fine of $5,000 and costs—

Mr. Hoffman: Five thousand dollars, Judge? Could you make that three and a half?

Len Weinglass When the trial was over they were all in jail. One by one they took them off. And they stayed in jail for seventeen days.

Stew Albert Abbie did not want to go to prison, in the worst way. Read Irving Howe's book *World of Our Fathers*. Jews had a peculiar fear of American prisons. There was a thing, to run away, go back to Russia, just not to let the goyim have you locked up.

Lee Weiner Who didn't think about splitting? I think it would've been irresponsible of us to the people who we worked with and to ourselves not to have thought about it.

Jerry Rubin Hayden and I hadn't talked to each other for the last three months of the trial. We just stared at each other with anger. And then we were put in the same jail cell. His first act was to say, "Let me read *Do It*." He said he liked it and we warmed up to each other. But then Abbie provoked a fight with him because Hayden marched down to get his haircut happily and willingly and Abbie threw a fit and had to be dragged to get his hair cut.

Tom Hayden I didn't even know that he was furious at me for that, because my recollection with haircuts is that you were taken into a room and they sit you down and in about two seconds chop some of your hair off. I didn't get the symbolism of that until it happened. Scalping, that's what it was all about.

Jerry Rubin The next day it was in all the papers, Sheriff Joe Woods holding up the hair. Abbie's hair became a symbol for the nation.

Violent protests erupted around the country following the verdict. The Bank of America in Santa Cruz, California, was burned down. Two weeks later, the defendants raised bail and were released.

Jeff Nightbyrd When they got out and got to the apartment, Jerry told stories about what jail was like. Everybody wanted to know what Abbie thought, but [first] Abbie locked himself in the bathroom with Anita and fucked for about thirty minutes.

Bill Kunstler Right after the verdicts, Foran addressed a Holy Name Society where he referred to Abbie and company as fags. I had to laugh because they were fucking every woman in Chicago that would hold still long enough to be properly fucked. If anybody were not gay it was the Chicago 8.

Len Weinglass Tom said to me, prophetically, when he asked me to take the case, that my life would never be the same. It's true. The trial completely changed me, introducing me to a major national political movement that I then felt completely committed to.

Bill Kunstler That trial changed me completely. I had just come out of the Berrigan trial, the Catonsville 9, which was very sedate with nuns and priests. Abbie and Jerry taught me a lot about how to be theatrical, dramatic, and humorous also.

Anita Hoffman There was this huge debt for the trial. So all the defendants and the lawyers continued speaking to raise money. Then Abbie was taxed for that income which he had handed over to the defense committee, so he had financial problems.

Jerry Rubin The trial made us complete, total, utter celebrities. Abbie's plan at that point was to go out and lead millions of people, a total cultural revolution. What happened is that we became the establishment. The media builds you up and then tears you down. So the destruction of our myths then began as soon as the trial ended. Dave and I and Abbie were sitting on the plane coming back from jail when the first *Newsweek* article came out saying how much we profited from the trial. The fat radicals living off the system. Book contracts, $2,000 speaking gigs. Of course it was 100 percent true, that was the problem. But we were trying to disguise it. Abbie would disguise it by saying, "I give away all my money." I don't know if he gave away all his money but he lived very well. It was downhill from there.

Stew Albert People started calling Abbie and Jerry pop stars. It's complicated because they had become very famous and SDS was dead. There was no organization around that could discipline and make use of their fame. So the tendency was to not recognize what they had achieved. That created a lot of grief and antagonism on both sides. Yeah, a healthy Left doesn't have two guys going around, making up the Left as they go along. But on the other hand, they weren't responsible for the unhealthy condition of the Left that allowed them to do that.

Abe Peck The standards of being a radical got so high that by 1971 being for peace in movement circles was counterrevolutionary. I think that year, '70–'71, it was impossible to keep up. It wasn't just the women attacking the men. Are you a feminist? Are you a lesbian feminist? A Third World lesbian feminist? The movement in its search for perfection became intolerant of people who were infinitely better than some armaments manufacturer or some exploiter.

Stew Albert That was the beginning of Abbie's turn to the harder political Left. His last theater may have been putting on a judge's robe during the trial. After that he's pretty much an angry, witty, brilliant leftist who goes around the country giving speeches, trying to stir up trouble.

ABBIE RELAXING WITH THE GOOD BOOK, AT HOME IN HIS PAD ON ST. MARK'S PLACE.
From *New York Daily News* Archives

Chapter Six

REBEL WITHOUT A PAUSE

Jerry Rubin We both went back to New York and then just started our mad speaking tours. Every night on campus, huge crowds and go, go, go.

Art Goldberg Abbie changed after the trial. You'd talk to him and you'd get a speech. It was very hard to have a real conversation with him. He became a media celebrity.

Sue Williamson was a college student in Lawrence, Kansas, when she met Abbie while he was on his speaking tour. They slept together and then were inseparable.

Sue Williamson When he spoke at the stadium, it was a wild scene. He blew his nose on the American flag in Kansas. That made the front page. There was a riot at his talk and he literally had to run away. We went off to this little college town in Kansas and we had a press conference and Abbie had a basketball and he said, "My name is Clyde Barrow and this is Bonnie Parker and we just robbed this downtown bank." All these reporters dropped their pencils and went running out of the room like "This is a hot story, they just robbed a bank!" After that we went to Texas, which was really frightening.

1970

Jeff Nightbyrd I was living in Houston. The public radio station I worked at had been bombed off the air twice by Ku Klux Klan, and these same people had shot up the alternative paper a number of times. Later we found out they were also members of the Police Department. And the same overlap of the Klan/Police Department had taken to blasting hippies' motorbikes. You'd be driving on the freeway and this yahoo drives up alongside you with a .44 magnum and blows a hole in your engine block, *boom, boom,* which tends to ruin your day on the freeway. The counterculture in Houston was a bit freaked out. So to inspire everybody, Abbie was invited down to give a speech at Rice University. He was taking a chance coming. The attitude of the local people was we're not gonna blow it and get him killed here.

Abbie Hoffman *(interviewed by Barry Shapiro)* I'm met at the airport, I said these must be the Yippies, because these were gun-carrying hippies. The cops would not come near me. We're walking through the airport with guys with shotguns. I get into a paneled Volkswagen with all the windows taped. "Pretty dramatic show," I said, and my friend Jeff Shero (Nightbyrd) said, "Last week there was a conference of army deserters and some of the guys were ambushed in their car." Shotgun ambush. "Where are we staying?" I said. He said, "We got the whole floor of the Holiday Inn." No one was allowed on the floor. And there was two karate guys who were with me, I could not step out of that room. They used a different truck to pick me up, I had to go out the servants' entrance, then they drove this car right into the middle of the park and I stepped up on the platform, the biggest rally in Houston's history, and I did a song and dance, Yip, Yip, go to Houston. Then we went back to the hotel and I'm locked in again. The Nazis put out a thing I'll never speak. So we stopped off at an underground press office and an arrow was shot out of a crossbow through the window, went six inches into the wall. I got a call at the room, they knew where I was, that the next arrow is going through my head. And I was getting pretty stoned. I wasn't too scared.

Sue Williamson The biggest problem was that when people would come to see him they would treat him like Jesus Christ. He would always throw it back to them, like you've got to come up with your own answers.

Since we were doing LSD a lot we talked about how it gets you beyond your own personal ego consciousness. We talked about God and that we are all gods if we just would become aware of ourselves as that, but not in the egotistical sense, in a more helping your brothers and sisters kind of thing. Abbie was what I would now call a bodhisattva, someone whose self was for service, here to help other people and the planet.

Stew Albert In one of his speeches, Abbie said he fucked Kim Agnew, Spiro's daughter. So the FBI determined that it wasn't true but then felt that they had to inform Spiro Agnew. In the FBI files there was this incredible discussion about just how to inform him that they had investigated his daughter, how they could somehow not get him angry at them for that. Agnew always used to really attack Abbie a lot. After I read those files, I realized he had a very personal reason.

Paul Solomon I started working for Merv Griffin in 1968. I kept pitching to have these radicals on the show. So we booked Abbie. He said for the show he's gonna be wearing a shirt made of the United States flag and I said that's great.

Randy Wicker Abbie comes in the store and says, "I'm gonna be on *The Merv Griffin Show*. I need that other flag shirt." So I said, "Those shirts cost me twenty-five apiece, Abbie. If you want that other shirt, you're not gonna just pay me for that shirt, you're gonna pay me for the shirt that you had torn up. Fifty bucks, right here, buddy." Abbie threw the money on the table and he took the shirt and as he went out, he said, "We're gonna hang you by the balls, Wicker." I yelled, "Abbie, we're gonna hang you from a red, white and blue tree."

Paul Solomon Virginia Graham came on first and talked all about her face-lift. Then these two kids from the Antonioni movie *Zabriskie Point* came on. Then Abbie came on and woke everybody up. He walked onstage wearing this fringed leather cowboy jacket and sat down and he said, "Gee, Merv, it's kind of hot under these lights, do you mind if I take off my jacket?" Merv said sure go ahead and he took off his jacket and he's wearing this American flag and Virginia Graham was so horrified, as if she saw a terrible vision. Then Abbie handed Merv's cohost, Arthur Treacher, a joint, and Arthur took the joint and held it out examining it for the rest of the night as if he'd seen something from another planet. Then Abbie takes out *Quotations from Chairman Mao* and started reading. He said, "You know, Merv, you ought to have this guy on your show. He sold a billion books. It outsold the Bible twelve to one. He's a neat dresser." It was great television. Merv was enjoying it, because it was commotion. You live for that kind of shit. Anyway, we taped at seven o'clock and put it on the same night at 11:30.

At 11:29 the director of programming of the network came on the screen and he said, "One of the guests on *The Merv Griffin Show* has seen fit to wear a shirt made out of the flag and in the interests of common decency we have chosen to edit out the offending shirt so nobody can see it." Right after there was a commercial for the movie *Myra Breckenridge* where Raquel Welch wore a flag.

Anita Hoffman The screen was blue on one side to block him out. Merv Griffin having this conversation with this blue screen.

Paul Solomon Abbie was breaking all the norms of talk show guest etiquette—walking down to talk to the audience, really raising hell.

Ed Sanders I remember watching him on the Merv show, creating this hate spasm in the audience, "Come on, come on, come on." He was already getting warped under that glare.

Paul Solomon *Revolution for the Hell of It* had just been optioned by MGM, and he was supposed to promote his book. But he never mentioned it. He was promoting Chairman Mao's book, not his own.

From the *New York Daily News*, 3/29/70

STORM OF PROTEST

CBS BLOTS OUT ONE OF CHICAGO 7

New York (UPI)

> . . . More than 2,000 persons telephoned the network's New York office to complain about the action which CBS President Robert Wood said was taken "because of the possibility of a violation of the law as to disrespect and desecration of the flag."

Jacques Levy convinced producer Hilly Elkins to buy the movie rights to Revolution for the Hell of It. *Elkins then sold the product to MGM. William Devane was cast as Abbie, but the project never got off the ground.*

Marty Kenner Jean Genet had snuck into the U.S. to speak around the country on behalf of the Panthers. We went to Max's Kansas City and we bumped into Abbie taking Anita out for her birthday. Abbie had just gotten a check for the movie rights, about $25,000, and I'm absolutely positive it was more money than Abbie had ever had. I told him how we were trying to raise money to get the Panthers out, that they were in jail on $100,000 bail. But Victor Rabinowitz, a lawyer we had, had come up with this brilliant idea that you could put up New York State bonds for the bail. We could get $100,000 housing bonds for $20,000 to $25,000. So for $20,000 to $25,000, we could bail out a Panther. And Abbie said here's the check. He bailed out a guy named Dorouba, or Richard Moore. Later, he lost it all when Dorouba split. And Abbie never even mentioned it. Abbie was certainly down on money in later years. But I never once got one iota of reproach. For Abbie, this was just perfectly natural and that was the end of it.

Abbie was well on his way to becoming a "brand name" around this time. He was anointed one of the four sexiest men in America by Mademoiselle *magazine. D. A. Pennebaker, the filmmaker who profiled Bob Dylan in* Don't Look Back, *offered Abbie $50,000 to be chronicled for a documentary. Abbie and Anita even met with William Morris agents to discuss merchandising offers.*

Anita Hoffman You know those little cans that you turn and they go "Moo"? There's a guy who wanted to do that with one that would laugh like Abbie. I remember seeing a prototype of an Abbie doll which had massive curly black hair and a flag shirt.

Abbie Hoffman *(interviewed by Barry Shapiro)* Every once in a while the ground gets shaky. You meet with some people clandestinely, who are high officials in MCA, William Morris agency, who are interested in managing your career and are convinced that they can make you a million dollars within six months. Whether it's for you or the movement, they don't give a shit what you do with the money. When you operate in that kind of milieu, you've got to have some way of pinching yourself to make sure you're still a moralist or a revolutionary or a threat to the society, and that was the way for me.

Jeff Nightbyrd I have talked about Abbie's sexuality as a plus. Not everybody saw it that way. Everybody got attacked for sexism. The *Rat* was actually taken over by women. By 1970 the rhetoric had gotten very gunny, full of macho violent talk—we're gonna fight for the streets, etc. One day, I was sitting in front of my St. Mark's Place apartment, looking at these dirty streets, and I said, "Wait, these aren't my streets. I don't even like these streets. I don't want to die on these streets."

So I went down to Greenville, Mississippi, and started working on a

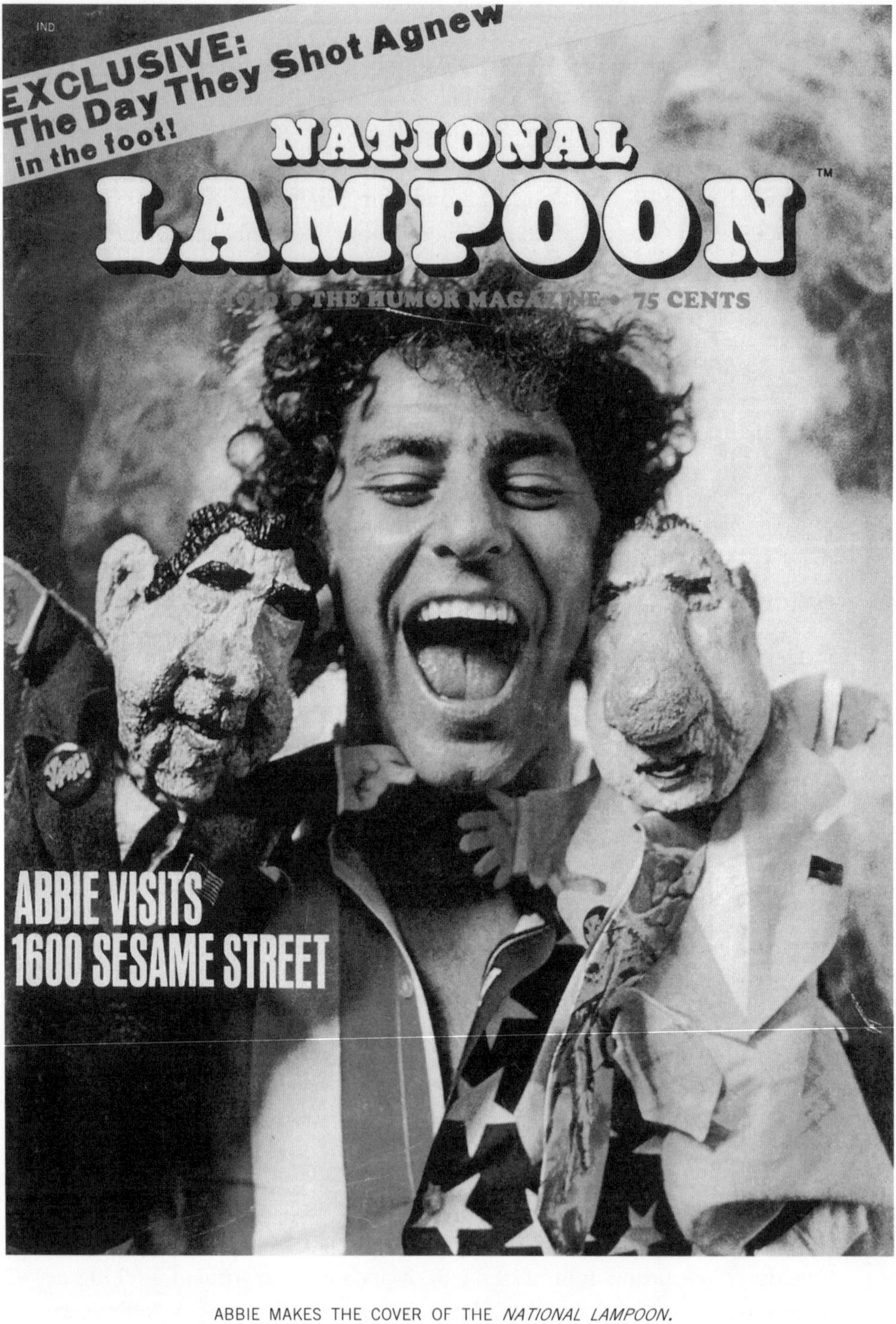

ABBIE MAKES THE COVER OF THE *NATIONAL LAMPOON.*

Photograph courtesy of J2 Communications/*National Lampoon*

book about the transformations going on among white people in the Deep South. A lot of my personal impetus was to try to figure out what my roots were again.

Back in New York, Robin Morgan and Jane Alpert and a number of women working at *Rat* did a special woman's issue and said hey—why should we give it up? So they told all the men they were wimps and sexist dogs and exploiters of women and got all the male guilt going and said we're gonna run the paper. They called me up in Mississippi to say, "What do you think?" I said we should basically support the women. And the women took over. I always felt if I'd been there there'd never have been a fight. It would have been part of the natural evolution for the paper. But I was the name, so I got all the bad press. *Off Our Backs,* a publication in Berkeley, printed this blow-by-blow description of how they came in and found me masturbating into the centerfold of *Playboy,* so they decided to take over the paper. It shows what an enormous cock I have because it stretched all the way from Greenville, Mississippi, to the Lower East Side.

From the liberated *Rat* Magazine

GOODBYE TO ALL THAT

By Robin Morgan

> White males are most responsible for the destruction of human life and environment on the planet today. Yet who is controlling the supposed revolution to change all that? White males (yes, yes, even with their pasty fingers in black and brown pies again) . . . Goodbye to all that . . . Goodbye to the notion that good ol' Abbie is any different from any other up and coming movie star (like, say Cliff Robertson) who ditches the first wife and kids . . . Women are the real Left. We are rising, powerful in our unclean bodies; bright glowing mad in our inferior brains; wild hair flying, wild eyes staring, wild voices keening; POWER TO ALL THE PEOPLE OR TO NONE.

Anita Hoffman Abbie was like Satan to her, the arch-sexist. I could never go to a women's consciousness-raising group or talk about any of the things that I was going through because it would be used as ammunition against Abbie.

Jim Fouratt You had a women's movement that now was feeling its oats. A lot of Left heterosexual women were denouncing men in a way that I've never heard a lesbian do. Then you had the men being really pissed off, feeling abandoned. We were king of the road and now suddenly we're the lowest of the low? I remember the famous press conference when Jerry and Phil [Ochs] blamed the women's movement and the gay movement for destroying the Left.

Susan Carey Anita was really smart. She was Abbie's equal intellectually, but when they were out in public, it was like she didn't exist. I could give you a list of people who sat with their backs to her. Alan Watts. And Ginsberg. Abbie was like God and it was gross.

John Eskow It's almost impossible during this period to imagine Abbie doing what he was doing without Anita there. And, as time went on, she began to get a little brittle, defensive and cold. So many people had descended on Abbie that she, in effect, became the broker of his time and attention, which is a very shitty job for anyone to have to do. That seems like a perversion of their relationship.

Sal Gianetta He was labeled brilliant, and he was, but he didn't believe it. The effect of what he said was that some of the dingy things he did were just to keep his name out there because if he didn't stay out there, he'd never get laid again. That was the gist of it.

Peter Berg I never registered Abbie as a coward but I always registered him as a thief. It affected me personally, very strongly, to feel that there were people that would use the ideas you were involved with to make money. By 1972 there were bank commercials, billboards that said, "Today is the first day of the rest of your life." To think that people we were involved with, who claimed to be alternative-culture people, had actually bought into fame, fortune or power was really depressing to me. If you wanted to understand why so many people got strung out on heroin during that time, myself included but also Peter Coyote, Emmett, Billy Fritsch, dozens of other people, it was this feeling of incredible loss. How could we have so underestimated the conviction of the people we were involved with? One of the reasons I've resented Hoffman was that that's exactly what he did. He bought out on fame. I think he always had a problem with fortune.

Peter Coyote I think Abbie and Jerry and these guys were never quite willing to give up the political, manipulative aspect of their events. Although everything was supposed to be free and open, there was always like a foot in the small of your back pushing you to a particular revelation or insight that they wanted you to have. That was the ghost of ideology that they wanted you to meet. And to us, that's like George Bush putting on bell-bottom pants and a Nehru jacket and a peace symbol. Thanks very much but no.

FALL 1969

Jeff Jones We analyzed the Days of Rage as a failure of our Bring the War Home strategy because it was too easy for the cops to repress us. We had to begin setting up clandestine structures to protect our leadership. And so we began groping our way toward creating an underground.

Robin Palmer Sharon and I only agreed to join the Weathermen as a couple. However, we were told that we could not remain a couple, they were into smashing monogamy. That was just before the townhouse explosion and one of the people that recruited me was J.J. and the other was Terry Robbins. I almost didn't join because Terry was on a tear. I remember afterwards saying to Sharon, "That guy's gonna blow himself up." Terry gave us a hint they were going to use those bombs to blow up soldiers at Fort Dix, something really counterrevolutionary. Yet we joined anyway because of gut check, that was the term we used, and because we were sure we wanted to join an organization and it was right to go underground, to do bombings, to take up the gun like the Panthers said. They put Sharon on the West Coast and me to Boston. We were supposed to look around to find something revolutionary to do. We went up to Bar Harbor to look over Rockefeller's place.

Sharon went through a depression on the West Coast. She wanted to get out. They were worried that she might crack and reveal stuff so they put me back with Sharon and decided to move me to be an overground contact of the Weather Underground and look after Sharon. It's at that point that I got permission from the Weatherpeople to organize my firebombing.

MARCH 1970

Marshall Efron The Weathermen blew up the house on Eleventh Street. By accident. These people were violent.

Jeff Jones The townhouse explosion forced our hand in going underground. Because they couldn't identify one of the bodies, the speculation was that I might have been one of the people killed. I knew that I might not see my family for I had no idea how long—it turned out to be eleven years—so I went to my father's house in Los Angeles for a couple of days, so he would know I was still alive, knowing that in a couple of more weeks, I would be gone.

The Weather Underground became the group that other movement groups measured themselves against. The townhouse explosion, albeit an accident, had shown that they were willing to die for their beliefs.

Gus Reichbach, *radical law student* These were people I had been friendly with, I remember them driving by in a car, screeching to a halt, rolling down the window, "Reichbach, there's a war going on, choose sides," rolling up the window and driving off. So there was an enormous amount of gut-checking going on, because you'd want to be as militant as the Weathermen without being fugitives. Abbie couldn't bear the thought of being a fugitive because he was at the crest of his fame. But on the other hand, he couldn't bear the thought that he wasn't as militant as the most militant Weatherman so he became a liaison for the Weather Underground. He passed messages back and forth.

The atmosphere of violence was intensified around this time by an FBI counterintelligence program called COINTELPRO. Many Left groups were infiltrated and, in the case of the Panthers, many leaders were murdered as a direct result of FBI operations.

Bill Zimmerman You look at those Panther letters, they were telling one side that this side was gonna kill 'em and then the other side that that side was gonna kill 'em. Those Cointelpro programs were very successful. But again, their success rested on our lack of connectedness to any kind of sustaining force in this society. Our analysis was of imperialism, not of how the country worked and where the people were at. The opposition of white working-class people to the antiwar movement really cut us off from any sense that we were part of America. We were against America, our heroes were foreign, our ideology was foreign, the people we wanted to win were the foreigners. So certainly the seeds were there for the movement to fall apart.

Anita Hoffman George Demmerle tried to entrap Abbie. George had told him that he had a source of stolen explosives from the navy if we wanted to plan some violent action and Abbie declined.

Ron Rosen, *Yippie* During that period of time Abbie used to have to go to other people's places because the toilet wasn't working in his apartment. He actually began to believe or at least say that it was a conspiracy, which seemed believable at the time because the landlord would get it fixed and then the next week something else within that same system would break down. So [over] this several-month period the toilet in his house wasn't working.

Grace Slick I went to Finch College and my maiden name was Grace Wing. Tricia Nixon went there about five years after I did. She decided that she was gonna have a tea for everybody that went to Finch College. That sounds like there'll be 8 million, but it's a real small finishing school. They teach you how to pour tea and catch Princeton men. I received this invitation and thought, "My God, they don't know who I am, otherwise they wouldn't ask me. This is wonderful." I assumed they're bringing their husbands. And the best husband I could bring would be Abbie Hoffman. So we got Abbie a suit. He looked like a budding Mafia hit man when we got through because his curly hair was slicked back. I think part of the mistake was that I had on a black miniskirt and high boots and a black top that was semi-see-through. The rest of 'em are all dressed the way straight, sixties college graduate types from the East Coast dressed—beige cashmere sweater, a skirt that comes down below your knees, regular-colored nylons and pumps and gold earrings and a nice coat. And the men all had suits that fit and short hair. So Abbie and I are in the line and the security guard says, "I'm sorry, you can't come in." I said, "Here's my invitation." So he goes back to the security booth and, after fifteen minutes of calling people, he comes back and tells us we still can't come in because I am a security risk. He said, "You are Grace Slick? I said, "Yes, I am."

From the *New York Daily News,* 4/26/70

"HE'S NOT AN ALUMNA," TRICIA SAID

ABBIE UNWELCOME AT LADIES' TEA

Washington (UPI)

To the startled looks of 300 kid-gloved ladies, Abbie Hoffman proved at the White House that the shearing of his locks did not clip his style. Shouting obscenities, Hoffman was muscled away from a White House gate when he tried to crash a ladies-only tea party being given by Tricia Nixon for fellow alumnae of Finch College.

Hoffman . . . arrived with pop singer Grace Slick. He claimed to be her bodyguard and said he was armed. "I wouldn't let Miss Slick go in there alone," he said. "I understand they lose a President every three years. It's a dangerous place."

ABBIE DONNED A SUIT AND TRIED TO ACCOMPANY ROCK STAR GRACE SLICK TO A RECEPTION AT THE WHITE HOUSE BUT GOT TURNED AWAY BY SECURITY. AP/Wide World

Grace Slick We had decided to dose Nixon. If I met Tricky Dick, I would've been standing with a cup of tea and gesturing. I'm an entertainer, I make a lot of gestures. And under one of my long fingernails is enough acid to make him weirder than he was. So I was planning to just gesture over his tea. Two or three hours later he'd be wandering around, watching the walls melt and saying peculiar things—they would have had to take him to Langley. And we might've read in the paper that Nixon is not feeling well. It was just hysterical thinking about it—the president of the United States crawling around on the ground saying, "I can see through my hands!"

Nancy Zaroulis and Gerald Sullivan *(from* Who Spoke Up?*)* On April 30th President Nixon made the public announcement: American troops, supported by B-52 strikes, had been sent into Cambodia to eradicate enemy strongholds there, specifically North Vietnamese command posts. In addition, air strikes against North Vietnam were being made. Within hours of the president's speech, college students across the country had turned out to protest. With the advent of the weekend, the protests became violent. At Ohio State the National Guard was called out and one student was shot. On the Kent State University campus Monday, May 4, 1970, Ohio National Guard troops killed four students and wounded nine.

Abbie Hoffman *(interviewed by Barry Shapiro)* I thought the apocalypse was coming. I had seen Nixon the night before on TV, announcing the Laos invasion. He was trembling. So Dave, Jerry and I went to New Hampshire the day after Kent State, we spoke and it was incredible. Every school in the state closed. We were pushing strike, and come to Washington.

Following the Kent State incident, riots broke out at City Hall and at Pace University in New York. Antiwar protesters were beaten by longshoremen while the police turned their backs.

From Abbie Hoffman interview with Barry Shapiro

Barry Shapiro: Did you think there was going to be a revolution then?

Abbie Hoffman: Six hundred schools closed. There was shooting, people firing at each other. What do you need for a revolution? I thought it was happening.

John Gerassi I saw Jerry Rubin in New York the week after Kent State. That's when he told me he was changing. I said, "Why?" And he said, "Look, Kent State proved to me that they're serious, that if we continue they're gonna kill whites. And I'm not ready to die." Now, that's something Abbie *never* would have done. Never.

Todd Gitlin It's something to realize that there really is a state and it really has a monopoly on legitimate force and they're willing to use it on you, privileged boys and girls. People don't necessarily drop out of a seriously revolutionary movement because they discover that the state means you ill. This movement was not revolutionary. It wasn't possible to be revolutionary for the hell of it.

Abbie Hoffman *(interviewed by Barry Shapiro)* We were going to Washington, a quarter million strong, and taking over the White House was in my head. I thought that some of us were going to die. If there was blood in the streets, then there was blood in the streets. This is it.

* * *

Tim Leary In January of 1970 I was sentenced to a federal charge of ten years for a half ounce of marijuana, and ten years for the two-roach charge in Orange County. That started the decade of the prisoner.

At the "Free Tim Leary" benefit in New York, Abbie and Anita interrupted a low-key festivity that had included Jimi Hendrix playing "The Star-Spangled Banner" and Allen Ginsberg chanting. Abbie was tripping on Orange Sunshine acid.

Abbie Hoffman *(interviewed by Barry Shapiro)* Anita and I got up on the stage. I was totally spaced out. There were all these Hare Krishna singers down there. Little altars with incense and candles. And it wasn't the message that was in our hearts. "They're dying all over the world, this isn't the time to burn incense." The people in the audience represented the vanguard in communications, the top of the hip culture, and if they could throw in their lot with people who are going to Washington, that would have been a really good thing.

So I said, "This afternoon I was down at Pace College. People showed me photographs of kids whose flesh was ripped wide open." I had this vision that the police could have come into this benefit and wiped everybody out while all the hippies were going "Peace and Love." The Hare

Krishnas started to try and drown me out with Om Om Brother Ommm. We're freaking out at the people videotaping it. One of them's going "Project. Project." Then Anita kicks over the altar.

Susan Carey Abbie and Anita both went up onstage to deliver this incredible rabble-rousing speech. Abbie said that same night that he was sure that the FBI or somebody was trying to break into his apartment. It was true. He was robbed.

MAY 15, 1970

From Abbie Hoffman interview with Barry Shapiro

Abbie Hoffman: I thought the Washington rally was gonna be the thing that put us underground. I didn't speak in Washington. We were in disguise. We were saying we were gonna take over the White House. And this is what we were accused of doing in the Chicago trial. We already had ten years piled up for crossing state lines to incite riot. We didn't do it then. Now we're doing it. We're doing it every day in every state we go to and we are going to culminate in Washington and when that happens I'm under. I'm not going to jail. And there's no way the government is gonna sit there and allow for the White House to be taken over. Lo and behold, Nixon got a few hippies, he went out by the fountain, told them all that he was just confused and concerned about their problems and they were very courteous and called him Mr. President. They should have spit at him, those fucking hippies.

They put buses around the White House instead of tanks, which was shrewd. Empty buses. Soldiers behind them. You didn't see a heavy show of force, but it was there.

The Trotskyites had control of the rally and they worked out a deal with the administration officials, the permit thing was neat and tidy. They got co-opted. I frankly was for ripping the city apart. I was for taking over the White House.

Barry Shapiro: Who's gonna be in front?

Abbie Hoffman: I was right there. I was nudging the troops. I wanted to see it go. And I was pissed that the fucking Trotskyites got control and I talked this over with the Vietnamese later in Paris, they said you know what we did with the Trotskyites? Slit their throats. I guess there are some principles of revolution that are universal. I was seeing the different kinds of personalities and factions that developed. If the revolution took over, I thought the only role that we could play was as a hero of the revolution. Which is essentially they make up all the stories about you but you're not allowed to be seen in public. And of course, ultimately they kill you.

Anita Hoffman On our first trip to Los Angeles Bert Schneider arranged for us to stay at Jack Nicholson's house. Jack had just become famous for making *Easy Rider.*

Gus Reichbach I think Bert played many roles for Abbie. Certainly financial was one. But Bert was also Abbie's entree to the glamour of Hollywood. While Abbie enjoyed the celebrity, he was also impressed by celebrities. I recall one time the awe and glee in which he recounted to me that he had gone to bed with Janis Joplin.

Alex Bennett, *radio personality* One night Abbie invited my wife and me up to his house for dinner. He made paella. At dinner he said, "We're having a special guest star." After dinner in walks Tennessee Williams. I remember him sitting in a chair almost at Abbie's feet, saying, "Tell me about the revolution, Abbie." Abbie almost acted like he had known him all his life, like "Nice of you to drop by."

Anita Hoffman We got a tour of the Manson ranch from Squeaky Fromme. Jerry and Phil went to visit Manson in jail but we didn't.

Jerry Rubin Manson wanted to meet with us because he wanted to use our trial as a model for his trial. Very brilliant guy, he just lectured to us for two and a half hours. We were so insane then that we thought maybe he was an oppressed hippie or just a victim.

Abbie Hoffman *(interviewed by Barry Shapiro)* After April 1970, I thought our work was really done here. The summer is a difficult time to organize, you lose the campus as a base for guerrilla activity. And I saw that we had suffered a defeat. On the surface it might have looked like a victory to some people, getting 200,000 people down there. I know Jerry and I were very down. We felt we had been taken by the pacifists at that point. The USIA, we later learned, made films of that demonstration to show the world what a democracy the U.S. was. So when you're actually being used as a tool, it's so very tempting to grab a gun and start shooting because you clear it up in your head . . .

SPRING 1970

Jeff Jones I was out in San Francisco. We'd only been underground for a month or two. Abbie saw the underground as something that could really be a tremendous inspiration and a new level of the whole cultural resistance. We met in Golden Gate Park and he said, "What can I do?" and we said, "You could help us with money." He told us to wait there and he went over to the Jefferson Airplane House on Stanton Street, and said, "Give me $100," and they gave him a hundred-dollar bill. He said, "I'm giving this to the Weather Underground, so you're a part of the conspiracy." My guess is that he liked what we were doing and I think he also realized that by keeping in contact with us, if he got into real trouble, he could come with us and maybe be safe.

Abbie Hoffman *(interviewed by Barry Shapiro)* There was also the alternative of going underground because I was pretty Weather-oriented. Anita was seeing this was the way out: we could change our names, live in a small house someplace and we wouldn't have to go to parties and reporters wouldn't be calling the house. But actually it was going to be almost a retirement.

Jerry Rubin Nancy Kurshan was saying we have to go underground. I said, "Nancy, it's over. No one's willing to die for this. It's gonna be a whole different situation now. America's gonna get very liberal, the movement is gonna disappear, people are gonna cut their hair, they're gonna start wearing suits, they're gonna merge into society, have kids, and it's gonna be the opposite of the sixties. And frankly, that's how I feel. As a matter of fact I'm doing yoga now. I'd rather do yoga than go underground. You want to go underground? Hey, have a good time."

POWER TO THE PEOPLE—ABBIE ADDRESSES A FREE BOBBY SEALE RALLY IN NEW HAVEN, CONNECTICUT. Archive Photos

From *Other Scenes* magazine, October 1970

CHICAGO: TWO YEARS AFTER

By Abbie Hoffman

Two years in a revolution, even a revolution for the hell of it, is a long time. The Lower East Side has O.D.'ed on heroin. People's Park was created by us and crushed by them. *Woodstock Nation* was born and diluted by the celluloid world of hip capitalism. The Black Panthers have emerged as the most revolutionary force in the land. The Weathermen have unleashed the rage inside each Yippie, and Yippies have turned on the Weathermen to digging culture . . .

It is true that our revolution must be born out of joy, but it's going to take more than some neat pranks to radically change this society. Never again will I spell America with a "c," for in the eyes of Amerika we have all been declared outlaws. An armed struggle is not only inevitable, it is happening, and the Yippies are part of that.

Folks will mumble, "Abbie sure has lost his sense of humor," but they never understood *Revolution for the Hell of It*. My book was written with treason in my heart. It was written with the knowledge that the institutions and values of imperialism, racism, capitalism and the Protestant ethic do not allow young people to experience authentic liberation. It was written with the intention of making fun subversive. And finally, make no mistake about it, it was written with the hope of destroying Amerika. Yippie!

In September of 1970, the Weather Underground helped Tim Leary escape from his California jail.

Superjoel Abbie's the one who set up the deal. Abbie did the introductions. I don't know who conceived of the idea, but Abbie's the one who presented it to Rosemary [Leary], who then middled it to Timothy and set it up.

Jeff Jones All we did was help him get away from the jail and get out of the country. The hardest part Tim did himself.

Tim Leary I arranged my escape from the inside and Rosemary had given $25,000 to Michael Kennedy, my lawyer at the time, to arrange my being met. We didn't know who it was, I thought it might be Mafia. I was picked up on the highway, and they told me that they were the Weathermen and I was very pleased. I certainly admired their skill in getting me out of the country. They knew exactly how to get passports for myself and my wife. And Bernadine shaved my head.

Allen Ginsberg Bernadine Dohrn or other Weathermen made Tim sign a statement published in the *Berkeley Barb,* addressed to me, denouncing pacifism and saying that armed struggle is the only way.

Tim Leary It was like an incredible summer camp of adventure and disguises. On my first trial run out, we all went off into Seattle and saw the Woodstock movie. Tripping with them was pleasant. Of course things went belly-up for both the Weathermen and me after that. They got carried away. This stuff when the Manson thing happened and the Weathermen were endorsing sticking a fork into the pregnant woman's stomach, that simply violates anything that anyone's believed in. The Black Panthers and the Weathermen seriously thought they were gonna have an armed revolution in America. At one point Field Marshal Cox of the Panthers was trying to get me to have my friends in California send maps of the Mendocino coast where they were gonna land like Castro in Cuba, and the whole thing became almost Monty Python, except they did have real guns and they did have enormous power over us at the time.

Leary was spirited away to Algeria, where the Panthers were being treated as an authentic liberation front. Eldridge Cleaver got the okay from the government for Leary to join them there. Stew Albert was sent by the Yippies to intercede on Leary's behalf, but his help wasn't necessary.

Stew Albert Leary came on his own, he didn't wait. So we didn't really do anything. The Algerians had given Leary sanctuary because they thought he was black. I remember seeing an article in an Algerian newspaper, referring to Leary as an Afro-American psychologist.

Abbie couldn't go to Algeria because of his bail situation. Anita goes. And it's all a disaster. We all got in on a special visa that Eldridge arranged and that necessitated a special way to get out that Eldridge controlled. Eldridge had become like the Emperor Jones in Algeria, he was really out to lunch. It was a dangerous situation 'cause he felt he was a law unto himself.

Marty Kenner All the Panthers there carried guns because they were all scared the other one was gonna kill 'em. In fact, [it was rumored] Eldridge had murdered another Black Panther there and had buried him, because he thought that he was having an affair with Kathleen.

Stew Albert Anita was brave. She went to the airport and talked her way out of the country. That was a real blow to Eldridge's authority, that Anita could get out of Algeria without his consent.

Tim Leary The way I escaped from Cleaver was that I told him we had a bunch of money and I had to have the passport to get the money.

Stew Albert When Anita got back to France she attacked all of us for collaborating with Eldridge there. Of course, Abbie was angry at us and Jerry was more sympathetic. I guess he and Abbie had gotten back to feuding over getting their names in the paper.

Gus Reichbach The rivalry between *Do It* and *Revolution for the Hell of It* was intense. *Do It* sold much more.

Anita Hoffman I met Abbie in Paris and we conceived America then.

Stew Albert All I remember about Paris was we had a lot of fun. We went to the cafés and met some nice French intellectuals.

Jean-Jacques Lebel Abbie and Jerry had asked me to organize large meetings for them to meet the French anarchists. So I organized some important meetings in the universities. The people composing the French radical movement were at least 50 percent workers, they were not university-educated. These guys were some of the most extraordinarily important activists ever. They had taken over the factories where cars, and television sets, and bombs, and all that shit were being made. And stopped the production of those horrors and said, "We want to live in another way, we want to produce other things." And they did it!

When the Yippies came over they behaved like "ugly Americans," as if the Americans owned the world. Jerry and Abbie were addressing these French people in English and not understanding that they didn't understand what they were talking about. And then they went out there saying drugs, sex, rock and roll. These guys were forty, fifty years old, saying, "We don't turn on, what is this stuff about drugs?" All my French comrades said, "They're a bunch of shits. Get them out of here."

Gus Reichbach Jean-Jacques overstates. First of all none of them had any contacts with the workers, so the notion that the workers couldn't relate to 'em is nonsensical. Certainly the leadership of the French student movement was culturally more conservative and much more intellectual.

Then Jerry and Abbie showed up and elbowed each other out of the way of the camera. A lot of those people were very turned off.

Meanwhile Jerry and Stew Albert took their Yippie road show to England, taking over David Frost's show long enough to smoke hashish on live television. Threatened with deportation, they went to Belfast, where they were jailed, made more headlines and then were sent home.

Stew Albert It's a pity Abbie missed that one, because he missed knowing what it was like to be a Beatle. As a matter of fact, John Lennon saw the Frost show and loved it and that was the start of our relationship with him.

NOVEMBER 1969

Robin Palmer *(explaining how Sam Melville got arrested)* Sam got caught because he recruited George Demmerle. He was going to do these bombs in the vehicles as a way to test George. Jane got caught because she lived with Sam. David Huie got caught because he and Pat Swinton lived on the floor below them. So they were prime suspects even though Sam had not confided to George [the names of] any other members of the collective. Then Pat split. She disappeared for five years.

So we stopped bombing. We had dynamite on our hands. What was left of the collective, four or five people, were somewhat depressed. Our head had been cut off, so we gave some of the dynamite to the Weathermen. Then I started to organize another bombing collective. This was to be low-level firebombing, Molotov cocktails. We had that planned for months and had it all set up for the First National City Bank at 91st and Madison. Only problem was that one of us was one of them. Steve Winer was a cabdriver and his job was to be the lookout. People later said, "You guys made the cop the lookout!" They let us go right up until actually putting the Molotov cocktail through the window of the bank.

They sent me to Attica. I got one to four years.

* * *

Abbie finally won a victory when his conviction for desecrating the flag was overturned on appeal by the U.S. Court of Appeals.

Chris Cerf Abbie would always know the little thing that everybody else would realize is ridiculous but that would get to somebody. The "Steal This Book" thing became that, though he didn't originally intend it as that. He just had the idea it would be a good little gag to say let's liberate this book from the bookstores. And we put "STEAL THIS BOOK" on the back cover of *Woodstock Nation* and the Random House sales manager went bananas. "We can't do this!" The crazier he went, the more Abbie loved it.

At that point Abbie decided that his next book was going to be called *Steal This Book* and that's at least part of the reason that Random House refused to publish it. Also, they had a few small problems with instructions for how to blow up things. I don't know if they ever noticed that the little Random House logo on *Woodstock Nation* was the little Random House being blown up.

Gus Reichbach Jason Epstein in his radical chic heyday at his *New York Review of Books* had a Molotov cocktail on the cover. But then that was still something that was happening in Europe. Suddenly, when bombs started going off in this country, Jason Epstein said Random House could not in good conscience publish a book that had a diagram like this in it.

Abbie approached John Eskow to help him compile Steal This Book, *which was basically an expanded, updated version of "Fuck the System." When Eskow was unavailable, he turned to Izak Haber, a young runaway who gladly signed on to the project.*

Anita Hoffman Izak claimed that *Steal This Book* was his idea. I don't know what the motive was. Maybe both of them had fantasies about the other—Abbie seeking Izak as this committed young soldier. Also, I think Abbie may have felt he needed a bodyguard too, and Izak was really big and brawny. Maybe Izak didn't get the attention from Abbie, I don't know. His later attacks on Abbie were such a surprise. I never understood, because the book wasn't his idea, it had always been Abbie's idea.

Stew Albert Izak seemed like a nice young man. Abbie knew a lot of interesting, talented people who he managed to impress and dominate. I put Izak in that category. Izak was different, though, because at some point he tried to kill his idol and replace him. Abbie was like a famous gunfighter in the westerns, and now people like Izak were coming along to make their reputation by shooting him.

Gus Reichbach No doubt Abbie used Izak. He made himself available to be Abbie's assistant and Abbie took full advantage of him as an assistant. But assistant is not the same as collaborator.

Izak went public with the dispute by attacking Abbie in a long article he wrote for Rolling Stone *magazine. The article was called "How Abbie Hoffman Won My Heart and Stole 'Steal This Book.'" It contained a litany of charges that Abbie had sold out.*

Jerry Rubin He had built up this incredible Abbie myth and all of a sudden this kid came into his life as a hero-worshiper and just told the world the guy is a contradiction. He stole the book, he lives fancy, he doesn't care, all that.

Abbie Hoffman *(interviewed by Barry Shapiro)* Haber had the code name of the Weather Underground. I knew that acting as a revolutionary, me or others close to me should have killed him. The blacks, if they thought they caught an informer, they'll kill him. But what did the whites do? They printed his picture in an underground newspaper.

Jerry Rubin I think Abbie aged fifteen years with that experience. The sad part about this is that Haber was using Abbie's techniques to get Abbie. His myth had been turned against him.

There was also a major problem getting the book published. Over thirty publishers rejected the book, primarily wary about the title. Then Tom Forcade, who published a small underground paper in Arizona and ran the Underground Press Syndicate, a struggling, free reprint exchange, offered to set up an alternative distribution system to get the book out.

Mayer Vishner Hoffman is rushing off to jail. Forcade embellishes his credentials and says he'll edit, package, publish, distribute the book. All Abbie has to do is go to jail and not worry about it. Forcade does a lot of work on the manuscript. Abbie comes out a few weeks later, he doesn't like the work. Forcade hadn't done enough of what Abbie wanted him to do, which was get the book into every bookstore. And had been doing too much of what Abbie didn't like, which was making it readable and fact-checking.

While Forcade's agreement to distribute the book for Abbie was being negotiated, Grove Press finally agreed to distribute it. Forcade was furious. He had done a major edit on the book and he still thought that he would be distributing it. So he sued Abbie.

Forcade and Abbie were persuaded to allow a "people's court" to arbitrate Forcade's suit. The judges set up a revolving credit plan where Abbie was instructed to pay Forcade off in books, not money. Forcade then had to distribute the books, keeping copious financial records. In essence, they'd have to trust each other, and an alternative underground distribution network would be set in place so other countercultural books could be distributed this way.

Even though the judges' decision made it clear that neither party had "won" or "lost," Forcade claimed a victory at the ensuing press conference, and the electronic media had a field day proclaiming that Abbie had "been found guilty by a jury of his peers." But neither Tom nor Abbie was pleased with the decision.

Fred Jordan, *editor* Grove was quite fair with Abbie and actually paid him a fair amount of money as the book sold. But Abbie always found a way of claiming that there was nothing paid. Barney Rossett was trying to explain to him that there's such a thing as returns, which he didn't want to accept. Many books were stolen and Grove got an awful lot of letters from stores that refused to carry the book.

Daniel Ellsberg Bookstores wouldn't show *Steal This Book* in their windows. It was an under-the-counter item. I remember the evening news in Cambridge showed a clip of Abbie in a downtown bookstore. The store manager is a very straight, bookstorish type, all dressed up, and he's saying, rather pompously, "Tell me, Abbie, how do you steal a book?" So Abbie says, "What's your biggest book here?" They bring out some huge art book. And Abbie puts it under his arm and you see him walk out the door. And the manager is saying, "Hahaha, what a funny guy." And then as the minutes pass, they start getting uneasy. Of course, he never returns. End of that interview.

Stew Albert *Steal This Book* sold well. Jerry thought Abbie was on the brink of a successful career in publishing and that he was going to be a rich businessman. Jerry was very impressed.

Rennie Davis I believed we needed one large civil disobedience action in Washington, nonviolent, broad-based but taking the pressure to another step. There was a lot of research coming out about the impact of Agent Orange, particularly on children in South Vietnam—children with webbed feet, who couldn't get their breath, born with no forehead.

I don't know if you remember an issue of *Time* magazine, in September '70, with a cover story called "The Cooling of America." The sense was that the antiwar movement had crested. Other than taking up arms, what more could we really do? I'd always operated within a collective context, but the antiwar coalition rejected the Mayday plan simply because of the perception that people wouldn't come. But somehow I knew we could do it. So Mayday was all my own. There was a commune of freaks across the street from where I lived in Washington. I solicited them to be the staff. Then a woman in New York gave me $50,000 to open offices and get set up.

One of the few people who really supported Mayday at that point was Abbie. Because the popular sentiment was still there, everywhere I spoke ten thousand people would turn out, huge crowds everywhere. By January 1971 everyone could see that Mayday was going to happen. Then the coalition came together and joined the initiative.

Ken Kelley One of my jobs was to get the rock and roll bands together. Abbie'd give pep talks around the country but as far as the organizing of it, he didn't have much to do with it. He was getting pretty burned out. I heard at the time he was getting pretty coked out too.

Rennie Davis So we had the April 15th demonstration with 350,000 people. The Vietnam Vets had their camp out in front of the Capitol. The Beach Boys played.

Ken Kelley Mayday was the last hurrah. Again, two successive weekends, plus the incredible coalition from welfare mothers to Vietnam Vets. Danny Fields, who worked for Atlantic Records, got us a hotel room right across the street from the Watergate Howard Johnson's.

Danny Fields There was a rumor that Aretha Franklin was going to appear at the Mayday protest so I booked a suite at the Holiday Inn. Aretha never came and as the festival went on everybody stayed there. We put pillows on the floor, we opened the sofas. Ken Kelley was there, Danny [Goldberg], Phil, Abbie, Jerry. They were coming and going. Then on Sunday there were stories that the police were going to do a vacuum cleaning of the streets and put everyone in RFK Stadium the next day. So I left. I told the hotel to keep this credit card open for another twenty-four hours, till noon on Monday, so that I wouldn't be evicting people who were necessary to keep this demonstration running. A week later the bill came in and it was somewhere between $6,000 and $8,000 for the one day. To this day, I don't know how they did it. How many room services can you order? But they were calling Hanoi! I didn't know you could do that. I was politely told that my department was being reorganized and that it would have a different shape. Without me there.

Anonymous I went to Washington on behalf of the *Ann Arbor Sun* and I saw Abbie there. There we were in this Mayday demonstration surrounded by regular army troops, National Guard troops with bayonets, helicopters overhead, a very tense and paranoid situation. What did Abbie do but pull out two tabs of LSD and said, "Let's drop acid." I said, "Are you out of your mind?" I was nineteen and still in awe of him, so I said what the hell and we did this acid.

Abbie Hoffman *(interviewed by Elli Wohlgelernter)* My self-image is so into conflict and being in the streets and being a political animal and seeing myself as out there to right the wrong, having a conception of myself that's engaged so that the experience of nirvana, meditation and that whole thing is risky when you're in the middle of a riot or chaos. So to be honest I have a very high percent of bad trips on LSD.

Gus Reichbach Going with Abbie I thought we'd be more in a leadership role. That was a miscalculation. By the second day, we had both thrown total caution to the winds. It wasn't like Abbie was directing troops or anything, he was there grabbing the car and overturning it and moving barricades into the street. It amazed me, the speed and glee with which he immediately joined it. We had both agreed we weren't gonna do it. And as soon as it happened, *wham!*

Rennie Davis Then the time came to see how many were staying to be arrested. There were 100,000 remaining for the second phase. Everybody was out in the streets at 5:30 in the morning. Most of the arrests had taken place by 6:30. This was the largest arrest in history.

Ken Kelley Abbie's being chased down this alley by cops. Just like the fucking Top Kat cartoon show, he jumps in this trash can. Well, the cops saw him and grabbed the trash can, dumped him out and broke his nose and hauled him away and stuck him behind bars.

Abbie Hoffman *(interviewed by Barry Shapiro)* Mayday was badly planned, badly organized. Crazy. Transvestites for Peace up on the stage. You don't know what freedom is until you put on a dress. I'm sitting there feeling like I'm an expert, feeling the separation between me and everyone else. I'll just be one of the troops. I'll sleep on the floor with all the people. I'll chant the slogans, I'll go with the people from the New York region, 5:00 A.M. Dupont Circle. I'm smacked. My fucking nose is cracked. I'm in jail. I'm thinking about getting mauled by the cops. For me Mayday was my last.

Stew Albert We were being held in a stadium. There was a hippie boy and girl there who said they wanted to get married and they wanted Abbie to perform the ceremony. So he did it. It struck me how despite all the criticisms, he was still a folk hero. Then somehow he escaped.

Jack Hoffman Nixon thought the whole Chicago 7 were Jews. He sent thugs to beat up my brother, it's right there in the transcripts.

Excerpts from the White House Tape, May 5, 1971

Nixon: They've got guys who'll go in and knock their heads off.

Haldeman: Sure. Murderers. Guys that really, you know, that's what they do. Like the steelworkers have and—except we can't deal with the steelworkers at the moment. We can deal with the Teamsters . . . it's the regular strikebusters types . . . and then they're gonna beat the [obscenity] out of some of these people. And, uh, and hope they really hurt 'em. I mean go in with some real—and smash some noses [tape noise] some pretty good fights.

Nixon: [tape noise] How did it handle it last night?

Haldeman: [tape noise] had some good footage of the big mob out on the Justice Department thing and . . .

Nixon: Some close-up?

Haldeman: [tape noise, unintelligible] Fortunately, they're all just really bad-lookin' people. There's no semblance of respectability. Rennie Davis has been spokesman and he's as good for us and he's a convicted conspirator and, uh, [tape noise] discredited.

Nixon: Hmmm.

Haldeman: I think getting Abbie Hoffman and, and this John—the other—they got . . .

Nixon: Aren't the Chicago Seven all Jews? Davis's a Jew, you know.

Haldeman: I don't think Davis is.

Nixon: Hoffman's a Jew.

Haldeman: Abbie Hoffman is.
Nixon: About half of them are Jews.

Even though Rennie Davis was the principal organizer of the Mayday protests, Abbie was indicted along with Rennie for crossing state lines with the intention of inciting a riot, a federal charge.

Rennie Davis Abbie and I were singled out by the Justice Department. We both felt that this was a much more serious charge than Chicago. We were facing twenty years. The movement was on the wane and it looked like it was just going to be the two of us together facing another trial.

Anita Hoffman His nose was treated by Dr. Spock and then he escaped and he came back to New York. I was pregnant with America. Maybe a week later, Abbie and I come back from the movies one night. We lived in this dilapidated office building on 13th Street, we had this apartment on the roof. So we walk into the hallway and four FBI agents jump out of the woodwork and jump on top of us and arrest Abbie. I must have told reporters that they jumped us in the lobby. The way *Rolling Stone* wrote it up, it sounded like we lived in a fucking penthouse. I really felt bad that I used the word "lobby." It was a hallway, a dumpy musty little smelly place where you got the elevator.

Abbie says somewhere in one of the books that I was always worrying. It's because I knew that he was vulnerable in a way that the cops didn't realize. I couldn't allow myself to think that he had a mental illness, there's no way that ever crossed my mind, but I'd have nightmares of him going out of control in a jail cell and a cop just coming in there and killing him.

Bill Zimmerman We went to Washington thinking we could close down the city. What happened? They arrested ten thousand of us in one day and filled up all the jails in Washington and Baltimore and surrounding counties. John Mitchell took over RFK Stadium in Washington and made it a prison camp, put up barbed wire and had a thousand people in the football fields under lights. But it didn't do anything at all. The war didn't end, America didn't rise in protest.

Abbie Hoffman *(interviewed by Barry Shapiro)* I had this nice-looking young lady doing this thing you're doing. We got stoned and she started to put the make on me. But it was a little weird. All of a sudden, I grabbed her handbag, there was a tape recorder in it. I said, "You're a cop." She broke down crying, no, she was writing for a true confession magazine what it was like to fuck me.

SUMMER 1971

John Giorno, *poet* As a work of art Abbie was going to fuck seven feminists. He had gone to bed with five, and he was planning the sixth one. But the seventh one on his list was Betty Friedan, and he said, "I don't know if I could do it!"

Jeff Nightbyrd Abbie told me he had slept with [a very famous feminist]. They were together at something and then he wound up going home with her, and he called me up and said, "Hey, Jeff, you won't believe what I just did." It was an affirmation of life, like "Whoopee, we broke through the categories," not "I conquered her."

Anita Hoffman Right after I came home from the hospital with America, Abbie had to go on a big speaking tour to raise money to pay for the trial. Now, it wasn't his fault but I resented that he wasn't there. He was just overwhelmed with all these things, so he really didn't play that much a part with America because he was always out there and then he did have to earn a living for us.

Ron Kaufman After the trial, I went to California. One of the things I got from Abbie is your politics are the way you live, not what you say. At that time, a lot of people were talking about kidnapping people like Kissinger. But it seemed to me the politics of kidnapping was the politics of Lyndon Johnson, it was no different. So I said if you were really into kidnapping you should kidnap buildings and free people, because your politics are then that you value people, not property. So I built this device which showed how you could kidnap a building and just make it not desirable to use for an extended period of time but not endanger anybody.

1971

This was after the Army Research building bombing in Madison, which was an attempt to destroy a building. That involved a whole truckload of explosives. This involved eight ounces of black powder in a safety-deposit box, at night, during a bank holiday, when no one was in the vault. There were time bombs placed in nine safe-deposit boxes, three major banks in each of three cities. I invented a timer capable of timing for seven months. It's time-locked so you can't get in there. So it's the only truly safe place in the world to have a firecracker go off. Eight ounces of black powder is

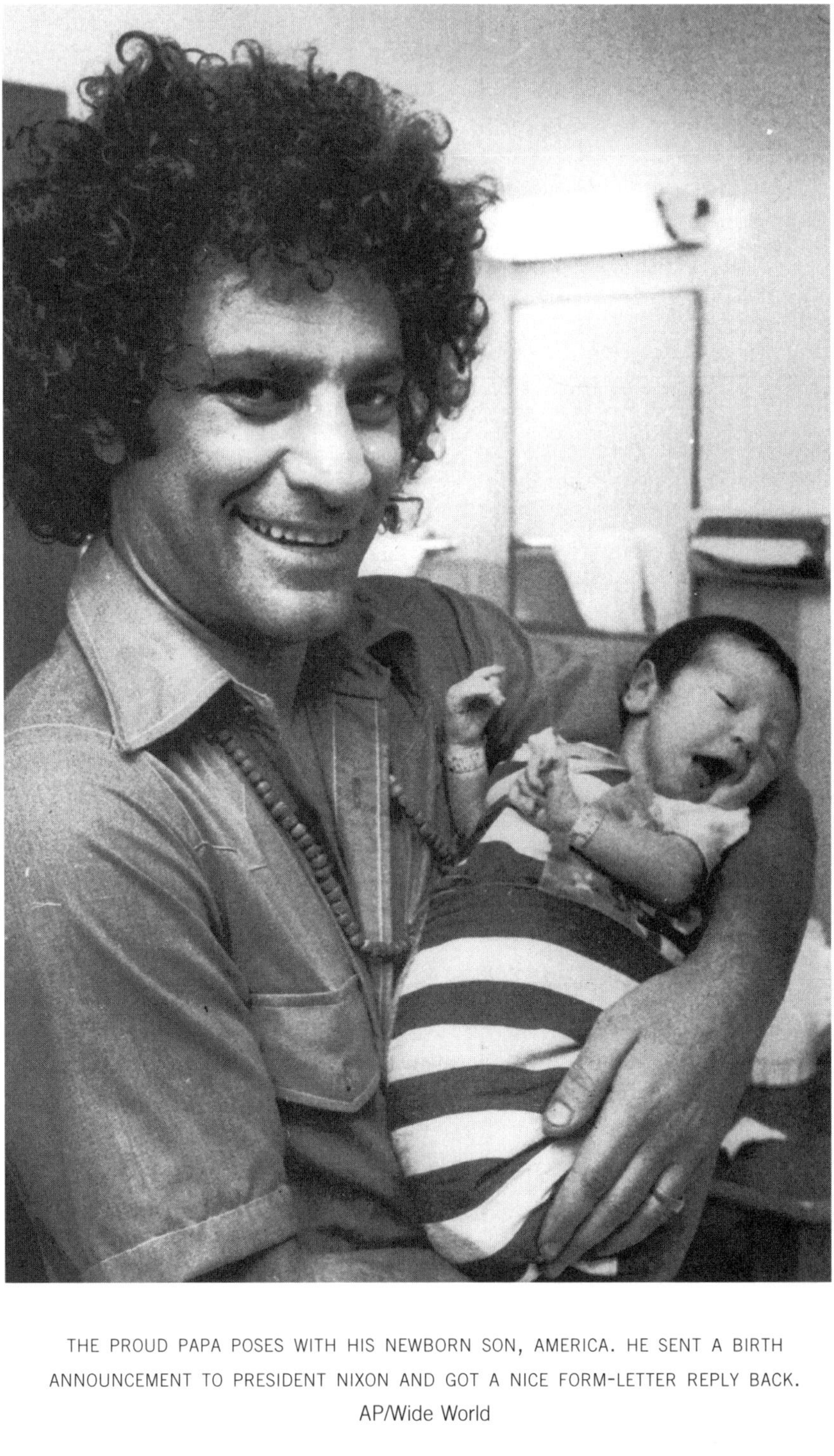

THE PROUD PAPA POSES WITH HIS NEWBORN SON, AMERICA. HE SENT A BIRTH ANNOUNCEMENT TO PRESIDENT NIXON AND GOT A NICE FORM-LETTER REPLY BACK.
AP/Wide World

questionably even an explosive. Maybe just a rapid combustion. But it's very symbolic. The whole thing was oriented towards the media. I put copies of either the Constitution or the Declaration of Independence in each box.

After I planted the bombs, sometime in the summer, I went underground. I changed my name, and enlisted in the infantry for three years with the idea that I'd be shipped to Europe after all my training. I went through all the training that they gave the Vietnam people. I was in the army five months and then I went on a leave. That's when I decided to turn in the letters to the media.

JANUARY 1972

One device had gone off on Labor Day weekend in the Bank of America in the middle of the night causing about $100 worth of damage. That was intentional. But the explosion hadn't made the press and they didn't know about the others 'cause nothing was going on there. There were just safe-deposit boxes; the rent was still good. So I turned over the keys to the media, with a lengthy document. By the time the whole thing exploded in the media, I was on the run. They immediately discovered who I was. It had this whole image of a one-man revolution type thing. Here I'm bombing banks in three cities and had infiltrated the military and there were articles in the *Chicago Tribune* about how the CIA was looking for me. But I hadn't done anything. It was not a destructive thing, I think about $100 worth of damage was done to one of those little doors to a safe-deposit box. There had never been anybody at risk at any time. They couldn't get into the vault for twenty-four hours after the explosion 'cause it was on a time lock.

One day, I saw myself on TV in my little hotel room. I was doing day labor in Dallas. It was five minutes on Walter Cronkite. It was a big deal, and my picture was in all the papers. So I checked out of the hotel, went to L.A. and I worked at one job for twelve and a half years.

Daniel Ellsberg I came back from Vietnam in June of 1967. I was the highest civil service grade, the equivalent of a lieutenant general. I went back to the Rand Corporation, which does contract work for the Pentagon. From then on I was at Rand and at the Pentagon as a consultant from Rand till September of 1970. When I finished reading the earliest part of the Pentagon Papers, I felt that the war had been wrong from the start, which was back in 1945. I had not realized that when I was in the government.

As of 1967, most people on the outside had no knowledge whatever of what people thought inside the Pentagon. They assumed that they supported what Johnson and Westmoreland were saying. Quite the contrary. The people inside the Pentagon did not differ in their sense of the prospect from Abbie Hoffman. Moreover, most of them felt the war should end. The thirty-six people who worked on the Pentagon Papers project, mostly military officers, had all been in Vietnam. That was among the criteria of selecting them. A bunch of them were very right-wing and later rose to very high right-wing roles under Reagan and Bush. They were all for ending that war. After Tet, in early '68, the public attitude switched to join them. So now there was no real difference between the general public attitudes and the Pentagon attitude toward the war after Tet. The question was what you did about that.

The difference from Abbie and the movement was not so much a difference as to whether the war ought to end but how urgent that was and what to do about it. And what responsibility rested on you as an American citizen if you were tired of waiting for other people to stop it.

Abbie had a serious desire to end that war, and he and Jerry and the others in the movement were the only people in the country who were acting responsibly to do it. I say many policy-makers were against the war, but unfortunately these policy-makers did not include the president. None of these presidents got to the point of being willing themselves to be the man who "lost a war." And they had the power to keep this thing going. One man was enough to do it if he was president, given the passivity and obedience, the silence and the secrecy and lies of all the others who disagreed with him but continued to serve him.

I started copying the Pentagon Papers on October 1, 1969, so the Chicago 7 trial was sort of coextensive with my own total commitment to the war. I gave the Pentagon Papers to Senator Fulbright in 1969 and 1970, and spent 1970 trying to get them out through Fulbright. Then starting in 1971, when it was clear that he wasn't going to put them out, I was looking for other people to do it. So I finally got to the *New York Times*. I was expecting to go to jail for the rest of my life when these came out, whenever they came out. Eventually I was indicted on twelve felony counts, facing a possible 115 years in jail.

JUNE 13, 1971

New York Times *publishes Pentagon Papers.*

John Lennon and Yoko Ono had recently moved to New York City. Village Voice *columnist Howard Smith was giving them a cultural tour of the city, including Washington Square Park, performing venue of street singer David Peel.*

David Peel I started singing my favorite underground music, like "I Like Marijuana," then "The Pope Smokes Dope," and I saw John jolt a little bit, and then I saw Yoko smile.

Ed Sanders Somehow David Peel had foisted himself on John and Yoko and they'd been swept up by this guy. Lennon had a penchant for the gutter. I'd see him at weird parties.

David Peel *Do It* was very big in Japan. Yoko made it a point to meet Jerry in America when she got here. Jerry brought Abbie.

Stew Albert Jerry hero-worshiped John Lennon and Yoko. Abbie wouldn't do that. In fact, he'd get competitive with John Lennon.

David Peel John and Yoko funded projects and they helped some of the Yippies, they did tons of stuff. John did things in Harlem. He donated money to WBAI. He helped us get street musicians on record. He got one of the radical bands, Elephant's Memory, started as the Plastic Ono Band.

Alex Bennett John and Yoko were always making promises they never kept. They were famous for that. I always felt that they were into that game of playing revolution, but what they liked more was the fawning.

From *Skywriting by Word of Mouth* by John Lennon

"WE'D ALL LOVE TO SEE THE PLAN"

Next came our "revolutionary period," which blossomed shortly after we landed in the States for a visit. Upon our arrival in the U.S., we were practically met off the plane by the "Mork and Mindy" of the Sixties—Jerry and Abbie: two classic, fun-loving hustlers. I can do without Marx and Jesus.

It took a long time and a lot of good magic to get rid of the stench of our lost virginity, although it was fun meeting all the famous underground heroes (no heroines): Bobby Seale and his merry men;

> Huey Newton in his very expensive-looking military-style clothes; Rennie Davis and his "You pay for it and I'll organize it"; John Sinclair and his faithful Ann Arbor Brigade; and dear old Allen Ginsberg, who if he wasn't lying on the floor "ohming," was embarrassing the fuck out of everyone he could corner by chatting something he called poetry very loudly in their ears (and out the other).

Roger Lowenstein Abbie and Jerry and I and Leslie Bacon went over to John Lennon's apartment. It was the first time I met Lennon. John was in a very serious mood. He was in pain, really going through a lot of shit. He'd curl up in a fetal position on the floor and primal-scream. We hung out there for a while and then it was one in the morning, the only time John and Yoko would dare to leave their apartment. Abbie wanted to see *Deep Throat,* which had just come out. It was playing up near Times Square. So we all hopped into a cab. It was really the first time that most of us had seen a triple-X movie on a giant screen. Abbie loved it. He thought it was a marvel of cinematography and biology. But John flipped out. He was so shocked and apologetic to Yoko for subjecting her to this sexist display. I remember Abbie and I just looked at each other, *whoa,* the old eyeball roll. It was really not a political event for us. We were like "Oh my God, she did it!"

Ed Sanders I had written this long poem called "The Entrapment of John Sinclair." John and Yoko read it and got turned on to getting Sinclair out. We had meetings to start organizing a series of concerts to free John Sinclair.

FALL 1971

The Lennons headlined the first benefit, in Ann Arbor, Michigan. Sinclair was released from prison shortly after that show. Then plans were laid for John and Yoko to play at the antiwar demonstrations planned for the Republican convention in San Diego.

Rennie Davis The first event on the national tour was incredibly successful. So much so that the Republicans canceled their convention plans for San Diego and moved the location to Miami, where demonstrations would be harder to mobilize. I think with the power that Lennon had and the mood of the country we could've kept building the momentum of opposition. But the Justice Department moved on Lennon, threatening to deport him on some marijuana charge. Lennon certainly didn't stand up very well with the pressure. From where I was it was unthinkable to buckle

ABBIE AND JOHN LENNON SHARE A DOOBIE ON THE ROOFTOP OF ABBIE'S "PENTHOUSE" APARTMENT ON 13TH ST. Reuters/Anita Hoffman/Archive Photos

to the pressure. But it was a very effective move by Nixon, and John, surrounded by his attorneys, was persuaded that he would be more effective pursuing another strategy.

G. Gordon Liddy Prior to the decision [to shift the convention to Miami], I had made my recommendation to move the convention but I recognized that it might not be accepted, that they might want to have the convention in San Diego.

That being the case, I offered a plan based on the Texas Ranger method of handling a riot. Have men stand on the periphery of the riot area until they identified the leaders. They would then maneuver themselves through the crowd and take out the leaders. The theory being that a leaderless riot was far easier to control, it just became a mob. And often when they did that they would be pretty tough on these guys. They beat the hell out of 'em. I thought a better way to handle that, if you know in advance who the leaders are, and we felt that we did, was to take them out earlier. And rather than beat them up, I thought that the thing to do would be to simply abduct them, drugging them if necessary or just knock them out, and hold them down in Mexico until after the convention and then sort of dust 'em off, sober 'em up and turn 'em loose. Any soporific would've done that and I would be certain that the dosage to be administered would not be harmful.

So this was the part of the plan which I outlined before John Dean, Jeb Stuart Magruder and Attorney General Mitchell. In fact Mitchell never approved it. I have said to people since that you have to consider my activities in the context of the times. It was my view at the time that what we had at stake here was general disintegration of the social order. It was civil war.

From Win *magazine, September 1971*

"I QUIT"

> I stay away from "movement" people these days . . . The movement now represents to me the petty ugliness of Norman Fructer's dribble in Liberation saying how Jerry Rubin and I "betrayed" the movement . . . This is a sort of retirement letter I suppose. Not that I'm going off to the country or anything. Let's just call it a parting of the ways. No more calls for me to do benefits or come to demonstrations or do bail fund hustles. Divorce is never an easy matter. After a few years perhaps we

can again be friends . . . Anything is possible, after all, you might not recognize me with my new nose . . .

—*Abbie Hoffman*

Susan Carey Anita wanted to move to the country with us.

Paul McIsaac Abbie was very depressed then, really black depressions. I talked to him about it. But he just wouldn't deal with it. There was a level at which he was not prepared to open up. The funny thing about Abbie is that he wasn't an intimate person.

Anita Hoffman We took off and went to the Virgin Islands for three months, to get away and to be a family and to just pay attention to ourselves. America was three months old when we went there. Abbie got a license for scuba diving, we went snorkeling, and it was just such a beautiful time.

Mayer Vishner If you give the kid the first six months, nothing bad can happen, they can handle anything, he said. Abbie the psychologist.

Anita Hoffman Abbie got into cooking and taking care of the baby and then he taught me how to drive. So we did try to live out some of that male-female women's liberation ethic of trying to express other parts of ourselves. Then one day, the FBI came, looking for Ron Kaufman. It was amazing because we were living under another name then. Then on another occasion I was cleaning house in a bikini and these two little groupies came wearing shorts, looking for Abbie. I chased them away with a broomstick.

Jerry Rubin I talked Abbie into almost every important decision that he made. I went down to visit them and I spent that whole weekend talking Abbie into coming back to New York and being political again. And he came back the next week.

Stew Albert Before the 1972 Democratic convention, Abbie got enthusiastic about the McGovern campaign. We went to Washington and we met with a top McGovern aide, Rick Stearns. The McGovern people were afraid that the Yippies were endorsing McGovern as a way of destroying him. We had to reassure them that no, this was really on the level, and then they said if you really want to help McGovern stay away. Maybe you could say that's a sign Abbie's reality principle was starting to go.

Memo from President Richard Nixon to Attorney General John Mitchell

EYES ONLY

June 6, 1972
TO: John Mitchell
FROM: The President

The fact that Abby [*sic*] Hoffman, Jerry Rubin, Angela Davis, among others, support McGovern should be widely publicized and used at every point. Here an ad or a piece of literature from a veterans' group might be in order. This must be carefully done but nailing him to his left-wing supporters and forcing him to either repudiate them or to accept their support is essential. In fact, one effective way to operate here is to have a prominent Democrat or Independent, or a veterans' leader or a labor leader, demand by letter or otherwise that McGovern repudiate the support of Abby [*sic*] Hoffman and Jerry Rubin and any others who are well known of this type that you can find. Keep calling on him to repudiate them daily until you finally break through the media blackout into the clear. I consider this a top priority objective.

cc: Bob Haldeman
Chuck Colson

Gabrielle Schang, *journalist* That whole summer in Miami was paid for by Yip, by Abbie, Jerry and Ed's contract for a book on the conventions.

Ed Sanders We got a $33,000 advance, enough to get an office and stuff.

Rennie Davis I was spending a lot of time in solitude, my diet and attitude had shifted, I was in communion with the sky and birds. I was still completely committed to the Vietnam cause but I was reevaluating my understanding. Were institutions and social structure and the fundamental engines of capitalism at the root of the human condition or was it really about thought, human imagination and how we perceive ourselves? I was questioning. I was feeling very high, not in a drug sense at all but from forty days of fasting. It was an amazing experience, just how sensitive you get to sounds and colors. I was experiencing the first inklings of my inner being. I think Miami started me on the journey of understanding I continue today.

Stew Albert Abbie had a theory that we could take over the Democratic Party. I think Abbie was even toying with the idea that he might run for office someday.

Marty Kenner The Panthers had split apart a year or two before. The Weathermen were blowing up toilets here and there. The movement had become a caricature.

Abbie invited an attractive young woman, Gabrielle Schang, to go along with the Yippies to Miami. In New York, Gabrielle had been going out with Tom Forcade, who had just founded the Zippies.

Gus Reichbach To a very large extent the whole Zippie thing was Tom Forcade playing out his anger and getting back at Abbie, organizing younger street counterculture people, who had much less movement experience but were attracted to the cultural and drug ambience. They felt that Abbie and Jerry were two old-timers, grown fat, soft, rich and conservative. And that it was time for a cultural revolution that would upend the Yippie bureaucrats and replace them by the rising stars of the Zippie hierarchy. So they launched unremitting personal attacks of the vilest sort, as well as acts of vandalism and sabotage.

A. J. Weberman We perceived Abbie and Jerry as selling out. We considered ourselves purists who couldn't be bought under any circumstances and wouldn't cut a deal with Warner Books.

Gabrielle Schang Tom showed up in Miami in a New York City taxicab with the meter running, outside of the dorm [where the Yippies were originally staying], demanding to talk to me, high on acid. Stew or Jeff went out and said, "Go away, she doesn't want to talk to you right now." I was right in the middle and I was really scared. I guess Tom was madly in love with me, but I didn't know it until then. I don't think he went back to New York. He sent the cabdriver back.

Aiming to avoid another Chicago, the Miami police went through a year-long program of training in sensitivity and self-awareness. There were no guns this time, since the police brass were determined to avoid confrontations. But Miami was full of undercover cops.

Gerry Rudoff, *Miami undercover policeman* We began hearing plans to trash Miami Beach. We were dealing primarily with the Vietnam Veterans Against the War, the VVAW. We were attending meetings.

ABBIE POSES AS A STEWARDESS IN A PARODY OF A THEN CURRENT EASTERN AIRLINES AD URGING PROTESTERS TO DESCEND ON THE 1972 CONVENTIONS IN MIAMI. AP/Wide World

Bill Zimmerman It was a totally different scene from Chicago. Chicago was a bunch of kids making a moral and righteous protest. In Miami it was like war. In Chicago there was still a feeling that we were right and could communicate our rightness to, if not Mayor Daley and the presidential nominees, at least some of the delegates and the public at large. But in Miami it was them against us. The war had gone on too long, there was no sense anymore that it could be ended. There was only a sense that it had to be won by the other side. That was the difference. In 1968 we were trying to get the U.S. out of Vietnam. In 1972 we wanted the Vietnamese to win.

Walter Philbin, *Miami policeman* Rocky Pomerance [the Miami Beach chief of police] used to tell us, "Just remember, every time you scratch your butt there's 10 million people looking at you on television. So be very careful what you do out there."

Flamingo Park was given over to the demonstrators as part of the co-optation strategy.

Gerry Rudoff There would be people screwing in Flamingo Park, right, and you'd just step over them. People doing dope, people swimming in the nude. I got the impression that Rocky's attitude was if we just don't look, in a few days it'll be over and everybody'll pick up and go home.

Ellis Rubin, *Miami attorney* I formed an organization called Operation Backbone, to stand up for your rights, because I really got angry when I saw the Vietcong flag marching down Washington Avenue, and Miami Beach Mayor Chuck Hall was there, joining with the protesters. I disagreed with their policy of co-optation. Rocky just didn't want a confrontation. I did. I wanted to stop them from espousing their ideals, which were very much opposed to mine and what I perceived to be [those of] the average American.

Walter Philbin Abbie and Jerry would have you think boy, don't fool with us. They'd talk almost like Hitler with their magic weapon. But in between that, they were comedians. They weren't our main concern. We could do business with them. They wanted fairness. And they couldn't believe it when they got it.

The arrests we made were mostly by scenario. In other words, we'd say, "We're gonna make some arrests." They'd say, "We'll give you seventy-five people in the intersection of Washington at the news time." This was what they wanted, news time, the publicity of arrests. And "There'll be no violence, you can make your arrests." And in many cases we just took 'em, put 'em in the vans, drove 'em around the corner and turned 'em loose. We planned all this over the table with them the day before.

Steve Berticelli, *Miami policeman* I doubt if there was two thousand people. And half the demonstrators were undercover people.

Rennie Davis There were plainclothes police everywhere, doing everything they could to support the Zippie position. The police were distributing Quaaludes in the park. Abbie was just trying to lay low and not take too many shots from his own people.

Dana Beal, *founder of New York Provo, cofounder of Zippies* The person who was running Abbie and Jerry's office, Fat Julie, was a fed. She got in there because nobody else wanted to be receptionist. Perfect job for a fed.

Walter Philbin Rubin and Hoffman were up in the Albion Hotel and we had that bugged.

Superjoel The fact that we all sat around the bar of the Albion Hotel and drank and watched television, instead of sitting around an apartment making acid cookies to straighten people out with, that was the most fundamental change.

Stew Albert I saw evidence of Abbie's manic-depression in Miami. He knocked on my door at two in the morning in a rage over something that had been written about him. He had walked from his room to my room through the hallway, naked. He didn't even seem to know it.

Jay Levin The Democratic convention was a party, from beginning to end. The first night I walked onto the convention floor, Larry O'Brien, the national chairman, was at the top of this huge blue podium, giving the welcoming address. At the bottom of the podium, on the floor, sitting cross-legged, looking out at the same audience as Larry O'Brien, is Allen Ginsberg going "Ommmm." I couldn't believe it. You could score any kind of drug you wanted, there was a transvestite section, lots of kids who'd been on the streets in 1968 were now delegates. Abbie and Jerry were greeted as heroes.

Ed Sanders There was not a clear message or image. We all had press passes. We were everywhere we wanted to be. So we were reduced to sound bites. There was Mike Wallace lumbering up to Rubin, "What do you think?" and Jerry made the mistake of saying something like Nixon is

POET ALLEN GINSBERG AND COMPANION PETER ORLOVSKY (LEFT) PROTEST THE CIA'S INVOLVEMENT IN THE HEROIN TRADE IN A UNIQUE WAY DURING DEMONSTRATIONS AT THE REPUBLICAN CONVENTION IN MIAMI IN 1972. Larry Sloman/Archive Photos

Hitler, which caused a big sound bite dearth afterwards. Abbie wasn't even good at that during the convention.

Stew Albert We showed some real political skill in Miami Beach. We came there with the whole town against us and we actually changed some attitudes toward us. Especially among the older people.

Jay Levin The Yippies tried to organize the old Jews. They told them the same administration that was gonna send their grandchildren to Vietnam was gonna take away their Social Security and their health care. But they did it in a playful way with a reminder that the Hasids were happy Jews.

Stew Albert We had picnics for them at the beach and speeches and they started coming to our office. I gave a speech saying, "Don't let the *meshugenas* get you down, we came here to give Nixon *tsores,* not you." Ginsberg chanted. Abbie wrote that poem in Yiddish, "Nixon Genug."

NIXON GENUG!

by Abbie Hoffman
(Translated by Motek and Jack Bramson)

Vos tutzick America?
Vuh bis der gaein?
Mit und ganise tacke Nixon
A vilder chiye tzmachen dem war in Vietnam
Un tucheslecher mit de ganse gesheft
Yentzer de urermer und kranke

(What's happened to you, America?
Where did you go?
With this smart-ass Nixon
A wild beast to make this war in Vietnam
An ass-licker of big business
Screwing the poor and the sick)

Vos tutzick America?
Vuh bis der gaein?
Mit un nishgutnick Nixon
Un shlump mit Mantovani records

Ver tzozugen un gansser yuntef in Miami
Uber tzegevden a shtickel white bread (Ech!)

(What's happened to you, America?
Where did you go?
With this no-goodnick Nixon
A shlump with Mantovani records
Enjoying a holiday in Miami
Here, have a piece of white bread [Ech!])

NIXON GENUG! NIXON GENUG!

(ENOUGH NIXON! ENOUGH NIXON!)

Lee Weiner While liberals may think of McGovern as their peak, I can assure them that the movement for change of America died on the streets of Miami. Or at least in that house on Biscayne Bay. We were being trivialized and lionized by people who had fantastic houses, huge lazy Susans filled with things which were not part of my mother's repertoire. It wasn't chopped liver. We were into more expensive drugs.

Carol Realini, *roommate of Jerry Rubin* I stayed at Margie Walker's huge, very luxe house in North Bay Road, a mansion with a swimming pool. That's where the hippest of the hip stayed during the conventions in 1972. Jack Nicholson was there with Julie Christie. Margie Walker's live-in lover was a very big mover of substances from South America. One day I came home and it was late at night and the swimming pool was filled with many people. Somebody grabbed me from underneath: it was Abbie. Abbie was going through a stage where he looked very ugly. He was a little overweight, his nose was very broken, his hair was a funny length. One of the first things he said to me was to apologize about his looks. I was a stranger and he was telling me that he doesn't always look like that.

Abbie went back to New York between conventions, where he met a beautiful young woman nicknamed Velocity. They started a torrid affair. When it was time to go back to Miami for the Republican convention, and because both of them were broke, Abbie concocted a scheme to get Velocity an assignment from Time *magazine to exclusively photograph the Yippies.*

Velocity aka Andrea Vaucher I told my husband I was going down but he had no idea that I was involved with Abbie. Jacques dropped me off and wanted to stay until my plane left. Finally we got on the plane and Abbie said, "Open your mouth," and I opened my mouth and he gave me my first Quaalude. Which kind of set the tone for this assignment.

Jay Levin Quaaludes showed up for the first time in a serious way in America that summer. The theory was that the CIA had brought 'em in to get everybody fucked up so serious political activity would not happen. And Nixon, paranoid that he was, feared McGovern. McGovern was the safe, clean edge of that myth that youthful energy could emerge in a wholesome form and heal the breaches between the demonstrators and the working class. So Nixon was worried.

Daniel Ellsberg The "plumbers" were hired to neutralize me. They included several people who had either advised or attempted to carry out assassinations in the past. Howard Hunt, for example, several times has reported officially advising the assassination of Castro. As Jonathan Marshall has revealed, Hunt, Liddy and others in the very spring of 1972 when they were operating against me and were caught in the Watergate were in the preliminary stages of an effort directed by the White House to assassinate Omar Torrijos, the president of Panama. This plan was aborted when they were caught in the Watergate.

Howard Hunt, Liddy, all these people involved themselves in an effort to "neutralize" me. At one point, in May of 1973, they were directed to "incapacitate Ellsberg totally." They used that euphemistic phrase but their prosecutor, William Merrill, who reported it to me, said that he had no doubt in his mind the intention was to kill me as I was giving a speech on the steps of the Capitol on May 3rd, 1972, which was just a month or so before they were caught in the Watergate. This was the same team that were simultaneously generating these plans for getting Abbie and Jerry. Jeb Magruder told his wife when she caught him burning thc documents about [their secret plan called] Gemstone in his fireplace that they had this plan for "kidnapping" Jerry and Abbie and taking them to Mexico. She said, "How would they get back?" And Magruder says in his book, "They might not get back." Meaning, they might be killed. And his wife said, "You can't do that, that's crazy." Magruder says, "I realized I said too much." Not that the idea was wrong but he shouldn't have mentioned it to his wife, who was, after all, a woman, and not reliable in such matters.

In this context we should remember that just six months earlier, in the fall of 1970, the CIA was implementing "Track II," directed by Nixon, to prevent the election of Salvador Allende in Chile. The plan was to "kidnap" General René Schneider, the chief of staff of the Chilean armed forces, who had refused to run a coup against Allende or block his election. This would be blamed on left-wingers and used as an excuse for martial law by other military. In the course of the "kidnapping," as could be expected, Schneider resisted and was shot to death. The similarity to what [Louis] Tackwood [an informant for the L.A. Police Department] reports that the Committee to Re-elect the President was considering as a possibility for San Diego just a year and a half later is very striking.

Getting back to my speech at the Capitol, I was going to talk about the mining of Haiphong that was shortly to come, so they wanted to shut me up. The plan was at least to break my legs and put me in the hospital, but Merrill thought undoubtedly they'd kill me. And the reason it didn't happen in this case was they came to suspect they were being set up to be the fall guys. So they blew the operation. But they didn't plan to stop with Watergate.

G. Gordon Liddy The Ellsberg thing, the break-in to the office of Dr. Fielding, who was a psychiatrist for Daniel Ellsberg in Beverly Hills, California, took place when I was a member of the White House staff, a member of the Special Investigations Unit. It was for national security reasons, after written instructions by superiors.

Ellsberg himself had said that he gave to the *New York Times* the large stack of top-secret cold war materials, documents, that goes now under the heading the Pentagon Papers. It was actually the history of the origin and development and prosecution of the Vietnamese War, a study in which he had been one of the contributors. And one can divide that study roughly into two parts: the first is that scholarly assessment of the war [with] countless citations from, excerpts from and references to top-secret cold war documents. The second half of the Pentagon Papers were full copies of all those documents. I think there were only seven people in the world who were cleared to have or review that study. Ellsberg had a copy of it and it was kept with the top-secret holdings of the Rand Corporation in Santa Monica, California.

The FBI found out several things. One, the Rand Corporation had been very lax in keeping the logs of its top-secret holdings, and so they really didn't know everything they had [or what] was missing. And the other thing was that Ellsberg, and he had several confederates, had admitted to taking out a lot more. No one knew what they had taken, where it was being kept, [or] what, if anything, Ellsberg intended to do with the remaining material that he had.

Then another thing happened. The FBI determined that someone, identity unknown at least at that time, had just given the whole shebang to the Soviet Embassy in Washington, D.C. Now, the significance of that was that it is my understanding that the *New York Times* actually did not publish everything received from Daniel Ellsberg. They looked at some of the underlying documents and said no, this is too hot. In effect if we publish this we're giving the Soviets the Rosetta stone. So the *New York Times* exercised restraint, for which I don't think they've ever been given credit. However, that was undermined when someone gave the whole shebang to the Soviets anyway. And we didn't know whether Ellsberg had done it or not. We were not sure whether Ellsberg was what he was being purported to be in much of the press, a loner acting out of conscience, or whether he had been recruited by the KGB. And so we said to the FBI, "What can you tell us about him?"

One of the things the FBI told us, which was undoubtedly from a wiretap, was that although Ellsberg had terminated the services of this psychiatrist named Fielding out in Beverly Hills, he nevertheless used to telephone him on an almost daily basis, all hours of the day and night, and discuss with him some of the most intimate details of his life. And we thought he might well have told the psychiatrist whether he was acting on his own or whether he in fact had been recruited by the KGB. So we said to the FBI, get the psychiatrist's files. The FBI tried and failed and it was then that we were ordered in writing to do so. Ultimately there was nothing of substance found in Fielding's office.

Daniel Ellsberg What they did against me gives a good deal of substance to the belief that they would have kidnapped or gone as far as [to] kill Abbie or Jerry. This gets to a point of a very great misunderstanding about Watergate and the war. Everybody says this was a mad operation by Nixon because he was certain to win the election. That's a historically wrong perception. Up until May 1972, it was touch and go and earlier Nixon was running third in public opinion polls, after Muskie and Wallace. He was slated to lose the election. A centrist Democrat, Muskie, was expected to be nominated and was first by a long shot, followed by Wallace. So if Wallace was in the race, Nixon was going to lose. They wanted to get Muskie out and they *had* to get Wallace out. And both of those things happened. Now, it may be that Bremer coming along and shooting Wallace was just luck. I think that's really quite implausible, actually. It seems more likely that Bremer was manipulated and his access to Wallace facilitated by others. But if Bremer acted totally on his own, and his motives remain very obscure, then I would say that he simply preempted an attempt by somebody else.

Nixon had previously been trying to get Wallace out by bribery to keep him from running as a third-party independent. And Wallace simply wouldn't agree not to run, to their great disappointment. And given that he wouldn't do it, they had an intense incentive to remove him from the race themselves. We now know that they had a team of professional assassins working on the election. So they had the ability, they had the people. It was only after Wallace was shot that the election became a sure win for Nixon. I believe that was a big factor in Humphrey and others not running and in letting McGovern take the nomination. It wasn't worth that much at that point. The point being that these plans for Abbie in San Diego were all laid well before Nixon had any prospect of any kind of victory.

Velocity aka Andrea Vaucher We met everybody. Norman Mailer and Daniel Ellsberg. I remember one incredible conversation in an elevator in the Fontainebleau with Clare Boothe Luce. We were on acid. Abbie turned to her and said, "Have you ever taken LSD?" There wasn't a hello spoken. And she said, "Yes, as a matter of fact I took it with Aldous Huxley," and she started telling us about her experiences on acid with Huxley. Then we got to the floor and said goodbye. That was a wild time.

Abbie was one of the greatest lovers I've ever had. First of all, when he's with you he's totally with you. I was married to a very, very handsome French racing car driver and Abbie wasn't my idea of a good-looking man. And he totally conquered me. He really appreciated my mind, appreciated my intellect. As a lover, he was wonderful, he was very kind, gentle, considerate. He was very passionate too.

Jeff Fogel, *Miami attorney, antiwar activist* The Yippies were going to go to the Republican Committee Headquarters at the Doral Hotel and throw up in the lobby as a symbolic expression of disgust with the nomination of Richard Nixon. I remember lengthy discussions the night before on what they had to eat. It was pizza and bananas and warm milk and peanut butter. So we got to the hotel but nobody could throw up.

Ed Sanders Abbie then was Mr. Fame. He was thinking about writing this book *Kiss and Tell,* chasing Shirley MacLaine around the Doral Hotel, trying to get a date with Gloria Steinem and Jane Fonda.

Gerry Rudoff Ellis Rubin got an injunction on the third night of the Republican convention to make Rocky [Pomerance] enforce the laws of the state of Florida. So then the arrests started.

Jeff Fogel Ultimately, I think about sixteen hundred people were busted in a couple of days there. The cops started using Mace and tear gas and there was some fighting in the streets. People were trying to get into the Miami Convention Center, they tried to bust through cordons of police.

Rennie Davis I was leading the march down the street and the police launched tear gas, the heavy Vietnam CS bad stuff. The first canister hit me right on the chest and exploded into my body. I hadn't had anything to eat for forty-two days and just took in all this poison and toxins. I almost died. I was unconscious for a while.

Velocity aka Andrea Vaucher We left a day earlier than we were supposed to because Abbie just couldn't take it anymore. We had come back to the Albion and they had pepper-gassed the whole place, and all the old people sitting on the porch were coughing.

Ed Sanders We were worrying about all these seniors getting teargassed, and right in the middle of an incredibly complicated confrontation Rubin said, "I am going to become a millionaire."

Walter Philbin There was a sense of disappointment in the press. There just wasn't any story. And after it was all over, we had to chase the kids out of the park because now it was going back to the public. They said they had nowhere to go. Don't you know, the police gave them money to get bus fare out of Miami. All the cops are giving two bucks here, three bucks here. I was a major, I gave five bucks. My own money. They wouldn't print that!

Rennie Davis After Miami, I spent three days in this bird sanctuary on an island off Tampa. My plan then was to take a year off and pitch a tepee on Gary Snyder's farm in California and go inward. Then the Paris peace accords were signed and I was invited to be a part of that. So I went. A friend of mine was on the plane as I went to Paris. He was on his way to India and offered to pick up my ticket. He said, "Let's go, the war's over, you deserve it. We'll visit the ashrams and sacred places of India." So I went with him and we wound up at this ashram where there were about thirty

Americans living with a young teacher. All of them had been in the antiwar movement. It was like a reunion in northern India.

I was initiated into a meditation. I was skeptical going into it but when I closed my eyes, a center opened in the brow of my head and suddenly there was light outside, inside, everywhere light. And I grasped who we were as a generation, that we had been present at the American Revolution, that we were a part of human evolution and that our juncture point would come in the 1990s with the turning of the millennium. Humanity would experience a quantum leap in understanding and consciousness.

All of this, in a moment, understood. The concept of inner light was something I had read about and felt an affinity towards. A true mystical experience was not something I was averse to. But Maharaj Ji, the young guru, in the beginning was difficult for me. I wanted to run the other way. But the experience he imparted to me was so beautiful that I dropped my resistance to him as well.

I was naive to go out and communicate all this in a twenty-two-city tour. I was just making my personal declaration. I was withdrawing from the antiwar movement. I communicated that we were entering a cycle of life where we reenter society. We'd have new lessons to learn, new experiences. We wouldn't be together as we had been. But we would come back together in the 1990s.

So a number of people, feeling betrayed by my new spirituality, threw eggs. That's what created the press stories. And that was basically the end of a public life for me. Abbie and Tom Hayden both had a similar reaction. Abbie made humor of it. Tom wondered if the whole time I was with the CIA. Abbie's reaction was more: where is this coming from?

Lee Weiner After Miami, I burned my fucking telephone book. I think the only person I talked to for the rest of 1972 was Ed. It was awful. It was very difficult to be in Miami and not understand that whatever fantasies one might have had about significant change in the United States were just that. And I will never ever be able to express the appreciation that I have towards the men's group who took me in, because I was really thrown out of every fucking other place. Which allowed me at least to have some sense of continuing connection. I was very lucky. Abbie wasn't lucky. Abbie didn't have a men's group. He needed a men's group. He needed something. We couldn't be friends. Look, I cared for Abbie very, very much and I think that if he had given either one of us the opportunity we would've come to love one another, okay? But I was busy saving myself and Abbie

RENNIE DAVIS RENOUNCED HIS PREVIOUS ANTIWAR ACTIVISM AND PAID PUBLIC HOMAGE TO HIS YOUTHFUL GURU IN A NUMBER OF CONTROVERSIAL PUBLIC APPEARANCES IN 1973.
Arthur Pollock

was having too good a time. So for Abbie I don't think that connection was there. Abbie went through terrible unconnected shit. We're talking about serious destruction. We're not talking small-time shit here. We're talking [Weatherman] Terry Robbins blowing himself into little tiny pieces of shredded meat. I'm not talking about symbolic endings. I'm talking about sitting in a restaurant in Brooklyn and pulling out my fucking telephone book and ripping out the pages and lighting them with a match. We're talking about people desperate to save their lives.

Carol Realini It was crystal-clear that Abbie and Jerry were over the hill age-wise. They could no longer represent youth culture. They had this book contract to do *Vote* and none of them wanted to do it.

Stew Albert They paid me $750 to take what they did and put it together. I couldn't synthesize Ed, so I just gave him a good title, "Ed Sanders Eats the Republicans," and I put Jerry and Abbie together and got *Vote* into something presentable. But the publishers didn't put it out until after the election. I think it was probably a conscious decision, because they thought it would hurt McGovern. That was the only theory I could come up with because the book is all about voting in the election.

* * *

Todd Gitlin There were two parts of the movement—a serious anti-war movement before students were themselves at risk, and a second, younger movement, a great deal of whose commitment to fighting against the war was based on the desire to protect its own collective ass. That part was mollifiable by the eighteen-year-old vote and especially the end of the draft.

Marty Kenner Nixon was smart. He ended the draft. He started an air war against the Vietnamese rather than a land war, and air war didn't take college kids, it took career air force soldiers dropping bombs on Vietnam. The movement began to slow.

Bill Zimmerman I think the main reason the movement broke down was that it didn't work. Every fall and every spring we had a half a million people show up in New York or Washington. Those were the largest, most democratic expressions of politics in the recent history of the country and they had no impact. Nixon watched the football game while half a million Americans were outside his door, expressing moral outrage at his policies.

Then they found this bizarre, horrible strategy, Vietnamizing the war, as they called it, which meant yellow corpses instead of white corpses, and somehow that was okay. As the antiwar movement widened to mainstream America, Nixon fixed it by bringing the ground troops home and reducing casualties by pursuing the same high levels of violence in Vietnam that he had pursued all along.

Wavy Gravy There wasn't much else going on, except trying to stop the war, twenty-five hours a day. So there was a vacuum when the war ended. For some of us, that's exactly what we were looking for, a little bit of a vacuum.

Chapter Seven

MAD ABOUT MOOLAH

Jean-Jacques Lebel At the end of the sixties, a lot of people went into diverse religious movements, or they became stockbrokers or teachers in universities, they became exactly those people that they were fighting against a few years before. You're a general without an army all of a sudden because the soldiers have disappeared.

Truusje Kushner At that point nobody understood the concept of flavor-of-the-month, Andy Warhol's famous for fifteen minutes. You didn't realize you were in vogue and then you weren't.

Jerry Rubin The real, vulnerable Abbie came out when his movement image was destroyed in the early seventies. There was this whole crushing of the movement leaders not just by Zippies, but by the mass media too. It was one day we're all heroes and the next day we're all jerks. I arrived once in Madison Square Garden and Peter Fonda rushed to touch my hand. Then a month later, Jerry and Abbie—oh, phonies, media freaks. It was over.

A. J. Weberman Abbie went through all kinds of craziness around that time.

John Lobell My wife and I are both architects living in New York and involved in the art world. It was the time of the sexual revolution, so we started having sex with our friends and writing about it. We had written this book *John and Mimi* and this agent, Marty Kenner, knew about us, and for some reason he told Abbie. One day the phone rang, "This is Abbie Hoffman. I hear you're writing a book. I'd like to see it."

After reading the manuscript, Abbie hung out with the Lobells and soon began joining them in sexual experimentation.

John Lobell One day he comes by and says, "I need your car." We had to do a radio interview so I gave him the keys to the car and just as we come back our car is pulling up and there's this huge blue tank of nitrous oxide in the trunk. He says, "You guys got to have an orgasm on this," so we're passing balloons around and staying up late into the night. After a while, we asked him how come he didn't come by with Anita. He says, "She's kind of suspicious of you guys. She's not ready."

Carol Realini Almost immediately, when I began being friendly with Abbie in New York, we became lovers. Everybody became lovers right away with Abbie; he had a fatal charm with women. His incredible humor and honesty is what did it for me. Aside from the fact that he was physically attractive. He had a very cute face and with those dimples, he had a great deal of boyishness about him. He did not have a good body. He was too short, and he had very short legs. But he wasn't fat, and he had a cute ass. But he had that incredible sense of humor. The unique thing to me about making love with Abbie was that it was always fun, it was never serious. So many times when you're fucking, your mind is wandering to 85 million places. With Abbie, he might be going down on me and I suddenly think of something that I absolutely had to tell him that was hysterical. And he'd crack up and then go right back to doing what he was doing before. He was very irreverent about something that people take too seriously.

Jeff Nightbyrd I've made love in the same room with Abbie. It wasn't quite an orgy but four people, that kind of thing. "How you doin' over there?" he'd call out from the couch. It was like you're all horseback riding. But very positive.

Carol Realini Abbie was having a million affairs that year. Hundreds of girls. I remember one day he came running into Prince Street, he was on cloud nine. I was in bed, it was late in the morning. My boyfriend, Jay [Levin], used to leave late in the morning to go home to Teaneck, then Abbie would come over after Jay left. So Abbie came running in and he said he wanted to jump right under the covers and fuck immediately while he was still hot from [this famous movie/television star]. He was so excited. He didn't make it with that many of them.

Alex Bennett I remember the night of Nixon's re-election at Jerry's Prince Street apartment with Lennon and Yoko and Ginsberg and Abbie and Phil. Here everybody had fought to keep this asshole from getting re-elected and forty-nine states voted for Nixon. Ed Sanders said, "Well, at least 45 percent of the public voted for sex, drugs and rock and roll!"

Carol Realini Jerry and I gave a party to watch the returns. Abbie had come right when the party was called for and there were maybe three other people there. He tried to talk to Jerry and gave up and then came in the bedroom and said, "What's going on, where's the party?" Then Abbie started asking me how I could stand to be Jerry's roommate. He was doing a terrible rap on Jerry, saying that Jerry was passé. By the time Abbie left there still were hardly any people there. Later on a couple of hundred people showed up.

John Lobell Abbie called up and he said, "I'm really depressed. I want to come over and hang out with you guys." I said, "Fine." We were flattered; like, gee, of all the people you know at a time of this political importance, you want to hang out with us, great! There was an interesting quote from that event. Abbie said, "I'd rather live in a country run by Richard Nixon than a country run by Tom Hayden."

Carol Realini There's one image from that party that I will never forget. Allen Ginsberg and Julian Beck lying in front of the TV, over there on the floor, stretched out in each other's arms, crying over the results and making out. It was very depressing. After a while the party thinned out and John and Yoko arrived with the Elephant's Memory band. They boomed in very noisily, raucous, very drunk. John Lennon had a half-drunk bottle of tequila in his hand and he was raving like a maniac, shouting at the top of his lungs, screaming for help, as was his wont. Up until let's say that afternoon, he thought there was gonna be a revolution, led by Abbie and Jerry, these great American radicals who he believed in. Now it seems like it was going down the drain because here is Nixon getting elected by this huge landslide. Lennon looked around and he saw Jerry Rubin and Judith Malina and Julian Beck and Ginsberg, these heavy faces that he recognizes as leaders of the so-called revolution, so what are they gonna do and when is it gonna happen and what can he do to help? And he wasn't kidding.

The truth was that he actually was looking at these people as some kind of heroes. That day was an epiphany in his life. He was screaming his guts out that he couldn't have any heroes either. How could he have been so stupid to be telling his fans and his public that he couldn't be their hero, when in fact he was doing the same thing, creating heroes in his own mind, one of whom was actually Jerry Rubin and was sitting there in the room with him?

Everybody was dumbfounded, but most of all Jerry. He was completely tongue-tied. Jerry had John Lennon for a hero, and John had Jerry for a hero. And here are these two schmucks, neither one of whom could be my kid's hero. As shitty and horrible as Jerry was, I'm sorry to say I think that John was a lot like that too. I had gone over to their place with Jerry a few times before the party. Almost all the times that I had gone over there, John was sitting in the bed watching television with the radio and the stereo on and this bed strewn with everything, and Jerry would sit at his feet, like paying homage. Yoko and I would be sitting in the other room smoking pot. Once she found out that I was enamored of Quaaludes, she confessed she too was enamored of Quaaludes, so we started getting stoned on Quaaludes and I would just listen to her tell me her whole life story eighteen times, totally kvetching about all her troubles. She's a big complainer. I never talked to John when we were over there because he basically didn't talk, he was like catatonic.

So here is Lennon, at our apartment, having a nervous breakdown, and Jerry couldn't say a word. It was left to Julian and Judith and Steve Ben [Israel] to do what they could to calm him down. He was really out there. He was getting more and more sober every second as the realizations were starting to penetrate, that this was like the end of his whole life. Because then, at the same time, it was "I don't want to be John and Yoko anymore. I'm through, I had enough, I can't stand it, I don't want her." He looked at her and said, "I don't want you." Then he said to everyone, "I don't want her." It was very heavy. He was practically having epileptic fits. This was going on in the bedroom. So finally John calmed down, he came in the other room where there were other people, and tried to start acting normal and socialize. It was back to having a party again. He came over to me—I used to wear a nose ring—telling me how fascinated he was with my nose ring. How he's been looking at me and my nose ring for the last few weeks every time I come over to his house and I shouldn't think he didn't notice just because he didn't say anything. And he's been dreaming all these weeks about sucking my nose ring. Now, is that a line? Even I have my weaknesses. I had to let the guy suck my nose ring. And so we were literally standing in the middle of the living room with him sucking my nose ring in front of everybody.

He was going "ummmm, ummmmm, this is so good." Eventually he was kissing me instead of my nose ring. I got very embarrassed. On the other hand, I didn't want to throw this guy away, I will admit, it was John Lennon. Two seconds earlier, I had just witnessed the guy having a nervous breakdown, and I wasn't ready to push him away and reject him. He was a complete wreck, his whole body and arms and hands were trembling. So I took him in the bedroom and put him on the water bed and I thought he'll probably pass out. I went in the other room and I said to Jerry, "Get people out of here, let him go to sleep. It's my room, he can have my bed, I'll sleep on the couch." Okay, so everyone left. And the only people left in the apartment were me and Jerry, John and Yoko, and Lola Cohen and this fellow James (a pseudonym), who was working for the Lennons at the time as their so-called secretary. He went everywhere with them. He turned out to be their dope-holder, because they were junkies at the time.

John woke right up and came out and took me in the bedroom. I totally cooperated with him and we got into a total sex trip. I couldn't stand knowing that his wife was listening to us in the next room since I had recently become friendly with her and I was fond of her. So I told him we should go downstairs to the basement. He was unclear on where he was, he was so fucked up. And he made me explain everything to him. He thought he was in Jerry's house and that I would have to go home somewhere and he wanted to take me home. "I'm sorry, we are home, this is where I live." That's when he snapped out of it and sobered up and he realized what was going on, and that his wife was in the next room listening to him making out with me. And he didn't care. His attitude was "fuck her." So we went downstairs to the basement and he told me that before he and Yoko married, they made a pact and were totally monogamous for all the time up until that moment. It's true, she told me. And he told me he wanted to break the pact. He wanted her to know that he was through with her and he had been trying to tell her this for some time and he couldn't get through to her. He felt the one way that he could get through to her would be to break the pact in a way that she would know he broke the pact. He wanted to use me for that. I agreed to let him use me.

He told me so many things that night. The first thing was that he was a junkie, addicted to heroin, because he was afraid he wouldn't be able to perform sexually. Eventually the whole house went to sleep. Jerry and

Yoko went to sleep in the bedroom, and Lola fucked James that night. Lola claimed that she heard Jerry and Yoko fucking. But I don't believe that Yoko and Jerry made it, no way. Are you kidding? Yoko and John had that pact. Even if he was breaking it, she certainly wouldn't break it with Jerry Rubin, the schlemiel of all time. So that was a heavy night, that election night.

Robin Palmer I was in Attica for three years. I was in with Sam Melville and Sam was like an icon. He was so stand-up, he was so respected by all the elements. He was one of the few whites that the blacks respected. I got some of that reflected glory because I was clearly Sam's rib. They put us in different parts of the prison but during the four days in the inmates' takeover of Attica, we were together. And Sam was murdered in the massacre. He was closer than you are to me when he was killed.

Anita Hoffman Those were very trying times. All the bad stuff from the fame was on Abbie's head, the fight over *Steal This Book,* the movement backbiting, the holier-than-thou . . . everybody trying to out-macho, gut-checking, "I'm more into violence than you." I just couldn't take the life, the surveillance, the groupies. Also, I had really had it with the city. I just wanted to have a normal life.

Anita's mother bought a house for them in Springs, New York. Abbie and Anita were to pay the mortgage.

Anita Hoffman I first moved out there as an act of rebellion against Abbie. He didn't want to come, so then he was really angry and jealous because this was the first really independent thing I did without him. But I think he really missed me and he came out to visit; then he really loved it. He started coming more and more. A lot of times he'd have to be in the city during the week but he'd come out on the weekends and he'd bring friends.

Carol Realini Jay and I went out there for the weekend and it was bizarre. They had planted a garden, they were growing tomatoes, they had Butterscotch the golden retriever. Six different kids came to mow the lawn. I said, "My God, Mr. Suburbia, I'm gonna blackmail you. Your image will be ruined."

Anita Hoffman We sent away to get these free pine trees from New York State as part of conservation efforts, and we planted them all around in the woods. We made this wonderful garden. If we were preparing a meal, you'd just run out and break off a few leaves of lettuce. We had one of those Mexican hammocks, and he built a swing for the kid, and we had a puppy.

Carol Realini He could never stay there more than three days in a row. That's why he spent so much time crashing at my place on Prince Street. He didn't keep another place in the city, so he had to be sleeping either with his girl of the moment or downstairs in the basement on Prince Street. You had the kid in the crib, Anita living this life of suburban housewife and Abbie alternating between this housewife life and raving out in the city.

Cora Weiss, *antiwar activist* He came to our summer home in Long Island when I was rototilling a garden. He taught me how to mulch with hay and how to use flowers in salads. That was in the early 1970s when it wasn't chic yet in the American gourmet cuisine to do those things. He also taught me how to fry blossoms in batter. Have you ever had fried nasturtium blossoms in batter? They're terrific.

America Hoffman I have some really small memories from the Hamptons of just being on the beach with him. I remember chasing a squirrel. We left there when I was three. He used to call me Junior a lot of times. Most of the time he just called me Kid. He usually referred to me as third person. Like "What are you gonna do with the kid?"

Carol Realini Abbie didn't have anything whatsoever to do with the raising of the kid. Abbie used to give the kid shoplifting lessons. At the time, he always used to say he hoped his kid would grow up to kill Rockefeller. He used to tell america that that's what he was being groomed for, to be Rockefeller's assassin.

Rudi Stern Posing, a lot of posing. The glib father, the close father, the father and the kid, a lot of family tableaus for other people's effect. Not the kind of hugging that's from inside.

Jerry Lieberman, *Abbie's brother-in-law* One night while we were all living in the Hamptons, I screened a reel of my commercials. Abbie came up to me later and said, "I really admire what you do. If I had to do it all over again, I would go into advertising, be a copywriter. As a matter of fact, I have some ideas for some commercials. Maybe you could peddle them for me, just don't tell anyone who came up with the ideas." He gave me some ideas. I didn't think any of them were good, so I didn't do anything with them. One of my clients at the time was Levi's. One of his ideas involved elves making jeans in factories.

Rudi Stern Abbie became a social quantity in the Hamptons. He and Anita were very popular with all kinds of people. It was a thing to have Abbie there with so-and-so, with Terry Southern there, Larry Rivers there. There were politicians, there were artists, there were scammers.

Truusje Kushner He would cook, that was his creative outlet. He'd have the blenders going and he was pretty messy in the kitchen. If you'd go out and buy a fish, you couldn't just broil it. Stuff it! It was always like some major production. If you weren't cooking, you had to be gardening. If you weren't gardening, go visit this one and that one. All these famous painters were there. De Kooning's daughter was the kid's baby-sitter. And Larry Rivers is as crazy as Abbie is so you can imagine what the two of them were like together.

Jerry Lieberman Abbie wanted to write. He did get assignments to do things for magazines and he tried to do it but it's a gray, depressing winter out there and I think that he got very disenchanted and he missed the city. He wasn't able to work out there.

Joie Davidow, *writer* When we were out in the country he left [to] go into the city. We were out there for days and he didn't call. I said to Anita, "Isn't that kind of funny? You would call me to tell me you got there all right."

Susan Carey I never understood how that open marriage thing worked. Although I know Anita did have a couple of affairs, it wasn't what she wanted.

From Abbie Hoffman Interview with Barry Shapiro

Abbie Hoffman: I think I got an illness, satyriasis. Pan, bouncing around the woods, playing the pipe, making love all the time. I've done other fucking more than Anita. I relate to women sexually.

Barry Shapiro: Why is it a sickness?

Abbie Hoffman: Because why should you? I don't relate to guys sexually. I picked up a guy once when I was seventeen. After I broke up with a girl. He blew me twice. Larry Rivers said you can't really understand being blown unless you've had a cock in your mouth.

Barry Shapiro: What kind of feelings do you have about Anita balling other people?

Abbie Hoffman: It's pretty rare. No problems. I encourage that. I would have feelings if she had a very close emotional relationship with a male.

Anita Hoffman We had this ethic about free love and all. I was not supposed to be jealous, so I was repressing it, which adds all the more to your resentment. I did know that he loved me and I loved him. But still, it was complicated.

Joie Davidow Anita started a women's group. We called it consciousness-raising but basically we bitched about the men.

Laura Cavestani, *video artist* Anita would complain that Abbie wanted sex too much, every night, and just kept doing it and doing it and doing it until she just wanted him to finish, because she would get sore. And all the other women were going "ohhhhh," rubbing their hands together, wanting some, "Oh, what a stud Abbie is."

Joe LoGuidice It'd reached the point where all of us had slept with everybody else. As always, Abbie was supplying most of the energy. He even brought in the Lobells, to instruct us all in how to be more sexually free and not get jealousies. They would come over out in the Hamptons and end up fighting all night between themselves because nobody wanted to fuck them. It was insane.

John Lobell We finally met Anita at a party on Long Island. She wasn't sure if she likes [all] this. We went upstairs to a bedroom with her and Abbie says, "Can I come in?" We said, "No, this is just for Anita." She really liked that because even though he's a nice guy and a real feminist, he's an overwhelming presence. Then I said, "What we're gonna do is number one, my pants are not gonna come off. And number two, we're gonna do anything you want and we're not gonna do anything you don't want." So the three of us played around in bed and I think we might've had a vibrator. After that we would all hang out together.

Mimi Lobell Once Abbie and John were both making love to Anita at the same time and she really got into it. It very much liberated her. She had been putting all of these energies into the political arena and she had forgotten that she was also this passionate woman.

John Lobell We're serious Buddhists but Abbie wasn't interested in any of that. He said, "My idea of complete serenity is at the center of a riot, that's my idea of serene."

Rudi Stern That summer Abbie was always fucking his brains out. Or wanting to fuck his brains out. I think Abbie had increasing problems getting it up. Abbie was with a lot of girls. But he did it in a way that was very, very insensitive. Everybody was out playing around but you didn't push it in people's faces, hurt people with it. Joie had a short involvement with Abbie that upset me a lot, not because it happened, but the way Abbie handled it with me. It's part of why a very wonderful relationship split up. He denied it and he was greasy about it. Joie told me about the impotence. She said, "Rudi, don't get upset, he can't get it up. It never happened." But I went bonkers. I promptly got involved with a much younger woman, of course, always younger, and went off with her to Haiti and devastated Joie. I handled it terribly.

* * *

Abbie Hoffman *(interviewed by Barry Shapiro, 2/21/73)* I'm an ultimate nonconformist. Death before work. It's a tragedy now that I gotta find a job. I feel very, very isolated. I don't see personal happiness. I liked being the hero. But I understand its limitations. It has to end in death. There's a lot of happiness being a moralist if it's connected with your creative impulses, your art, and your pleasure. There's no separation between what is fun and what's good. 1966, '67, that was the happiest that I've ever been.

The opportunities to defy authority don't come that often now. I think my brushes with the law from now on will be of a criminal nature if there are any. Well, if you read *Steal This Book,* you tread the boundary between criminality and revolutionary activity. There were big debates in *Win* magazine after *Steal This Book* came out about whether the ripping-off ethic is revolutionary or not.

I'll tell you why I said I'm moving into criminality. One of my best friends and I had a good discussion here a couple of weeks ago. We're writing a screenplay about it. He's talking to his automobile insurance agency, right, a receptionist, and all of a sudden there's a free connection, which'll be the title of the film. And they hear two Mafia types discussing a dope transaction and $300,000 in cash, where they're gonna meet, a newsstand here in New York.

Abbie told Shapiro that he, his friend and his friend's wife actually went to the drop-off site and planned to create a diversion and rip off the dealers but, as they later learned, the receptionist from the insurance agency had informed the police and the area was saturated with undercover agents, so the dealers wisely called off the transaction.

Abbie Hoffman See, my mind is back into the criminality, ripping off a bundle. Life is play, death is work. Although criminality in itself is a kind of work. I bet a lot, on the football games. I've been talking to bookies a lot more, thinking about playing poker again. I hustled some pool at a fucking intellectual party and they didn't pay me, they said I was too fucking good and that I hustled them. So I got to sharpen up so I'm not so good. I forgot, I just opened up and was putting on a performance which is not good if you're gonna hustle.

Barry Shapiro Always gonna be somebody that's gonna beat you.

Abbie Hoffman Not in the little role that we carved out. The little Yippie role. Who's the next generation? Who are the next leaders? Who's gonna go to jail? Let's talk like business opportunities, there were openings in the revolutionary biz for good women leaders. Although they had to go more feminist than Left. Then there was another area—the violence. Violence was a new area opening up for whites. There was Mark Rudd and Bernadine. Then we got into the underground movement. Because we became famous, we got thrust into a national leadership position because we were able to mobilize a number of national demonstrations without being forced to go underground, exiled, dead, be in prison. But in a sense, that number had been done. We were the last national mobilization leaders as personalities.

I conceive of dying as a revolutionary act now. I see suicide now in a different light. I had flashes of committing suicide. I think it's time for me to die. I got three years. I'm supposed to die in my thirties. People I admire generally did. Modigliani, Che Guevara, Lenny Bruce, Marilyn Monroe, Christ. People get superenthusiastic about life, I'm not as enthusiastic as I was before, I'm not sure that I have the talent.

Barry Shapiro But this role is not one you see yourself overcoming?

Abbie Hoffman Which role? The El Yippie? I'm trying. I'm considering going into the movies. I've had offers but they're all offers to play myself. I want it not to be a rip-off thing, like a Jim Brown, like the athletes that go into the movies. I want to try it as a skill. But not as a career. If you were to say to me here's $200,000, you would never hear or see me again. I would leave the country. I would give it to this accountant and he would take care of those kids.

* * *

Jerry Lieberman Abbie was always talking about deals, about trying to promote some idea of his. And they never worked out. He was a loser, in a commercial sense of the word.

Joie Davidow He was still a star. The trouble was he didn't have money. He was taking reviewer's copies of records into New York and selling them on 14th Street to raise money. They were broke.

Abbie Hoffman *(interviewed by Barry Shapiro, 2/27/73)* I gotta help my kids. So now I gotta get some bread. But it's not a big thing. It's not gonna ruin my life. No, no. I'd die before that. Like I told you we had all those offers. It's a crazy area, where I really had to take a purist stance. Saying no, none of these deals. There's no way of dealing with that kind of level of fame and do what I want to do, which is going around to campuses, start riots, end the war, those kinds of things.

I'm a product of my environment. I'm more a symbol than a leader. When Ali got beat, that became a symbol for me, of the death of our kind of heroes. Now we're gonna see Nixon heroes. D. W. Cooper, the skyjacker, Clifford Irving, somewhat? Mark Spitz. Bobby Fischer. There's something in common with all of them. Personal greed.

Patsy Cummings, *Joe LoGuidice's girlfriend* I think he wanted to get together a pile of money and just go off somewhere. We had just discovered Zihuatanejo at this time.

Joe LoGuidice Zihuatanejo is where Leary hid out for about two years. It was this isolated little Mexican village with a long history of speed and amphetamines and acid. There were these Indians walking around and then you went to the pharmacy and you said gimme one hundred Quaaludes and they gave 'em to you. When we came back I says, "Abbie, I think I found heaven." So we decided we were gonna set up this artists' hideaway spot, a little colony for writers and filmmakers.

Stella Resnick I met Jerry in San Francisco in 1973. I was a psychologist and I had a very successful practice by that point. Jerry was getting into the human potential movement, healing himself of his rage. He had given up smoking and he'd lost weight and been doing psychotherapy and he'd become a vegetarian and he'd done yoga and he went running. He did everything that he could to reprogram himself.

I met Abbie that June of 1973. He was leaning on the door to the bedroom at that apartment on Prince Street. I remember being impressed with how soft-spoken he was and how humble he felt to me. His voice was soft, he looked down a lot, and he seemed a little shy. I could sense in Abbie a lot of disappointment with how things were turning out. Money was such an issue for him. The first day I met him he said money's tight and he had two families to support.

Jerry Rubin Abbie said, "I used to have sex fantasies, now I have money fantasies. I just go to bed at night dreaming about money."

Anita Hoffman Abbie was very bad with money, careless and not well organized. We were living in my mother's house in East Hampton and we were paying the mortgage. That's one of the reasons that he wanted to do a sequel to *Steal This Book*.

Rudi Stern Abbie was promoting his telephone box, the blue box that enabled you to go into a phone booth and dial around the world. It was being sold for a lot of money but it was well worth it.

One of the offshoots of the Diggers and the Yippies were the phone phreaks, a loosely organized group of pirates who delighted in ripping off Ma Bell by devising ingenious ways to make calls for free.

After a while, Yippie phone phreaks were distributing many different boxes that produced tones that accessed free phone service. One of these, the black box, enabled anyone to make a free long-distance phone call from any pay telephone. The blue box gave the user free long-distance service from both a pay phone and a home phone. The Boxman, a former grass dealer, was one of the first distributors of these devices.

Boxman The box that we made, the blue box, we were selling for $500 per. I got a call from someone who claimed to be Howie Samuels. Abbie used that pseudonym whenever he called me on the phone because of his general paranoia about the telephone. Of course when he came over I knew who he was. But he stuck to the name nonetheless. Abbie bought one for himself and he was thrilled with it. He must've used it to death because he kept coming back for repairs. In one year, he brought it back four or five times for repairs, but each time he came back he bought another one. My sense was Abbie was a scam artist. And a guy who was desperate for money.

* * *

Abbie Hoffman *(interviewed by Barry Shapiro, 3/5/73)* In a period like now, you get down about the feelings everyone has about no cause worth fighting for. When there's an active movement you feel that your individual actions are part of a general force, so that it's not a meaningless gesture.

I remember living through the fifties and getting along quite well without doing any good. I wasn't raised in a commie intellectual-type family. As the sixties became the sixties, that's when I got it. I got to see blacks demonstrating outside of Woolworth's, being carted off to jail in small southern towns. I remember seeing them on TV singing freedom songs and saying there's something happening in their lives which is not happening in mine right now, maybe there's something about this working for good, putting your energy into something else than making money or a career. There was also an exhibitionist quality about it. A way of getting known, having an identity, whether to yourself or to the world. "Who are you?" "I'm a freedom fighter." It felt better with me if people said, "Oh, he's a civil rights worker" than "He's a doctor" or "He's a psychologist." Or "He's a nice Jewish boy."

Barry Shapiro You seem more depressed today. Last week you were so excited.

Abbie Hoffman Anita and I were together and we're now apart. That's why I'm down. Right now I have fantasies of being with Anita in the woods with the kid and a dog.

Barry Shapiro Why don't you do that?

Abbie Hoffman Money. I've been having money fantasies. I haven't had that for ten years. I'm going to make this killing. The get-rich-quick schemo. That's a money fantasy, right?

Now as I look at myself I've got the same kind of goals as most people in the world—I want to make some money, to have some security, to make sure my kids are provided for. So I don't know if that's selling out or what.

* * *

Gus Reichbach Abbie was being trashed for being rich and he didn't have a dime. He was moving and welcomed in a celebrity-filled high-flying world, where there was wealth beyond imagination. He probably at that time would've entertained some merchandising things, but [in] the Nixon era, he was not that merchandisable. Of course he was going around speaking where he could, he was always trying to peddle a book project. And I guess the time comes to get into the whole interaction between the counterculture and the drug culture.

There was a celebration in the counterculture of living outside the system. The early drug entrepreneurs were by and large hippies who were supplying drugs to the counterculture. As pot crept into the mainline structure, it was becoming a more profitable undertaking, but the sensibility was still rooted in the counterculture. These were people who gave money to various political causes on the sly. And there was certainly a romanticism of the smuggler outlaw which fed beautifully into Abbie's own image of himself as an outlaw and a hustler.

Jay Levin Cocaine was hot from 1971 on. Originally people thought it was just like marijuana. It was from the natives, a natural, organic substance. It did not have any of the dark, criminal sensibility, for the counterculture at least, that it would later develop in the culture. And of course, since it was more expensive than marijuana, it was done often in the hipoisie circles, the hip capitalists who would talk the talk but never walk the walk. Abbie knew some of those people. Then it became popular among the artists' and musicians' set.

Carol Realini It's such a wonderment to me that he liked cocaine, because he had so much natural energy. And he really loved coke, it was his drug of choice. But he didn't abuse. I don't remember him getting that horrible cocaine personality.

Marty Kenner We'd go out to East Hampton when I was Abbie's literary agent. We'd shoot guns in the backyard at beer cans and have laughing gas and coke at night.

Anita Hoffman He never got into it heavily because we couldn't afford it. We never paid for coke. But I think it did have the effect of setting off his illness, setting off a manic state.

Joe LoGuidice Everybody was doing a lot of coke, everybody. As much as you could get your hands on. And there was a certain amount of that kind of dealing that comes with well, we'll split an ounce and you'll get this, and we'll cut the cost down. But Abbie always had a different metabolism from the rest of us. I did a snort and I'd get high. He'd do the same snort and he'd get completely out of his gourd. He had a much more hyper, significant reaction to almost anything.

Superjoel This might be kind of gnarly to have to cop to but I was one of the people who turned Abbie on to drug dealing. I was in the closet about my drug thing in those days because it seemed to take away from the legitimacy of our antiwar efforts. So I kept my little secret life that provided me with the funds to do this shit. You know what my kids got for the seventies, after the Vietnam War was over? Money—millions and millions and millions of dollars. When I got really disillusioned with the political stuff, I just went full out into the drug business. I was manufacturing LSD and then I branched off into the coke business. My kids grew up skateboarding up to the door of our Lear jet. My son, when he was twelve, knew how to call the limo service and get the ultrastretch. Little Francesca was the hostess on the Lear because she was the only one who could stand up, full up, and walk back and forth to serve drinks. So I'm one of the people who turned Abbie on to the benefits of drug dealing. I always did feel bad that maybe his third time out he got popped.

Sal Gianetta Cocaine is a strange drug. When certain people get their hands on it, it becomes so much a part of their support system that they're not even aware of it. He was among the worst I've ever seen. I should've known he was starting to set up a network to move shit, because now I can look back, the conversation came a lot to certain aspects of smuggling. But we talked about the stupidity of trying, especially in the 1970s, to move shit in. I had told him there's only two or three ways you can get caught smuggling. The telephone and strangers.

A. J. Weberman I said to Forcade, "We're gonna fuck up Abbie good." He said, "Weberman, don't waste your fucking time. I got news for you, man. Abbie's gonna get himself popped."

Sportsman Abbie and I had gotten to be friendly because he used to like to come up to my house to meet women, because I was dealing coke. He talked about needing money for some causes. I guess he supported a lot of people.

Diane Peterson I met Abbie through my friend Linda. She made me go out to dinner with them. And he did his usual thing, if you've ever been to dinner with him, playing with the chicken bones and flipping spoons and making hats and brassieres out of napkins. He did a back flip in the lobby of her building on East 61st Street while people are coming out of the elevator. He went into a market down the street and stole a couple things. He'd just taken two Quaaludes and he was just flying.

MAY 1973

Daniel Ellsberg We had lunch in Washington after my trial. It was a time when I perceived us both as being very out of key with the country. After the Paris accords the country just accepted what the administration was saying, which was the war is over. I'd say, "The war isn't over. We're bombing!" In that spirit I remember being impressed at how committed Abbie remained and how depressed he was about the situation.

Sportsman We had done some business. The first time Abbie came he said, "Look, you have a good reputation, here's some blow, pay me when you have the money." It was white, regular blow. The first time he brought me either half an ounce or an ounce. When I sold it, he gave me more.

Laura Cavestani Our friends came back from the Hamptons and said we're really worried about Abbie because he's going to these bars and dealing coke openly.

Frank Cavestani, *video artist* Abbie thought he was gonna make $30–$40,000 in a night. If he thought about it, it's too good to be true.

Carol Realini For days at least, if not weeks, the product was being batted around the Chelsea Hotel and Abbie was asking people to help him off the stuff.

Joie Davidow One of the first times I ever did coke was that coke. It was pure. I didn't have much to compare it to. I got really paranoid.

Stew Albert I knew that Abbie was dealing. Later on he made this big painful confession to me that he had really done it and was guilty but he forgot that he had offered to cut me in on the deal.

Jerry Rubin He tried to get me to invest. He wrote me a letter saying I wouldn't do anything like that without letting my buddy in on this. Send me two grand but I need it by Monday. I went to Western Union with $2,000 in cash. Western Union doesn't take cash anymore. They send $2,000 but they charge like fifty bucks. I said fuck this, man. I thought hey, till Monday, he can wait. So I wrote him a check for $2,000 and I mailed it to him. About a week later he sent me the check back and said, "Too bad, money came too late, next time." Then he was busted. Am I lucky or what?

Sportsman We built up a nice relationship. I had given him some money, I think $6,000, to buy some blow, maybe two weeks before he got busted.

Diane Peterson He explained to me that he had been accompanying various underground types, doing various kinds of crimes and writing about it and this was going to be another one, and we were gonna hang out, and would I like to come along? It's gonna be a lot of fun.

Gus Reichbach Carol Ramer was Abbie's secretary/administrative assistant/gofer. She had worked at the Law Commune. Carol had some guy John Rinaldi who was an Italian from Brooklyn, who knew some other Italians. Through winks and nods Abbie was led to believe that the friends of the friends were somehow connected to the mob. The idea was to do a dope deal and rip off the mob by stepping on the product a couple of times. Abbie was not gonna put a gun to someone's head, but short 'em on the weight, again showing Abbie's sense of invulnerability. He thought he could tweak the mob's nose and get away with it. Here's one of the most famous faces in America; that's a recklessness born of enormous ego. And a certain hubris.

Ken Kelley He said, "I was stupid, stupid, stupid, stupid." He was convinced the guys were both Mafiosi and cops. Cops on the take.

Arthur Nascarella I had been in Brooklyn South Narcotics Division for a year. I had tried to become an undercover on a couple of occasions but I was too big, I didn't fit the profile. I had a friend in Queens, the kid brother of a guy I grew up with, a kind of a peripheral wise guy, and he had always told me that if I ever got to Queens and he could help me out with anything, give him a call. So lo and behold, I got transferred to Queens. I got in touch with my friend and said, "You hear anything in the street?" He said if he heard anything he would call.

One day we were working on a buy operation. We had an undercover on the beach in Rockaway, we were up on the roof making surveillance of him attempting to make buys. And we were floating in from Rockaway, I called the office and I had a message from my buddy. I gave him a call. He says to me, "Listen, I got a guy who wants to sell three pounds of cocaine. You wanna buy it?" I says, "Yeah, of course. Who is the guy?" Again, you have to take this with a certain degree of skepticism. In 1973 three pounds of cocaine was fucking unheard-of, particularly on a one-on-one sales situation. I guess guys had made a kilo-or-better arrests but essentially they tripped over them. To my recollection, nobody ever sat down and bought that much coke at a clip. I said, "Who's the guy?" He says, "He's a Jewish fellow, he's always on *Johnny Carson.* His name is Hoofer, Heefer, Hoff . . ." I said, "You talking about Abbie Hoffman?" He says, "Yeah, Abbie Hoffman, that's right." I says, "Yeah, Guido, yeah, right." You gotta understand this guy's a heavy Italian guy, from Brooklyn. For this guy to have a way into Abbie Hoffman is like I fucked Raisa Gorbachev. I says, "All right, I'll listen." He says, "Be at my store about ten o'clock tonight, he's gonna make an introduction." He had a small superette on Seagirt Boulevard, in Far Rockaway. So I went back and got the team together.

We decided to go in as Italian wise guys. That's not much of a stretch for me nor the kid I picked as my partner, Bobby Sasso. Ten o'clock that night we drove out to Rockaway and we meet my buddy and he makes an introduction of us to a guy named John Rinaldi. Rinaldi's driving a Mercedes, nice-looking kid, and he asks us to follow him into Manhattan. So we get into the car and we go into the city and we wind up across the street from the 10th Precinct, somewhere on the West Side. Rinaldi brings us up and it turns out to be an apartment of a woman named Carol Ramer.

Ramer lets us in and it's a pad of the day, 1973. You sit on the floor and you burn incense and listen to fucking Ravi Shankar, a lot of sitar solos. We engage in a conversation with Rinaldi. After a little while, the doorbell rings and fucking Abbie Hoffman walks in the fucking door with this skinny, waspy-looking chick named Diane Peterson. Introductions are made. I told him I was Louie, Bobby said he was Frankie or something like that. Abbie introduced himself as John Mitchell. He's got a sense of humor, the guy. We spent maybe an hour at Ramer's apartment. We didn't cop to knowing who he was. Look, he perceived that we were bullshitting him in terms of who we were. So he made a game of it. But he thought we were wise guys.

As a rookie cop, I had been sent to Columbia during the riots. I knew who the guy was, I'd seen him plenty of times. I had read a couple of his books, to be honest with you. Understand something: unfortunately, because you wore a blue uniform, people packaged you and categorized you. I was twenty-nine at that point. I had a lot of things that I agreed with in terms of the antiwar movement, but because I was a cop, I wasn't allowed to have an opinion. I guess that's one of the reasons I wound up going to college for nine years and I got a master's degree, only because I didn't want to stick around bars and listen to "Guess who I beat the shit out of today?" I knew there was more to the world.

Anyway, I had read *Steal This Book* and I thought him going to the House Un-American Activities Committee dressed up as an Indian and him lighting up a stinkpot at Con Edison, I mean the guy was a master media manipulator, there's no two ways about it. Every time he fucking opened his mouth he had five hundred cameras, you understand?

Diane Peterson One of them was *very* good-looking, I was thinking he's the Al Pacino type, and the other one was big and loud, he was supposed to be the pistolero. Something was supposed to happen that night and then it wasn't gonna happen that night, it was gonna happen the next day. That was the first time I'd met Carol and John Rinaldi. He was the one who did all the introducing. And it seems that Sasso, the Al Pacino type, was connected, but was also a cop. But John had no way of knowing.

Arthur Nascarella We sit down with these people and they break out some cocaine. They pass it around to us. You fake it the best way you can. Thank God, every time they would hit it they would go into this ecstasy kind of a situation, you would have to go "ooh ooh far out," which would give me two seconds to fake my shit, 'cause it only went around once.

So Bobby says to the kid, I understand you got a package to move. We start talking business and Abbie says, "I got the best coke in New Yawk," blah blah blah. I says, "Look, I want to taste it." He had the three pounds on him right then and he wanted to do the fucking package as we sat there. This was our first inclination that we're dealing with someone who didn't know what the fuck they were doing, because what he did then is he takes out a fucking little vial of blow and he gives it to me. Now, remember something, we're doing a three-pound, $36,000 package. He charges me for the taste! He wanted $75 for a fucking taste on a $36,000 package. This guy's a fucking socks salesman, he don't know what the fuck he's doing.

I say to him, well, you want seventy-five but you'll take fifty though, right? He says, "Oh yeah, I would take fifty." I says good. I had about $1,500 on me of photostated buy money. So I gave him a fifty-dollar bill for the taste. A lot of people don't know there's two buys on this guy. When we take him the next day at the bust, he's still got my photostated fifty in his pocket, which is proof of the A buy.

Then the fucking problem started. We need thirty-six grand if we're gonna put the fucking package down the next day. Thirty-six thousand dollars is every fucking penny of the entire Narcotics Division and half the money that the fucking police department is walking around with in their pockets. We got serious shit to take care of here. We got to work out the tactical part of this thing, what the deal's gonna be, who the fuck we are, what are we doing, and more important, where the fuck do we get the money from? There's five boroughs, five Narcotics Divisions, and my boss is dispatching couriers to each borough to pick up whatever buy money they got. Hey, the Bronx has got $8,000, Manhattan's got $14,000, terrific. They wind up borrowing some money from some bullshit bank on Pearl Street, just to get it all there. So we throw it in some fucking suitcase.

Joe LoGuidice The day of the bust Abbie was at my house. I was trying to talk him out of it. I just had this feeling he was gonna get busted. He felt no fear about it, he was completely without any apprehension, none whatsoever.

Patsy Cummings We tried to warn him, we said, "Look, you're a famous guy, this is ridiculous."

Joe LoGuidice I started to realize that there was something going on on a much higher, bigger level and there were more people involved in it, and I started saying to him, "Abbie, this doesn't sound like a good idea."

He's saying, "Nah, as a writer I need this experience, and nothing's gonna happen, nobody in the world would even suspect that anything like this would be going on with me, it's too obvious." It was on a Sunday, I think. I do remember that it was the day before the Rockefeller law went into effect. I said, "Look, this is like a message from God." He took it the exact opposite way. He said all the more reason. I couldn't talk him out of it. I think finally it was that decision, for him to do what he did, that ultimately is what killed him. I've always believed that.

AUGUST 1973

Sportsman Governor Rockefeller's new law on drug dealers was going to go into effect, with a mandatory sentence of fifteen to twenty-five years. Sunday, about 11:00 A.M., the morning of the day he got busted, I went to see him so I could give him some money that I owed him for the coke he had fronted me. He told me somebody's gonna have to test the new law. He prophesied his own bust. I will swear in court on a Bible to this. He thought the law was unjust and ridiculous and somebody would have to set the example. He was a player, he would push somebody and see how far he could go, am I right? He said he had a deal in the afternoon, that's all he said, that he had some business in the afternoon. I have to surmise that he did know he'd get busted.

Rudi Stern I was with him and Joie at Cafe Ferrara the day he got busted. The three of us were sitting having coffee. He was on his way for some big thing. He didn't tell me where he was going. Big deal, big score, big money thing. He's looking at his watch, and he put one hand on this railing and leaped over it to whistle down a cab coming down Grand Street.

Arthur Nascarella After phone calls were made, we were gonna meet the girls somewhere and they refused to take our car. They wanted to go in a cab wherever we were gonna go. Something like four o'clock, we were supposed to meet the girls on the corner of 23rd Street and Seventh Avenue. So we commandeer a fucking taxicab and we put John Donovan in a cab and we park his ass there.

I got my suitcase full of fucking money. We meet the broads. How's everything? Oh, we're gonna go to the Diplomat Hotel, 43rd and Sixth. Terrific, oh we need a cab. There's Donovan right there. He's reading a newspaper. I walk up. Bang, bang. "You working?" "Yeah, I'm working." I says, "C'mon, let's go." We throw the broads in, the fucking car is wired. Perfect. Now here's Donovan, one of my best friends, I love the guy, but he's playing the role of a cabdriver. He's parked on the north side of 23rd Street facing west. Behind him is about ten fucking surveillance cars. Donovan being the weird New York City cabdriver he thinks he is, pulls out of the curb, makes a fucking U-turn on 23rd Street and goes the wrong way. He leaves ten tail cars behind us. Now the broads are babbling, and I look out the window and here's the fucking commanding officer standing in the street with his shield in his hand, stopping traffic, and all the cars are making the turns. I was gonna beat the shit out of him, he could have blown it right there.

He drops us off on 42nd and Sixth Avenue. So the broads say we're gonna go ahead, you hang out here, there's a Papaya King, so we had a hot dog, and we got the captain and his second-in-command, John Keane and Bobby Lamm, two good guys. Look, they love Arthur Nascarella, they love Bobby Sasso, fuck the both of them, don't lose the bag of money, you lose that bag of money we're all fucking gonna be directing traffic on Staten Island for the rest of our careers. If it's a stickup, get shot. Don't come back with no bullet holes. I don't want to hear no stories, I want to see blood.

So what happens is the girls see them and go "Jesus, these guys look like fucking cops." They're right behind us walking, they make Bobby Lamm and the captain, they're a hundred percent fucking right. You know me, I'm telling them a joke, ba be ba bop, just get their fucking heads off it. They calm down. We got into the hotel and go upstairs. Carol Ramer had counted the money in the cab. We went up to the room, everything was everything. Then it was agreed that Bobby would stay in the room and I would go downstairs and meet Hoffman and a bodyguard that he was bringing with him, a guy named Michael Drosnin.

Diane Peterson I was supposed to go down and call Abbie and tell him that we were there. And a lot of people seem to think that the cops didn't know who Abbie was. They *did*. Because as we were walking to the phones, Nascarella said, "Is this Frankie"—that was the name that Abbie was using—"Is Frankie that guy Hoffner or Haffner, the guy who's on *The Dick Cavett Show* all the time?" I said no.

Arthur Nascarella Diane Peterson was wonderfully enamored with him. She loved him. Before he came to the hotel, she had us in the hallway saying, "Do you know who that really is?" "No, who is he?" "That's Abbie Hoffman." "Are you kidding me, no shit?"

A PRESCIENT ABBIE PONDERS HIS FUTURE JUST DAYS BEFORE HIS OWN DRUG BUST.

From the archives of Jerry Lieberman

Diane Peterson The minute I called Abbie, the first thing I said was "They know who you are." He giggled and said, "First of all, *Cavett*'s the one show I've never been on." As I recall he was sort of hesitant about it but didn't think it was important enough to do anything about.

Arthur Nascarella After a while, Hoffman comes. There was a brownout in the city. The elevators were down. The air-conditioning was down. He had to walk up. He comes in with a shopping bag, I can see he's got a scale. The girls are in the room. So he brushes by me in the stairwell, he feels my gun. He says, "You got a fucking gun on you." I say, "Absolutely I got a gun. You ain't got a gun? I lose this money I'll be in the East River in twenty fucking minutes. I got a gun, if you ain't got one that's your fucking fault." He figured that sounds cool. Remember I was supposed to be a fucking Italian wise guy. So he leaves Drosnin downstairs with me. He goes upstairs and he does the deal with Bobby. The team is out in the hallway. Bobby's got a wire on. They had a little banter, a little bullshit conversation. They scale out the fucking coke, Bobby gives 'em the money, pulls a gun on him, the door goes down, he's busted.

Diane Peterson Abbie had to come up the fire escape because the elevators weren't working. Ten floors, huffing and puffing, giggling, his hair all over, he comes in the window with grocery bags, he had groceries to disguise the fact that he's carrying drugs. Abbie was wired, of course, his usual self. So he's hopping around and doing all this stuff, and I guess Sasso had to wait until he actually said something, and he got it on tape. So finally Sasso pulled out a very small pistol, pointed it at us as all these cops came in the windows and banging on the door and all of a sudden there are all these shotguns pointing at our heads. I've never seen anybody sweat so much as Abbie did, I mean it just poured out of him. And Abbie, being Abbie, lurched towards Sasso, who was holding a gun on him. I said, "Don't do it!" And he stopped, and he did it again. I put out my hand, I stopped him, and Sasso said, "She's right, man, I'll kill ya." But you know Abbie, he's just so spontaneous, he just didn't think. I don't know if they immediately identified themselves as cops, I really don't remember. I don't think the door was locked. It may have been. I don't remember those details, I really don't. I just remember that the next thing was all these very long barrels. I just stood there. I wasn't gonna do anything to make 'em shoot me. The money and the drugs and everything were on the bed and we were standing with our backs to the bed so when the other cops came in they made him sit down and they cuffed him in back. And then because all of his sweat was coming down, Nascarella asked me if I wanted some towels so I could wipe it off. My job for the next few minutes was just to wipe the sweat off of Abbie's face. Abbie didn't say anything. He was just very quiet and just looking around like a trapped animal, which he was.

Arthur Nascarella Abbie tried to bullshit his way out of it, which of course ain't happening. You know, "You guys keep the coke and let me go." The blow sucked anyway, it was like 17 percent some odd shit, it was garbage. It was coke nonetheless. Three pounds and change.

Diane Peterson We found out later from a hooker who had gotten busted the same day in the hotel that everybody in that hotel knew something was going down. She said there were cops on the roof, there were cops on the fire escapes, shotguns everywhere, and she was wondering what was going down herself. So when we got out to the parking lot, there was a huge crowd of people out there. And this other cop whose name I don't remember yelled at the crowd, "Look, we caught a bunch of commies." So that stuck in my computer to tell the lawyers. The cops knew who Abbie was.

Arthur Nascarella So we take him and we book him at the 14th Precinct. None of us called, we didn't give a fuck, but all of a sudden there was a lot of press. The word went out that he had taken the flop. When we brought him in, the attitude inside the precinct right then was disbelief. They perceived him as an enemy. The guy had just cost the federal government $10 million to prosecute the Chicago 7 and they beat it. They walked away with a couple of misdemeanors apiece. I guess for the feds, I learned this later, he would have been a tremendous target. For me, remember, I was the fucking last guy in a bullshit little fucking narcotics team, no place. Fucking Abbie Hoffman, I'm trying to get fucking Luis Sanchez with a twenty-dollar bill. I'm looking for a guy selling loose joints on the fucking sand in Rockaway the afternoon we meet the guy. This is a quantum leap. He was no target of mine.

From the *New York Daily News,* 8/29/73

NAB ABBIE HOFFMAN ON DOPE CHARGE

By Patrick Doyle and William McFadden

Abbie Hoffman, the radical left-wing leader, and three other persons were arrested in a West Side hotel yesterday after they allegedly tried to sell three pounds of cocaine to undercover agents.

Diane Peterson Did he ever say he was sorry? Not exactly. But I've always thought of Abbie as the sort of person who runs along throwing banana skins in front of himself and expects other people to grab them. And everybody always did. I remember the day we were arraigned and the quarter million dollars bail each, and the "most heinous crime" business. As they took him in one direction and me in another, he looked at me and he shrugged his shoulders but looked really sad at the same time. I guess it was an "I'm sorry."

Mayer Vishner I was watching the ten o'clock news on channel 5, and there on my little black-and-white Sony is Abbie being busted for the cocaine. I couldn't believe it. He looked like I felt, beaten up by the temperature, New York in August with no air-conditioning, sweaty and dirty and scared, handcuffed, surrounded by cops and photographers. I just started to cry. I started calling people that we knew to try and figure out what needed to be done.

Anita Hoffman Out in the Hamptons I get this call from Gerry Lefcourt. I just picked up and drove into the city. Joie Davidow was living with Rudi Stern in a loft on Hudson Street. Joie let us stay there. Visiting hours were maybe 7:00 P.M. It was the summer, twilight in New York City, empty streets, people no longer working. So I would walk through those streets carrying America and then we'd go in the jail. You see them behind a thick, old glass partition, everything is dirty. And there's phones connected but it was like a child's toy phone with rope. You can imagine, the first sight, me holding baby and him on the other side, it was so devastating. The Tombs was horrible, horrible. I remember rats, hot and overcrowded, just hellish.

Joie Davidow Abbie'd call and if Anita wasn't there he used to try to get me to talk dirty on the phone to him.

Abbie spent six miserable weeks in the Tombs, knowing he was facing a sentence of fifteen years to life.

Sal Gianetta My impression is that he thought he might die in the Tombs. He lost part of himself. Even in the deepest fucking manic-depressive place, I heard him say, "It's all right. Tomorrow." Now he didn't know that there were any more tomorrows.

Gus Reichbach I went to see Abbie in the Tombs and at some point in our meeting he broke down and cried like a baby. His sense of shame was palpable.

Carol Realini I was in Ibiza and Jay sent me a telegram to call him. He said the way I could be most useful is raise bail from all the dope dealers in Ibiza and then fly up to London and collect there. I very quickly found out that not a single living soul in Ibiza was gonna give one penny for Abbie Hoffman. Half of them were out there living under false identities from dope busts. Abbie Hoffman, he's supposed to be political, what's he doing fooling around with coke deals, leave that to the pros. I made a reservation and came home.

Diane Peterson Geraldo Rivera had been doing a piece each night during the week on the fact that our bail was so ridiculously high. It was a quarter of a million each, and there was another guy who'd been busted for the same thing, who wasn't anybody, whose bail was set at $20,000.

Joe LoGuidice A lot of celebrities really backed off it completely because all of them were doing coke. I even had a couple of them say to me on the phone, "It's either help Abbie or give up coke and I don't think I can give up coke."

Diane Peterson Carol, Abbie and I all got out the same day. We wound up staying in there three weeks. They brought the bail down first to $50,000. Mike made bail when it was $50,000. Ultimately they brought it down to $10,000 for Abbie and John and Carol. Mine was $7,500 'cause I didn't do much.

The charges against Mike Drosnin were dropped after he proved that he was actually on assignment from Harper's Magazine *doing research for an article on the drug scene.*

John Lobell After Abbie got out on bail, we all went to Joe LoGuidice's loft for Chinese food. Abbie wanted Chinese food. So Abbie comes and he's got all these stories about the Tombs. He was in there with Carlo Gambino, the godfather of godfathers. Abbie says Carlo Gambino says to him, "You and I gotta stick together. All them other guys here is animals."

Joe LoGuidice Going underground was a topic of discussion even in jail. He was convinced if he was convicted and had to go to jail they'd kill him in jail. After he got out of the Tombs, we had a big strategy meeting. He came out of jail like a general. Who was gonna say what, deal with that, get it straight. Somebody complained about him giving orders. He said, "You have to understand there are the generals and there are the soldiers."

Jay Levin At that point it was already seen as a counterrevolutionary, self-absorbed indulgence to be involved with cocaine, rather than with serious organizing. I think what was starkly apparent to him was the fact that it was gonna be very hard to muster the troops.

Jack Hoffman How could you fuck up and do something so stupid? You get busted fifty-four times for things you believe in politically, and the fifty-fifth time it's for some stupid fucking coke bust, because you want to fuckin' test the limits. How fuckin' dumb can you be? You start to lose a certain amount of self-esteem at that point, without a doubt. So what do you do? You try to set up yourself some sort of defense mechanism. You attack people, but you don't give them a chance to get their little punch in, you don't give them that chance to ask a question about the drug bust. You isolate yourself, you break off friendships, you become obnoxious, you become arrogant, you become all the things that were negative about Abbie. And you change, because you're so ashamed of the fucking thing. God, he was fucking ashamed.

Norman Mailer I think Abbie was a serious man when all is said. He hid it for years but I think he was damn serious, maybe more serious than any of us. I think the drug bust burdened him. I think he felt that he had let down the movement and hurt things badly. I think Teddy Kennedy is like that. I think after Chappaquiddick Teddy Kennedy has faced himself in the mirror every day of his life and that's one reason why he's so serious about whatever he does. I have a similar tale to tell. When you fuck up seriously you do hurt the ideas you believe in.

Marty Kenner A week before he was busted, we were at the Luxor Baths and my father was asking Abbie what he was up to and Abbie said that for him politics was okay, it was like going to *schul* or church, something you had to do. But what he really enjoyed was being an outlaw. Now Abbie gets busted as an outlaw and all of a sudden he's writing a book. He's not an outlaw, he's a journalist.

Jeff Nightbyrd Abbie put out the thing how it was all a setup, and then his next story was he was only middling the deal.

Paul McIsaac Abbie went through a period of a month or so in which my impression was he was really putting himself in Gerry's hands. Gerry was pursuing some of these lines that it was a setup, that the evidence couldn't stand, what a lawyer would do. In the midst of that process, Abbie realized he was guilty, in their sense. The bust was really hard on him. I think it may have been partially the way it ends him up with his family and history: he's a dope dealer. And that kept him going with this sort of halfhearted denial. Maybe he just didn't want to cop to the fact that a cop outsmarted him. He certainly couldn't deny it to those of us who were closest to him. But it was amazing how he could do that other rap about how he was set up.

Mayer Vishner I didn't know what to believe. I didn't believe that he was stupid enough to be trying to sell three pounds of cocaine. And I couldn't think that it would be such bad cocaine, like 2 percent watered down. Then Abbie's saying he was set up, that John Rinaldi, Carol Ramer's boyfriend, was a cop. But the guy is being charged. Something is wrong here. And for me it's a very awkward situation because I know I'm not being told the truth.

But we go into gear. We collected information about cocaine and how it shouldn't be included in the drug law. We also attacked this aggregate-weight section of the drug law, which said that a teaspoon of cocaine in four pounds of baking soda is four pounds of cocaine. What Abbie was selling was so bad, so diluted, so stepped on, that he would've gotten off with a misdemeanor if they were only counting the actual cocaine. While I wanted to attack the aggregate weight, it meant (1) that he was selling cocaine and (2) that he was selling bad cocaine. So I told myself that it was just a backup defense and that that's a lawyer's job, to have as many defenses prepared as possible, and that in some way supported the contention that he was set up or that cops were involved on both ends because they would be using bad cocaine for such an operation. I never asked him the specifics because I already knew that I couldn't get a straight answer.

John Gerassi When I came back from Europe, Abbie and I had a very long conversation about the future. I told him that I was so frustrated and so upset and didn't know what the hell was going on, that I'd become impotent for three months. He said, "You're the first man that's told me honestly that he was impotent." And he told me that he had periodic terrible impotence problems. It was the political despair, it certainly was for me. I was so down and so convinced that we were getting nowhere.

Stella Resnick The Chicago 7 contempt trial was November of 1973. That was fun. First of all, it was a complete recapitulation of the conspiracy trial. All the people were present, except for the judge. Now Lenny Weinglass and Bill Kunstler were defendants, because they were also charged with contempt. Leonard Boudin was the defense attorney. I was there with Jerry and Abbie. Abbie's state of mind was more up.

Tom Hayden We had a different judge and all the defendants behaved differently and we won the case. The times had changed.

Bill Zimmerman I went with Tom to the trial. Rennie gave everybody copies of the guru's book. He was wearing a white suit and was blissed out. He just smiled patronizingly to everyone. It was bizarre.

From the *New York Daily News,* 11/22/73

OVERTURN CHI 7 CONVICTIONS

Chicago, Nov. 21 (UPI)

> A Federal Court of Appeals reversed the convictions of five of the Chicago seven defendants today, criticizing the "deprecatory and often antagonistic attitude" of Judge Julius J. Hoffman during their turbulent 1969–1970 trial. Hoffman declined comment.

Stella Resnick Jerry and Abbie and I went to visit Judge Hoffman's chambers. We walked in and Abbie and Jerry both gave him a little wave and sat down. The man got so flustered. We didn't say anything, we just sat down in the back for about five minutes. He was staring at Abbie and Jerry the whole time, and then we just got up and left. He did look just like Elmer Fudd.

Len Weinglass In Chicago after the contempt case was over, we were standing on a street corner, Hayden, Abbie, maybe a few others, and it was snowing. People were talking about the future and Abbie said, "I could walk right in front of this bus, right now, and that could be the future for me." It was really very macabre.

LATE NOVEMBER 1973

Alex Ducane I went to a friend's house and there was Abbie, carrying on about this dreadful situation he was in, about his bust, and he had to go underground, he didn't know what to do. I thought he was so gross, so disgusting, so aggressive, so ungraceful, I despised him. But he kept badgering me and somehow I ended up leaving with him and we were walking along looking for a cab, and he was carrying on and I was thinking to myself no, no, no, this guy is so awful. And somehow, with this sinking sense of doom in the pit of my stomach, he ended up crawling into the cab with me and ended up where I was staying. I wasn't even attracted to him. I couldn't stand him! But from the moment we got into the cab, I fell in love with him.

He told me he had been busted for a big coke deal and it was a put-up job, the government or whoever had manipulated the circumstances in order to create the situation whereby he was going to enjoy fifteen years of fidelity behind bars. So very quickly, all of my pores burst out into this thing of wanting to take care of him, just like instantaneously going from hating him to mad, passionate love. And basically we could never get it together. He was completely impotent.

There were several things that he talked about. One was the pressure of the bust and the possibility of having to go underground. The other one was the thing with Anita, they'd split up and he was in a great quandary as to what to do about that. She was living upstairs at the Chelsea. At a certain point I had moved into the Chelsea with Abbie. I spent Christmas with him already, the gefilte fish and all of that, and we had gone and spent Christmas Eve midnight at the Russian Tea Room. It wasn't romantic because when you can't get laid . . . I was living with him! I slept with him every night for two months! It wasn't that we were just kissing and making out, we were trying to make love and he couldn't. The only time he could do it was the last night I was in New York before I went to the airport, in the basement of Carol Realini's apartment. He came in saying he knew he was gonna be able to do it that time because it was the last night.

Laura Cavestani Frank was instrumental in convincing Abbie to go underground. Frank and I knew this girl named Carrie whose grandfather was a lawyer. They were rich Republican Jews, had a house in Nyack. We were up there for a day of swimming. And one of the people up there was a supreme court judge from Philadelphia.

Frank Cavestani We were like the kids, so we were swimming up to the edge of the pool listening to their conversation. They had no idea who we were. At one point the lawyers were talking about Agnew. They said he's finished, he's going away. So then one of the lawyers asks about Abbie Hoffman. And the federal judge says, "He's going away for a long time."

Laura Cavestani He said, "We're gonna lock him up and throw away the key."

Frank Cavestani And the other guy says, "Why?" The judge says, "Because he's got a big mouth." So we go back to New York and I tell Abbie this whole story. And he says, "I know, they got it in for me." I said, "So you don't have a chance." And he said, "Well, there's a plan afoot. And this story is like the nail in the coffin. I'm gone."

Jay Levin He had to get the ID. He'd gone to cemeteries for dead people's names. He was in contact with the Weatherpeople; they offered to help.

Jeff Jones He asked for a meeting with the Weather Underground organization, and I went. We met at a movie theater in Queens and sat down in the front row and sat through *The Way We Were* four times while we talked. People kept yelling "Shut up!" Abbie was telling me he wanted to become part of the Weather Underground. And he wanted to become part of the Central Committee. He wanted us to take him in but he also wanted to come in at the top. I had expected him to say, "I want to come with you guys," but it never occurred to me that he would say, "and I want to be your leader." We felt that he was too much of an individualist and too inconsistent and too out of sync with our politics for it to be safe for him to come with us. I had to tell him not only were we not going to let him be one of our leaders but we weren't even going to let him come with us.

So we went around and around and around with him trying to convince me and me knowing that there was no way. I just had to hang tough. We had decided that we would help him with ID, help him by sharing our knowledge, which we always thought was more valuable. I talked to him about the psychological rivers he would have to cross, the long periods of time where no one would know who he was, and I sort of predicted a lot of what came afterwards, which added to my misery because I personally was powerless to do anything about the troubles that he had later on.

Mainly we told him that he would have to build his own network of friends and given how many friends he had and the money he could tap into, we also felt that in some ways he was better off than we were. After we said goodbye I didn't know if I would ever see him again. He was pissed off. I remember riding back into Manhattan standing in the front on an elevated subway, just thinking this is the saddest thing and I don't know what's going to become of this guy. I don't know if he's going to make it.

Lee Weiner Allen Ginsberg and Abbie and I were schmoozing in a corner at some party at the Village Gate for Abbie's defense after the coke bust. Then Allen got up to do a poem and Abbie pulled me over to the side. He asked me, "What exactly did people take with them when they run?" I would know what Jews historically took with them. Was it diamonds, was it currency, was it this, was it that? Abbie was so fucking unprepared. He had some romantic notion of being on the move all the time. I remember saying, "Everything I know about it is you go to one place unless you want to be dependent upon other people who don't really like you very much. Find a fucking place, find a place."

Joe LoGuidice Abbie and Anita came to Zihuatanejo before he went under. He had already made the decision, he was practicing walking and not making eye contact. He was psyching out the territory, where he was gonna be, who was gonna cover for him. We were setting up code names for different contacts, and telephones, the drops and so forth.

Mimi Lobell In those months before he went underground, after the bust we had a lot of fun. They were the best times.

John Lobell Just before the bust we got in with Anita so now we became two families that would spend more time together. After the bust that was picked up, plus Eleanor [Bingham] being there as a catalyst, introducing this whole other level of fun.

Ira Landess Abbie's demons were ferocious and if you want my professional opinion I suspect that the demon is, as is almost invariably the case in all manic-depressive situations, unconscious homosexual wishes. As a species we are bisexual. We have a sexual desire for our mothers and we have a sexual desire for our fathers. If that homosexual desire is repressed and remains totally unacceptable to us, it becomes the agent that haunts us and always threatens our self-esteem. If we can make conscious our bisexual wishes and maintain a balanced self-esteem in the presence of those wishes, we don't have to run as far. And being a cocksman was central to his life and he was never able to let go of that as far as I know. Doing it to that kind of extreme [is] like screaming, "I'm not a homosexual."

Joe LoGuidice One night in that period we were all in the Hamptons and Abbie was trying to talk me into the idea, although neither one of us were homosexuals, we owed it to ourselves to try to have homosexual experiences to have some frame of reference. We all went to a gay bar and Abbie sort of danced with me and then after the dance he tried to attract guys and then the first guys who came up to us and asked us to dance, we couldn't do it. It was a strange period.

John Lobell Abbie felt that as a matter of political responsibility he should have homosexual sex. He felt embarrassed he hadn't. So I felt responsible to help the situation along. We got together at their place in the Hamptons. Eleanor and Anita were already out on the Island. I had a bad cold so I curled up in the back of my car and Abbie drove it out there. And the big help on getting everything through was Quaaludes. So the first night I gave everybody my cold. We had a big pileup and finally Abbie and I each fucked each other. The next day Abbie says to me, "Well, did you convert?" I said, "No, I think I like girls better." He says, "Yeah, I feel the same way." It was only with lots of extra women around that each of us could really get it up for each other: "Mimi, could you sit on my face while Eleanor is jerking it off to get it hard enough to get it in there?"

Jay Levin I remember Abbie describing giving head to John Lobell. Here was this macho, total womanizer, talking about giving head to a guy. I said, "How the fuck could you do that?" He says, "Because I never did it, I had to find out what it's all about. You climb Mount Everest 'cause it's there." And he said it very scornfully, disdainfully, like how could you have such a small imagination not to even want to try something?

Robin Palmer One day Abbie calls me up and says he wants to meet me. So we go down to Washington Square Park and he tells me that they're offering him a deal. Five years. Do I think that he could do five years and still be Abbie Hoffman when he got out? I thought about it and I said to him, "That's the kind of question that can only be answered by you, Abbie.

I would say, given my own experience, that you could. But on the other hand, Sam Melville's dead. So you've got to make up your own mind about that." He was saying either he could do five years or he could go underground. He wanted to know if I felt I had made the right decision not to go underground but to go to jail instead. I said I thought I had.

Then he asked me, "If I go to jail what do you think if I became a homosexual? If I became a homosexual, I could write a book." I said, "Abbie, do not do that. That is a bottomless pit. If you become a homosexual in jail, you're a sex slave and sooner or later you're going to be the trigger for a riot, a stabbing, some really serious violence. If you think our society has a low consciousness about homosexuality, there's absolutely no consciousness about it in jail. You're just a piece of meat."

Roger Lowenstein Abbie gave lip service to an open marriage but he didn't believe it. That's why the thing with me was so bad. Anita and I really had a romance. It wasn't a casual thing like Abbie had with women. I don't think Anita would allow herself to have casual sex at that point. We began a romance and that really threatened Abbie terribly. He would half-joke, "Hey, man, it was supposed to be a quickie." He would say it to Anita too. He'd say, "Look, when I get laid it's quick."

Jay Levin Abbie got incredibly jealous because she would in fact start making dates with other men. Of course, Abbie would go crazy and say, "She slept with him and she made the appointment the time she was supposed to see me." He'd cover up his jealousy and say he was angry for some other reason, like standing him up. There was a part of his personality that, from time to time, saw other people as betraying him.

Around this time, Abbie decided to get a vasectomy. But Abbie saw his vasectomy as a political statement, so he enlisted the artist Larry Rivers to videotape the operation.

Anita Hoffman We discussed the vasectomy before he did it. He didn't like the fact I had an IUD that got lost in my body. He was very upset that that would have to happen to me and he wanted to take some responsibility. Plus he really didn't want another child, neither did I. But I think that it was also true that he was fucking a lot of women who wanted to have his baby in order to name the kids Abbie! I don't think he wanted to be caught in a paternity suit, either.

Alex Bennett I said, "Weren't you afraid it was going to make you impotent?" He said it did. He claimed he couldn't get it up for a year after the vasectomy. He said he made that videotape because he wanted everybody to see how easy it was to get a vasectomy but it was so gruesome that nobody would ever want to get a vasectomy after looking at that video.

Jean-Jacques Lebel I thought that was an obnoxious thing to do. How far can the fucking star system go? Next thing you know you'll be filming him shitting or pissing.

EARLY FALL 1973

Joe LoGuidice I was going with Patsy at the time but I had this on-again, off-again fantasy romance with Johanna Lawrenson. Johanna and I arranged to meet down in Mexico. I had put this trip off a week until we were able to raise bail money for Abbie. Then Abbie came down to start checking out the possibilities if he had to go under. Johanna was there and I introduced them. I could see that he had terrific eyes for her right away. But in the meantime, I had left Patsy back in New York and she was really fucking furious with me. I decided to go back to Patsy then. Although Johanna was wonderful, beautiful, I realized that life with Johanna would be very much like life with Abbie, in a different kind of way. So the last thing I said to Abbie before he split—he kept saying oh, she's fantastic—I said, "Look, man, you can't think about these things right now, you better concentrate on what you're gonna do with your old lady and your kid. Johanna's gonna be living in Mexico City and I'll give you her number. But don't use it, only in an emergency," because I wasn't sure that Johanna could be that cool. She's great but she can also be very naive. Of course, she was the first person he contacted when he finally did go under.

Laura Cavestani He always said, "I'm going away." I don't think he ever contemplated taking Anita and the kid. I got the impression that his attitude was I gotta be able to move fast.

Alex Ducane Abbie was talking to me about going underground with him. I said, "Are you kidding? How can I possibly go underground with you in my ankle-length fur coat?" At first I laughed at the idea, and then eventually, actually, I got really sort of intrigued by the idea and then I became really devastatingly in love with him. I probably would have, but at that point he realized that it was the wrong idea. He was seeing Johanna at the same time he was seeing me.

One night in December Abbie was at a meeting in this church in St. Mark's Place. I was supposed to meet him later, so I went to Max's, and I saw Johanna, who I hadn't seen in a couple of years. She was talking about that meeting. I said, "That's funny, because I just left my friend Abbie, he was on his way there." Then she said that she had just come back from modeling in Mexico City and she had been involved with this married man who was Mexican and who wanted to leave his wife for her, but he had a son. She said she didn't know what to do.

It turned out that Abbie had been in Mexico City with her and then I met him when he had come back to the States. So he had been in Mexico briefly, long before he went underground! I had no idea that she had been with Abbie, and there I was sitting saying that I was with Abbie. Since she brought up the subject of the meeting, obviously she was also seeing Abbie in New York, which I didn't know.

At the same time, Abbie was telling me that the only person that he was really sort of in love with and having an affair with was this woman who was a psychologist. Obviously, it was Johanna. So I decided I'm not gonna go underground in my fur coat with him.

Anita Hoffman Abbie wanted me to come with him underground and I think it was hard for him to believe that I wouldn't. There were just all these reasons why I couldn't go. I think he changed because of the illness. That's part of it. Now I realize it was the illness, but it was hard to be with him, it was really hard! He was so egotistical. I had that kind of personality where I could be totally absorbed in him. I was this zero at this point. I said even if I'm zero I have to find it out on my own. The women's liberation movement had made me realize the extent to which I was totally overwhelmed by him. So to go underground was even less than what it would have been before, less than zero. And once you made that decision . . . He was just very hard to be with and I loved him so much.

Once he was gone it would be simple. Maybe there was poverty and all these problems with me and America, but I called the shots. With Abbie, everything would be subordinate to his survival, as it should be. It also seemed like it would be easier, at least initially, for him to be underground alone. I think basically it ended between us the way it had to. Then I had my own life, which was extraordinarily difficult in the years separated from him. It's only now at forty-nine that I can buy myself a living room couch. Before that it's all been struggling for food and for day care and support the kid and everything. I feel that he would like me now maybe more than he did when we parted. I think he would be proud.

Truusje Kushner Abbie came to me and he basically encouraged me to encourage Anita not to go underground. He really felt, and I think this was from the bottom of his heart, that it would do her no good to become his partner underground. I would have encouraged her to do that anyway. Abbie came and asked for my help. He's a brilliant strategist.

Anita Hoffman If I had known he was crazy when he went underground, I just never would have let him go alone. God, I didn't know that he was ill, that he was so vulnerable. It was like another adventure, he'll do okay, and sooner or later, day by day, or year by year, we'll figure it out. It wasn't the death-definitive parting. I did get put off by the manic behavior, I didn't know what was going on, he was fucking all these women and I just couldn't take it. I'm a really simple person and I just wanted a simple life and that's all I really want even now. And now that I'm alone, it's easier to be simple. I don't know whether any one person could be a sufficient mate for him, actually, but I know I've never loved anybody like him and I don't ever expect to.

Carol Realini After Abbie got bailed out, he used to come around to the Defense Committee office. He used to try to beat me in there and open the mail and take the cash out and put it in his pocket. One day I find him doing this, I said, "What are you doing?" He took the money out of his pocket and said, "Here, take this and buy some pot and turn everyone on. That'll be a good thing to do with the money."

Since Anita was not going underground with Abbie, he decided they needed to get a divorce. Abbie convened a countercultural court.

Joe LoGuidice I represented Anita and Joie Davidow represented Abbie. Joie showed up with a German chocolate cake and coffee. Abbie and Anita had very little cash. Abbie felt that he needed all or most of that money to go underground with. He knew he couldn't work for at least the first six or seven months, he needed some surgery, he needed papers, he needed what you need. The argument was that Anita had the kid and no money and that Abbie couldn't take all the money. It wasn't that much, about $10,000. He says, "You don't understand. When the enemy is about to capture the general, the troops have to throw their bodies in front of him." He was deadly serious. When we really thought about it he was right. He felt that Anita's friends would all make sure that nothing happened, and it was true, we did. He knew that we were never gonna let Anita or the kid starve.

Alex Ducane In February of 1974 Abbie and I moved out of the Chelsea without paying his bill. He had the whole hotel mobilized. Every day, every hour, every night, Larry Rivers and other people were taking little handbags of clothes and stuff out of the hotel till the final crunch came and he and I split. By this time the suite was empty.

Stanley Bard, *owner, Chelsea Hotel* I don't remember how much he owed. Several months rent. Maybe he owed a thousand dollars, which was a lot of money for that time. Before he left, he paid some money. He was a very honest person. I felt very badly for him. To think of someone having to go underground and splitting from his wife and baby is a terrible ordeal.

Carol Realini The day before he split, Abbie was going around town with America, paying calls on all his friends. He wasn't saying, "Goodbye, I'm leaving," he was just dropping in and spending twenty minutes. It was very touching. And then he was gone.

Anita Hoffman We had a plan for the last day. We were going to take America to his day-care center and then Abbie and I were gonna have lunch and then I was going to drive him to Newark airport in our little Volkswagen Beetle. I remember when we kissed goodbye at the airport before we walked to the gate for the airplane. I think his last words were "Don't start smoking again," because we had stopped smoking together and it was this big deal. I remember not looking back because it was superstitious, you're not supposed to look back.

Jerry Rubin I was totally against Abbie going underground. Of course, maybe he had no choice. His coke bust was the nightmare of all times, right? The final act of that whole self-destructive breakup of his being on top of the world. And then all of a sudden everyone's turning against you. And boom!, you're just spinning out of control. Abbie became the prisoner of his myth, the prisoner of his media story. So going underground was just a total extension of the sixties.

Lee Weiner I wish Abbie hadn't sold dope, okay? I never heard anybody say it to Abbie. Not in my presence. "Schmuck!" I said it, we had that fight, okay? Should we maintain the fictions? To what end? Abbie's relationship to the real world gave him his real energy and his real focus.

And when that connection was broken, in a much harsher way than it was for me, much harsher, look what happened. Ren had a psychotic break, Tom splintered into a hundred pieces and tried so hard to pull himself together, Jerry got lost in some fantasy world of money and responsibility. The truth is my high school class didn't do so good.

Chapter Eight

QUOTES FROM UNDERGROUND

Truusje Kushner The day after Abbie split, these guys are on the roof of our house in the Village. I said, "What are you doing?" "Oh, we're from the phone company." "Well, what are you fixing?" "Uh, well, there's a problem with the line, lady."

Jack Hoffman You know why Abbie went to Mexico? Because I had a factory in Mexico, and my sister lived there. Abbie couldn't be alone. It was the perfect setup. Aside from the FBI chasing us. There was a guy parked on my street for a year. They had over a hundred agents on Abbie the first year. There was no doubt in my mind, the first two years, they got him in the corner somewhere, they would have fucking blown him away. I lost a lot of friendships because he became a fugitive. I had a guy rip up a $25,000 contract right in my fucking face. Oh man, I could tell you stories, oh please, how I suffered.

Florence Zuckerman, *Worcester resident* Everybody felt Abbie's father died of a broken heart. The anxiety and worry took so much out of him and he was ashamed.

Jack Hoffman Abbie took it to his grave, it was his albatross. He feels that the drug bust killed my father.

Anita Hoffman I think Abbie was in Mexico for most of that first year. I later found out he taught in this girls' school in Guadalajara. I would mail letters to friends who had his real address.

Jack Hoffman The first contact I had with him was a tape that I got in the mail from Guadalajara, and it was with his passport. So I knew he had gone. I listen to the tape. He opens with "Oh, I want a corned beef from Weintraub's, Jack. Come on, make it fucking lean, lots of mustard."

From the *New York Daily News,* 4/7/74

ABBIE SKIPS A COURT DATE; SOUND NATIONWIDE ALARM

By Ellen Fleysher

Special Narcotics Prosecutor Frank Rogers announced yesterday that a nationwide alarm was issued for Yippie leader and alleged cocaine salesman Abbie Hoffman after Hoffman failed to appear in court. The alarm was sent out after Acting Supreme Court Justice Mary Johnson Lowe ordered a bench warrant for Hoffman's arrest and issued another order forfeiting the $10,000 cash bail put up by his wife, Anita.

Carol Realini Abbie sent me a key chain with a huge, ugly plastic big toe attached. It was like a takeoff of when Getty's ear was cut off and sent to his mother.

Letter from Abbie Hoffman to Carol Realini Barbizon Plaza Hotel

4/14/74

Dear Ca:

I'm working hard and never bored. I'm into this more than I thought I would or could be. I've not seen a soul for 3 months but read everything and watch all the news and talk shows—any plans anyone thought I had were changed 2 weeks after I took the dip anyway . . . Where have all the game players gone? "I hope he hasn't been hit by a truck" and all that other shit—"Tell em I'm up in the Catskills with all the other good Jewish boys waiting on tables for the summer." Make me laugh!!!! Tell me America just shot Rockefeller. Tell them I took an acid trip and tell Jay I love him. I don't do nomodope. I look like the guy in Love and Anarchy—

RIP VAN WINKLE
zzzzzzzzz

* * *

Anita Hoffman When I was on my own, I founded this self-help center for mothers and children receiving public assistance. I wanted to get support for what I was doing from the Prairie Fire Support Group because they were the support group for the Weather Underground and Abbie admired them in the early stages. I was doing good work, welfare organizing, that's respectable, Marx would love that. But they were cliquish and dogmatic and closed off from me. One woman in the group and her boyfriend were sweet and she volunteered to baby-sit.

America Hoffman My mother told me they were FBI agents. She said they'd go through the trash and stuff, and I remember now that they'd suck up to me and try and get me to say stuff. But she said that they made the best baby-sitters. They took care of business.

Diane Peterson The lawyers said if you put more of the blame on Abbie you can plead the "dumb broad" excuse. I said, "We're thirty-five years old. He didn't drag me in there, you know."

The pretrial motions were one circus after another.

Arthur Nascarella We weathered storms of people who said we had wiretaps at his mother's house, we had done this, we had done that. Total bullshit.

Diane Peterson One motion involved this super in Carol's building, this wonderful woman who had two little children, about eight and nine years old. Her name was Best. Best was a Jehovah's Witness, and she would not come into the court. So we all went out into the hall. Judge Lowe asked her questions out in the hall. "Did two men come pretending to be telephone men and was it these two men who are right here in the hall?" indicating Sasso and Nascarella. "Yes, they were there, and yes, they did do something in the basement," Best affirmed, trying to establish that there was a tap on Carol's phone. And every time she would answer a question

"Yes," her two little daughters would nod, yes, like little birds on a fence. And the judge believed her.

Arthur Nascarella Complete lie. Hoffman's wife, every time I used to testify, she used to sit in the audience and try to put a hex on me, voodoo shit.

Diane Peterson At the end, the judge said she was proud to be in a profession with lawyers who had done as well as our lawyers had done during the pretrial motions, but we hadn't proved it. That was the end of the motions. So at that point we decided to cop a plea.

Angela Dorenkamp Abbie's mother used to send him toothpaste and toilet paper when he was underground. I would ask her how Abbie was and she would say "Abbie?" as if "Who's Abbie?"

Mayer Vishner I had certain tasks. At some point I was to call his mother and tell her that he was fine, which I did. One time I'm on the phone twenty minutes and Abbie's got this grandiose idea that the Defense Committee was gonna take a position on the Israeli conflict or something. They weren't gonna do 'em when he was around, why should they do 'em when he wasn't there.

From *To America with Love: Letters from the Underground*

LETTER FROM ABBIE TO ANITA HOFFMAN, 6/27/74

I know this little kid same age as junior who adopts me as his "new daddy." I don't want him, I want junior. The kid stuff drives me to tears. I just sent a few drawings to him as you suggested. Sent them days before even. We are on the same wavelength. We feel exactly the same. I'm sure of it. I have feelings of unworthiness in our relationship, though, that I have to deal with. My manhood is definitely jolted by the idea of being an appendage to your strength . . . After all, my most creative act is staying alive . . . Maybe your successes are a threat? . . . Way back in the corner of my mind sits a little "me" that's unsure of the future, a little "me" that's been belted once too often by life, that doubts the past, that longs for death, whose legs are not as strong as they once were, and feels his talent is gone, the times are run out and he should learn the big lesson of life—nothing comes easy. It's just a little me but it's the one that wakes me up at night. The Failure. But then, of course, I'm really strong and getting along so well, and I wonder how others would function and, well, I accept myself.

LETTER FROM ABBIE HOFFMAN TO CAROL REALINI AND JAY LEVIN, 8/74

Dear U-2!!
Things are slow here in New York. I'm getting to be such a has-been—why just yesterday I went up to a cop and told him who I was and would he mind watching my car for me while I double parked. So I ran into the bank cashed a check came out and drove off. Shit I haven't been busted in 11 months and it's the longest I've gone in 10 years without a fall. Ah well what can you expect from our permissive society.
Your faithful Indian compassion
Toronto

Joe LoGuidice Abbie contacted me. I was supposed to be in Mexico City on a certain date and he says find a hotel. It's now maybe five months after he went underground. So I found this fantastic hotel off the beaten track, the María Cristina. I say I'll sit out in the garden in front of the place. I walk out to the front door and there's this bus unloading the fucking Harlem Globetrotters. And Abbie knew a lot of them. I couldn't fucking believe it. I go back to the room. He calls. "What the fuck was that? Are you setting me up?" I says, "Yeah, I brought the whole fucking Harlem Globetrotters down here, and I got the cops. What the fuck are you talking about?" He was like totally crazy.

So I go way the fuck on the other side of Mexico City at twelve o'clock at night. I'm sitting there waiting and I see this guy walking around and around the block. He's got on a fucking porkpie hat, I swear to God, this is Mexico City, it must've been 150 degrees, he's got a porkpie hat on, with a full fucking-ass trench coat, with the collar pulled up, and dark fucking sunglasses in this deserted neighborhood. I'd bust him just on general principles. Finally he came up to me and he said, "Wait five minutes and then start walking in the opposite direction around the block," like something out of Dashiell Hammett. He's glad to see me but I sense there's something wrong. He starts talking to me about Johanna. I said, "What do you mean, what about her?" "Well, do you still like her?" I said, "She's a good friend but . . ." He says, "Oh good, I've been living with her for the last five months." He was afraid that I was gonna be very upset, which I wasn't at all, but they had kept it secret. He says, "I'm really fucking relieved, man, because I thought maybe I was gonna have to dump you and find a new contact."

Mayer Vishner We were all glad he didn't tell her who he was right away. That shows that he's not totally stupid.

From *To America with Love: Letters from the Underground*

LETTER FROM ABBIE TO ANITA HOFFMAN, 8/12/74

> You should know of her existence and that it's more than a casual relationship, and you should feel free to pursue your desires, not only carnal but emotional. She's no lightweight and she teaches me a lot about survival. She is better at this than me, as you are. I get sad sometimes. Very sad. I think we'd get along very nicely. Do you think we made a mistake having a child? I never asked that or felt it ever before. Somehow it all doesn't seem quite fair to him. He doesn't get to make a lot of choices. Give him a hug and kiss for me. I can't write more.

Anita Hoffman I was relieved 'cause I knew he had a helpmate and I know she really loved him and I think she's responsible for his survival underground. He may have been more in love with Johanna than he let on in the letters to me, but I think he was torn, I think he really did love both of us.

It was an incredibly exciting time for me. I changed in very fundamental ways. I had to restrain myself from writing how exciting it was for me, and I could never write that I was having lovers, which is the first time, but which was something I needed in the face of his seven years' worth of! I didn't want to hurt him.

Jean-Jacques Lebel Johanna and I lived together in Paris and America. She came from an extremely strong, communist, American Left family. Her father was a very important dock organizer, union guy. And a tragic death, he was drinking a lot and sleeping on the streets and he caught pneumonia. Johanna's mother was a high-class, intellectual leftist. Magazine writer.

Alex Ducane I first met Johanna on the opening night of Max's Kansas City, in December of 1965. Johanna was a very successful model. She had worked a great deal in Paris, and she was like *the* hip, beautiful young woman of New York of 1965 among painters, artists, fashion photographers, models. I met Malcolm Morley ten months after I met Johanna. Johanna had been a girlfriend of Malcolm's in 1964. She had just started this relationship with Frank Jones [a pseudonym], a famous sculptor/painter. We used to go to Max's every night, Viva and Johanna, myself. It was the place to be.

I left and went to England, and then Malcolm and I lived here for a year in 1969. We spent basically every day with Johanna and her new boyfriend, Johnny Kidd [a pseudonym]. My impression at the time, based on what she said, was that she wasn't getting any [modeling] work anymore. She must've been about twenty-eight then. She was a go-go dancer in some bar just above Max's. Johnny beat her up constantly. But she'd go back with him, just like she did with Frank. During that period she went to California, she'd gotten pregnant by Frank and had an abortion, then she came back to New York. And she was back with Johnny. Then Frank stopped and Johnny stopped and Abbie started.

Abby McGrath I went to junior high school with Johanna. Johanna had terrific boyfriends, all very nice and good to her, but somehow she would gravitate to those who weren't as good to her. I'd say, Johanna, go for the money. Marcello Mastroianni thought she was the best thing since sliced bread. Take him. No, I want this crippled-up one over here in the corner that needs me.

Viva, *actress* I've known Johanna since we were young teenagers. Johanna really introduced me to the art world, taught me how to dance, lent me clothes, gave me money, found me a place to live in Manhattan. I used to go to her house in the Thousand Islands whenever I had a fight with my dysfunctional family, which was at least four times per summer. You'd go through her visitor's book and every other entry is "Thank you for rescuing me one more time." I guess she rescued Abbie.

Carol Realini Naturally the first thing that happened when he hooked up with Johanna is a mad dash to get the vasectomy reversed because Johanna wanted a child.

Joie Davidow She would make sure his coat was buttoned. She devoted herself to him 100 percent, not just like a mother with a child, like a mother with a retarded child, that level of caretaking.

SUMMER 1974

Ken Kelley Jerry Rubin called me up and said, "You want to go see our friend Sam?" So we flew into Mexico City, met Johanna, and we went out to a small village outside of Cuernavaca. Abbie lived on the outskirts of town in this really nice modern house, with a swimming pool and two horses, that he was subletting. It was really cheap.

Marty Kenner We spent a couple of days with Abbie and Johanna on our way to Cuba to visit Huey Newton. Abbie was complaining that Huey got all the money and he didn't. "I must be the only fugitive in the world who has to support two families aboveground." He was in a good mood.

Ken Kelley Abbie said to Jerry, "Listen, when you go back, I want you to call up Paul Kantner [of the Jefferson Airplane] and tell him that I need some money." And later on, Paul gave him money. He said Francis Ford Coppola had helped him out with disguises and showed him how to do makeup. Abbie had gotten a nose job, at least he said he did. He had bandages to prove it but it sure didn't look any different to me.

Anita Hoffman Johanna and Abbie attended the Max Factor school in Hollywood when he was underground in order to learn how to do makeup and disguises.

Ken Kelley Abbie wasn't doing much. To stop from going crazy, he was working on this script. He said he was in this communist collective. "I'm a communist now, no more of this Yippie shit." And he was subject to the discipline of his communist cell. From what I could ascertain it consisted of him and this guy Paul Williams, in Los Angeles. Williams and some of his friends had this big ranch in Ventura County. Abbie's job was to stay out of trouble and work on this script about Fidel Castro.

He said he felt lucky that he hadn't been caught, he alluded to some psychotic episodes. Johanna told me he was on some kind of drug. But he seemed very animated and not flipped out at all. The cell was top-secret stuff and he enjoyed playing that game. That's all he could talk about, he was reading Marx and Engels.

Joe LoGuidice That was the first sign I saw of Abbie consciously or unconsciously trying to manipulate something he didn't really believe in. We had quite a few disagreements about it.

Jeff Jones All of a sudden, while he was underground, Abbie's language becomes much more Marxist-Leninist. He talks about establishing a communist party. I think part of what he was doing was trying to make himself more acceptable to us.

Sal Gianetta Mexico was bad. He came back to L.A. and I saw him for a while in 1975. He was totally fucking depressed. Plus he was afraid of dying in Mexico. I shouldn't say dying. He was scared shitless of getting busted in Mexico. Being forgotten. And he was really using drugs. He was wrecked when I saw him.

Joe LoGuidice After the first year he was underground, I said, "I think that you can make a deal. Resurface, confess and get back to business." It was romantic at first; he had met the perfect woman to go through this trip with him. But it became more and more expensive. There were some problems with [Abbie's sister] Phyllis's husband. He was Argentinian by birth and high up in the Mexican government, so he was afraid of a scandal. Abbie started getting very schizy, crazed. He started taking a lot of chances.

Frank Cavestani Anita was really broke, and I was at this company TVTV and I said would Abbie be interested in doing a show? So we worked it out and I think overall we paid them $5,000.

Michael Shamberg They hooked up with [the writer] Ron Rosenbaum, and the big thing was they wanted money. At first it was going to, like ten, fifteen, twenty thousand, but it was right after CBS paid Liddy for an interview, so there was a real stigma. TVTV was working with WNET and the lawyers said don't do it. They finally said, we're not giving you money for the interview, we're giving you expenses to arrange the interview, which I had to get in cash. And then Ron Rosenbaum and I were told that on such a morning at eight o'clock we had to go to a phone booth in Hollywood at Las Palmas and Sunset. We go there, the phone rings, they say, "Look under the counter," so under the counter are these two airline tickets. We go to the airport, the tickets are to Sacramento, we go to Sacramento, we get off the plane, nobody's there for about forty-five minutes. Finally, this very straight-looking couple comes and meets us, who, I later realized, I'm pretty sure was Bill Ayers and Bernadine Dohrn.

They were secreted to an unknown destination by van.

Michael Shamberg We're in a cheesy motel or apartment, we set up, and Abbie comes in. He kept saying how great he felt and how healthy he was. I'd learned even then that when people say that, they're exactly the opposite.

So we did the interview. It was all really just a polemic and so it came out as pretty dull stuff, I'm afraid. And that was it. They drove us to the San Francisco airport, and in about thirty minutes I realized we'd been somewhere around Berkeley, that's the only place these people could really be comfortable and have a network of support. The idea that they were living somewhere outside of the communities they sprang from was simply not true.

Because we'd paid him, that overshadowed everything else. There was a big piece in the *New York Times,* "Should you pay these guys?" It was really a disaster. It's funny, we never did have any response from the authorities.

Jeff Jones I was worried on two levels—I was worried that he would damage himself and I was worried that he would damage or expose us. Contact was with intermediaries. We heard the story about him flipping out in Las Vegas and it was all the more clear that we could have no contact with him.

Jay Levin The freak-out in Las Vegas came fairly early on. He'd absolutely gone off the fucking wall, running around screaming "I'm Abbie Hoffman" in the casino rooms and on the floor of the hotel. He had that hemorrhoid attack simultaneously. I think it was the pain that drove him over the edge. Of all the beatings he had been through, that was the one level of pain that really got to him. He was sitting there for days with this biting cloth.

Joe LoGuidice Johanna's making all kinds of emergency calls; he was getting a little violent.

SAIGON FALLS TO THE VIETCONG, MAY 1, 1975

Ken Kelley I remember getting a frantic phone call from Bert Schneider himself. He said, "Meet me at the Airport Hilton at LAX at 11:30." I saw Abbie in his room and he had a couple of magnums of champagne.

"The Vietnamese won, goddammit, they did it!" It was all he could talk about!

That's when I started to see Kinky Friedman a little bit too. He was the only one who could out-Abbie Abbie.

Kinky Friedman, *songwriter, novelist* Abbie talked to me about Jews a lot, about the two kinds of Jews in the world. There's a kind of Jew like the German Jews that just didn't want to cause any trouble and the family on the right of them disappeared one night, the family on the left disappeared one night, they still said, "Lay low here, take it easy for a while and everything'll be fine." The merchant class of Jew, the shoe-salesman-in-Seattle type of Jew. And then there's the other kind of Jew, Spinoza and Freud, Einstein, Tony Curtis and Abbie Hoffman. That kind of Jew, they're troublemakers, they're different, they aren't happy. Being Jewish is very much a part of Abbie. As a mystery writer, I think there's something very Jewish about all detectives in that they're on the outside looking in. Judaism, at its best, should be on the outside looking in. It should not belong, should be out of step, out of time with whatever is going on. Hopefully that will bring us some insight into how we may be able to make things better. Yeah, Abbie was one of the Jews who change history. And he saw himself that way.

Ken Kelley I know Kinky was giving Abbie money. It was a real love relationship. There were some heavy drugs going on. Also a lot of drinking. He was still doing cocaine and Johanna had a big conspiracy to keep it away from him because she said he just gets wacko on that. The one thing he did like, though, that she said was good for him, was marijuana. It mellowed him out.

Kinky Friedman I went to a few Hollywood parties for Abbie. Every celebrity wanted to be around him. Abbie was a character, Abbie was colorful.

Ken Kelley He'd applied for a California driver's license so he had me drive him to the Roosevelt Hotel, he was getting mail there. He says, "Go in there and ask if there's any mail for—" and then he looked around like the CIA is going to be in the lamppost and then he says, "Barry Freed." So I went in and there was one piece of mail for him from the Department of Motor Vehicles. I remember him opening it up and he says, "Ah hahaha, Barry Freed! Do you get it, freed, I'm freed!" It was a picture ID and he did look different in the picture. Coppola must have taught him something.

Jay Levin He was putting the bite on Hollywood for money. But also, (a) he wanted to be a movie star, and (b) he wanted a movie made about him as an American hero. He enjoyed Hollywood people, he enjoyed their drugs and he enjoyed the flirting. He had an incredible crush on Tuesday Weld. I don't know how close he got to realizing that crush but that was his fantasy.

John Eskow I think that he burned some bridges there. He just thought he could try to put a move on anybody's girl. It was like he was entitled to it all and that shit don't play on the street, you know?

JUNE 1975

Ken Kelley There was this major SOS call. First it was from Kinky, and then one from Schneider and then Abbie himself. He was just causing too much hassle for people, he was not being careful. Hollywood quote unquote definitely wanted him out. I was anointed to be the guy that goes with him and Johanna to Mexico, to set up shop. We load everything up and Kinky gives him a lot of cash and we head out. At night in a Volkswagen bus with a sleeper in back. Abbie seemed okay. He knew why he was going there. The fact that he was able to talk about it was reassuring to me. Temporarily.

[The next afternoon] Abbie says, "Let's pull over." He's looking at the map, he said, this is a really neat town called Guimas. He said there's this one hotel there, you just rent a room and you're right on the beach. We have lunch and go back to the room and Abbie's pretty wasted, so Johanna pops a pill in him, I'm sure it's Thorazine. And he crashes. I'd found out they were having this dance in town that night. I said, "Maybe we'll go out and check it out." He says, "Well, just be careful."

We split and found this dance at an old high school gymnasium. There was a live band. They took a break. I asked Johanna if she wanted anything and she said not yet. There was a commotion going on, very far away from us. I looked over and I felt this whizzing go past my ear. A full can of beer plunked Johanna right on her lip. I don't know how this motherfucker had done it, he wasn't aiming at us, but it made a perfect arc, all the way across that fucking room. She's turning ashen, bleeding rather profusely.

Everybody's going *"Aaaahhhhhh, la gringa está wounded,"* whatever. We go to this Red Cross place. This was a Saturday night and it was filled with people that had gotten into accidents. There was blood everywhere. Johanna kept saying, "It's very important they use a butterfly stitch so I don't get a scar." So I said, *"Mariposa stitcho,"* but the Red Cross lady spoke English. So they sew her up real quick, a really nice job. I drove back to the hotel.

Johanna said, "I don't want to go in and have him wake up right yet." She said she'd sleep in the van and told me to wake her up before he wakes. I remember lying in bed there, thinking, "Holy fuck, something major's gonna happen today." Abbie wakes up kind of groggy, he says, "Where's Josie?" I said, "She's sleeping in the van. Now, look, I gotta tell you something. Don't freak out." Immediately, he starts to freak out. "What the fuck is going on here! I fucking go to sleep, we're supposed to have a quiet night and all of a sudden you guys go out!" He duck-walks out to the fucking car, slams the door behind him. Maybe twenty minutes later they both come back and I guess she'd sort of explained the situation to him and so he's just going, "Now what are we going to do? Let's go up to the hotel and get some breakfast." Before they got breakfast, they stayed back there to fuck. She said that always calmed him down. And she said, "We should call Bert and tell him what's happened."

So it's seven in the morning and I go next door to this fancy hotel to make the call. And I do a double take. We've taken all these incredible precautions to get out of Hollywood so that he'd stop having this Hollywood mentality. I see, walking by the big fountain in the middle of the courtyard of this hotel, Burt Reynolds, Liza Minnelli, Gene Hackman and Robby Benson. They were filming *Lucky Lady* there. I just saw big trouble, capital *T*. So I call Bert and he said one of the producers was his friend and if we run into any trouble he should help us out.

Kelly was unable to steer Abbie away from the movie people.

Ken Kelley He goes up and acts like this flipped-out Hollywood mogul, "I'm making this Fidel movie." Now, he's making really nasty comments, mumbling "You motherfuckers" under his breath, and then he'd flip back into "I really am a producer." I looked at Johanna and she said, "Did you take your pill this morning?" "I don't need no fuckin' pill! You're all trying to poison me!" I thought, I want to get the fuck out of here because it's not my job to baby-sit a psychotic.

Through Bert Schneider's friend, arrangements were made to fly Johanna back to Los Angeles. Kelley accompanied her back. Abbie was left to await a call from Bert.

* * *

Diane Peterson Our case had gone on for two years. Carol had tried to split and she'd been caught at the airport. So before we copped a plea she did ten months in Rikers. The judge, who was called Hanging Mary at the time, wanted me to do a year. The night before the sentencing, Cunningham, the assistant district attorney, went to her and said that he thought I should get probation, because he liked my demeanor in court. I showed up.

Mayer Vishner Ramer did time. She was taped extolling the virtues of this product. Diane was on probation for a few years and she behaved herself.

Ken Kelley Johanna went down to Mexico again, after Abbie had calmed down a little bit. I had planted the idea of doing a *Playboy* interview with him. He said fine, maybe I could get him some extra bucks for that. That fall I went down briefly to see Abbie. I came back Thanksgiving and we did a lot of sessions.

Jeff Nightbyrd Abbie called me before he went underground. He said, "If I ever come down to Texas can you take care of me?" He was just checking out his options. "Sure, of course we can do it."

Kinky Friedman Abbie came and stayed with me at my ranch in Texas. It took a measure of courage on my part. I didn't know whether the feds were gonna come in and arrest me and take us all away. I'm not a paranoid person but maybe there were people constantly monitoring where Abbie was. It's like what the old Federales said about Pancho Villa. They could've had him anytime, they just let him slip away through kindness, I suppose. That's what the song says. The real reason is because had they taken Abbie away they would have created a martyr.

Abbie stayed with me a few times. He rode horses, he fished, hiked around, went into town, shot pool.

Though he didn't want to give any interviews, Abbie was so hard up for cash that he accepted a wager with Nightbyrd.

Jeff Nightbyrd I said if you win [the pool game], you win $150; if I win, you get $150 but I get an interview. He's a better pool player but I got a shot at an eight ball, a real tough shot, a cross bank shot on the eight ball into the side pocket. Bang, I was lucky, I made it, and he always was an honorable gambler. He was so pissed off. "Goddammit, *Playboy* would pay me thousands for this and you got it for $150." In the article, I embellished this big account of all this plastic surgery but the fact was he looked pretty much the same. His nose looked a little more fucked up.

From the *Austin Sun*, 12/4/75

CONVERSATION WITH ABBIE HOFFMAN ON THE RUN

By Jeff Nightbyrd

. . . As the highway whistled under the front wheels, the beer had given the conversation energy. In this year of cynicism I wondered what Abbie thought the important issues were. His answer startled me. "I think we better talk globally because I've adopted a much more orthodox communist view." My mind reeled—the apostle of individual action and theatrical stunts which won avalanches of criticism from hardliners was now calling himself a communist!

"Do you want me to print that?"

"Sure!" he answered enthusiastically. "I think it's time people should say they're communists. I used to say I was an anarchist or maybe a hedonistic communist, but around the world people understand the force that's fighting for them is communism."

Ken Kelley I went back to Mexico around Christmas with Toby Rafelson. She brought this big piece of video equipment, because *Playboy* was thinking maybe *Saturday Night Live* could do a segment to promote the piece. We put a bandanna around his face; that's when I took the still pictures for the interview.

Jeff Nightbyrd One of the most interesting things he told me when he showed up in Texas on the lam was he and Josie would stay at KOA campgrounds. All these old people would go "Oh, look at the sweet young couple. Would you come over to our Winnebago and have hamburgers tonight?" Abbie said, "You know, Jeff, this country is pretty racist. I go around and all kinds of people tell me anti-Semitic jokes and jokes about niggers. Abbie Hoffman never heard those jokes before."

From the *Austin Sun,* 12/11/75

PART TWO: LOVE AND PAIN IN THE UNDERGROUND

By Jeff Nightbyrd

"You know what I learned from being on the road?" Abbie asked me as he gazed out the window of the car . . . "There is a denial of the spirit of the Sixties. That spirit meant one thing: that people had a hope of changing things through an incredible kind of optimistic energy. Whether it was naive or not, it's a spirit that people felt inside themselves. And they believed that they had the power to change the society and affect their own destiny. Whether or not that's an illusion, it's an incredible adrenaline, and an incredible psychological cure for what ails a person, a generation, or a society. Now that Spirit is missing from young people today. They're unhappy and they talk about suicide."

Ken Kelley Back in Chicago, every day I'd face the next stack of transcripts and just go "Holy fucking shit." Abbie kept saying, "Make sure that my politics comes through." I said, "Believe me, your politics will come through." We had rapped about his mother and father, first marriage, his going to Brandeis, Maslow, his involvement in the civil rights movement, the Yippies and the Village, it was really terrific.

Kelley wrote a sidebar that placed Abbie at a sprawling Texas ranch.

Ken Kelley Later Abbie told me Kinky had this ranch in Texas. Had I known that, I would've put it in Arizona 'cause I didn't want to get him in trouble. I was very careful to disguise the whereabouts to preserve his identity. So everything is going to press, and I get this call from [radical attorney] Michael Kennedy's office. There's a package here for you from somebody. I knew it must have been Abbie. It was this huge manuscript that he'd written that bore absolutely no relation to the interview whatsoever. He had decided to interview himself and he preceded it with a note, "This is the most important thing in my life, make sure that they run this. I went over this with my cell and this is what my people want me to say." Now, I didn't know what was in his head and what was real. I wasn't going to say, Sure you have a cell, who doesn't have a gweat big wittle communist cell. But then I read this interview and there was not even a snippet of anything that we had talked about. It was like I was interviewing some Marxist scholar for the Albanian *Daily News,* where all he talks about is the importance of communism and discipline and how he's renounced all of his bourgeois past. I flipped out. *Playboy* was literally on the presses. I'd sent him the galleys. Plus, this wasn't the deal!

Two weeks later I get a call from Kennedy's office. Abbie had a shit fit. How could I! They say we've got to pull the interview, you can't run that. Kennedy says, "How much would it take to stop *Playboy* from publishing it?" I said, "Nobody in the world has that kind of money. But even if we could, that wasn't my agreement with Abbie that he'd write his own version of it." *Playboy* asked me to go on a P.R. tour and I went everywhere, defending Abbie, presenting his plight, saying he's a good guy.

From the *Playboy* Interview, May 1976

Playboy: If you could choose your way of dying, what would it be?

Hoffman: I used to imagine Richard Nixon losing his temper and strangling me on national television. But I think Eric Sevareid would be a better choice, because he stands for all that's true and rational. If he blew his cool and leaped over his desk to strangle me, everyone in America would find out what I already know—that he's always naked from the waist down. So if I could make him show his pecker and hairy white legs on television while he strangled me—yeah, he'd be much better for the role than Nixon.

Playboy: What would you say to people who claim that because you were driven underground, the Government won and you lost?

Hoffman: To me, the issue has always been defined in terms of hide-and-seek—and I'm on the loose. You know what Che Guevara said, that he was looking for one person to carry the flag, just one person. And Che is *the* saint of Latin America.

Playboy: And you feel you're that one flag carrier? Aren't you romanticizing this underground life of yours?

Hoffman: Shit. This going underground can be done. This is nothing. You got to have been chased by the Ku Klux Klan through Mississippi at five A.M. without a road map, trying to play someone from Tennessee who's just visiting. *That's* trouble. That's what the media don't know about me. Nobody knows that about me. Most people just think I appear on TV as a radical clown who throws money around and has long hair and acts crazy. This underground stuff isn't glamorous, but what most people don't know is that I've been practicing for it all my life.

Jeremy Larner I was sad when I read the interview in *Playboy*. The Abbie who, in his wildness and bravery, his idealism and confusion and suffering, had touched beauty, had by then become an "image," a product concocted and marketed, I thought, for the revolution of the asses.

SPRING 1976

Abbie, claiming his cover was blown, left Mexico for Canada.

Abe Peck I'm at *Rolling Stone* and I get a call. Abbie is denouncing the *Playboy* piece. There's an unfortunate mistake in it, where it says radical sheep instead of radical chic. But most of all Abbie really feels that Johanna, Angel, has been exposed and he's freaking out. Abbie's version of being worried about having your cover blown is to call a lot of people to come do something and use the media. So I went up to Toronto. It's the first time I saw Abbie manic. He wants to go to the track, and people are trying to restrain him.

Ken Kelley All of a sudden I was being painted as this monster who had deliberately set out to destroy him, that I'd printed false stuff. Abbie brought pictures of him and Johanna burning their documents in this open grill to prove it. Then Johanna got it in her mind that I owed her $2,000 for the plastic surgery when she got hit in Mexico with the beer can. I never talked to Abbie again.

Mayer Vishner A standard Abbie operation, everybody feels ripped off by the other person. The *Playboy* interview was like a beer to an alcoholic. It was back to talking politics, being famous, and it made him nuts.

Jeff Jones After early 1976 I didn't have any more time to worry about Abbie because I had to worry about myself and my whole survival in a whole new way. The Weather Underground fell apart. We all went our separate ways underground. Eleanor and I and our kid became a working-class family in the Bronx.

* * *

Anita Hoffman Abbie was underground when Phil Ochs was cracking up. They were both probably cracking up at the same time, although I didn't make the connection then.

Jack Newfield A lot of people lost their way after the movement. Phil stopped writing songs. He became obsessed by Sonny Liston and he came to see me at the *[Village] Voice* a few times about the Kennedy assassinations.

Stew Albert Phil definitely saw himself as a supporter and critic of American liberalism. [His song] "Love Me, I'm a Liberal," that was his making fun of it, but when liberalism collapsed, Phil made efforts to psych himself up for being a revolutionary. But it really wasn't him. Then he tried to revive fifties rock and roll six months too soon. Phil ran out of a position, and his position may have been his creative stimulus. He didn't know what to write about or why to write it or how. The whole world knew about Phil's mental illness, you couldn't miss it. He acted it out in a very public way.

Stella Resnick Phil had given up alcohol and he hadn't recouped his spirits by any means, but he was back in New York and he was enjoying himself. When I left town for the summer I gave Phil my apartment at the Chelsea, because he wanted it so badly. While he was there his soul took a rapid decline; he went back on alcohol.

Bill Kunstler I was in Folk City and Phil came in with a meat hook, and he banged it into the table and just glowered at everybody and then left.

Jay Levin Phil, to his great misfortune, had an alcoholic background. And whereas Abbie had the inner survival quality of fixing on a woman who would balance him, Phil didn't have that quality. Phil had many more problems with women. And Phil didn't have as many moves as Abbie, either. Phil was adrift.

Larry Sloman I had taken over Jerry and Phil's apartment on Prince Street from Carol Realini and my roommate and I let Phil crash there for a while because he literally had no place to go. He was in desperate shape. When he was John Train, this alter ego he had concocted, he was flamboyant and scary. But most of the time, he was just Phil, depressed and meek as a lamb. Every morning he would get up and pace the living room and recite out loud, "I can see it now. My obituary in the *New York Times.* 'Folksinger Found Dead.' "

Stella Resnick He couldn't write anymore, he couldn't sing anymore, he was paralyzed. Phil hung himself, he strangled himself. This is the self-expression chakra. Phil was enraged that he couldn't produce anything anymore.

Stew Albert When I got a little bit out of shock, I said I miss Phil, I really loved Phil, but the worst part of it is Phil has legitimized suicide for our generation. As a result of this, other people are gonna do it.

* * *

Jay Levin Before the Barry Freed personality emerged and they settled in Fineview [New York], there were some extremely serious moments with Abbie when the manic stage came out. After they left Mexico, they had gone to Montreal thinking that Canada would be a good place to be. Abbie was taking out a lot on Johanna. For the first time he began hitting her and she split, very shaken up. I went up for a few days before I had to go to Vegas on a trip. Abbie was all over the fucking place. First of all, he was being very psychic; he had been seeing all these numbers in his head, and he gave me a hundred dollars to play these numbers on Mayday. When I went to Vegas, I played them just a few minutes before Mayday expired at the baccarat table and I won twelve hundred bucks for him.

Anyway, in Montreal, he was stalking around a hotel. In those days I was beginning to learn a lot about psychology, so I had my first experiences trying to talk to him from a therapeutic mode. He'd rant about Johanna. He'd rant about somebody who had fucked him over. He'd talk a mile a minute about some close call he'd had with a cop. Of course, even in the worst periods, he was never without astute statements about life, but he was on overwhelm. He'd been having trouble sleeping, he had this incredible restless energy. And the thing to do was just try to ride it out with him, divert his attention. Remember, it wasn't until later that he learned that he really had a disease. So the experience itself was frightening to him in a way that he was a little too macho to communicate. Even if he hadn't been manic-depressive, here's his big, big soul confined to hiding out from cops, not being able to do what really was his work. Without a disease that's destabilizing. So I spent a couple, three days just hanging in, hanging out.

Stew Albert Abbie called me and he certainly sounded very optimistic, big things going on, big this, big that, big networks. It sounded a little crazy. And he asks if I could come up to Montreal. I took the train and we spent some time together. He certainly seemed sane. He was telling me he was thinking of writing a manual on how to be a fugitive. I told him about the Phil Ochs tribute concert that was coming up that I was gonna speak at. Somewhere along the line he decided he was gonna come down to the Phil Ochs event. I advised him against that. But he was gonna do it. So we went back down to Woodstock together on the bus. We didn't sit together. Abbie had some friends there. He got off the bus and I went one way and he went another. His friends were waiting for him at the bus stop.

Marty Carey I get a call from Stew, he says, "Hi, I'm in Kingston [a town near Woodstock] with our friend." I said, "Oh?" So now he's gonna pass our friend on to me.

Susan Carey Stew said he can't handle it anymore.

Stew Albert The next day was the Phil Ochs memorial at the Felt Forum [in New York]. Abbie went down for it. It was a great evening.

Marty Carey [Back in Woodstock] I deposited Abbie out here in the Mount Pleasant Hotel. And he proceeds to shit in the parking lot, go riding, pull a knife on the horse guy because he couldn't ride wherever he wanted to. I was in town, he jumped out, he saw Ed Sanders at the library, he panicked Ed. I'm going crazy, "What is he doing? He's gonna get caught, he wants to get caught." I don't know what to do.

John Eskow I hadn't had contact with Abbie for years. One day I was sitting in my little roach-infested apartment on West 93rd Street, struggling over some obscure surrealist poem with a big tumbler full of Scotch in my hand and the phone rang, and this very familiar voice said, "Hi, it's me, don't say my name." I said, "How you doing?" He said, "Good. I want you to come write a book with me." He was writing this autobiographical book with heavy emphasis on the '67 to '70 period. I asked him why he wanted me to do it and he said, "Because you were around all the time and you didn't take that much acid, so you probably remember it."

I made a reconnaissance trip to Woodstock to meet him. Abbie was staying in a run-down, shabby little motel. My girlfriend and I and Marty Carey went over. We all went into the room, he had a big bottle of brandy, he was drinking a lot, and it was the seventh game of the NBA play-offs between the Suns and the Celtics, his hometown team. There'd been the whole thing of "you won't recognize me, don't be shocked," but he looked exactly the same, except that he had a bald spot. He seemed to have convinced himself that he looked totally different.

Our conversation during the first half was largely about the momentous issues of him being busted. But he kept interrupting to say like "Oh, did you see that jump shot!" and then he would go back to talking about what it was like to be a fugitive, [then] he'd say, "Oh no, out of bounds, I don't believe it." And he became much more consumed with the basketball game than with his own status as a fugitive. And finally—it's a legendary game, it was like a double-overtime, seventh-game play-off, and he had us all, of course, rooting for the Celtics, and we were screaming and the room was also completely, needless to say, suffused with marijuana smoke. Suddenly there's a pounding on the door and a voice saying, "All right, that's it, open up in there." To be trapped in a hotel room with Abbie at that point was to really face the possibility of getting killed, because you knew he was not about to go quietly. So the door opened, but it wasn't the cops, it was the motel manager saying, "Hold it down, people are complaining." We felt like we had gotten away with murder because the guy had no idea it was Abbie. And we went into another overtime, and Abbie started screaming again and we started saying, "Abbie, man, the guy said he would call the cops if it happened again." But Abbie's excitement was so great that he could not control himself and he was jumping up and down, yelling "Yes! yes! yes!" And this guy came and smacked on the door again and said, "I'm warning you, I'm gonna call the cops." The cops never came, that was the luck of Abbie at that point.

I got home that night and I realized that $140 was missing from my wallet. Marty said, "I saw Abbie holding your wallet at one point, he put it down on the bed." I knew Abbie had stolen it from me. It was clear to me that he considered it dues to the people. But I was really poor. I couldn't confront him, it was still too much younger brother/older brother. So Marty called him up that night and said, "Why'd you take $140 from John's wallet?" Abbie said, "I didn't take any money from John's wallet." Marty said, "Come on, I saw you." Abbie said, "No, I was just rearranging the bills in it." He didn't want to cop to it. But the next day he gave me eighty bucks back. When we went back in the morning, I found him on the front lawn of this motel playing mumblety-peg, throwing a long knife into the lawn over and over, and making it stick upright so the blade would quiver. There were some very horrified motel patrons walking by. Abbie was screaming semi-incoherently and throwing this knife and running and picking it up out of the ground and then throwing it back, shouting about being in L.A. last week with Candy Bergen. I realized he was having a psychotic episode. Then he seemed to calm down a bit and he and I went to a coffee shop to talk about the book. This was the first time I'd been alone with him and I was really scared. I felt trapped between two enormous forces. The American police system, which was trying to hunt down Abbie, and I don't think it's paranoid to say wouldn't have minded killing him given any provocation, and Abbie, who seemed equally bent on some kind of insane confrontation with them.

I felt an incredible sense of drama. I was with one of America's most wanted fugitives, sitting in a coffee shop, and he kept saying to me, "Don't call me Abbie, I'm Barry Freed, if you want to talk to me I'm Barry." He said it so often that all I could think of was "Okay, don't call him Abbie, don't call him Abbie." About five minutes later, a state trooper came and sat down right next to me. Abbie was on my right, the state trooper was on my left. Abbie and I finished our conversation, but at a leisurely pace, and I just thought, "What kind of idiot cop, sitting two stools away, wouldn't recognize him?" With all his warnings to me—"I'm undercover now, they'll fucking kill me if they find me"—he was talking just like Abbie Hoffman. And the state trooper's going "Marge, another cup of java." Finally the time came to go and we stood up and Abbie said, "Okay, John, this is on you." And because he had stolen my wallet I was really pissed off. I said, "Fuck you, Abbie." His name just slipped out. Now we were hovering over the state trooper, and the guy never looked up from his coffee. I began to tremble as we walked out, and as we got out into the parking lot I said, "Man, I'm so sorry, I can't believe I did that." And he said, "It's okay, I just did a Carlos Castaneda thing when you said my name. Didn't you see that the state trooper didn't see me?" I said, "Yeah." He said, "I wasn't there. I've been reading Castaneda and I know how to do that shit now. When the cop looked up, I was invisible."

Marty Carey I'm trying to get him out of the hotel and find him a private place. So I called Eric Anderson, the singer. Eric is thrilled, privileged to have Abbie stay at his house. Ten hours later, Eric calls up. Abbie had made $400 worth of phone calls . . .

Susan Carey . . . and is he gonna get paid for them?

Eric Anderson, *singer/songwriter* The Careys needed to unload him on somebody. I was an innocent lamb. Who would ever suspect me, this WASP? Abbie basically wanted a place to meet his wife and son. So Anita came up with america. I think they were trying to get it back together. He was with somebody else, actually. But I think he wanted to get back. He wanted both of them.

Stew Albert Abbie punched Ed Sanders in the balls at one point. I think he apologized for it later. He was in bad shape.

Ed Sanders After the incident where he hit me at Eric Anderson's house, I didn't have anything to do with him from 1976 till God, I don't know.

Eric Anderson Anita and america left. Then one night I just said, "Do you want to go out? I know it's risky but we'll paint a mustache." So we went to the Bear and we started having fun and drinking and he was talking to people and it was human, real life. Then we started going out. He got so fed up with the absurdity of having to hide. I took my daughter riding and he liked that and he wanted to go riding. He had a little too much fun.

Stew Albert He started hanging out in the Bear Restaurant, basically telling people who he was. The word was all over Woodstock. He was driving all his friends crazy. That's the craziest I ever saw Abbie. Bar none.

Marty Carey Finally I called Johanna and I said, "You just have to take him away." Abbie wrote a check out to me for a million dollars. Then they went to New York.

Stew Albert We actually had a barbecue party and celebrated. It was like we were liberated.

Susan Carey I think the underground thing was the thing that killed him because he just couldn't do anything. He would probably blame it on her that he would be able to be himself if not for her. She'd say to us, "He tried to kill me, he tried to smother me with a pillow." They called us down to the city, and she wanted us to take him.

Marty Carey They were at the Gramercy Park Hotel and we went there. I didn't want to believe that he was attacking her, it was too scary to believe, but I had never seen that kind of behavior.

Susan Carey We told Johanna he needed a doctor, not people like us. I felt that he should be in a hospital. Yet Abbie pulled me aside and told me that I should make sure that I keep in touch with Anita. It was hard because that Abbie was always there, the loving Abbie, the one who really cared about people.

Jay Levin They had found a nice little house in this beautiful town on the lake, north of Montreal. And again, he and Johanna had gone at it. He was into this macho thing of throwing these knives around the house. I went up for several days, it was really an emergency.

Just before Jay's visit, Abbie had been picked up for a minor offense and had been in the Montreal jail. He managed to talk his way out before the fingerprint reports came back.

Jay Levin At that time of my life I had really begun to believe in the powers of the therapeutic dialogue. I didn't know about manic-depression as a disease treatable by chemicals. I always thought of therapy as emotional education. So I began to talk to him about fear mechanisms, and he couldn't deal with it. There was nearly a violent outburst once when I started talking about his father.

He had a hard time looking at himself. And he had very high demands for people in his closest circle, like the children. So he replicated his father's behavior. I can't say in those few days I had a great success in getting him to use me as a surrogate therapist. So I nursed him, we walked around town.

Mayer Vishner His craziness was manifesting itself in things like making plans to come to New York for America's fifth-birthday party in July because he'd be so well disguised no one would see him. At the same time he was convinced that they, whoever they were, were closing in on him. In the meantime he's calling all kinds of people he shouldn't be calling, sometimes with grandiose ideas and sometimes just with crap.

It evolved that the best team to deal with this particular crisis was me and Dellinger. Abbie always had a lot of respect for Dellinger. So Dave and I flew to Montreal and we drove up to this little town, St. Adèle. Abbie was on his best behavior. He got into some kind of political discussion with Dave right away. Then Dave had to leave and I had another night. He argued with me about vegetarianism. He wanted me to defend vegetarianism, meantime he made me a great vegetarian dinner. Then we went for a walk through town. He said he was crazy. He played me tapes of him talking to himself. He would walk down the streets of St. Adèle, talking into a tape recorder about how nuts he is. It was an argument between the paranoid Abbie and the one who wasn't worried. There was the frightened Abbie who was trying to figure out if he was in imminent danger, and there was the other one who was trying to reassure him that if he would just shut up and go on being Barry or whoever he was that week, everything would be fine. This argument evolved until I remember distinctly at some point the paranoid one is saying, "Someone's taping us right now," and the other one says, "Of course, someone's taping us, *I'm* taping us."

After dinner, we go to this bar and Abbie wants to shoot pool. He puts his quarter down. I go to the pinball game. Abbie asks me to justify, in Talmudic fashion, my interest in this game. So I explain to him that you can be very skillful, very lucky, some combination of the two, and it varies from game to game, so that this game is the perfect metaphor for life itself. He takes that in. He suggests that the next game be a contest. He goes first and he's just flipping wildly. He hits it a few times and then it's my turn. I remember deciding as he plays the second ball that he'll probably be more comfortable if I'm not hovering. I go watch the pool players, but something is amiss, because there's no noise coming from the pinball game. I turn around and he's crouching by the pinball machine. He's found a discarded matchbook, he's folded it up and stuck it under one of the front legs of the pinball game, and now he's scanning the floor, looking for another matchbook. No one is paying any attention to him but my imagination is racing. I'm thinking someone's gonna see him, there's gonna be an argument, maybe a fight, cops. I say, "What the fuck do you think you're doing?" And he says, "It isn't fair. The machine has gravity on its side." At that point I got our asses out of there. By this time, he was fine and I was nuts.

Joe LoGuidice Abbie couldn't handle the obscurity. He was bothered that the cops weren't looking hard enough, he took it personally. He was hysterical. That was the point where Johanna decided to take him up to the Thousand Islands, figuring that would cool him out.

Annie Gefell We're right on the Canadian border. It's like the fjords without the cliffs, rocky islands in the middle of the St. Lawrence River. The river at some points is eight miles wide, at some points it's a quarter of a mile wide, barely wide enough to fit two ships by each other. It's very beautiful. In the summertime there's more of a visiting population. Less than 10 percent of the people stay for the whole winter.

Johanna's place was on the river, in Fineview. A white house with landscaping and trees and a garden and a dock. It's a very old house, five, six generations maybe.

Jay Levin Abbie probably felt secure enough that the FBI had not identified her as Angel and therefore would not come knocking on her door looking for him. So the strategy was to bring him slowly into a place where he could feel secure and try to live something more close to a normal life with him. It was incredibly good for him. She was so happy.

FALL 1976

Annie Gefell Johanna brought Abbie to the river right after this horrendous oil spill. Three hundred thousand gallons of crude oil had dumped into the river because this ship ran aground on a rock the week before the American bicentennial celebration. I met him that fall. He was very aloof and detached. When I came to know him, I realized that he was just figuring out if I could be trusted. They were a mile from the Canadian border, so it was a relatively safe place.

John Eskow My girlfriend and I joined Abbie and Johanna in the Thousand Islands. Abbie and I were going to work on the book. At that point I told him that I wanted to write a movie called *Soon to Be a Major Motion Picture,* and he filed away the information and then ripped it off. That was my title. I think we spent three weeks there and the rest of the time we worked by correspondence or he would come to New York or I would just write or edit the manuscript on my own. But the period up there was the intense period of writing and remembering. That was very stressful for him too because he was going in and out of Barry Freed and back to Abbie in the course of our sessions. We would go up to the second floor of the Lawrenson house, and he would blast this Eagles tape so nobody could hear us. But he would become so excited in remembering things about that period that he would start yelling. I would say Barry, Barry, what about the cover? "Fuck Mayor Daley!" It was close to the other houses and there was a little old lady who lived next door, who Abbie/Barry would have long discussions with about weeds.

Abbie was getting $20,000 to write the book, which was a pretty big advance for that time. He offered me $5,000. So this is the odd, rough justice that Abbie would dispense. He'd steal $140 from my wallet, and then he'd offer me $5,000, which was, I think, very fair actually. Believe me, I did the work for it. As always, he was carrying around trunks full of manuscript pages about his childhood, his adolescence. He had nothing about the Yippies. He had nothing about acid, the East Village, any of that, because he didn't remember it.

The most striking memory I have, aside from going on madcap boat rides down the St. Lawrence, is of me, Abbie, my girlfriend and five or six of Barry Freed's friends gathered in Abbie's house. These people really had no idea that he was Abbie Hoffman. And we're watching the *NBC Nightly News,* Garrick Utley reporting, and suddenly on comes a broadcast about a "Free Abbie Hoffman" rally in New York. My girlfriend and I just looked at each other in utter disbelief. We're lying on the floor, next to Abbie Hoffman, with all these people around, and one of the people says, "God, I wonder where that guy is?" And Abbie, without missing a beat, said, "Ah, he's probably down in Mexico having a great time, getting drunk and hanging out in cantinas." I thought, "That's style. He's the Errol Flynn of psychedelia."

Out of concern for both Abbie's psyche and her own existence, Anita proposed a small community to provide more support for Abbie and some fresh air and trees for their child. She and America, Johanna and Abbie, and friends Sam and Walli Leff rented a house together in Santa Fe.

Anita Hoffman I guess my hidden agenda was that I saw it as partial relief from child care. But [the Leffs], who didn't have any kids, would say, "Oh, it's sunset, let's take a walk." I was burning with jealousy but I didn't have the nerve to articulate it, so I acted kind of bitchy, and nobody quite understood why.

America Hoffman They got along well, surprisingly well. He's a great guy, but he needed to be taken care of. He was very demanding, people who were close to him know that. He was funny though. Even when I was a kid and I wouldn't understand half of what he said, I still thought he was funny.

Anita Hoffman It lasted maybe two months, and then Abbie and Johanna went to Florida. I was so in love with Santa Fe and New Mexico that I stayed there with America for eighteen months.

Gus Reichbach He was writing articles and tweaking J. Edgar Hoover's nose. But then the Carter administration came in and Abbie Hoffman was not viewed as a major fugitive.

Joe LoGuidice Abbie told me he had a job for a while as a tour director at the FBI Building in Washington. He probably just took the tour.

JULY 1977

America Hoffman The first real contact I had with Abbie as a father was when I went out to the Thousand Islands. I was about five or six. I hadn't seen him for two years, he was like some mythological figure by then. They told me he wasn't my dad. I remember being with him for a while and then realizing that this was actually my dad. My stepmother spent a lot of time with me. And I was on my own a little bit. All the kids used to make fun of me because I was from New Mexico. They used to put a hat on the ground and start dancing around it. I never wanted to leave the house 'cause the kids would always abuse me.

Of course, my dad would abuse me too. My dad would try to teach me ball and he'd just throw the ball at me really hard. I'd just think of it as this weapon being hurled at me. It would hit me in the head and I go "Owww, I don't want to do this no more." Then when he'd get really mad he'd say, "Okay, you've been lazy and you've been sitting around pretending that you're sick all day, you never play out with the kids. I'm taking you to the soccer field." I'm like "No! no!" And he'd drag me to play with all these older kids because he thought that would toughen me up. There was no game, they'd just kick me around the field. They wouldn't want me on their team. First I'd have to suffer the humiliation of not being wanted on anyone's team, and sitting in my slouch position, and they'd just kick me around the field. I'd think maybe I could get some protection from him or something but then he'd be out there watching, like "Good game." I guess he was tough when he was a kid.

Mayer Vishner Abbie loved the kid, he called him Superkid. He really taught him that he could do anything. I liked that because my parents taught me I couldn't do shit. I went up to the Thousand Islands. America must have been five or six and it was terrific, the way they were together. If America wanted to get cereal from the cupboard, he put the chairs together and climbed up and got the cereal. I said to Abbie, "You're not afraid he's gonna break his neck?" Abbie said, "No, they don't hurt themselves. If they know what they're capable of, and if you let 'em, they're not gonna do anything that they're gonna hurt themselves."

Stew Albert He didn't hit the kid or anything like that, but he certainly didn't make America seem like a welcome guest in his house. At one point, with Abbie gone and no food in the house, Judy and I took America out for lunch. Abbie was trying to get the kid to be self-sufficient. But the way he was going about it was hideous.

Lee Weiner I was walking in the Village and some fucking Orthodox Jew with the pais and the hat sticks his head out of a fucking phone booth, says "Lee!" Abigail had pais, yes. I actually sat on the curb I was laughing so hard. We went to my place, spent the afternoon. He was fine. But he was hard on himself like he always was, critiquing his performances. I don't think Abbie ever trusted himself after that Vegas crack-up, ever.

Gus Reichbach I remember once meeting him on 23rd Street. He had a beard and a yarmulke. We had cheeseburgers. I told him that was probably not a good cover, wearing a yarmulke and eating a cheeseburger.

1977

Lola Cohen, *actress* I was at the Actors Studio and I had a very good friend named Ellen Chenoweth, who's now a big casting director, who loved Abbie and was involved in the antiwar movement. Abbie was writing *Soon to Be a Major Motion Picture.* He didn't have a publisher, he had nothing. He was so upset he had no money and what was he gonna do? So Ellen said that Peter Masterson, who later directed *A Trip to Bountiful,* was interested in the manuscript. I met with Peter and Ellen, and Peter through Thom Mount's people bought the option. Abbie said he'd give me money and he got $100,000 but I never saw a nickel. He said he had to give it to all his ex-wives. But that was great because I felt like I helped somehow.

Dave Lubell, *Abbie's entertainment lawyer* There was always some talk about Abbie coming aboveground and appearing in the movie. His dream was to do movies.

Anita Hoffman They went to Europe for the winter. He must have been driving his agent, Elaine [Markson], crazy because every other letter to me was he was always worried about money so he'd list all these article projects that Elaine was trying to sell for him. But there were always delays and disappointments. He did an interview with R. D. Laing, he interviewed these French intellectuals.

Jerry Lieberman While he was in France he forged some kind of official letter from *Playboy* saying that he was a restaurant critic. He went with Johanna from one restaurant to the other and they just pulled out all the stops trying to feed and entertain them everywhere they went.

Mike Elias, *television writer* When we heard about it later everyone thought it was terribly amusing. But when I started to think about it, a great restaurant in France is not an enemy to the people nor a corporation like Con Ed that deserves to be ripped off. It's a family business and these are people who work their asses off. I worked through college as a waiter in the Catskills and I'm saying to myself, "I wonder if he tipped the waiters?"

Joie Davidow They were in France doing that restaurant scam. He called to give me a recipe for rabbit. I couldn't believe it. You're risking death to give me a recipe for rabbit stew?

Dennis Roberts, *radical attorney* Anita gets hold of me. Abbie needs a divorce. He's underground, how the fuck am I going to get the forms? So I prepared a divorce pleading. I filed it in Alameda County Superior Court and it had to be served. So I mail it back to Gerry Lefcourt, I don't want to know. One day the papers came back to me, there was his signature on them.

Rick Spencer Abbie came up to the river in 1976, I met him in 1977. I was still sailing in 1976; I used to be a merchant seaman. I intuitively knew he was somehow involved in counterculture and the underground. He and I got along real well. You know, the Jewish sense of humor, it's not too common around here. And he got totally into the gardening.

Viva I had picked out this house up here [in the Thousand Islands] when I was about fourteen and forced my father to buy it. When we first arrived when I was twelve, we could see the water to the bottom. Of course this is the story of every river in the world now. We would dip our glasses in and drink. It was the cleanest water.

Then the Seaway gave my father lots of money to blast off forty feet of our property in the middle fifties. "Oh," Mother says, "there goes another blast." Nobody ever imagined fighting them or even saying there was anything wrong with blasting off forty feet of solid rock peninsula. It changed the current, it changed everything. All those heavy metals dumped in from Lake Ontario and all the Great Lakes ended up at our front door. In the sixties I began noticing the dirt in the water. I saw this really hideous moss growing on everything. Then you couldn't swim in our harbor anymore, it was so clogged. I remember a woman telling me how the detergent was making these grassy, spongy weeds grow and choke everything. That was the first time I heard that detergents were pollution. But until Abbie showed up, we just thought it was great to see all those ships going by. We never connected them with pollution or government interference in your life, or seven thousand people being displaced, or flooding seven communities and several islands downriver, or destroying the whole sturgeon population by destroying the rapids and therefore destroying the livelihood of the Mohawks from the St. Regis Reservation. We didn't know about it.

Annie Gefell People had jobs in restaurants, in hotels, in trinket shops, on boats, being gardeners for golf courses and summer cottages. Since tourism had been cut off drastically because of the oil spill, people just said, "We might as well go make twelve dollars an hour working on cleaning up the oil." So the oil spill got cleaned up in 1976 and some environmental effects remained but you could swim in the river so tourism came back. Then in 1978 the Army Corps of Engineers decided to run ships up and down the river during the winter months.

Rick Spencer These scientists did a half-million-dollar Department of Energy Conservation study and concluded that winter navigation would be a disaster. The Winter Navigation Board, a group of federal agencies, were going to go ahead anyway, they didn't care. So the scientists were trying to drum up local opposition.

Steve Taylor, a dock builder and liaison between the scientists and the community, distributed the six-hundred-page study to his friends.

Viva Nobody up there would have gotten organized if it wasn't for Abbie, nobody. They would never have even thought of opposing winter navigation. The Seaway is bad enough, but winter navigation? There would have been ships going to different ports all winter, breaking the ice, disrupting the whole ecology. I don't know how many houses they destroyed in the Thousand Islands downriver where they put the dam. They destroyed the rapids, built a reservoir without asking anybody. Entire islands with cattails and birds on them used to float past our house. Fishermen would weep because their fishing grounds were now gone. No one was asked, no one was consulted. Apparently Rick and those guys were sitting around moaning about what a bad thing it was. But they wouldn't have thought of organizing. They should make Abbie a saint. St. Abbie of the St. Lawrence.

Rick Spencer The next day, five or six people showed up at Barry and Johanna's and we started talking about it and then Abbie said, "We'll start a committee."

America Hoffman In four weeks there was a $1,200 phone bill. He was on two different phones at once, one on each ear.

Rick Spencer The bureaucracy was stacked against us. Congress had been supporting this project since 1965. The local congressman was a guy named Bob McEwen, who didn't like us too much either. He was just a Republican conservative, old-boy politician. He was up for reelection, so he was trying not to rock the boat.

The Corps was going to hold an informational meeting August 1st. So we started organizing and then about 450 people showed up for this meeting. This was unprecedented. There was this incredible anger and outrage because people around here know that ice has always saved this river. It shuts everything down for the winter months and gives it a chance to replenish.

Bea Schermerhorn We've been year-round residents for forty-five years. I gave a speech in the Alexandria Bay High School auditorium and I got a standing ovation.

Rick Spencer I don't think Abbie publicly spoke at that meeting. But afterwards he went up to these colonels with all their epaulets and he just looked them in the face and said, "We're not afraid of you. The U.S. Army hasn't won a war since 1945."

Annie Gefell That meeting completely threw the Army Corps of Engineers off. They were not prepared for this. Most people were definitely against it, on environmental and boondoggle tax money arguments.

AUGUST 1978

Bill Kunstler While Abbie was underground we gave a benefit for him at the Felt Forum.

Carol Realini Abbie planned the whole thing. He wrote all these long, handwritten memos on how he wanted the thing done.

Abbie gave instructions regarding fund-raising and entertainment, as well as providing the benefit organizers with specific reasons for his charges to be dropped.

Joe LoGuidice Terry Southern and I wrote that play for the Felt Forum thing. We got terrible reviews, but it was a great show. Abbie was in the audience. He was taking a lot of chances.

* * *

Rick Spencer Abbie tried not to be the up-front person at first. But nobody else knew how to deal with the media up there.

From the *Watertown Times*, 10/7/78

WRITER LEADS OPPOSITION TO WINTER NAVIGATION

By Larry Cole

Barry Freed, the fast-talking, ambitious public relations chairman of the Save the River committee is dredging up opposition to the proposed winter navigation on the St. Lawrence River.

Tucked away in an impromptu office in their home at Fineview on Wellesley Island, Mr. Freed, 42, and his wife, Johanna Lawrenson, 38, are surrounded by mounds of pamphlets and flyers about the committee and its work . . .

Mr. Freed has lived on the river for about four years, but his wife, the daughter of novelist and short story writer Helen Lawrenson, has spent summers on the St. Lawrence since childhood.

Miss Lawrenson, a former model, is now a free-lance photographer. Mr. Freed describes himself as a free-lance television script writer. They live six to eight months on the river, according to Mr. Freed. "The rest of the time we're nomads," he added.

Annie Gefell He couldn't depend on his notoriety. He had to explain what it was that he wanted [people] to do and why he wanted them to do it, or they weren't going to do it. We're talking about rugged individualists, we're not talking about people who see something and run with it. And the river's not a place known for its graciousness to Jews. He felt that he was a real outsider.

Bea Schermerhorn My first impression of Barry was that he was very loud and somewhat authoritative and he wasn't exactly my kind of person. Finally I said to my husband, "If I'm going to be part of this group, I'm going to go see what that office looks like." I came back from there and I said, "I don't care what you want to say about this guy, I have never seen such organization." He had a Rolodex and files all over the place.

Rick Spencer Abbie got [the journalist] Robert Boyle up and he wrote an article for *Sports Illustrated* that came out in November. It was our first national media exposure. Abbie understood exactly what had to be done, from day one. The moment I realized we had a chance to win was when I walked in the house one day and Abbie's on the phone talking to some guy in Governor Carey's office and the guy was buying Abbie's line. I remember saying to myself, "For the first time in my life I'm actually working with somebody who knows what he's doing."

By that fall the organization had rented an office, mounted a letter-writing campaign and was garnering media attention. Then Barry and Johanna left Fineview. Annie Gefell was designated by them to run the office.

Annie Gefell In January of 1979 they decided to shelve the demonstration project. I think that Abbie must've known that was going to happen, so he felt he could leave.

Rick Spencer The Winter Navigation Board said, "We're gonna send it back to Congress, let Congress decide, that's what they get paid to do." Everybody was really psyched. Abbie and Johanna were in California, but they called all the time and Abbie was just ecstatic, "Ah, you guys are doin' great." Then I said, "Let's go to Washington."

Jay Levin Abbie was absolutely out of his fucking wig. He called the *Herald-Examiner* reporter, had him meet him at the Hollywood sign and had his picture taken. He was running up and down Hollywood Boulevard saying hello to people. He showed up at my offices at the *L.A. Weekly* with a million ideas, but most of it was stories about how he was gonna be the only underground movie star.

DECEMBER 1978

Larry Sloman I get a call from Abbie. He's in town. I had met with him periodically when he'd come into Manhattan. One time we had lunch at a Jewish dairy restaurant on Canal Street. We discussed one of his typical media schemes but what I remembered most was his paranoia about getting recognized. If he was Myron Cohen maybe he'd get recognized. As it was, I'm sure nobody in the place even knew who Abbie Hoffman was.

Carol Realini Someone called me from some hotel in midtown and wanted me to come over. When I got there they were with Abbie but they didn't want to mention that on the phone. Abbie was in the throes of a very bad manic episode. He couldn't be left alone. As soon as I got there, they showed me which medication to give when, and gave me all the instructions about tying him up if necessary, and then they left me alone with this raving lunatic. Of course, I always had a very good relationship with Abbie and we very much loved each other, and I never feared him, ever. But if I ever came close to it, it was that day. He threatened me, he was ugly with this disease. He wanted to go out and play pool and he wanted to go be Abbie! He was calling people up, saying, "This is Abbie."

It became four in the morning and I was getting panicky because I had no way to get out of there until I could find someone to replace me. He did manage to get some people to come over and there were people in the hotel room, none of whom I knew or trusted to leave with him. One guy was a very big coke dealer and Abbie was doing coke on top of his craziness. I don't remember how I got out of there. I just remember being in that room for many, many hours while he bounced off the walls. I had to threaten him, I had to make out with him, I would have done anything to keep him from walking out the door.

He'd constantly be calling room service and they'd come in the room and he'd say, "Guess what? I'm Abbie Hoffman." He did everything short of go to FBI headquarters.

David Fenton, *publicist* We started planning his return a year and a half earlier. It became very apparent that he was having very, very bad mental breakdowns and episodes. Johanna was bearing the brunt of them, largely by herself.

Barry Gottehrer I'm working for this insurance company in Massachusetts, it's right around Christmastime and the phone rings. My kid answers and he's saying, "Yes, I've been a good boy, yes, I listen to my mother and father." I said, "Who is it?" My wife says, "Kevin says it's Santa Claus and he wants to talk to you." I pick up the phone and it's fucking Abbie. I said, "Where are you?" He says, "I can't say." He said he'd like to come in, could I try to work out the arrangements. I got Gerry Lefcourt in touch with a judge. Abbie wanted assurances that he would get no time and this liberal judge wisely said he wouldn't say it out front publicly. He said most likely he would not give Abbie time, he'd sentence him and then suspend it. Apparently after a series of conversations with Gerry, they couldn't work it out.

* * *

Rick Spencer Every two years Congress tries to put out a water resource development bill. And these March 1979 hearings were on the bill. What we did was bring up the project. So we sent a delegation down and

Abbie and Johanna flew in from California. He was a little nervous. But not too bad. By then I knew he was Abbie. I figured it out through the *Playboy* article. I didn't tell Abbie I knew until he told me later.

At the hearings, the congressmen asked, "How do you know there's chemicals down there?" I started saying, "It's the Corps's job to tell us." That's when Abbie talked. He says we had Mirex scares, and lead, he cited three or four chemicals and heavy-metal stuff. Abbie understood you had to know what you're talking about because environmental issues are essentially scientific issues. That doesn't mean that he didn't sometimes exaggerate or take credit for things that we weren't totally responsible for. But I don't recall Abbie ever saying anything on winter navigation that was factually incorrect.

Fred Jordan, who helped distribute Steal This Book *when he was at Grove, was now an editor at Grosset and Dunlap. He bought* Soon to Be a Major Motion Picture *and enlisted Catherine Revland to help in reconstructing the story.*

Fred Jordan Eventually he told me that he was finished with the manuscript and he wanted to bring it to me and could he stay with me? I was living in Croton and he and Johanna came for ten days. I edited it, and he was marvelous to work with, totally cooperative.

In June the Senate had additional hearings. Senators Moynihan and Domenici were pressing for sweeping water resource reform, but Senator Gravel, the committee chairman, just wanted to get a bill passed. When he determined that a major bill was destined to be written, he called for additional field hearings. He wanted them to be held in Michigan, but the Save the River people put pressure on, and the hearings were scheduled to be held in Alexandria Bay at the end of August.

Rick Spencer Everybody's bitching, "How could they only give us two weeks?" With nobody having any notion of what a coup this was. Finally Barry says, "Forget about it, we gotta do it, how are we gonna do it?" He got everybody refocused and we just pulled out all the stops. We did the media, the flyers, the word of mouth. Abbie spoke at a lot of places.

Annie Gefell We got eight hundred people to come to the Alexandria Bay High School for the field hearing, the same auditorium where the first hearing was held the year before. Senator Moynihan sat there for eight hours. I swear to God, I don't even think he got up once.

Rick Spencer We had 'em on the stage, sitting in the aisles, in the hallways, outside the door to the auditorium. Another hundred people or so couldn't even get into the building. It was unbelievable. The politicians spoke first. Flack, the commissioner of DEC, was the first one. Congressman McEwen didn't speak, he didn't show. But some of the State Assembly people did. And then Abbie gave a great speech.

Howie Glatter In the eighties I asked Abbie if he was worried that Moynihan would take one look at his face and say, "Holy shit, this is Abbie Hoffman!" and call the cops. He said, "You're damn sure I was scared. I was shitting a brick."

Rick Spencer One of his great lines was "There's nobody on the Winter Navigation Board that lives within five hundred miles of the river." He got a standing ovation. Everybody was screaming and yelling and all these kids turned around and they had written "Save the River" on their backs, one letter on each back, like at a football game. We weren't responsible for that, that was a spontaneous action by a bunch of kids. Moynihan said, "In my entire career I've never seen an audience like this," because everybody stayed to the end. After the hearing, as an aside to Abbie, Moynihan said, "The sixties aren't dead. They're alive in Barry Freed."

Annie Gefell Everybody was having their pictures taken with Moynihan. Abbie had a few other purposes for having his picture taken with Moynihan. I didn't know it then but it was part of his schtick for coming up the next year.

Rick Spencer Moynihan said it just ain't gonna happen on the St. Lawrence while I'm your senator. We were ecstatic. That afternoon Jeremy and I were jumping in the river, screaming, "River, we saved you today, we saved you!"

Barry didn't have an ego. He couldn't allow himself to have an ego. I really believe the reason he thought Save the River was his best organizing was simply because so many people really emerged, discovered things about their abilities. What was his line? He says people around here don't even know what an area code is. Half of us didn't have phones. We're all on different islands. We all come here to get away from everything. And look what we did.

* * *

BARRY FREED (ABBIE) WITH NEW YORK SENATOR MOYNIHAN AT A 1979 UNITED STATES SENATE HEARING ON THE ST. LAWRENCE RIVER. WHILE UNDERGROUND, ABBIE-AS-BARRY, AN ENVIRONMENTAL ACTIVIST, ORGANIZED SAVE THE RIVER!, AN INTERNATIONAL GROUP THAT SUCCESSFULLY SAVED THE ST. LAWRENCE RIVER FROM WINTER NAVIGATION.

NOVEMBER 1979

Jack Hoffman Abbie did an interview in Boston with Danny Schecter. Then he came to Worcester. He was a fucking speed train, totally manic. He had a bodyguard, he had a fucking plastic machine gun. He told me he robbed a liquor store. I don't know whether it's true or not, but he said it just to get me scared so I'd be concerned. In other words, get me some money.

Joe Abooty, *owner of El Morocco restaurant, Worcester* This local Worcester writer said to me, "You gotta do me a favor. They're gonna give me a column and I have to start off with a bang." I said, "Okay, what do you want?" I figured he was gonna pick some movie star. He says, "Can you get me Abbie Hoffman?" I knew Jack, I knew the family, and he liked to eat here. So we're having dinner in that private room. I'm serving and the reporter got up and went to the phone and called the FBI, while we were eating, just to tell them where he is. I guess the FBI just didn't want to do anything about it.

Jack Hoffman We were here at El Morocco one night and Sheila called up. She said, "You tell your fucking brother to get on the phone and get me some money or I'm calling the FBI and telling them you're there." I swear to God. I went over to Abbie, I said, "Let's get the fuck out of here, she's gonna call the FBI, I don't trust her. And since you ain't gonna give her any money, I'm getting out of here."

Kinky Friedman Abbie stayed up in Westchester with me for a while. He was more weather-beaten by the time he got to Westchester. Living underground took its toll on him. No question about it. By that time, almost everybody knew that Abbie was not a bad guy, that he was a Pretty Boy Floyd type. And everybody hoped that he wouldn't get caught.

Fred Jordan The galleys of *Soon to Be* had come back. Elaine [Markson] had passed them on to him and he said he would come and bring them back himself. The minute he walked in I knew he was basically different from the way he was last time. He established himself in our living room and he screamed at the top of his voice, in this ebullient fashion, "Now you're gonna throw a party for me." I said, "Abbie, you're underground, remember?" He said, "Doesn't matter, we're gonna have a party at David K's." And before you know it, he's on the phone calling Paris and Los Angeles and San Francisco, inviting everybody to come to his party. I said, "Abbie, I think it's insane. You want to get arrested, get arrested, but I am not going to be there." He says, "So we'll have a party without you."

David Fenton Everybody tried to stop him from throwing this party. As if it wasn't crazy enough to have this party, he invites reporters to it! There's a Page Six *New York Post* gossip columnist there and somebody from *New York* magazine. Meanwhile, he's just bouncing off the ceiling.

Catherine Revland Abbie said the dinner was going to be done communistically. Each according to his appetite. During the meal Abbie'd go by and he'd say, "How are you doing? How are things financially?" "Well, can't complain." I thought that's rather inappropriate of him. Well, later on, when it came to pay for this, he'd already cruised around to see who was doing well and pointed them out. "Cough up the plastic money, come on, we know you got it."

Marty Kenner Later on the FBI called [me], they were tracking down the people who had paid by credit card.

David Fenton Eventually we had to get him out of the restaurant because the reporters were there and word started spreading all over the public part of the restaurant. He came very close to being caught that day.

Fred Jordan I didn't go. I've known him long enough, I know he was a rip-off artist. Later on, his brother told me that he had spent the worst night that they remember before he came to my house. He was so manic they had to literally tie him down to his bed during the night. And they had no idea where he went to. Johanna also called me to apologize. She said, "I know that you had a rough time with him. We have to take him to a psychiatrist."

Oscar Janiger, *psychiatrist* He came to me in several capacities. One, because of his troubles, his illness. Two, because it's a contact in Los Angeles and maybe I could be of help to him in a trial. He knew I had done a lot of forensic work. So he began telling me about his background depression and it was informal. I let him tell his story.

It soon became clear to me that, looking at just the history of the illness, I was dealing with a case of classic manic-depressive. We call it now euphemistic bipolar illness. His record showed the characteristic peaks and valleys. It began relatively late in his life. I think the best I could do with that is to think that his temperament was that of a person who had mood swings to begin with.

He equated his first episode with the time when the cops beat him up. Mayday in 1971. Broke his nose. That's where he establishes the crossover between just being high and going into these wild, sort of uncontrollable states. His real illness might have started roughly then. It seemed to me that all of his protestations about living and dying were after 1970. I don't think he had these very morbid thoughts before that time. In other words, a lot of the depression prior to that time we call depressive reaction, which are depressions that people get because of circumstances. And God knows, he had enough things to get depressed over. But that was a different order of depression. I think probably one could shade into and impact on the other, for example, when he got beat up and his nose was broken, Mayday, was also a time that the movement was crumbling. He felt to some extent that he was not really listened to, that his voice was failing. In him, external events triggered that other thing and then he went into a totally disruptive pattern. But to somebody else it may not pull that trigger.

Manic-depression is one of the scourges of all time. And yet when people think of it, there's almost a feeling it's a very special kind of disease that very privileged people somehow are into. Little do they understand that it's terrible. People foolishly will say oh, man, I don't mind being high like that. I'll tell you, it's a torment. Because there's still that nagging feeling that you're just artificially revved up, and you know there's gonna be a price for all of this. He told me he felt horribly ashamed and guilty. Of course the public never saw that.

Now, when people get manic they can become very destructive and totally impossible to talk to. They get you by the collar and they're yelling at you. So if a man has a forceful, extroverted personality, that could add another dimension and make him a total pain in the ass. But Abbie suffered in his depression and he didn't let on, which is typical of him. He suffered horribly.

So we put him on a lithium regimen and he responded very well. Then Lefcourt came here and we planned the strategy for the defense. Abbie was clearheaded and we began to make plans for his return to New York. I said, "There's only one guy in the world that I'll recommend to you and I'll tell you right now, Abbie, he'll take no shit from you." I called Nathan Kline, I said, "I've got you a hot one, baby." He said, "Okay, I'll take him." I thought they'd work well together. You gotta know Nathan's personality, Jesus. He's a gruff, fatherly, no-nonsense man who really gives it to you, no euphemisms. He gives 'em a *zetz,* like you gotta do this, I'm telling you! He's a charming man. And very bright. So they got along real well.

Alex Bennett In August of 1980 Abbie calls and says, "Why don't you and your wife come up to the Thousand Islands and spend a week?" As soon as I get there, he says, "Quick, get in the boat." He takes the speedboat as fast as it'll go, right down the center of the St. Lawrence Seaway, and starts yelling at the top of his lungs, "I'm Abbie Hoffman, I'm Abbie Hoffman." Then he looks at me and says, "I gotta do that at least once a week to keep my sanity. I gotta remind myself who I am."

The first night, we went to a town meeting. Mary Ann Krupsack, the lieutenant governor of New York, was running for governor and was there courting Abbie/Barry's favor because he was one of the most powerful political people in the area. I was amazed that the lieutenant governor of the state of New York was trying to curry the favor of America's number one fugitive.

Annie Gefell They come back spring of 1980. At that point Save the River had 2,500 members and we knew they weren't going to have winter navigation. Out of the blue Abbie resigned. Barry called Karen autocratic.

Rick Spencer Only a few of us knew, but a lot of people suspected he was Abbie by then. He figured he was going to have to split and create a new identity because of the visibility of the Save the River thing. His lawyers thought if Reagan got in, it would be worse for a deal. Abbie said he was tired, he wanted to be himself again. What we mainly talked about was what the impact on the committee would be. I remember saying to him, "Don't worry, we basically won our issue, it'll be fine."

Marty Kenner I remember meeting at Michael Kennedy's house in the Hamptons with Michael, Gerry Lefcourt and Bert Schneider, trying to persuade Josie that Abbie had to surface because he was gonna get caught and he'd die in prison, it would just be a horrible thing. It was better for him to try to take control of his own destiny by surfacing and making a deal.

Gus Reichbach I think Johanna felt very happy there on the river. Abbie was able to do at least some political things without being the celebrity that inevitably creates difficulties in personal relationships. Bert and Gerry Lefcourt were anxious for Abbie to surface. They no doubt wanted the old Abbie back—the zany, funny, well-known political activist.

Viva Abbie was getting a little itchy about the Thousand Islands. He complained to me that he didn't know how to carry on a conversation with

Kitty, the postmistress, when he went over to get his mail. I said, "Why do you think you have to carry on a conversation with Kitty? I don't feel I have to." He said, "Well, that's because you're a mystical artist and nobody expects you to talk. But I'm a community organizer."

Jerome Washington I was in Green Haven prison then. My thing was Abbie, don't come in. Your spiritual force being out there is really giving a lot of support to a lot of people. It was a lot of guys' dream to find some way to slip away and go under.

Alex Bennett One day when we were up there, Abbie and I took a walk. He said to me, "I think I'm gonna give myself up." And he told me how he'd gone to Hollywood, sold the movie, how they picked him up in a limo, wined him, dined him. I said, "Abbie, you're probably the most successful fugitive of all time. You got a 300,000-buck advance royalty for a movie that may never get made, people are publishing your stuff. You're doing better as a fugitive than you might do as Abbie Hoffman overground." And he said, "Yeah, but I just can't stand having people not know I'm Abbie Hoffman. I can't take it anymore."

Either that night or the next night, we went to dinner and we all dropped a Quaalude. Abbie had a rule of not doing drugs when he was going to be in public because of the fear of relaxing a little too much. But he was starting to get sloppy. Abbie had had a few drinks, and he started arguing with Johanna over Jerry Rubin. She felt the same way I did, she didn't like Rubin. Abbie started getting mad at her, he said, "Jerry's been my pal, Jerry's been with me through all this, he may not be a perfect human being but I'll defend him." Then it got more and more animated, and finally, in the middle of this restaurant, at the top of his lungs, he said, "Whaddaya mean, I know what it's like, I've been in jail four times!" These people know who he is, he's Barry Freed, this local hero. I whispered, "Abbie, hold it down, hold it down!" And he looked back at me, he says, "What? Is it five times?" This man wanted the world to know he was Abbie Hoffman, and stripped of being Abbie Hoffman, at least to himself, he was nobody.

David Maloney, *student activist* His resurfacing not only came from his safety and identity being in jeopardy but from what was happening in Central America with the CIA. I believe he really thought that it was possible for him alone to lead that battle to revolutionize American consciousness. It was like here I go again.

Jay Levin There was a big campaign building up to the resurfacing. We were all getting people to write letters. Abbie was doing a great job of organizing this from underground.

Gus Reichbach His biggest vacillation turned on whether he was gonna be made an example of. Gerry was not gonna try the case because he felt he was just too close to Abbie. I also think the prospect of Abbie going to trial and potentially getting a long sentence was too personally devastating to Gerry. Ramsey [Clark] had told Abbie he would do it without a fee, but he would need about $250,000 to cover expenses. I think that also was a factor in deciding to take a plea.

Jay Levin There had been several attempts to test the waters [through] Robert Morgenthau, the Manhattan district attorney.

Morgenthau had recently married Lucinda Franks, the journalist who had won a Pulitzer Prize for her work on the explosion at the town house on Eleventh Street. As Jill Seiden was a friend of Lucinda's, Gerry asked her to call and try to pave the way for negotiations.

Jill Seiden Bob said that there was no way Abbie could not do time. It was three pounds of cocaine. But he said the special prosecutor would probably agree to a sentence of one to three years and it would end up being a year and most of it would be done in a halfway house.

Jay Levin Johanna had grave reservations about Abbie resurfacing. But once Abbie had concluded it was time to come up, nothing was gonna stop him. They got a deal he could live with, and there went Barry.

Chapter Nine

THE JEWISH ROAD WARRIOR

Sam Mitnick, *editor* Perigee Books [a division of Putnam] bought Abbie's autobiography from Grosset and Dunlap. Fred Jordan had already left. We scheduled it on the fall 1980 list as the leader. Then I got the first of many calls from Abbie, from various phone booths. Abbie said, "You know, I'm gonna do it!" It was very carefully orchestrated.

David Fenton We wanted somebody who would be sympathetic and show the positive side of Abbie's life. We ultimately settled on Barbara Walters. All I could say [to ABC] was you have to trust me that I will bring you to Abbie Hoffman in hiding. They agreed and Abbie and I started planning this operation that ultimately involved at least fifty people. We had various checkpoints where we had lookouts to see if anyone else was following; we had different fail-safe points built into it so we could abandon the operation if there was any problem. Abbie loved all this, the more stealth the better.

Sam Mitnick Right before Abbie was going to resurface, when it came time to get that first advance check out, the Treasury Department showed up and demanded that we turn the check over to them.

David Fenton I rented a Lear jet. Just before we were to board the plane Barbara starts yelling at me that she's not going to get on that plane till I tell her where we're going. I just had to hold my ground and say, "I'm sorry, then you can't go. I'll have to give the story to someone else." At that point I couldn't tell her about Barry Freed, and saving the river, and posing with Senator Moynihan, which would have really made her want to go do this. I was afraid this whole thing would fall apart. Abbie had already set the date for turning himself in. The D.A.'s Office knew this was about to happen. A lot was at stake, but I could not tell her with the crew standing there. So finally she relented, we get up in the air and I tell her. And she's thrilled.

Bob Fass Barbara Walters' camera people told us that we had better security than Arafat, ours was more confusing. From Watertown we flew to Fineview. Now we're on these small four-seater planes, landing on this island in the river.

Catherine Revland It was a beautiful day and there were all these boats and Barbara goes in one and Abbie and Johanna were coming in their boat out of the west, flying in the breeze.

Bob Fass They each went out to the middle of the river and she stepped into his boat and he took her off downriver.

David Fenton It was like Jewish mother meets Jewish son. Love at first sight.

From *20/20*

Barbara Walters: Barry Freed. Mark Samuels. Howie Samuels. Abbie Hoffman. What do I call you? Are you now Barry and not Abbie in your own head?

Abbie Hoffman: I know I'm Abbie but I'm a hunted animal and when I hear the name Abbie or I see it on TV I instinctively do what I call the Kennedy flinch. I physically duck because that is a danger word. Even "Dear Abby" I turn the page in the paper real quick.

David Fenton We have the *New York Times* scheduled to interview him as soon as he gets back to New York just before he turns himself in. We made other promises to other media. But ABC, contrary to our planning with them, issued a statement that Barbara Walters was off interviewing Abbie Hoffman. Someone up there recognizes her and finds out she's interviewing Barry Freed. Bang. The *Daily News* breaks the story who

Abbie is while Abbie's still up there. So all our careful plans get completely out of control. So we got him to Manhattan and the *New York Post* finds out where he's staying and they have a reporter go knock on his door. We have to move him to another hotel. The next morning, we bring him down to the courthouse. There was a mob scene. The cameramen were literally pushing each other down onto the street trying to get next to Abbie. He loved all this.

Arthur Nascarella I was assigned to the Queens District Attorney's Office as an undercover. I never got a promotion. They brought me and Bobby back 'cause it was our fucking collar, so we were with him that day. But he was crushed. And he had a problem of continuously defecating on himself. I think he shit himself at the arraignment. He just was not the same guy. That conviviality was gone. Over those seven years his personality just got wiped out.

David Fenton That same day, we had another mob scene at the press conference at Putnam's.

Catherine Revland At the press conference, he was everybody's favorite. It was that great American love of the outlaw. We thought, "Gee, the sixties are back, everything's going to be fine, Abbie's not going to do time, Ronald Reagan isn't going to win."

Sam Mitnick The only comparable story that I can think of was the day that Elvis died. That press conference at Putnam's was held in this little conference room. Abbie arrived, typically, about two hours late. We had a lot of reporters running around, wondering why we didn't have liquor for them. Who keeps liquor in a publishing office for a press conference at noon? He finally came in and everything got crazy.

Catherine Revland The room was packed, and Fenton shouts, "Print to the rear." Of course, the TV cameras are all in front and the *News* and the *Post* and the *Times* are all moaning in the back about how they'd been abused and the next day they were not nice. It just soured immediately. I have never seen such a backlash and I think that was something from which he never recovered. He was seen as a criminal rather than a political person.

Headline in the *New York Post*, 9/5/80

LAUGHING AT THE LAW

ABBIE'S LIFE WAS A SERIES OF SCAMS

From the *New York Daily News*, 9/10/80

THE MARKETING OF ABBIE HOFFMAN

> Abbie Hoffman, the revolutionary who created a media event last week when he surfaced after six years as a fugitive, has already: signed with a lecture agent; sold the film rights to his life story; sold the film rights to a still-unwritten book; and persuaded Norman Mailer to round up a star-studded committee whose members will testify in court as to Abbie's character.
>
> A few months ago, via "intermediaries," Abbie signed up with New Line Presentations, the lecture agency. Abbie will get $3500–$5000 per speech. "He could get much more," says New Line's Michael Harpster, "but he told us not to ask as much as we could." Why? "To make himself more generally available, and not to be accused of cashing in."

Sam Mitnick There was never really any serious attention paid to him finally as a sensibility. I think he started to sense that very early on, because some of the glee and the smart-ass wasn't there anymore. Without ever articulating it, I think he began to realize he was an anachronism.

Country Joe McDonald He was in show business, he didn't see himself as show business but he was a popular figure. And so with his going into hiding, disappearing, which happened to many of us, the press just found other things to write about: Madonna, the Eagles, whatever. When we were at Woodstock we were happening. But that was ten years ago and he had a real hard time dealing with it. So did I, because you take it personally when everybody's paying attention to you, especially when you're pouring out your heart and soul. You think, "I'm not selling corn chips, I'm selling real ideas for people to live by," but it's corn chips, in a way.

Sam Mitnick All I remember was the nose, the nose was a shocker for me because he used to have a beautiful, almost Roman nose and in came this altered sort of schnoz, the equivalent of Barbara Hershey's lips in *Beaches*. There was a time when Abbie was almost beautiful. But when he emerged he was not beautiful anymore.

Sal Gianetta He left Abbie Hoffman in Mexico or wherever. He had a mind that saw the only hole in the fucking matting and he could go right straight fucking through it and haul everybody with him including the opposition. That ability to do that was gone.

Don Epstein I was working for New Line's speakers' bureau when Abbie surfaced. Within a few months he did a thing on *Donahue* in Syracuse where there were thousands of people there. And then we started booking him.

Kenny Rahtz I booked Jerry Rubin. So when Jerry called to say Abbie is surfacing, I got totally psyched. I booked loads of dates on Abbie, never having spoken to him. About a week before his first date, Abbie called me and said, "I hear you booked me here and there and I don't like the time that I'm speaking here and I don't like the subject there." Not who are you, not thanks for anything. Just criticisms and *tsores*.

Rick Spencer When Abbie turned himself in, I was up at the river trying to handle our version of a press mob. Most of the Save the River people thought it was funny. But a few people quit the committee.

Bea Schermerhorn I have said this at Save the River meetings when Abbie was being put down by some of the newer blood in the organization. I don't care what you want to think but the man came among us at the most opportune time. Without him we would now have winter navigation on this river.

Rick Spencer I went to New York to be executive director of his defense committee. It was one of the worst six months of my life. I hate New York City. Basically, I'd just run around and try to get letters from people. Gerry Lefcourt wanted it low-key. Of course, Abbie wanted massive demonstrations.

Rennie Gross I ran his office. He got a ton of mail from women. He certainly seemed to sleep with half the world. I felt like I was reading some movie star's mail.

Rick Spencer When I was down in New York on the Defense Committee, Abbie would gamble five hundred bucks a day sometimes. He won $15,000 on the Super Bowl and he bought a boat. One day I said, "Abbie, I can't believe you bet the way you do." He says, "I'll tell you the reason why I do it. It's good training for leadership. It teaches you how to make decisions." He always had an answer.

Rennie Gross It didn't matter that he broke the law, it didn't matter that he had a lot of cocaine. What I got from him was they're gonna get me because I'm so important, I have to be stopped and they know it. But I didn't get the feeling that people bought it. I don't think he could manipulate the media anymore. And I didn't get why he and Johanna were in love, it didn't quite make sense to me, but I did get the feeling of great protection, almost motherliness. I remember being at her apartment, putting together the scrapbook of clippings of him resurfacing and he got up late, and he came out of the room in a stupor. He had no clothes on and Johanna and I were embarrassed. She went up to him and said, "Abbie, someone's here, put your clothes on," and sort of took his clothes to him. It was an awkward scene, like a mother talking to her teenage son.

Abbie spoke at an activist gathering at the Rowe Conference Center in western Massachusetts. One of the participants was a young antinuclear protest organizer named Al Giordano.

Al Giordano They had maybe sixty, seventy people there for this workshop. Abbie was smaller in frame and far more reserved than I would have imagined him to be. People kept asking him, "Hey, Abbie, where's Jerry?" or "Hey, Abbie, I was there for the levitation of the Pentagon." Finally he snaps at the group and he says, "Why do you always want to talk about the sixties? I've studied with Abe Maslow and he taught me that nostalgia is just another form of depression so don't be nostalgic. I want to talk about how you organize and win in the eighties." I loved the guy from that moment on.

From the *Tomorrow* Show, 1/12/81

Tom Snyder: How did a revolutionary, a man who professes to love his country which you do, get mixed up in this business of cocaine? Why let it even get near you?

Abbie Hoffman: It's impossible to go to a party without it getting near you. Not now of course. Now I go to a party there's absolutely no dope at all. I should just be hired by the mayor to just keep going to parties, clean up the whole city.

Elli Wohlgelernter, *journalist* I was working then as a reporter for the *New York Post,* and I interviewed Abbie a few times before he was sentenced for the cocaine arrest. He told me he was afraid of being raped, that guys would love to say they fucked Abbie Hoffman.

From the *Los Angeles Times,* 4/8/81

HOFFMAN GETS 3 YEARS FOR DRUG SALE

New York (AP)

Abbie Hoffman, the political activist and former Yippie who surrendered last September after nearly seven years in hiding, was sentenced Tuesday to three years in prison for a 1973 cocaine sale. He must serve at least one year before becoming eligible for parole.

From Pete Hamill column, NTT Special Features, 4/10/81

SHED NO TEARS FOR ABBIE DESPITE SOB SISTERS' PLEAS

I say to hell with Abbie Hoffman . . . In court the other day, he tried to explain why he had become a drug peddler. "It was an act of stupidity," he said, "and it was an act of insanity." At the time he was "very depressed." Of course. How simple. You stand for something, you have many people who believe in you, even admire you; you represent a set of principles and beliefs that were sometimes dangerous to hold. And then you become a drug peddler because you are "depressed."

There are a lot of drug dealers now in jail who will be there long after Abbie Hoffman walks back into the sunshine. He should be pleased that his crime will not cost him any more of his life. Instead he's behaving like a card-carrying member of the Me Generation, whose values he so long despised and scorned. The laughter is gone. The principles are shabby. In the end, he sounded like a cheap drug peddler, although even a drug peddler ought to know that if you can't do the time, you shouldn't do the crime.

Jerome Washington A lot of guys were so pissed off they were threatening me. "Your motherfucking friend, man, if he was black, he would've gotten twenty years like me. That's because he's a fucking honky. And he's a fucking friend of yours, man, I oughta bash your fucking . . ."

These were the same guys who were holding him as a champion as long as he was under.

David Fenton I visited him up in prison in Fishkill. He was really depressed up there.

Jill Seiden In jail, Abbie was picked on because he was a celebrity. He was beaten up a few times. I think he lost some teeth. He had to complain until they put him in the halfway house.

Marty Kenner What amazed him was how different the penitentiary was from what he thought. We had lionized George Jackson and the revolutionary black prisoners. He said with black and Third World prisoners there was not a hint of any politics. Their vocabulary was about fifty words, motherfucker this and motherfucker that. He couldn't get people to watch sports programs, much less political programs. The only thing people wanted to watch was cartoons. It was a very different atmosphere from the sixties.

* * *

Out on work release, Abbie was sent to do community work at Veritas, a drug treatment program.

Bruce Paskow, *musician, Veritas client* He came to the program ostensibly as a counselor. That's a good one, arrested for coke, next stop—drug counselor. As it turned out, the real reason he was there was as a fundraiser, which he was quite brilliant at.

With the help of Jill Seiden, Abbie arranged fundraising events, including a benefit at Studio 54.

Jay Levin He said he didn't know what he was gonna do with his life when he got out. I said, "Ab, the fact that you're good at this Veritas stuff and you feel grounded here is important. Maybe it's time you really looked to run some major program and just settle down, you're gonna hit fifty." He says, "Who's gonna give me a job like that?" I said, "You could create your own organization, raise money. The thing is to have an office you go to every day, some sort of structure would be really good for you." And he said yeah, he understood that but he didn't know if it was possible.

Jill Seiden Abbie's time was up in February of 1982. Then he immediately asked me to start working on this other party for medical aid to El Salvador.

Gus Reichbach The coke bust was a shattering experience for him mostly because he felt it destroyed his credibility on the Left. I think his whole relationship to the more traditional Left changed. He needed much more acceptance from them, so in a certain sense his political viewpoint became more orthodox. For instance, in the later period he was an orthodox supporter of Fidel. He had to, in a way that he didn't before, prove his anti-imperialist bona fides.

Sam Mitnick *Soon to Be a Major Motion Picture* hit the best-seller list in late October. Then we bought *Square Dancing in the Ice Age,* a collection of essays. To be blunt, we were cashing in. By the time the book was ready for release, any vestige of an audience that Abbie had was gone. I don't think people understood his humor or what he was talking about anymore. If there is a political equivalent of somebody who appears on *Hollywood Squares,* that's what Abbie had become. The personality who's out of work.

Ellen Maslow I saw Abbie again at a Jack Kerouac conference at Naropa. He stayed with us. I had three sons who were fairly young then. At one point Abbie told me he was disgusted that I had not abandoned my children. He said those words, that I had abandoned political work and it was revolting to him.

I was a practicing Buddhist at the time, and my mission was to introduce him to Rinpoche [the spiritual leader of Naropa]. Allen Ginsberg and I were very concerned about Abbie's state of mind and thought maybe he could wake up. Rinpoche did one of his numbers with Abbie which for many other people changed their lives. Abbie was singularly unimpressed. He just thought we were all full of shit, which might very well be true.

Mike Brownstein, *poet* I remember seeing him standing in the middle of this crowded room. A lot of these people were Naropa students and I suddenly realized that they didn't really know who he was. And he was waiting for that recognition, this forlorn figure, standing in the middle of this noisy crowd.

Elliot Katz, *student activist* There was a very interesting panel at Naropa on Kerouac and politics. Timothy Leary talked about building utopian colonies in space. William Burroughs's vision seemed a bit too paranoid for me. Allen Ginsburg was very insightful in advocating a Buddhist concept of moving beyond winning and losing. I'm a student and great admirer of Allen's poetry and politics. But that day, I thought Abbie was the most convincing, accepting Allen's ideas but arguing with wit and humor that we needed to create a just society first. He was very inspiring.

Ron Kaufman I lived in L.A. I worked at a convalescent hospital for twelve and a half years. I had no contact with anyone for fifteen years. The FBI were hot on my relatives, tapping phones, just furious about this. I met Marti in 1982 and we got married two years later. I tried to make a bargain and surface but they were not willing to talk about it. I was facing a very heavy thing, three districts, thirty-seven counts, 365 total years.

Don Epstein Abbie was not happy with New Line. I left New Line Presentations and opened Greater Talent [Speaker's Bureau] in 1982. When I left, I took a lot of these guys with me. I came up with the idea of packaging Liddy/Leary debates. Then Liddy did a debate with Abbie.

G. Gordon Liddy The first debate was to take place at the University of New Mexico in Albuquerque. I thought Abbie was behaving very strangely. He would refuse to ride in any automobile in which I had ridden, he refused to walk through a door through which I had walked. They had set up the debate in what I consider to be bizarre fashion, in a gym [with] a boxing ring. They had me in one corner, Abbie in another corner, some representatives of people who do the lecture things in a third corner and the local press people in the final corner. Abbie was just off the wall. If someone in the audience asked him a question such as "What do you think of foreign policy?" he would discuss oral or anal sex! He had a prepared speech which he jumped up and started shouting at the top of his lungs. He then left the boxing ring and started circulating out in the audience and the students were rather frantic, trying to get him to come back. It was just bizarre.

Don Epstein Abbie said, "I massacred him, I killed him." He wanted to do more of those.

Joe LoGuidice Abbie and Johanna were coming down to Zihautanejo. I went to pick them up at the airport, and he came off the plane with his head down. I said, "What's the matter?" He says, "Jesus, look who's behind me." I thought it was cops again. I look behind him and there's Jerry Rubin and his wife. It was a complete coincidence. They were on the same plane, coming to the same place. He wouldn't talk to Jerry. So I finally forced them into having dinner together at our restaurant.

Patsy Cummings Johanna didn't like the idea at all. She thought Abbie should not be his friend for political reasons.

DECEMBER 1982

Mimi Rubin We hadn't spoken for a year. It was just obviously fate and the moment we saw each other we fell into each other's arms, kissed, hugged, spent the whole time on the way down talking.

We spent every other day for three weeks together. Abbie and Jerry would swim together and Jerry doesn't swim well and Abbie would help Jerry. It was just the most wonderful, wonderful vacation. Abbie talked to us about being trapped in his radical persona.

Jerry Rubin He shared how being Abbie Hoffman is a drag so much of the time. How he feels his life's really over. How he couldn't do what I'm doing, because he doesn't want to. [Jerry was throwing networking parties for upwardly mobile young professionals.] It was kind of tragic. He's a classic hedonist. And he told me that he wasn't having a good time. Politics had become a chore, a way of making a living.

Al Giordano I went to the Bronx to see my dad on Christmas Eve. I called my home back in western Mass. and my roommate says to me, "Abbie Hoffman's in a real hurry to get in touch with you." I gave Abbie a call and he says, "We got to go to Delaware. The Philadelphia Electric Company is trying to destroy the Delaware River with a nuclear plant." He wasn't even clear what the issue was about. It was just the electric company and they had to be stopped and this group DelAware was going to hire us to stop this. He said, "I'll work for a dollar a year and you ask for whatever salary you want." I said, "When do you want to go?" He said, "Tonight." I said, "I can't go tonight. It's Christmas Eve." He said, "Where would this country be if George Washington hadn't crossed the Delaware on Christmas Eve?" We were down there by two o'clock in the afternoon, the next day.

The pump was part of a plan to divert 100 million gallons of water a day from the Delaware River. Half the water would go to a nearby nuclear plant, and the other half was to go to drought-ridden central Bucks and Montgomery Counties so that giant real estate development could take place.

Although most of the members of DelAware were Republicans, they hired

Abbie—at $1 per year, with Al as his $250-a-week assistant. To the chagrin of Bucks County officials, Abbie and Al immediately helped organize a protest at the pump site. They supplied the protesters with a variety of patriotic hats, American flags and "Don't Tread on Me" flags purchased from a local gift shop. Because of the protesters, it took the construction company eight hours to get their equipment anywhere close to the pump site.

Al Giordano In some ways the tension brought out a manic episode in Abbie. Abbie started becoming very concerned about his standing within the organization and there began to be the kind of glazed look in the eyes on occasion and a little bit of white foam on the side of the mouth. I called up Johanna and I said, "You've got to come down here" and she said, "I can't. I can't be around him." So she sent Sam and Walli Leff and Marty Kenner down. Walli Leff was saying, "He shouldn't be here at all. You should stop putting responsibilities on him." Johanna had only recently explained to me that he was manic-depressive but even then I didn't know what that meant. Johanna was telling me to make him take his white pills, his lithium, but he was refusing.

Sometime after Nathan Kline's death, Abbie attempted suicide by taking seventy-five sleeping pills.

Ira Landess Johanna found Abbie and got him to Bellevue.

On April 12, 1983, Abbie wrote Anita a letter from his hospital room. In it, he reported that he was recuperating and doing fine. He said that he was reading his doctor Nathan Kline's book about manic-depression, From Sad to Glad, *and was certain that this whole incident could have been avoided if he had read the book earlier, since he would never have stopped taking his medication just because he was feeling "well."*

He promised that he would be a good patient from then on, and he vowed to work on the "community of one." But Abbie instinctively saw his illness in social terms and urged Anita to send him any literature she could find on depression, and any writing, even poetry, about suicide. He was planning to write a book and speak on campuses about this problem in the future.

The old Abbie wit was even in evidence when he closed the letter by noting that this was the only one he'd written while hospitalized, since it was too tiring. He characterized the whole episode as an attempt to operate on himself to remove the pain in his head. "Good thing I'm a lousy doctor," he noted.

Ira Landess I spoke with Abbie about what happened. He said he suffers from an intolerable sense of loathing and self-hatred, and he gets an auditory hallucination, a command instructing him to kill himself. The command on this day told him to take the pills. The further command was to put on all the gas jets. He said he had to follow it like a robot. At that point I called up Artie Zelman, who's a psychiatrist and a buddy of Abbie and mine from Brandeis, and we met with him. Abbie described his imprisonment . . . I remember him telling us how unhapy he had been since the loss of Nathan Kline.

Jay Levin Abbie went into these depression groups when he was living in New York. They were very interesting because Abbie began to learn you could measure depression, and you could do the same thing in the manic stage.

Gus Reichbach For a brief period of time he was talking about organizing manic-depressives.

Marty Kenner He'd go through the list of famous people who'd been manic-depressive, from Abraham Lincoln to Winston Churchill to Leonard Bernstein. Abbie was proud that if he had to have a mental illness, it was this one.

The pump was eventually defeated in a referendum. The county commissioners, however, claimed the vote was nonbinding and went ahead with plans to start building it. By July 12, protesters had reoccupied the construction site. They kept a summer-long encampment and nineteen people were arrested.

Al Giordano In November the Democrats won the County Commissioners' seats for the first time in about two hundred years and they started appointing their people to the board of this Water Authority. They hired Tracy Carluccio, DelAware's executive director. Abbie came back in December. They had a $100-a-head victory dinner and I arranged for Abbie to get free tickets. We made peace and Abbie and Johanna came together. He was doing better. He was back with Johanna and that was always a positive sign. One would worry about Abbie when he would stray too far from her.

Jon Silvers Abbie bought a video camera so that he could make porn movies of himself and Johanna. He had a lot of porn movies in his permanent collection. His favorite was *Little Girl Blue,* about a little girl in an English boarding school. I told him I had never had a really good blow job.

He says, "You gotta see this," because he's a big blow job fan. He gets the tape. The girl is giving head, she's sucking, but she's also like twisting at the end. He said, "That twist, that's very important, they gotta twist when they reach the head." Johanna comes in and I'm red, and Abbie says, "Hey, you know what I'm showing him?" And Johanna, without even looking at the screen, goes, "I know, I know, the twist at the end."

* * *

Intending to bolster the Sandinistas, Abbie organized tours to Nicaragua, taking along politicians and high-profile media contacts. But he was unable to get an audience with Sandinista leader Ortega or his wife. While there, he bartered counterfeit watches on the black market.

Jack Hoffman He told me he gave Ortega a gold phony Rolex. They were my watches. He used 'em for bait in Nicaragua to get a deal in the hotel. And he got food. Abbie didn't sell 'em. You gonna trust Abbie selling Rolexes, are you kidding? He gave 'em away. Then he took a dozen to the Amazon. I said, "Who's gonna buy the watches in the Amazon?" He said, "I guarantee you I'll sell some down there." He didn't do so good with the Indians in the Amazon, they didn't care about time.

Robin Palmer I saw Abbie as a lost soul when he was doing the Nicaraguan thing. Still in that whole communist lockstep. That's my beef with Abbie and the Left. They don't understand what doomed communism from the beginning is the dictatorship of the proletariat. Any dictatorship won't work. I understood that with my epiphany that Fidel Castro was considered a counterrevolutionary throughout Africa. I had to do considerable soul-searching. I never voted for Reagan. But I had to admit that on the question of Nicaragua, Ronald Reagan was right. The Sandinistas are just a bunch of communists.

Don Epstein The country was really starting to swing to the right and that's why Abbie was falling out of favor with all the college kids. Although when he went there, there was no bigger draw, they loved him. But it was harder to book him. People like myself, who were considered hippies in the sixties, were moving into the eighties and now everybody was calling us yuppies. I came up with this crazy idea, a Yippie versus yuppie debate. And everybody turned and went, "Wow! Who do we get?" I said, "Who else do you get? You get Jerry Rubin and you get Abbie Hoffman." Jerry loved it, of course, because it was a way of making money. Abbie didn't like the idea at first. I said, "Ab, come on, let's try it." We did one date and then I brought them to the *Donahue* show. Donahue loved it, the audience went nuts.

Abbie Hoffman Note to Don Epstein at *Donahue* Show

Rubin will crack in seven minutes. I plan to take no prisoners.

THE LAST YIPPIE.

Don Epstein It took off. We did hundreds, it was the hottest attraction in the country.

Alex Bennett I moderated the debate in San Francisco. Abbie comes out with this blender and says, "Jerry, I'm gonna make you a yuppie cocktail." He put a Rolex watch in there and some Perrier water and turned this blender on and just absolutely devastated this Rolex. It was the old Abbie. The audience loved him.

Jeff Nightbyrd They came to Austin and it was the worst night of my life. It reminded me of two veterans of the Spanish Civil War who were in different factions getting up and denouncing each other. Jerry was getting baited by Abbie and then Jerry would say, "I guess I should follow your revolutionary example of dealing cocaine. You call me a sellout, you're a drug trafficker." Then Abbie says, "Well, how about the time that Johanna and I came to your house for dinner and the first thing you did is lay out a couple of ounces of coke, and we did some lines . . ."

Kinky Friedman Abbie got caught, but not by the government. I guess the yuppies caught him. He lost those debates. The audience was cheering for Abbie and they laughed at Abbie and championed him, but they went out and did what Jerry Rubin said. They became Young Republicans.

Rick Spencer I was in graduate school, I was working with [another environmental group] Great Lakes United, so I resigned as president of Save the River.

After Rick resigned, Abbie felt that the Save the River leadership might fall into conservative hands so he promoted Johanna for the presidency. The ensuing election turned bitter and ultimately Johanna's victory backfired.

Marty Kenner Abbie did things that created irreparable damage up there. Save the River fell into the hands of people diametrically opposed to Abbie and Johanna, who defanged it and made it a very respectable organization that didn't do very much. I make a living by trading currencies, and Abbie had wanted to give me some money to trade, and I just said I couldn't do it. My wife was on Save the River. I couldn't work all day trying to make the money and then come home at night and hear what a shit he was to other people. So he started trading with a friend of mine who I had told him about.

Steve Tappis What Abbie really wanted to do was learn how to trade commodities. He was a gambler and he thought he had particularly good insight into world events.

Marty Kenner It was just another game for Abbie to bet on. He liked action, and the futures market in Chicago provided a lot of action. The casino is always open, and it's not like baseball or basketball where there's a season.

Steve Tappis Abbie got a few speaking bureau people to put some money in [to a fund Steve managed]. We called it the Cronkite Fund. I said, "Why Cronkite?" He says, "It's a name you can trust."

Don Epstein Abbie says, "I'm making a fortune." He would call me up every couple of days and say pork bellies are doing this today and orange juice is doing that. So we put up a sizable amount of money, close to a hundred grand. Suffice it to say we lost everything.

Peggy Farrar, *friend of Anita and america* Anita and america moved to Seattle for a while. He got into some trouble there.

America Hoffman I was twelve when we moved there. I started doing a lot of drugs. I met some guy at a bus stop who made his living by emptying the parking meters. He had a way of manufacturing keys to all the meters. I bought a couple from him. I'd come back with like sixty dollars' worth of change in an hour. It was fun. I'd just go up to a homeless person and dump a load of change all over them.

I used to get beat up by all the black kids at school. My big thing was that I could take pain more than any other kid in the whole school, they'd be punching me in the face and I'd be laughing at them. I wasn't hurting, because I'm so good at nullifying my feelings.

John Eskow At a political fund-raising party in the Village, Abbie came up to me and said, "I hear you're doing really good in the movie business now." And he just started asking me all these questions about agents. It was like a scene in a movie in which I flash back to the Pentagon and Chicago, these just momentous events, and wonder is this the sad residue of all that grandeur?

* * *

When he returned to Nicaragua, Abbie's relationship with the Sandinistas was so poor that even his radical friends in the American delegation couldn't get him an invitation to Ortega's inauguration.

John Gerassi He tried to get Bert [Schneider] to intervene but Bert couldn't do it. We did see Abbie at the inauguration. He passed as a newsman and he was way in the back and he climbed a telephone pole so he could see.

JULY 1986

Ron Kaufman I finally got caught by an FBI Most Wanted poster. I was in San Francisco, working at the World Affairs Council, working with the intelligence division of the police department, providing security for people like Caspar Weinberger.

That day, I was coming home, turned the key in the lock and I was nailed. I thought I was being mugged. They were out there with the flak vests and the whole works. This was fifteen years later. It was a dead case. My FBI agent never even had any questions for me. They reduced my charges to three counts: possession of an unregistered explosive device, one in each city, run it concurrently, nine-year sentence. The deal was that I'd get out after forty months. So I go into prison in September, go to the parole commission hearing in December. They say we just raised your guidelines, it's now fifty-two to eighty months. Do it all. So instead of forty months I was looking at seventy-two months.

Don Epstein The debates ran two years. Toward the end we could've done eighty to ninety a semester but Abbie was getting really ticked off at Jerry. One night Abbie called me up. "From now on, two flights, two different cars, two different everything. I don't even want to see the guy."

Then Abbie would come in over the summer when the colleges had shut down and say, "I need money, just get me anything." That's when I started him doing the comedy clubs.

SEPTEMBER 1986

Mark Caldiera I was writing for the UMass paper. Abbie was doing one of his comedy shows at the Ironhorse in Northampton. I was just blown away. He had his Boston Red Sox hat on and he was going on and on about isms and schisms and wasms and how the eighties had replaced the fifties and drugs had replaced communism and not changing the world but cleaning up that river. "Act locally, think globally."

John Gerassi Towards the end, we really didn't talk politics at all, we talked football. We watched the games at Lenny Weinglass' house. Everybody hated Dallas, right? We also hated the Redskins, because of their name, although then we found out the Redskins had more blacks than anybody else. So we would switch. Then the only coach that was black was the Raiders, right? So we switched to the Raiders.

Don Epstein I think our rift came in because he started betting a lot. Every Friday afternoon, three o'clock, there was a call from Abbie to every agent in the office. "Who're we taking this weekend?" When he had a favorite, forget it. You could take him to the cleaners. Then he would come up here Monday morning to collect or pay off the bets. If some of the agents won and he owed them fifty or a hundred bucks, he'd say "I got a Rolex man, it's usually fifty bucks, I'll give it to you for twenty-five. And now I'll only owe you twenty-five." He'd always be here that next morning to pay but he'd be bargaining with you.

* * *

NOVEMBER 1986

Nancy Cohen, *filmmaker* I read *Soon to Be a Major Motion Picture* and I fell madly in love with this character. Then this film idea came up. Abbie wasn't exactly being pursued by too many people at that point. We shot it before his fiftieth birthday.

One time he got really angry about some of the questions we were gonna ask and this dark thing came over his face, it was real scary. He said he was a manic-depressive and I didn't have a clue what that really was but I could see it in his face.

From the Film *My Dinner with Abbie*

Nancy Cohen: Feel guilty about anything?
Abbie Hoffman: Are you using guilt in a psychological or legal sense?
Nancy Cohen: I don't know what you mean by legal sense.
Abbie Hoffman: Well, I do. [Long pause] I have had some doubts that it was the right thing for me to do to get busted for cocaine.
Nancy Cohen: You didn't do it on purpose, did you?
Abbie Hoffman: Getting busted was probably good because if I didn't get busted I might have kept doing it. Cocaine can turn a philosopher into a pervert quicker than anything I know.

Nancy Cohen Abbie said he needed adversity in order to thrive. He told me he would just sit home and watch TV and scream at it and that's how he got through a lot of the days. He would just sit there and scream, "No, no, no, lies, lies, lies, lies."

Ron Kaufman I talked to Abbie sometime around his fiftieth birthday. He sounded okay. But I was wrapped up in my own case.

Marti Kaufman As soon as Ron was arrested, Abbie wanted to know if he could help. But they were really nervous about publicity in the case, because everybody thought it would be counterproductive. Abbie was one of the ones who was most aware of that. So he just kept it low-key.

* * *

Art D'Lugoff, *owner, Village Gate* When we came back from Nicaragua, Abbie wanted to do a radio show.

Jon Silvers, *writer* A friend of mine at WBAI said that Abbie Hoffman was going to start a New York *Prairie Home Companion* and he needs some writers. I went to the Village Gate the night before the premiere. Abbie was doing fifteen things at once, all of them wrong. He was very good with impromptu remarks, but when it came to anything structured, he couldn't handle it. His timing was bad. And probably the worst thing I think any person onstage could do is laugh at your own jokes. Whenever the jokes wouldn't work, Abbie would try to say something profound. That didn't

ABBIE WITH COCONSPIRATORS CARLY SIMON AND KAREN BLACK HARMONIZING AT A FUND-RAISING BENEFIT FOR VERITAS AT STUDIO 54. UPI/Corbis-Bettmann

work either. He kept trying, week after week. I helped out as much as I could. After six weeks, the show was canceled. He took it hard.

From the *Watertown Daily Times,* 12/1/86

HOFFMAN AT 50: "WE'RE TALKING MIDLIFE CRISIS"

New York (Knight News Service)

. . . So Abbie Hoffman, the irrepressible prankster of radical politics, just days from his 50th birthday, is sitting with his mail, and it looks like all the world is hassling him at 11 in the morning . . . "We're talking midlife crisis here," he says. "I miss my youth. I've got taxes to pay, I've got hemorrhoids, I don't have any real estate, I've got kids and they got problems, and I'm nervous about the future. Know that flick *The Road Warrior,* where the character Mad Max is fighting alone for justice in a post-nuclear world? Trying to hold on to his can of gasoline so he can keep going? That's me, man. I'm the Jewish Road Warrior, and I don't fit in."

From Mutual Radio Network Report

by Elli Wohlgelernter

Elli Wohlgelernter: Once upon a time he said never trust anyone over 30. This Sunday the activist, the ex-hippie, the original Yippie Abbie Hoffman turns fifty . . . Back in the sixties, Hoffman was the clown prince of the protest movement, the joker who used humor as the cutting edge for getting his dissident views heard. Like the time he threw money down on the stock exchange.

Abbie Hoffman: I wouldn't throw out money at the stock exchange today when we're at 7 percent unemployment, when we have 34 million poor people, where you know steelworkers are being chucked out by the tens of thousands. It would be an insult to those people.

At the beginning of the Iran-Contra scandal, the CIA came to UMass to recruit. After some Radical Student Union members were arrested for blockading the building being using for CIA interviews, there was a protest that Abbie attended. About sixty-five people were arrested, including Amy Carter, who had come from Brown with some friends.

Mark Caldiera Abbie was arrested in the building with us. I don't really think they knew who he was. Abbie was telling a group of us that he had been arrested forty-nine or fifty times and since it was coming up to his fiftieth birthday, it was almost one a year for life.

Betsy Tomlinson practiced law in Northampton and often represented people arrested at political demonstrations. She first encountered Abbie in the courtroom where people were sitting around waiting to post bail or to go to jail for the night.

Betsy Tomlinson The first thing Abbie said was "You have to talk to Lenny Weinglass. We have to have a jury trial. We'll use the necessity defense." He was so positive and definite about everything. At first I thought he was really jumping the gun, since we had not even gotten people out on bail. In retrospect, I realized that Abbie had a vision about that trial from the onset.

Abbie and I traveled together to New York, the day after the arrests. By the time we reached midtown Manhattan he had me convinced that we could put the CIA on trial and win.

Mark Caldiera It got down to about fifteen who decided that they would go to trial and work on this full-time. We were soon to be known as "Abbie Hoffman, Amy Carter and 13 Others." I was an "Other." Amy was the most quiet, passive person you could ever meet. She hated the spotlight and was a little reluctant to do this. We just told her, "Look, we need you. You have this celebrity that none of us have."

Len Weinglass Amy really liked Abbie a lot. He was very gentle and respectful of her. They always were after him to get Amy up front, and he would say Amy doesn't want to be out front.

Shortly after the radio show ended, Abbie asked Jon Silvers to collaborate on a book on urine testing.

Jon Silvers We put together a modest proposal. Viking-Penguin picked it up, and we wrote a book. We thought that unreasonable search and seizures were a symbol of deteriorating civil liberties that affected everyone. It seemed that drug testing was a very funny way of starting, you know? Urine? Yet a lot of people were making money off it and, more important, a lot of people were being harassed and had their careers derailed by it. That was Abbie's genius—to see one frivolous issue encompassing all these things.

Don Epstein He really felt he was gonna happen again. But then when he went out there the kids loved him, but they would do nothing. He wanted to do these workshops while he was on the campus for free, for Nicaragua and so on. Maybe ten kids would show up and he got really pissed off.

Abbie spoke at an anti-CIA recruitment rally at Rutgers University and he met Christine Kelly, one of the radical leaders on campus. He invited Christine to Amherst to participate in a meeting to form a national radical student organization. She and two other Rutgers students agreed to host a student convention at their school.

Christine Kelly Abbie put us through a series of tests. First, "I want to see you think through the idea. Write a proposal. And I want to see a budget." A budget!

Jeff Nightbyrd Abbie loved Johanna. I think he didn't want her to screw around, so he probably screwed around less. He told me she had a rule for him that if he was out traveling and speaking that was okay, but she didn't want him to screw around under their roof.

Jon Silvers We'd been working together about three weeks on this book and I was just starting to get to know him. He was on the college lecture circuit and he stopped by my place en route to the airport. He opened his bag to get some notes out. His underwear flew out and there were bacon strips on the underwear, by the way. And there were condoms in there. He called them safes. I said, "Hey, don't let Johanna see those." He goes, "Oh, Josie put them in. I love her, but hey."

MARCH 1987

Tim Leary Abbie and I had many wonderful times in the last couple of years of his life because we did a lot of co-lectures. We did one in Seattle with Hunter Thompson. Hunter and Abbie wouldn't leave the hotel room; they were watching Seattle and Houston play. They'd bet $100 on the game, the two of them are lying around in their underwear, it's only the third quarter, Hunter was ordering eight-balls on the phone, and it's time to go to the lecture. So I went alone and there was an enormous crowd and I had to walk onstage and say, "Listen, I'm the warm-up act." I was lucky I did get a chance to talk for about twenty minutes. Suddenly the two of them roared onstage and I never got a word in after that.

Mark Caldiera We decided to use the necessity defense, which says that you can violate a law if the reason for doing it is to prevent a higher law from being violated. We had to prove that there was imminent danger and a threat, that we had exhausted all our other means and that our actions could clearly abate the danger.

Betsy Tomlinson Abbie was instrumental in contacting many of the expert witnesses. We had an impressive lineup that included Daniel Ellsberg, Ramsey Clark, Morton Halperin and Howard Zinn. Abbie also decided to represent himself at trial.

Mark Caldiera The trial lasted a week. Daniel Ellsberg testified about leaking the Pentagon Papers. After that, we heard the testimony of Ralph McGeehey, who was at that time in the CIA. He was involved in the decision-making as to whether or not to assassinate Daniel Ellsberg, who was sitting right there.

Florence Hoffman I went to that trial. Abbie looked like a lawyer. He was dressed so well, I was so proud of him. At that time Johanna didn't pay any attention to me at all. I'm not going to talk. But Abbie loved Johanna, and he wouldn't say a word against her.

Mark Caldiera Abbie used none of the sixties theatrics at all. He sat at the table with the legal team and he wore a suit.

From Abbie Hoffman's Closing Argument at CIA Trial, 4/15/87

When I was growing up in Worcester, Massachusetts, my father was very proud of democracy. He often took me to town hall meetings in Clinton, Athol and Hudson. He would say, "See how the people participate in decisions that affect their lives—that's democracy." I grew up with the idea that democracy is not something you believe in, or a place you hang your hat, but it's something you do. If you stop doing it, democracy crumbles and falls apart.

Thomas Paine, the most outspoken and farsighted of the leaders of the American Revolution, wrote long ago:

> *Every age and generation must be as free to act for itself, in all cases, as the ages and generations which preceded it. Man has no property in man, neither has any generation a property in the generations which are to follow.*

Thomas Paine was talking about this spring day in this courtroom. A verdict of not guilty will say, "When our country is right, keep it right; but when it is wrong, right those wrongs." A verdict of not guilty will say to the University of Massachusetts that these demonstrators are reaffirming their rights as citizens who acted with justification. A verdict of not guilty will say what Thomas Paine said: Young people, don't give up hope. If you participate, the future is yours. Thank you.

Al Giordano The point about his father bringing him to town meetings in Athol and Orange, that was all bullshit. He said he made it up. It was a very moving speech nonetheless. Then we went to lunch together and both of us declared absolutely that based on the judge's instructions, the jury was going to find them all guilty.

Mark Caldiera One of the jurors said that the CIA has no right to be its own government, conduct its own laws and to be unaccountable, and basically that's what we showed. So we were acquitted. The whole courtroom erupted. Abbie was jumping up and down with his fist raised. When we all came out there were hundreds and hundreds of media people outside. We stood on the stairs and unfurled a banner about a protest at CIA headquarters on April 27th. Then we had a little press conference there. It was so powerful, you really felt that you could use this system against itself.

Jon Silvers When you worked with Abbie you became his life. He would call sometimes three or four times a day. He never said hello. Sometimes he said, "Johnny"; but usually it would just be, "Listen, I was thinking about . . ." He never asked how I was. I knew he cared for me a lot. But he never once said, "How are you, what's going on in your life?" And maybe that's what separates genius from the rest of us, being so self-absorbed.

I think he was really lonely and that's why he liked working on projects with people. The way I like to think of him is sprawled out on this rug, in a starfish position on his belly, with a yellow pad in front of him and a red pen in his hand, furiously writing hundreds and hundreds of pages, of which maybe two or three lines were salvageable. But he was so happy, so in his element. He'd stop the second a basketball game came on. For months we lived off of cold pizza and Pepsi.

Christine Kelly In May the New Jersey public television network wanted to do a CIA campus debate. The host had appeared quite liberal before the cameras started rolling. Abbie said there's a Contra training camp right here in New Jersey; this is a documented fact. This TV host says you can't say that, that's not a proven fact. Abbie said, "Don't you read the newspapers?" The host said, "Don't believe everything you've read in the newspapers." This sets Abbie off. We drove him back to New York that night and he was screaming, "PBS, public bullshit."

In the car he went into this really dark mood, saying, "You don't know what working hard is all about, you don't know what organizing is about, you people have to work harder. In the sixties I had friends who were killed over this stuff." I remember him saying, "I miss it, I miss it, I miss it."

The next day Abbie called up and said, "I want to apologize. I was too hard on you. You're really doing a great job. You're leaders, you have to keep going."

Jon Silvers Abbie's participation was limited to encouraging me and to scribbling these wild and lengthy stream-of-consciousness segments on what drugs in America are all about. He'd stand behind me massaging my shoulders as if that would make the words come faster, as if that would transfer the energy. It was like a mind meld. We wrote the book in about four months. Abbie was very proud of it.

* * *

Jeremy Kagan wrote and directed an HBO movie of the Chicago conspiracy trial.

Jeremy Kagan I arranged to have all of the real defendants and the lawyers come out on the second-to-last day of shooting [to] mix with the real people and that would be the last image of this piece.

Rennie Davis I got a lot of information internally at that HBO thing in L.A. Particularly about Abbie and who he was and who the Chicago 7 were. I was getting pictures of the American Revolution, the 1960s and what was in front of us in the 1990s as one simultaneous event.

The 1960s was a unique historic era, an adventure emerging suddenly and unpredictably out of the shadow of McCarthyism and the cold war. In one moment, the American perspective was military containment of an iron curtain abroad and political witch-hunts by HUAC at home. In the next blink of an eye, an entire generation was embracing freedom marches, antiwar protests, recreational substances, participatory democracy, cultural revolution, a return to nature and the rejection of every xenophobic national policy.

Abbie was a beautiful symbol of this social explosion. He was curious, passionate and completely free of any need for validation or approval. He and the spirit of a generation were closely bound. That was his beauty. When the movement ended, just as suddenly as it had begun, and everyone seemed to turn back like Cinderella's carriage into Goody Two-Shoe pumpkins, Abbie could never accept that, that the passion and power was over.

I tried to drop my hints—that the passion for life that we saw in the time of the American Revolution and then briefly again in the 1960s would occur again in the 1990s and the early part of the next century. The condition of the earth is much more serious than the environmental movement understands. It's going to be apparent within the next couple of years, I think, how serious it really is. I think at that point we'll see leadership and structure and a world response. Countries going onto a war footing and an extraordinary mobilization, unprecedented in history. The sixties were only really the preparation for it. We're all gonna come together at high levels of cooperation and alliances. I actually tried to tell Abbie that this was coming and to hang in. Not, maybe in hindsight, enough.

* * *

Jon Silvers We'd been working together on the urine-testing book for so fucking long, we were sick of each other. Somehow we started talking about tennis and I said, "Let's go play." So we met at the Central Park courts.

Let me try to describe his costume. The image you get is of Bozo. His hair was long and shaggy and he had on this Day-Glo T-shirt that said "Eat the Rich." But it was about two sizes too small on him and he had an enormous gut at the time. He had these Keds canvas sneakers, old tube socks that were sort of falling down the ankles, and—should I say this?—he smelled. Abbie's hygiene left a lot to be desired. It was almost embarrassing to look at him. I'm thinking, "Oh, I'm gonna kick this rube's ass." I was on the Penn tennis team.

So we start volleying around, and he's missing, swiping the clay, and people are looking. They vaguely know he's someone but they're not sure. He finally says, "All right, I'm ready." Okay, Abbie, you can serve first. He arched his back and he cocked his right arm, threw the ball up, and this two-hundred-mile-an-hour serve comes perfectly placed in the box. *Whphht!* What the fuck was that? He routed me. And he taught me a lesson: don't judge a book by its cover. After that we both felt very good and came back and did work.

Gus Reichbach I saw a real degeneration in Abbie the last couple of years, mostly in his relationship with Johanna. I'd seen dismissiveness before, or contempt even. But not meanness. I remember sitting in a restaurant, the three of us, and I think he was a little paranoid, because he took offense at something Johanna said or did, that struck me as being very innocent. That enraged him. And once he was enraged, he was unremittingly cruel.

Lee Weiner Listen. We're talking about a guy who beat the shit out of a woman who was running around the country nursemaiding him. I think I would feel a little bad the morning after. "Here, honey, rest your eye, go in the supermarket and get a raw steak." I don't mean to be grotesque about this, but come on! I'm sure it hurt him.

Ira Landess I learned Abbie was seeing some psychiatrist who was giving him lith and as usual Abbie couldn't stand taking it and he was going off it and he was freaking out. He was being grotesque and brutal and insane with Johanna, a steady diet of verbal hostility. Plus he'd whack her around. And there was something about the sex in particular where he'd become totally fiendish. Johanna said he became an uncontrollable beast. This all came out in connection with a dope deal.

He was supposed to get me an ounce of pot. He said, "Here, let me cut it up." I said to myself I don't want to watch Abbie do this. I want to give Abbie a chance not to screw me. And for all I know he didn't.

A few weeks later, we were watching a tape of Abbie on some show and he said something positive about Sheila which Johanna was very offended by. Abbie stalked out and left and that's when Johanna told me about what she's been living with. I made the mistake of indicating that two people are always involved. She said, "This is some friend of yours that you're protecting. That friend of yours two weeks ago was laughing his head off at how he beat you in that last dope deal."

Anita Hoffman Some friend of mine was having some fathers-sons sweat lodge. I had written to Abbie to ask if he could participate in that with america.

Letter from Abbie to Anita Hoffman

As to the Sweat Bath—I'd love to do it and will say yes . . . My family connections are very important to me and there are many times I'm very sad about not seeing children, loved ones, even friends more. Seventy-five percent of my thoughts, and it goes 24 hours a day, are centered on my work. I'm as dedicated as ever, probably more so. Just worked successfully to free a marine who went AWOL in Vietnam and they were threatening to execute. I serve an important role in my country and that is my life. Sometimes, I have to actually smother certain feelings because if I follow them, I would drop out. It's very hard for others to understand this and I'm always lonely and isolated. Being complimented and lauded by lots of people really does very little to overcome this loneliness. I just want to do what has to be done so much. I'll never understand why everyone else doesn't feel this way.

LOVE
ABBIE

America Hoffman I've read those things and they made me feel better, but he never told me that. That's what hurt, he was too macho to admit it. He wanted to be everything to everyone. And he was in some ways. He was a great tennis player, he played golf well, he even played Space Invaders really well.

By the spring of 1987 the victory in the pump fight was turning to defeat. Abbie returned to help, concocting a new strategy to stir up publicity by handcuffing himself to the nearby reservoir fence.

JUNE 1987

Fred Duke, *Dump the Pump activist* He'd wrapped himself in an American flag, he made a big show of pain. They arrest him, they stick him in the car. And he was charged with criminal trespass. Abbie wanted to do this one on his own, but this rather elderly woman, a very committed radical, wanted to get arrested too. And she starts screaming at the cops, "There's only one way a woman can get arrested in this country." And she starts taking off her clothes. So they arrest her. And as they're taking her to the police car, I see Abbie in the back going, "No, no! Not the stripper. No! No!"

After his arraignment, he and I and some other people go to get some-

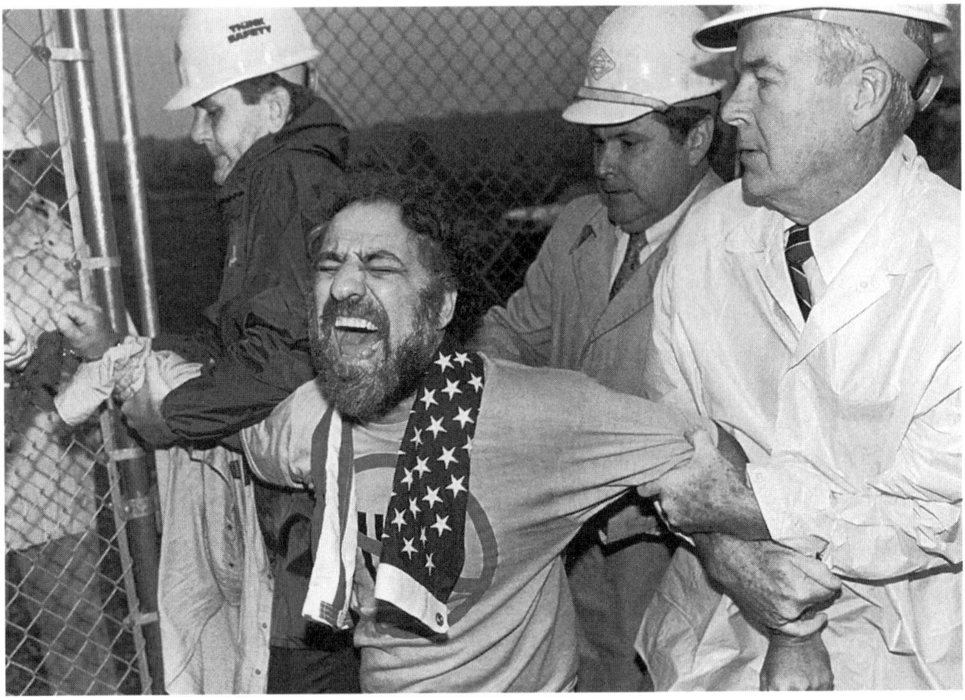

ABBIE CONSCIOUSLY CREATED THIS ARREST PHOTO OP BY HANDCUFFING HIMSELF TO A CHAIN FENCE IN A PROTEST AGAINST A PLAN TO DIVERT WATER FROM THE DELAWARE RIVER IN 1987. AP/Wide World

thing to eat. Abbie's lost the key to the cuffs so somebody had taken a bolt cutter so they were still on, but they were separate. He's pissed and his arms are moving. "You promised me I would be alone, you let her get arrested. You don't understand what the press is gonna do with this." And every time he makes this gesture he hits the table with the cuffs. The next day, I think the *San Francisco Chronicle* had Abbie getting arrested for stripping in Pennsylvania. And he's like, "See, see!!"

Jon Silvers When Abbie and Johanna started having problems, Abbie wanted to get a place of his own. He had some money saved. I said, "Let's go look at apartments." He said, "I want Greenwich Village, that's my place." And he couldn't afford anything. I got very sad, for Christ sake, Abbie Hoffman can't afford a one-bedroom apartment in New York! Then he started talking about homesteading up in Harlem.

A. J. Weberman He wanted Johanna to sell her country home and throw the money into a place in the city. This was the only thing that Johanna had in the fucking world. I says, "Johanna, don't do it, man, I'll tell you something, the guy's a little *meshugener.*"

Fred Duke After those charges were dismissed, Abbie ran out of ideas. We stayed in Stockton through July. We had a mutual friend who was into real estate, who called me about a place. She said it's a turkey farm and it doesn't have a kitchen but they're gonna put one in. It was real affordable, a few hundred dollars a month. Abbie moved into the turkey coop and was pretty happy there.

Jon Silvers If you didn't approach it from the outside, you would think this is a great place. The landlord kept llamas, right next door to Abbie. A few months after he'd been down in Bucks County he got himself a girlfriend, named Ann. She was about twenty-five years old and she was one of the earthy, crunchy types, a little heavy. She really idolized him. She moved in. But he told me he was impotent with her. "Oh, Josie, Josie, I miss Josie! Ann, she's so nice, she's young, she loves me, but I keep thinking of Josie. I love her, I love her."

David Kirshenbaum, *student activist* I went up to Rutgers for a National Student Organization meeting. They had this telegram, "Urgent national call to help save democracy and the Delaware River," from Abbie Hoffman. It sounded like a good cause, so I said okay, I'm gonna go.

Al Giordano Abbie called up america and said, "Come on, boy, come on down. It's time to inherit the family business."

America Hoffman He said, "We'll go on the Delaware River, there's all these girls that want to meet you, and we'll go inner-tubing and we'll go camping and we'll do all this great stuff." It sounded great. Well, he didn't even pick me up at the airport, some other guy from the Delaware River committee did. That got me mad. And they gave me this forty-page paper on the history of river battles and the Delaware. I was supposed to read this 'cause there's a press conference, the very next day. Like I'm supposed to feel emotional about this battle? He conned me into coming.

So I get there and there's a press release and I think of all these clever things in the car, because somehow I want to make him proud and get that out of the way and then do our thing. At the press conference I say all this stuff like "Us kids, we're organizing, we're in the streets, we're not that Pepsi generation, we're fighting." They loved that Pepsi thing.

Fred Duke He was talking about his kid coming in. He talked about two things, getting him laid and getting him arrested.

America Hoffman We got in a huge fight 'cause he wanted me to like involve youth. How am I supposed to get youth involved in a city that I don't even know any people there? I wanted to get laid. And he wanted me to get laid too. I thought that was cool.

At Abbie's urging, a small group of protesters broke into the pump site during the night and waited for the press to arrive the next morning.

David Kirshenbaum The media got down about 7:30 and the hard hats were about to come in and the cops were outside and the protesters were picketing, yelling "Dump the Pump." We were about a hundred yards away, tops. Then we followed Abbie's lead and we jumped up on top of the crane. Then Abbie and america whip out these little American flags and start leading us in "God Bless America." We're singing it as loud as we can. The reporters were all watching us and filming us. "Oooh, Abbie's here with his kid, ooohhh." Then the cops go, "Do you guys want us to take you out of here or you want to come voluntarily?"

America Hoffman It was such a silly trip, the whole thing, me doing a press release, Abbie goading me into getting arrested, and then he handcuffs himself to me. The only way I could even deal with the whole situation was to flirt with some girl while I was inside the bus.

I never felt shitty about the whole thing till after I got back from New Hope. I never really digested my feelings about the whole childhood thing. But then I was really pissed. I never told him because he always had more problems than me. He never said he was neglecting me. He never admits he's wrong. That's something he told me I should learn from him.

David Kirshenbaum Abbie resigned from the board of DelAware. There were too many people who, behind his back, weren't supporting him. You can't be a revolutionary without support no matter how much you want to be on your own.

Fred Duke By now, mostly what he was doing for them, which is something he did with an extreme loyalty always, was when he'd be off lecturing, he'd bring up their issue. He kept it alive.

Christine Kelly One of the next tests was to bring Abbie onto Rutgers campus, paid for by the student government, and he would give us the honorarium. So we brought him on for like $3,000 and he wrote the check back to us. So now he knew we were really serious and we had $3,000. Right after the speech, we had this big party in the Dead Head frat. Abbie said, "Here's my address book, go up to the bathroom and copy as many names out of it as you can." Then we knew we were in.

Fred Duke Abbie voted locally in November and he used the DelAware office as an address and somebody challenged his vote. And it went to court. The executive director wasn't willing to vouch for him living in the office, so his vote was declared invalid. To make matters worse, the one council candidate in New Hope had won by one vote, and he had voted for her. So they were gonna flip a coin to determine the winner of the race. Not only had Abbie lost his voice, he had been replaced by a coin.

Letter from Abbie Hoffman to Don Epstein

> These provincial assholes are really screwed up here in Bucks County. The news that I was denied the right to vote was in Pravda! I'll never know how a nice Jewish kid like me ended up this way. Shit. In ten days I'll be 51, the oldest juvenile delinquent in the fucking country.
>
> ABBIE

Pennsylvania law mandated a coin toss to determine the victor if an election was tied. Ironically, the candidate Abbie voted for won the coin toss.

David Maloney He was preparing to promote his *Steal This Urine Test* book. He wanted Johanna to go with him but she didn't want to do it so she called me. I dropped all my classes at school. He really needed somebody that he could depend on for everything. "You can't let him forget his briefcase, you can't let him forget to take his medicine."

It was a super-demanding trip. We would start the day out with a morning television show at six o'clock, at eight o'clock we'd be on a live radio talk show for an hour. This went on all day long, radio, TV, news and late-night talk shows. On top of it he continued his college speaking throughout. We'd go to the university for an eight o'clock talk and then talk for two and a half hours, and we'd always go out and have cocktails with students afterwards and we'd get back to the hotel at two o'clock and start the day again the next morning at five o'clock.

By the completion of the three-and-a-half-week tour, he collapsed in the airport. He couldn't make it to the next venue, he was so physically burned out. But what really impressed me was that when he had to, regardless of how exhausted he was, he still could blast out with this tremendous energy.

But Abbie always had to fight for credibility. Nine times out of ten the interviewers had no idea what the subject matter was. He called them Ken and Barbie TV talk show hosts. One time, in D.C., he said straight out to one of these ladies, "What do you want me to talk about? You haven't even read the book, you can't ask me questions. Why is the book even out here?" He picked the book up and he threw it off set and hit the cameraman. The audience loved it.

Fred Duke Abbie and a few others started their own campaign to convince me to become DelAware's new executive director, which meant a massive campaign against the Republican mode. So I finally agreed to do it, and I started in January of 1988. Abbie's all excited. We got the organization back, finally. Well, not quite. It's a seventeen-member board, and I'm hired by a vote. Not exactly what you'd call a mandate.

David Maloney Three weeks after the trip Abbie called me up and was completely hysterical. He said, "You gotta come down here, they're shooting at me from the trees."

Letter from Abbie Hoffman to Don Epstein

> Donny—My life's getting more complicated by the hour now. Not only was my right to vote taken away in Pennsylvania, there were several death threats against me. My landlord saw men near the woods with guns outside my apartment. The chief constable of New Hope, William Brooks, stated before several people that I would never live in Bucks County. I had to sleep in a motel under an alias and disguise last night.

CHRISTMAS 1987

David Maloney I was back at school. Abbie says, "Why don't you come down and start researching this next book with me." It was gonna be either Great American River Wars or the Last Generation—how if this generation didn't take charge that it very well could be the last. I never worked on either book project, but I did go down and live with him for about a month and a half. Johanna and Abbie were planning a trip to Mexico, to rekindle the romance and try to work out the problems. Mexico went well. He came back happy and optimistic. There still wasn't a complete resolution about where they were at.

While on the book tour, Abbie had continued to shepherd the Rutgers convention from a distance.

David Maloney He had faith that National Student Action was gonna be the next SDS.

Although close to eight hundred people showed up for the Rutgers convention, even Abbie's powerful speech could not prevent it from disintegrating due to the antinational and anarchist contingents.

Jeff Nightbyrd He called me after they had the meeting. "You wouldn't believe it, Jeff. It's not that they were anarchist, they were ineffectual. They debated all morning about opening a bank account." He saw them as a bunch of kids that didn't know how to get things done. The product of American suburbs and privileged classes. That depressed him a lot.

Kinky Friedman Abbie Hoffman was punished by God. God made him go on these lecture tours speaking to college students in America. And the sight of so many young Republicans made Abbie very sad and he realized he was a spiritual dinosaur. Abbie saw college campuses from a time when everybody understood what he was saying to a time when everybody was cheering him on but just like you'd cheer for the bull at a bullfight, when you know he's going to lose. When it gets to be the Charge of the Light Brigade, if you're running into a wall of yuppies and young Republicans everywhere you turn, young people whose minds are closed, a steady diet of that for a year or two could depress anybody. This is a legacy? This is a result of all of the great adventures of the sixties, of Gnossos Papadopoulos and Richard Farina and all Bob Dylan's protest songs? You have a generation of mild-mannered llamas.

* * *

Jon Silvers The urine book came and went. The reviews were good to excellent and the sales were moderate. I think to date we've sold fifty thousand copies. Then we said we had so much fun with it we were gonna do it again. And we put together a proposal for a political book in the footsteps of Theodore White, *The Faking of the President.* We gave the proposal to Viking, they said okay.

Abbie loved being on the campaign trail. Everywhere we went, the minute he'd walk in, cameras would always spring around and turn on him.

I remember one Dukakis rally we went to, they wouldn't let him into the room because they thought he would upstage it. One of the Dukakis workers came over. She was beautiful, about twenty, and she says, "I'd like to talk to you, Abbie." Abbie comes over to me and whispers, "Jon, give me the car keys." I would never let him drive. "Why?" "I'm gonna try to fuck her in the car. I'll be back in an hour." He wound up getting a hand job. I always wanted to ask the women who fucked him or blew him or jacked him off, why would you do that? He didn't radiate sexual energy. I'll tell you how he did it, because 99 percent of the women would just tell him to go fuck himself. But there was always that one.

* * *

Jeff Nightbyrd I was a consultant to Oliver Stone's film *Born on the Fourth of July.* Oliver said, "What do you think of Abbie being in the scene as one of these campus speakers?"

Oliver Stone It was funny, because when he showed up, I'd written some text and he said it was almost exactly the way he said it.

Abby McGrath He did an Oliver Stone film for scale, wrote the script himself, and was afraid to ask for billing. He didn't even have an agent make the deal for him. The sucker did it for scale. He was afraid he was gonna lose the part! "Abbie, who else is gonna play this part? Who's gonna play Abbie?" "Oh, a hundred actors can do it."

Oliver Stone He had such charisma with gray hair that I opted to make him like those older radical types who'd show up on campuses. Abbie really got into it. There's a big tear-gas riot-type situation and he was great. All his actions were spontaneous and ad-libbed and the cops were hauling them off and he was protesting and continuing to scream and shout as they were pulling them off.

Jeff Nightbyrd He didn't screw anybody on the movie set, which was a first.

Oliver Stone During the sixties, I thought he was a threat to national security. Coming back from the Vietnam War and between the Panthers and him, I was terrified of all that stuff. I thought they were forces of unrest and disorder. My eyes opened maybe late but at least they got opened. After fifteen years I began to see him. And as a symbol I loved him. As a man I can only say that I liked him from that day that I first saw him. He seemed full of spirit and energy and optimism and he was so pleased that the picture was being made, that finally the sixties were being given some credibility, some due.

Jeff Nightbyrd He said, "God! This is a great career! Beautiful girls all over that love you. We're giving a good message to everybody, it looks good, catering truck, this is great. I think I should be in movies, don't you, Jeff?"

Jon Silvers After he finished he told his agent, "Get me scripts, get me scripts." And she got him scripts. None of them ever panned out.

Jeff Nightbyrd They offered Abbie a job on *Miami Vice* but the role was something that he politically disagreed with. He really needed the money, but out of principle, because he thought it gave a bad message to the public, he refused to do it.

* * *

Jon Silvers Shortly after the Iran-Contra scandal broke, there were rumors floating around that Reagan-Bush campaign advisers, during the 1980 campaign, had made overtures to the Iranian revolutionaries that they should keep the hostages until after the election, embarrassing Carter and making Reagan look like the American savior. Abbie decided to write Jimmy Carter and ask him if there was any truth behind it. And lo and behold, Jimmy Carter wrote a letter back and said, "I don't know whether these rumors are true, we have long had suspicions about this." I got the letter and I sent it off to *Playboy*. They said, "Do it, do it." So Abbie and I did it.

Abbie had somehow set up an interview with Bani-Sadr, the deposed Iranian president now in exile in Versailles. Abbie nearly blew the entire expense allotment from Playboy *on the plane tickets, but Jon Silvers managed to make other arrangements.*

Jon Silvers I got us there and back for $1,200. He really had no concept of money or how to set the groundwork for a piece. At this point he was doing ten different things at once. He was Dumping the Pump, he was doing lectures, whatever. Anyway, the Bani-Sadr interview was his baby, he wanted to handle that. So I said, "All right, I'll get us there, you just get the address and get us in the room." He said he knew Paris and he was gonna make arrangements at a great hotel for us. It was my first article for *Playboy* and I wanted to be very delicate on the expenses. We get there and it turns out to be the Paris Hilton. Three hundred bucks a night. There are great hotels for twenty-five, fifty dollars. Fucking Paris Hilton. I mean there's not even a sense of France in that place.

So we get there, exhausted from the flight, and Abbie can't find Bani-Sadr's address, can't find the phone number, nothing. At that point I just let him have it. He got angry at me, too. It was *The Odd Couple,* it was Oscar and Felix. I'm very precise and climbing the walls, and he's screwing everything up. He was heavily medicated at this point too, so that might be one excuse. Anyway, I engaged an interpreter. I made the arrangements, we conducted the interview.

Bani-Sadr didn't know who he was. No one in Europe knew who Abbie was. I'd never seen a man walk with a chin thrust so far out, hoping to be recognized. He had no women in France, no women at all. It like dawned on him, I think a little bit, that maybe he's fucked up.

Robin Palmer The last time I ever saw Abbie was at a twenty-year reunion for the Columbia rebellion. That was the first time that I'd seen him in a number of years. Marty Kenner and Abbie were trashing Jerry as a sellout. I said, "Well, that's your opinion but I'm an anticommunist now. I'm sure you heard that." Abbie said, "Robin, you're the one that taught me to be a communist." I said, "Abbie, I'd take a stake and drive it through Fidel Castro's chest now." Abbie went, "You're the one who convinced me that Fidel Castro was a great guy. You're the one who told me that Fidel was trying to get rid of money." They both turned on their heels and walked away from me.

Jeff Nightbyrd He put a lot of energy into that New Hope fight, and it wasn't saving the river.

Steve Ben Israel Ultimately they couldn't stop the nuclear plant from using the water. That was one of his first big losses.

Fred Duke When I was director of DelAware, I used to have press conferences about every two weeks, to keep headlines. It got to the point where it was just getting more desperate and there was less to say. One night in May, I called Abbie and I said, "I'm doing a press conference." He hadn't gotten in any trouble for a while, so it seemed like a good time. He says, "What do you want me to say?" I say, "Anything that's on your mind. I'll take my chances." So the next morning he shows up, it's nearly dawn. He pulls out his legal pad and he makes a speech; then he says, "If I hear a bang in the middle of the night I won't be afraid." Well, that opened the whole issue of whether people are gonna blow up the pump.

A. J. Weberman Abbie wanted to get dynamite to blow up that power station. He put the word out.

Dana Beal I says, "Abbie, you know I've become totally nonviolent and I just don't know where to get that stuff anymore."

Aron Kay, *Zippie, pieman* He said, "What good are you guys?"

Abby Fields, *Latin America activist* There was a period where all he wanted was for Johanna to marry him so he knew he had a house to live in. He was very insecure about financial things. Everybody had this impression that he had a lot of money. He didn't!

Jon Silvers Johanna wouldn't marry him. They had a marriage counselor—and he drew up a list of ten demands. He said, "I got her doing one to five now." I guess six through ten they were still trying to work out. I never saw the list but he told me a couple of things on it. They were mostly sexual.

Christine Kelly She'd say, "Look, I don't want to move to New Hope." But she was in New Hope most of the time. When she wasn't there he would go on the phone binge. Abbie would call, "Ah, me and Josie got in another fight, she's not talking to me." But two days later, they would be back together.

Jon Silvers I saw one phone bill, it must have been $1,000, for a month.

David Maloney Abbie and Johanna had a year of being separated and during that year I think Johanna developed a sense of independence. It had the reverse effect on him. She really was his backbone in the later years and he was falling apart slowly from the deterioration of the relationship.

Jon Silvers He and Johanna had been fighting really, really awfully. To top it off, we were working on the *Playboy* piece—rather I was working on it, he wasn't able to contribute anything—and he wanted to put something into the article that I thought would defeat a lot of what we were trying to say. Abbie believed that one reason that the ayatollah wanted to get back at America was because the shah had posed with David Rockefeller and Henry Kissinger in a photograph here in New York, and that infuriated the ayatollah. It was just so stupid to me. I didn't want this frivolous piece of crap in there even if it was a line. He blew up. First he went white and then he had echolalia. I said, "Abbie, calm down"; he would go "Calm down, calm down, calm down." He started foaming at the mouth and pacing the room. He turned white, he turned red, gritted his teeth. I really thought he was gonna kill me. He started crying a little bit. Then I freaked out. Finally Abbie calmed down and he just walked out and I got my way. But he wouldn't forgive himself for losing it in front of me. He never apologized to anyone, not that I saw, but he came very close to apologizing to me. He thanked me for all the work I'd done on the article. He said, "I know it's yours, thanks for putting up with this." It was clear to me that he was a mess at the time. And then, shortly after that, he had his accident.

Al Giordano Abbie was on his way to the airport to go to Chicago to meet with *Playboy* about the October Surprise article. He was driving and he was eating an ice cream cone and he drifted into the wrong lane and a truck hit him and the car ended up flipping over and he got a little mangled up. The police and the paramedics were there and they were saying he should go to the hospital and get checked out. He said, "No way, I've got to catch this plane." There's a crowd of onlookers gawking. He goes up to the crowd, holds up a wad of bills. He says, "I've got $100 for anyone who can get me to the airport on time to meet my plane." This kid says, "I'll take ya." So he grabs his bag, hops in the car, goes to the airport.

Fred Duke He was unconscious for about five minutes. They thought he was dead, they couldn't find any pulse. Then he came to. He was a terrible driver to begin with. And it got worse when he got the car phone.

Jon Silvers We were supposed to meet at Newark Airport. I got a page over the P.A., Johanna's on the phone. Abbie was in a tragic accident, but he's on his way. An hour later he limps in. He's all bandaged and bruised and he's obviously in another world. But he won't go to a hospital, he insists we go on the plane. We have to get this through, this manuscript is of national importance, it'll bring down Bush, it'll bring down Reagan. He had an awful lot of faith in the work we did. Too much faith sometimes.

Al Giordano Abbie gets on the plane. By this point, he's pissing blood and his ribs are crushed, his hand is bleeding and his foot's mangled and he's limping around. He has a very disastrous meeting with *Playboy*. He's upset with them because they're not promoting it on the cover. On the plane back to New York he was in pain and he goes back to the bathroom and he lights a joint and the alarm goes off and they kick him off the plane and he's threatening to sue the airline and the maker of his car for the car accident.

America Hoffman I was so pissed at him and into my own thing that when he told me that he almost died I just said, "Go ahead and die. Don't whine to me." Yeah, I'm a mean guy.

Florence Hoffman He should've been hospitalized. I said, "Jack, it's foul play. I won't accept anything else." I went to the CIA trial. That's why I figure foul play. Jack says, "No, he was eating an ice cream cone."

Becky McSpadden, *West Coast activist* Abbie said his mother said, *"Silkwood! It's just like Silkwood!"* But he didn't say that he thought his brakes had been tampered with or anything like that.

Fred Duke Later he started dropping hints that maybe somebody had tampered with the brakes. He said that on the air to Howard Stern. If he had died in the accident, the conspiracy freaks would've been out. I'm not gonna sit here and say that it's not possible. Although when it comes to car accidents, he would've been an easy target.

Don Epstein After the accident, he was more scattered. He was in pain all the time. He was really getting paranoid. Every single letter, every single conversation, was people in Bucks County really wanted him out, the sheriff hated him, the CIA was after him. He said that they were gonna kill him.

Rick Spencer I saw Abbie that summer, during the tenth anniversary of Save the River. He was on crutches and he looked like he aged ten years. I was shocked.

Marty Kenner Jonathan Winters performed at the benefit. There were maybe five hundred people in this dark, kind of Las Vegas nightclub room, and Abbie came up to me. Again, no hello, just started this talk *at* me about how he was funnier than Jonathan Winters. And then he walked away.

Annie Gefell There was a little printed mention in the program, but in the speeches that night, there was no mention of the history of the Save the River committee. There was no commendation or public pronouncement, no little talk about how the committee got started, who the founding members were. I think it was a conscious whitewashing of history. They knew Abbie was there. It was very deliberate to not include him.

Stew Albert In Chicago in 1988 at [the conference marking] the twentieth reunion, he was nuts. Manic. He was in pain. He would talk beyond his time limit and interrupt on panels. He got into an ugly confrontation with Carl Oglesby.

AUGUST 1988

Todd Gitlin Abbie hated [Carl's speech] and he commenced this diatribe in which he was screaming. I've never heard anything like this in a public dialogue. He was a caricature of the Wild Man Revolutionary. I walked to the back and ran into Jeff Nightbyrd. I said, "What is it with Abbie?" He said, "He's off his lithium."

SOME OF THE CHICAGO CONSPIRACY REUNITED IN GRANT PARK TWENTY YEARS LATER. FROM LEFT TO RIGHT: ABBIE (WITH CAST), PAUL KRASSNER (UNINDICTED COCONSPIRATOR), DAVE DELLINGER, AND BOBBY SEALE. AP/Wide World

Steve Tappis Todd Gitlin wasn't any better.

Stew Albert Abbie was acting intemperately and you might say rudely on the panels. But you know what? On the whole, the audience was with him. He did it in an entertaining enough fashion. Abbie had a bad thing with Paul Krassner at this event. Paul was recounting the Yippie/yuppie debates in his monologue. He mentioned that Abbie and Jerry got $5,000 a debate. Abbie just fucking blew up, yelling Paul down from the audience. It was really awful to see.

Paul Krassner I felt bad about that. We talked later. Johanna said, "Look, that's one of the reasons why we're apart now, because of this money stuff. He gives away money to avoid his Jewish guilt." Remember he gave the money to the Panthers. I asked him, "Why'd you do that?" He said, "Jewish guilt."

Stew Albert We did a very nice thing together. Judy and I and our daughter Jessica and Johanna and Abbie took a drive around Lincoln Park. We saw it one more time. It was a rainy day and we took this very sentimental drive. "God, we got worked over here." "This is where my head was split open." We were both saying, "Boy, we must've been nuts."

Anita Hoffman The last time I saw him was when he came out to L.A. to do the stand-up comedy thing. He had the flu and he wanted to cancel but he had to do it for the money. He had $16,000 in an IRA which he had carefully saved from his speeches, I think it's the only money that he really ever saved and he was setting it aside for his old age. But he had to go into the IRA to pay back taxes. He didn't want me and America to come and see him. But we came anyway. He was in bad shape. He was drinking and that was unusual because he always hated alcohol. I thought his performance was rambling, but the audience really loved it.

From Stand-up Performance, 8/30/88

> Speaking of being born again, where's Jerry? Hey he was a good organizer in the sixties. He had a complicated life. In the seventies, he became a black separatist for three years, then he was a Croatian lesbian. On October 19th, on the crash, he got yuppie fatigue. He died of a computer virus. Small private funeral on the East Side. I traded him for Amy Carter, though, you may have read about that. I didn't even give up a draft pick.

Alex Ducane He did that comedy thing on the West Side. Abbie came out with his leg in a cast, and did this slightly pathetic routine. Johanna was there. I was very shocked. She looked weary, depressed.

Carol Realini I went with Alex DuCane. Towards the end we were dying of embarrassment, I was crying for him. Johanna was sitting by the door, selling his books, so we decided to go commiserate with her. We already knew that they had broken up and she was just kvetching the whole time about Abbie and money and being used.

Alex Ducane I had the impression that there was no possibility of them getting back together again. After all of these years of them being together and underground and what has she got left? The guy's paying her a few bucks for selling copies of *Playboy* magazine with some interview of his in it at the fucking door!

Carol Realini When the show was over we spent a half hour talking. He was in a terrible depression, so he had to work triple hard to pull this off.

Jon Silvers Abbie was really trying to remain contemporary, he was trying to get back into the thrust of things. And if you think about it he had an awful lot of success. He beat the CIA on trial, he raised the issue of urine testing, tried to bring Iran-Contra into the limelight, but he was routinely ignored. He was ignored not because the subjects weren't worthy, but because he was Abbie Hoffman and therefore had had his say and was considered some relic. We had done one interview promoting the *Playboy* piece on some schlock morning show. I watched it and superimposed below Abbie's face was the name Abbie Hoffman, [and] below that, "Sixties Activist." That would have upset him a great deal.

Abbie Hoffman Letter to Don Epstein

> Your line about no agency advances any money is simply ridiculous. i.e. I read in the paper that Robert Bork had been given an— advance. I was promised that there was gonna be a comedy week in April. No dates. I was promised again by Stanky that yogurt commercial, big money. That was in January, we talked about that. Nothing since. What's with this guy? Start taking over.

Don Epstein His mind was pure socialist and his pocket was pure capitalist. I don't say that in a bad way, capitalism was not meant to benefit

Abbie Hoffman, it was meant to benefit what he was doing. All the money that he was always trying to gain went to Save the River or the DelAware thing. Plus he was always worried about his children with insurance. That was really his big fear, that he was getting older and he hadn't really provided for the kids.

Jon Silvers He wanted to sell out. Some yogurt company had this idea of having old sixties guys endorse the yogurt. They wanted Abbie to endorse it. One commercial would be Abbie, another commercial would be Jerry in a suit. They would have paid him an awful lot of money but Abbie said no just because Rubin was involved.

Don Epstein The thing that I've always been very upset about is our relationship really ended right before his death. I think the rift came in because he started betting a lot too. He was starting to eat through a lot of money. Our relationship got stormy because of the advances. Abbie didn't realize how much money he was really taking out. It was $5,000 here, it was $5,000 there, it was $10,000 here, it was $10,000 there. Then he would hold me hostage: I'm not going on the date until you give me some more, I'm not doing this. Then he wasn't happy with the amount of dates that he was getting. I kept telling him, "Abbie, you've gone to these schools ten times already. How many more times can we milk these guys for it?" And he says, "I've got something new to tell them." That's when Jack stepped in. And things got real volatile. Jack didn't understand how much Abbie had really been into us for. I had to take the company posture, because Abbie was really annoying the agents, hurting a lot of them who had really believed in him for a long time. There was no rhyme or reason. He'd come in on a Tuesday, have an hour meeting with every agent in the office. We all loved him so we dropped everything. And he'd say, "Look, whatever you need me to do I will do. Anything. Seven-hundred-dollar date, whatever it is. Now go out there and really go do it." These guys would go bang away and book him a date. Three days later, we'd send the paperwork, and he goes, "I'm not taking this date for $700."

Letter from Abbie Hoffman to Don Epstein, 10/31/88

Dear Don:

Because of extreme differences and difficulties extending over the '87–'88 lecture season, I've decided to terminate, after all these years, my association and connection with Greater Talent Network. My lawyers have read the alleged exclusive contract and found it outdated on your end. I have selected American Program Bureau to represent me beginning January 1, 1989. Let's just end this amicably. We simply have come to the end of the road. There is no thought on my mind of reconsidering.

SINCERELY, ABBIE.

Don Epstein That wasn't Abbie's style, it wasn't his words. I think after that we had one conversation, in which I said to him that I believed that the contract's in force but I would never try to enforce a contract with you. We've been together for a long time, let's just part amicably and move on. I honestly believe that had Abbie lived, six months or a year would've passed and we would've been back together. I know APB didn't get that many dates for him. That's why that letter is so bizarre, because that was a letter of closure. And Abbie would never close the door.

Chapter Ten

FREE FALL

Jon Silvers Abbie was burning a lot of bridges. He had a falling-out with Fass. He would call Fass's show from Bucks County, and want to talk about whatever Abbie wanted to talk about. Bob would try to focus him. At one point Abbie said, "Oh fuck you, your show is boring anyway." Bob said, "Ah, Abbie, go take your medication." This was on the air.

Anita Hoffman He alienated a lot of people because of his illness. Whenever I spoke with Abbie over the last few years it was clear that he was unhappy. He would reveal his loneliness and ongoing money problems. After the auto accident, he was always in pain. His foot hurt and he couldn't play tennis. It must have been tremendously depressing.

Al Giordano For nine months he'd been hobbling on this cane. When we went to the Delaware River in 1983, he told a reporter something I'll always remember. He said, "I might not be the best, but I'm the fastest." I think that losing his physical abilities was a major contributing factor in his death.

America Hoffman I told Abbie I did acid when I was fifteen or so. What was his response? Probably "Put Anita on the phone." No matter what I said, it seemed like he never listened to me. Sometimes he'd try and quiz me on political things and if I didn't know the answers, he'd treat me like I was dumb. He said, "You really should know your shit." It was important to him that I be political in case I'm gonna be interviewed I shouldn't look bad.

I didn't talk to him almost a year. That was really my decision. He was really sad with that. And he'd heard that I tried to stab my mother. I didn't really though. Actually I went berserk and I picked up a knife and chased her into the street. She called Abbie and he's like "Oh, more bad news, just get him to see a shrink. I don't want to deal with it now." Then she'd say to me, "Talk to him, it's Abbie on the phone." I'd say, "I don't want to talk to that motherfucker. It's none of his business." That's when I went into therapy.

Susan Carey Abbie talked a lot about how he wanted to be like Maslow. He wanted to be special to students. But he felt old because he said the kids weren't interested, they didn't know what he was talking about. And they didn't know who he was!

Don Epstein Abbie and I were sitting here and one of my agents came in and said, "I just pitched you on the phone. Great pitch. The girl from the school is ready to book the thing. And she says to me, "How much is she?" I says, "No, no, you know, Abbie Hoffman?" She says, "Sure, I know who she is." Abbie cracked up, he thought it was the funniest thing he'd ever heard.

Coca Crystal, *cable TV talk show host* He was disillusioned with the new generation of students. He told me they would raise their hands and say, "Who is Malcolm Ten?"

Don Epstein The last conversation that I had with Abbie was probably sometime in December. It was a dispute over advances.

NEW YEAR'S EVE 1989

Rick Spencer When I saw him he had just had a hemorrhoid operation. But he was in pretty good spirits. Then about the middle of January he went into his depression.

America Hoffman What I figured out in therapy was that I didn't need him and that I never had him as a father in the first place. That helped a lot because I killed him for myself. If someone's just causing you problems and you're trying to love them, and every time you want to love them more they hurt you, it's better to just shut 'em out.

Jon Silvers When Salman Rushdie got the death sentence, Abbie was literally the first one to say we have to help him. Abbie called Viking and said, "Get me in touch with him, I'll give him advice on how to survive underground." Abbie was on the phone to Mailer, Doctorow, saying we have to get a reading together, and then events started to happen without him. When a bunch of PEN writers appeared on *Donahue,* Abbie was sure he was gonna be on and he wasn't invited. It hurt him a lot. A lot.

Becky McSpadden He was upset that Johanna had this job and didn't want to live in the country. Then he started in about how much he hated the city. And he said that Johanna had never even read any of his books. He was really hurt.

Jay Levin There was always the fear that a genuine, existential depression would coincide with a physical depression. Meaning that the objective circumstances of his life, no money or fruitful outlet for his energies, fighting with Johanna, whatever it might be, might coincide with his biological depression. And except for the period around his earlier suicide attempt, that never happened.

Christine Kelly Abbie hated taking lithium. He felt he was losing his creativity on lithium.

Jay Levin So he went to this new doctor, and the guy put him on Prozac. Now Prozac's an incredible drug for 95 percent of the people on it. But it has to be carefully monitored in the early stages. For some people it's just wrong. Abbie may have been one of those people or he may've been so badly monitored that the dosage was wrong. What happened was he kept taking more and more.

A. J. Weberman Johanna told me the psychiatrist had recommended institutionalization. I wish Abbie would've told me, "Hey, man, I'm up against the fucking wall. I'm trying to check into the fucking loony bin, and I don't wanna do it under my own name and the insurance thing won't cover it. How about some fucking bucks, man?" But he never asked me for any more than what I gave him to get by.

Ira Landess At the end, he was gambling on anything and everything. The saying is if you're still playing and you got money, you're alive. Are you still alive in the double? If you're not alive you're dead.

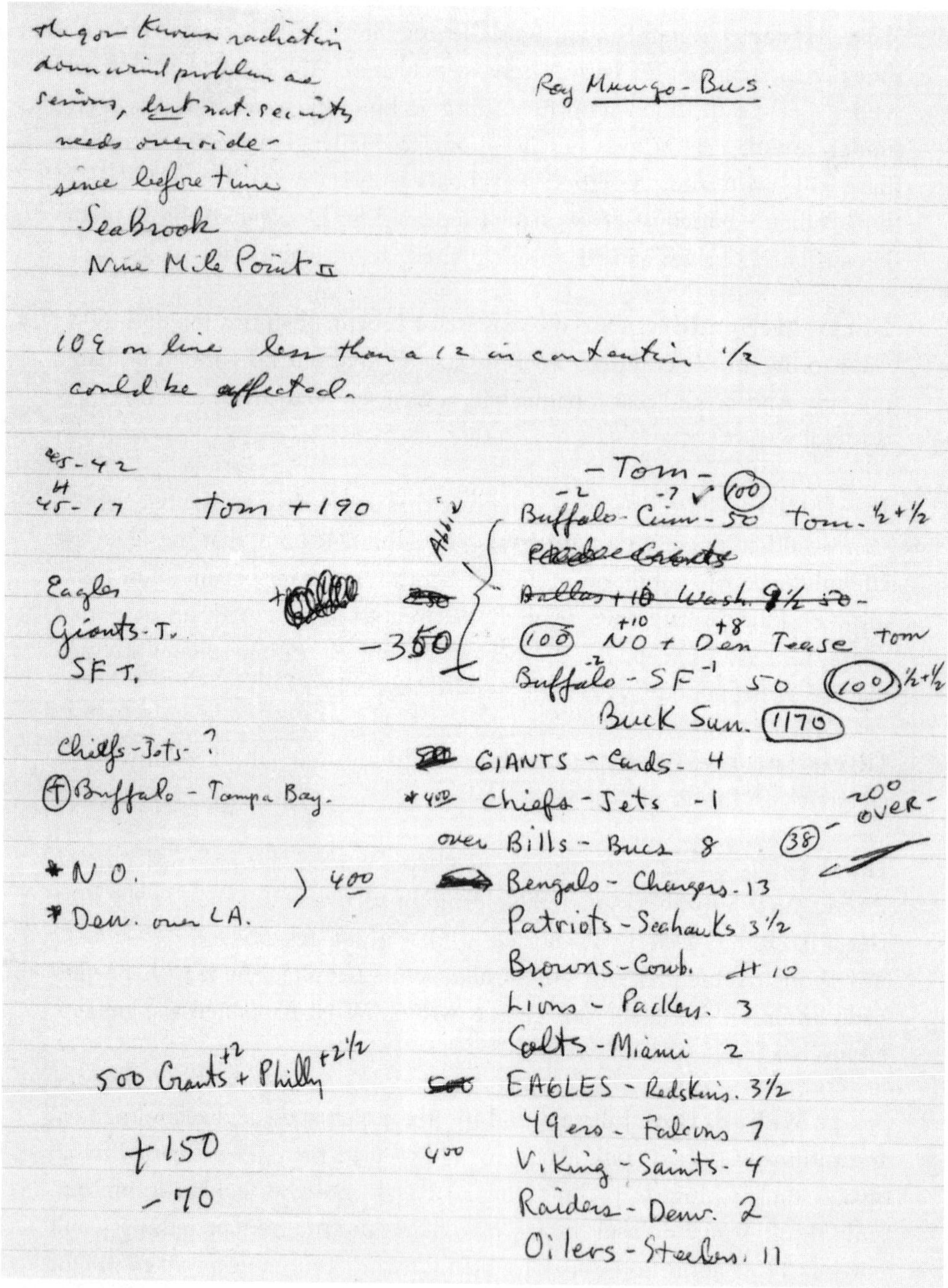

they [illegible] known radiation
downwind problem as
serious, but nat. security
needs override -
since before time
SeaBrook
Nine Mile Point II

Ray Mungo - Bus

109 on line less than a 12 in containment 1/2
could be affected.

45 - 42
45 - 17   Tom + 190

Eagles
Giants - T.
SF T.

Chiefs - Jets - ?
(4) Buffalo - Tampa Bay.

* N O.
* Den. over LA.   } 400

500 Giants +2 + Philly +2 1/2

+150
-70

- Tom -
Buffalo -2 - Cinn -7 - 50 (100) Tom - 1/2 + 1/2
~~Rams Giants~~
~~Dallas + 10 Wash. 9 1/2 50~~ -
(100) NO +10 + Den +8 Tease Tom
Buffalo -2 - SF -1 50 (100) 1/2 + 1/2
-350
Buck Sun. (1170)

GIANTS - Cards - 4
* 400 Chiefs - Jets - 1
over Bills - Bucs 8 (38) - 200 OVER -
Bengals - Chargers. 13
Patriots - Seahawks 3 1/2
Browns - Cowb. +10
Lions - Packers. 3
Colts - Miami 2
EAGLES - Redskins. 3 1/2
49ers - Falcons 7
400 Viking - Saints - 4
Raiders - Denv. 2
Oilers - Steelers. 11

ONE OF ABBIE'S LAST HANDICAPPING SHEETS. HE WAS ALWAYS MIXING POLITICS (TOP LEFT) WITH PLEASURE (FOOTBALL HANDICAPPING). From the archives of Jonathan Silvers

Al Giordano Abbie bragged about doing Steal This Game, a computer program to help people with betting.

Jon Silvers He ended up calling Jack for a couple of hundred or a grand. You know what made Abbie broke—he had a very bad season gambling. He could have made a lot of money if he had taken more speeches but he didn't feel up to speaking.

Al Giordano Jack might have lent him a small amount, but the money in that relationship flowed in the opposite direction, that I guarantee you.

Christine Kelly Abbie talked to me a lot about how he was trying to help his brother out. In one sense it was very warm and in another sense it was kind of like this is a very major pain in my ass. One time in that period I called him and I knew he was in a bad way because he said, "What do you want?"

Fred Duke I walked up to him in the supermarket in early March. I hadn't seen him for a good month or so. I said, "So what are you up to?" He said, "Absolutely nothing." I never heard him say that before, it was always something. He said he was thinking of moving to Cuba. He said, "I think I got Johanna convinced."

Mike Lerner He called me in March with a plan. He said we should get a trip together of famous performers, I think he mentioned Dylan, Joan Baez, somebody from the Dead and somebody from the Rolling Stones, and go to Israel to demonstrate support for the peace movement. In that conversation he told me that he was much, much more interested in his Jewishness. I was particularly taken by the indication that he was seriously thinking about spirituality as something that he wanted in his life. I said, "Yeah, okay, fine, let's do something," but in fact the attitude underneath that I'm sure he must have picked up, was "How do I get this guy off the phone? I got three thousand other things, he's never gonna follow through."

John Schultz I was doing research for my book on Chicago 1968, so my next dealings with Abbie were three major telephone interviews. The first two interviews in March were really rather exuberant and quite lengthy and he seemed up. He also seemed very conscious of history at this point.

Letter from Abbie to Anita Hoffman, April 1989

> I've been in an acute depressive episode for almost two months. This is the most I've written, and I don't read. I'm scared to cross the street without Johanna.

Frank Cavestani So you're sitting in this place in New Hope and it all comes down on you. You don't got your girl, you don't got any money, your body's not working, you got nothing to say anymore. Why continue? Why come out of the trailer and do the scene if you're gonna be bad?

Jon Silvers I think what was different about him toward the end was that he wasn't deluding himself as much. Because all his projects were falling apart. He wanted to do a book on battles to save our national rivers: that was going nowhere. His comedy album was in tape and no distributor wanted to touch it. I was off in my own world doing this political book. Johanna was in New York. The Bucks County pump battle was over and lost and people were blaming Abbie. All he used to do was talk about that thing. It was so important to him. It bored the fuck out of everyone else.

Fred Duke He called me later in March. "So what you doing?" "Nothing." We talked about maybe now's the time to go back to New York. He had been saying all the time—in the press conferences—that he'd moved to Bucks County and he was gonna live there until he died because he was getting this accusation of being a carpetbagger. So he was a little concerned that he was going back on that and I said, "Oh fuck that, I wouldn't worry about that."

Tim Leary Abbie and I were booked into Vanderbilt University with Bobby Seale. Often before the lecture, you meet with the students and the faculty. I usually don't do it, but I heard Abbie was gonna be there so I went. I was shocked. Abbie was slumped over like an old man and instead of flirting with the girls, he was in this state of acute depression. He told me about the accident and he was upset because his mother was dying. Later, when we were introduced, Abbie shuffled on like an old person. I was worried. But when he got up in front of the microphone, suddenly he came alive and gave this dynamic, incredible speech.

Abbie Hoffman *(from Vanderbilt speech, April 1989)*

> So you are the famous Vanderbilts, in this fortress of radical subversion. It just oozes out of the name. I'm making this up as I go along just like

the sixties we just made it up as we went along . . . In the 1960s apartheid was driven out of America. Legal segregation—Jim Crow—ended. We didn't end racism, but we ended legalized segregation. We ended the idea that you could send a million soldiers ten thousand miles away to fight a war that the people do not support. We ended the idea that women are second-class citizens. Now it doesn't matter who sits in the Oval Office. Even George Bush has to talk about child care . . . The big battles that were won in that period of civil war and strife you cannot reverse. We were young, we were reckless, arrogant, silly, headstrong. And we were right. I regret nothing.

Jill Seiden About a week before he died, in the crossword puzzle of *New York* magazine, there was a clue—ex-rebel Hoffman. Five letters. I immediately called Abbie and said, "You better tell *New York* magazine that you're still active, you haven't given it up." He said, "Ah, who cares?"

America Hoffman I heard from him two or three days before he killed himself. He was already depressed. But I ignored it. I didn't know how bad his leg was. And what was I supposed to say? He'd come up with fifteen terrible things that've happened to him. He had a terribly painful tooth problem. And the battle, and breaking up with Johanna and the car accident. He had money problems. Jack was telling him his mother was dying of cancer. It was just everything at once. I just said I've got a car, I've got a girlfriend, I'm going to college soon. I was out committing crimes and we were fucking in our car outside of school and all kinds of tough teenage stuff. I wanted him to be really proud of me. But his response was "Put Anita on the phone."

Susan Carey Anita told us that Abbie called her that week and he was acting really different, being really nice and caring and going over all the things that he felt he had done wrong with her and with Alan [America]. Now that she looks back on it she realized that he was saying goodbye.

Al Giordano Abbie's mother had been in and out of the hospital and just a few weeks earlier Jack had called Abbie and said, "She's going to die tonight, you've got to come up." Abbie flies to Worcester and his mother picked him up at the airport. "Mom, I thought you were dying." It's my understanding that right before this weekend, Jack called him again and said, "She's really dying this time. You've got to come up." Abbie said no. Then Stewart Hutchinson [a WBAI producer] called Abbie up and said, "You sound really down." He goes "Well, my mother's sick."

APRIL 9, 1989

David Maloney Monica and I went out to spend my birthday with Abbie and Johanna. Johanna was spending four days a week there and working at a chess shop in New York three days a week. I think she was pretty happy with that arrangement. But I don't know if it was enough for him.

Christine Kelly Johanna and Monica and David were taking care of him. Abbie had had a really bad two weeks before this, and he was assuring them that he was feeling better. So my sense of it is that it was pretty orchestrated on his part. He insisted that Johanna not come back down and drive him to the airport to go to a speaking engagement he had booked for that week. But he also told David that he didn't want to do it. He had ambivalence about whether he could do it or not. He was giving really mixed signals. Depressed but very nice and polite, extremely sweet, which might be considered uncharacteristic of Abbie.

Jeff Nightbyrd I talked to him a few days before he died. We were betting on NCAA at the time. I didn't know he was going through a depressive period because we were jiving and talking, my bets are better than your bets, back and forth. We talked about his previous suicide attempt a little bit. I said if he ever wanted to kill himself he should contact the Hemlock Society and find out how to do it right. His first attempt he took pills and alcohol and didn't do enough and got sick and threw up and fucked it up. This time he emptied all the capsules.

John Schultz I called him on Sunday night for a final wrap-up interview. He slurred his words, but he seemed as intent as ever. He was very direct and substantive in his answers. He sounded depressed. I've worked in a psychopathic hospital, I recognized the voice. His very last words to me were "John, I have to go now." I remember sitting just staring at the phone for a while after I hung up.

Christine Kelly While she was down in New Hope, Johanna was telling him if you don't want to do the speech, don't do it, but if you're gonna do it, she wanted to give him confidence 'cause that was the big thing that was missing. His bag was packed and his sweater was there and he had a stack of our brochures next to his bag. Ready to go. My sense is that all along he had an exit plan. It was just when he was gonna use it.

Abby McGrath The day he committed suicide, Johanna says, "I'm really worried about him, I don't think he's gonna live another five years."

Christine Kelly Abbie was articulating clearly to Johanna that he was feeling better. That day she bought him a new cookbook, she bought a frame for his photo that he had just had taken. She had just come back from shopping and she started phoning and couldn't get through.

Florence Hoffman I was going for a cancer evaluation because they found little things. The doctor said it looks like cancer but you can't say for sure. I went to the clinic. And I had a clear ticket. Can you imagine that? That was the day he committed suicide.

Christine Kelly Johanna panicked, she couldn't get through and she knew he had to be back. She called his landlord, Michael Waldron, and asked him to go over. Michael came back to the phone and said, "He's dead. Should I call the police, or what?"

Gus Reichbach Johanna called me, saying, "What should we do? Somebody walked in there and they think he's dead. Should we call the police or move the body?" She wasn't shocked at all. I said, "The first thing is to find out if he's alive or not, because it makes a difference who you're gonna call." But then she called back and said the landlord had called the police.

David Maloney I immediately assumed it was suicide. I knew the way his moods fluctuated, and I knew that suicide had been an issue in the past in his life. But then, in Abbie tradition, I knew that he would've left it vague to make it as confusing as possible for everybody, to create some sort of controversy like was he killed by the CIA?

Gus Reichbach Here's a fucking guy who filmed his own vasectomy. So the fact that he should not leave a note says volumes. He was very consciously trying to say that he was not making a political statement. I think what he was saying is this is merely an act of personal pain. It's probably the only private thing he's ever done in his adult life.

Christine Kelly When Johanna got there the authorities had come in and swept already. His body was gone.

David Maloney We took a bus the next day. His house was still quarantined by the cops. Johanna and Jack were able to go in, nobody else. Jack was staying there in the apartment. He was pretty manic.

Al Giordano I got down there early afternoon, Jack was already there, staying on the bed Abbie died on.

John Schultz Somebody called me to tell me, and I practically threw the phone at the wall. Then I got into the car and I turned on the radio and I heard that he was [found] in bed, a blanket pulled partly over him, his knees tucked up, on his side, and he looked peaceful. I remember thinking that Abbie had made sure how the image of him would be reported. He even picked the time when he knew that there would be nothing else on the news.

Front-page headline, *New York Post,* April 13, 1989

ABBIE HOFFMAN DEAD

52-year-old '60's radical leader found in his bed by neighbors

America Hoffman I was looking at colleges in northern California. We were checking into some sleazy hotel and there was a guy at the counter and his TV happened to be on. It says, "Abbie Hoffman dead. Details at eleven," and then it shows a picture of him being dragged off by cops. The first words out of my mouth, words that I've never said before, [were] "Wow, bummer, dude." Then I went to the hotel room and I acted cool in front of my girlfriend Mary, and she cried for me. I couldn't cry. I wasn't sad yet. I'm only sad now, to be honest.

Mary, *america's girlfriend* He saw this anchorman saying something great about his father. And then all of a sudden he started to cry.

America Hoffman Tom Brokaw said the coolest thing, it hit me so hard it made me cry. He said, "Abbie Hoffman is gone. We've ridiculed him for so long but now he's gone. Let's have a minute of peace for Abbie Hoffman." I respect Tom Brokaw. They did twenty minutes on Abbie Hoffman when he died.

Paul Krassner For a solid week I got calls from media people. You could hear a certain poignancy as they asked questions. Countless people that I knew in the underground press are now in mainstream journalism. And the perception of him was that he never sold out, so he remains their dream.

ONE OF THE MANY EDITORIAL CARTOONS THAT WERE PUBLISHED AFTER ABBIE'S DEATH.

William Bramhall

Stew Albert It was a little surprising that the media did well by Abbie. Abbie didn't die on page 27 in a little AP article. He got on the cover of *People* magazine. He died big.

Tom Hayden There was a sixties radical recruited by *People* magazine to write about Abbie as if he really knew him and they were kind to him. But if they had been as kind to him in his life, I have the feeling he wouldn't have acted in such self-destructive ways. This was "Abbie dies. He was a reckless and misguided individual but he fought for a lot of important causes which we in the media will keep alive in a more rational and understandable way."

Al Giordano I came to the conclusion that Abbie with his knowledge of pharmacology had figured out a way to kill himself that was autopsy-proof. This would be the last scam, to steal this suicide. Then the autopsy came back and they said phenobarbital, a lot. Abbie used to work a lot with phenobarbital when his father was in the pharmaceutical business.

From the *New York Post,* 4/19/89

ABBIE ENDED LIFE WITH 150 PILLS

By Timothy McDarrah

> DOYLESTOWN, PA.—Abbie Hoffman committed suicide with a "massive overdose" of prescription drugs that could have killed at least 15 men. Bucks County Coroner Thomas Rosko said an autopsy showed Hoffman downed "150 doses" of phenobarbital, a powerful, long-acting sedative and anti-convulsant . . . The drug's lethal effect was magnified because Hoffman was also legally drunk, Rosko said.

Jon Silvers There was an anniversary of Phil Ochs' death about two weeks before Abbie killed himself and that set Abbie off. "Phil died, he was a friend of mine, boy he must have been a mess." Abbie wasn't putting out the right distress signals, because he was making jokes on the phone. About a year earlier, when Robert McFarlane tried to kill himself, with Valium and a glass of milk, Abbie and I were laughing about it. Abbie said, "If you really want to kill yourself you take a hundred phenobarbital and wash it down with a half pint of Jack Daniel's." And it's eerily close to what he did. What was it, 150 phenobarbital, washed down with half a pint of Glenlivet? He loved drinking Glenlivet because it was what Mailer called the drug of defeat. And if it was good enough for Mailer it was good enough for him.

From the Associated Press

DRUGS IN FRIDGE

> DOYLESTOWN, PA.—Small quantities of illegal drugs were found in the home of Abbie Hoffman, who committed suicide earlier this month, authorities said yesterday. The drugs were found in a box in Hoffman's refrigerator, Bucks County District Attorney Alan Rubenstein said. The box contained 9.38 grams of marijuana, .31 of a gram of hashish, a cocaine residue and trace amounts of LSD, amphetamines and psilocybin, Rubenstein said.

Joie Davidow Johanna's main thing for the next couple of weeks was guilt. It wasn't really rational but she just kept beating up on herself.

Angela Dorenkamp Florence didn't want to think about it being suicide. She never got along with Johanna and because Johanna and Abbie weren't together when he died, as the mother, you think, would this have happened if she had been there?

America Hoffman I had this very bizarre dream that I was at the house on the St. Lawrence and his ghost would be ignoring me. I'd just be saying, "Look at me, look at me, *look at me!* Don't get into your own thing, I want you to look at me." But he never did. I woke up really upset.

Faye Schreibman When I saw the paper, I said, "That's it, they finally got him."

Stew Albert He's one of the last people in the world that I ever thought would commit suicide. Abbie was vitality and energy, imagination, creativity, wit. I thought of Abbie as life itself. And you don't think of life itself dying. So I was devastated. Still am.

Tom Hayden Abbie was a difficult person but America shouldn't be a place where difficult people have to commit suicide. I just think he had a broken heart. Yes, he had a massive ego that nobody had a responsibility to satisfy but basically what he wanted was less egoistic than most politicians or businessmen I know.

John Giorno A month or two later, we were downstairs around a big table, Debbie Harry and Chris Stein, Keith Haring, and William Burroughs was sitting next to me, and it's just all this drunk and stoned talking. William says to me, "He really let us down." I said, "Who?" He says, "Abie." "Abie? Who's Abie?" It takes me a second and I realize he's talking about Abbie and then there was sort of this great moment that indeed he let us all down.

Oscar Janiger What the fuck, letting us down? The man is ill, for Christ sakes, Burroughs knows better than that. Did Burroughs let us down when he's lying in his own shit and couldn't move? Only because he got better could he write about it. And his writing about it didn't change it that much. Who's Abbie letting down? What, has he got some debt to the world that he hasn't discharged so that if he's dying, he's gonna have to still do it? Abbie had to stay afloat. It's a dangerous, difficult world and a dangerous, difficult condition. How he did it, boy, is a triumph to this man's endurance. It was his toughness and his goddamn sense of reality and sense of humor.

Mike Rossman If anything, Burroughs' is a reiteration of the attitude which, introjected, helped to kill Abbie. This demand that the man's life should not be his own, that the very fundamentals of his life should be distorted to coincide with the media image and expectations that we hold of him. It appears to me to be an inhumane demand. Whatever you say, this was a man who loved life, he did it to excess, was maybe tortured and driven, but he was above all an affirmative personality, that's what made his politics so interesting.

Mike Brown, *radical professor of sociology* When you try in your life, the way you live, to comprehend the whole of humanity, you either have to become a religious nut, a priest, whatever, or you run the risk of suicide. You try to make room for every imaginable instance of suffering and struggle. I think that was true of Abbie in some way. And I think that part of his despair was his sense of the impossibility of it, not from the standpoint of I'm bigger than it all, but from the standpoint of not being able to evade that responsibility.

From Reuters wire service

ABBIE HOFFMAN LEFT ESTATE OF $37,000

PHILADELPHIA, Reuters—Yippie leader Abbie Hoffman left an estate of $37,000, his will revealed Friday. The will, filed for probate in suburban

> Bucks County, put his net worth at more than $37,000 rather than the $2,000 reported after he committed suicide April 12, 1989, by taking an overdose of barbiturates and alcohol. Hoffman left everything to Johanna Lawrenson, his lover for more than 15 years. Most of Hoffman's estate came from his share of a family-owned property in Massachusetts, said Gerald Lefcourt, his lawyer for 20 years. "He never owned a house, never took the proceeds from his books and never bought anything for himself."

America Hoffman I wasn't shocked that we didn't get anything. I didn't expect anything. Ilya [Amy] was pissed. I think Andrew was expecting something shitty like that.

Jill Seiden In the will he left notes to his kids saying you're all great, you're all terrific, you can do without. Everything goes to Johanna because she really didn't have any marketable skills.

Stew Albert They did a memorial for Abbie in L.A. It was at the big Unitarian Church and the place was so packed they had an overflow crowd and the sound system going outside. The remains of the Doors played. And Whoopi Goldberg was there.

Whoopi Goldberg *(from Steal This Wake, L.A.)*

> The man we're honoring told me early in my life that it was okay to be different, it was okay to do the things that you wanted to do as long as you could bring other people with you. And one of the things that Abbie Hoffman did was brought a lot of peoples [*sic*] along on the dream that America could be all of the things that we all knew it should be . . . He taught people what they could do and gave them a sense of who they could be and said that I could help too then, I could be a part of the revolution without having to hate, or hurt people or maim them. He said it was okay to walk that edge, so I did. I decided that the edge was where I wanted to be because there were lots of people like Abbie Hoffman there to help me not fall. And so I'm going to keep him alive in my heart because fuck 'em if they can't take a joke.

Laura Cavestani She didn't say it as Whoopi Goldberg, the biggest, blackest comedienne on the screen making the most money. She said it as a welfare mother with nothing to live for. I thought, "God, if he could just be alive to hear this, this would keep him going for another ten years."

Tim Leary *(from Steal This Wake, L.A.)*

It's impossible I think for any of us to really appreciate what Abbie helped us do the last two decades. As we well know, American fascism is an extremely polished and skillful machine. There are no Siberias, there are no tanks and there are no beheadings. The three techniques of the American fascist machine in dealing with dissent are trivialize, demonize and ignore. And certainly Abbie has felt the honor of being treated this way in a major league fashion. We hear so much in the establishment press media about the sixties. Nancy Reagan would have us feel it was just another temporary naughty aberration, something on her carpet. What went wrong? Nothing went wrong, my friends. People grew and moved out from where they were. I have been reminded of the power of Abbie's symbolism in the last week watching the evening news, 150,000 students in China revolt. Abbie. Abbie. And in the provincial university towns as well but in the Boulders and the Berkeleys and the Columbias of China. I wonder where they learned all those tricks. The police are there and they don't know what the fuck to do with this. Their students lighting Chinese celebratory firecrackers, see, we're not doing it with bombs or grenades. Firecrackers. That's guerrilla politics as Abbie taught us, isn't it? How about the Soviet Union? How about North Korea? North Korea, of all the buttoned-down Mafioso countries of the world, here come the students there, where'd those Korean kids learn the trick of doing it just when you're gonna catch the evening news?

Peter Townshend, *leader of the Who (interviewed in* Rolling Stone *magazine, 12/23/93)* I was thinking the other day that Abbie at Woodstock was correctly despairing. He was fucking right. All those people at Woodstock saying, "A new dawn has come," and John Sinclair was in jail for a joint because the FBI didn't think that he was the right kind of political animal. And the FBI's lawyer and I would be sitting on the Concorde together.

Jim Fouratt Abbie left many messages. One is yes, you do matter and yes, you can change the world. But also that you can die from drugs, your loneliness and your pain and your isolation are not helped with chemicals. That politics do not pay your rent, that never being able to admit to making a mistake leaves you always on the run, and that the government didn't win but that unless one really knows how to love oneself and love other people, in the end you become a victim of the system that you fight against.

America Hoffman I would've liked to talk to him now. I never had a really good discussion with him. I feel a little bit more developed mentally than when I was fifteen, because I had all this shit to prove when I was fifteen, and now I don't really. So I just would have liked to talk to him.

Allen Ginsberg The idea was right but it was premature. And the fruition didn't come in America. It came in Eastern Europe. The Eastern Europeans picked up a great deal from the American tactics of the sixties. The rock and roll, the Fugs, the Velvet Underground, my own poetry and the American sixties flower power psychedelic. That's their inspiration. It took them twenty years but they learned a lesson about organizing and how to do it properly and how to have it as a hippie rebellion under the flower people angle and it was successful there. The revolution was won not by guns but by Levi's and rock and roll. That Yippie thing of dope, sex, fucking in the street, which was hyperbole to begin with, caught on in Eastern Europe. So it seems like the sixties did have a fruition, not in America where the repression is more subtle, but in Eastern Europe where the repression was so overt that people recognized it and found that the one way of combating it was spiritual warfare rather than physical warfare.

Jean-Jacques Lebel Several hundred thousand farmers in Brussels were demonstrating about the price of milk. The farmers had come from Spain, from Italy, from Germany, from France, and blocked up the whole city of Brussels with their tractors. A bunch of farmers came with cows. They knew that all the ministers of these governments of the Common Market were meeting at this building in Brussels. So with the cows, they pushed their way into the giant elevators, and they went up on the fortieth story, where all the ministers were making speeches. They barged into the meeting with the cows, and they squirted milk into the ministers' faces. Abbie will never be forgotten, because of things like that.

Burt Chandler Every item that Abbott protested about in his humorous way—that many of us were thinking, "My God, what is he doing?"—every single one of them has been accepted as part of mainstream society. I wouldn't be surprised but that Abbott and what he spawned ultimately caused the war to end. Every major college in the country's had its curriculum reformed. Lyndon Johnson's Great Society, the welfare aspect of our society, which Abbott was into before Johnson, is an accepted bit, the making way for minorities in institutions and banks and businesses and government and schools. Even pay toilets have had a great downswing. I think history is going to be extremely kind to Abbott.

Rabbi Joseph Klein I think he did damage to Judaism, oh yes, absolutely, absolutely. Abbie was a smart aleck who defied the establishment and got applause for it. That kind of person has existed in every generation. A hundred years ago, Abbie would have been hung. In our day it was tolerated. In any other part of the world, he could not have gotten away with it.

George Lois, *art director, advertising agency owner* Here's a guy who was totally dedicated to trying to wipe out injustice wherever he found it. So dedicated that in many more ways than one he offered up his life for it. That's something that I never did. I gave up my time, gave up my energy, gave up some talent, but I never said, "Okay, here's my fucking everything." It's beyond a hero. I found him saintly. Abbie was as spiritual a man as I've ever met, a lot more spiritual than any priest I've known.

Kinky Friedman Abbie was a troublemaker in the great tradition of Jesus. Essentially, he lived nowhere, he never held a real job, never stayed married. But he was on top of things before most people were. Abbie had a great deal of courage. Things happened to Abbie every day that would have derailed most people in their mission. The only hard-on Abbie had was for having a good time and stirring up as much shit as he could. Then he was happy. Sometimes this worked to help a lot of people.

America Hoffman I think he'd like to know that I was doing okay. I like to be able to be free to do something I want. Something above working at a restaurant, maybe having health insurance, that's what I consider as being rich. Being rich enough to actually decide, "Hey, let's have children," or something corny like that. I want to have my own son I can push around.

Anita Hoffman There's nothing that's ever gonna be like that again for me and there's a truth that for years I was unwilling to recognize. Abbie was one in a million. When I wake up from a bad dream he's the one I think about. I've never loved anybody the way I loved Abbie and I don't expect it to ever happen again that way. I never stop thinking about him. The main good thing about dying is that I'll be able to say hello to Abbie again.

Stew Albert Who knew that the sixties would happen? Nobody, nobody. Mailer came the closest. Nobody predicted it. Some beat poets in San Francisco, there was a note of cultural rebellion and apocalypse in some of their stuff. But certainly none of the conventional wisdom was predicting it. Even the Marxists weren't predicting it.

Abbie Hoffman (*from* Soon to Be a Major Motion Picture)

> There is absolutely no greater high than challenging the power structure as a nobody, giving it your all, and winning. The essence of successful revolution, be it for an individual, a community of individuals, or a nation, depends on accepting that challenge. Revolution is not something fixed in ideology, nor is it something fashioned to a particular decade. It is a perpetual process embedded in the human spirit. No amount of rationalization can avoid the moment of choice each of us brings to our situation here on the planet. I still believe in the fundamental injustice of the profit system and do not accept the proposition that there will be rich and poor for all eternity.

A Poem by Anita Hoffman, 8/18/89

Abbie
you brought me my first feelings
of fear in the gut leaping
barricades at the Pentagon
Mr. and Mrs. America
declaring liberated territory

and the first feelings of love
so powerful we flew
over city streets together
and saw each other age
in ten seconds on acid

you gave me my first orgasm
and child
and death that tore my heart apart.

Tom Hayden There are not many opportunities to experience another dimension of life, the inspired dimension. Not much. Although, these moments keep happening. Nicaragua in 1979 and the Soviet Union a few years ago, and Prague and the Philippines. When you've been through it nothing else measures up. And I think Abbie waited twenty or thirty years for it to come back and he couldn't wait any longer. He may have been right, it may not be coming back, for Americans. But just as you get to a point of gloom, it can happen. There's absolutely no way of predicting in January 1960 that something was about to happen that would change Abbie Hoffman and Tom Hayden's life forever. Nothing. It was a quiet time, people called it a silent decade, they said students were apathetic, nothing was happening. And then four people get arrested in a sit-in in North Carolina and the sixties happened. So we shall see. I'm gonna wait it out.

A performance artist since 1980, Andy Soma had read much of Abbie's writings and viewed him, in part, as a precursor of performance artists. After Abbie's death he decided to do a piece, "Free's Last Laugh," as a memorial. He began by giving away free books from the sixties. Then he went onstage holding up a huge cutout of Abbie and harangued the audience. The audience was encouraged to throw tomatoes at Andy, tomatoes that he provided.

Andy Soma The performance piece ends with me projecting a slide of the American flag in reverse colors. There's a dot in the middle and I tell the audience that they gotta help me to create this flag, because unless they help me, it's not gonna work. I tell them to stare at the dot and we'll create a retinal flag that only exists in the mind. And while they stare, I'm doing this stream-of-consciousness thing about depression. Then I repeat this mantra based on what Abbie said, that "politics has become theater and magic," till it gets to be a trance thing. And then the reversed-color flag slide goes off and the screen's white. And if people stared at it, they actually see the reverse colors. So when the green disappears, you see red. So they see a flag floating in space. That's the last image. A flag that doesn't really exist.

Where Are They Now?

STEW ALBERT lives with his wife, the former Judy Gumbo, in Portland, Oregon. He is still active in local community affairs.

D'ARMY BAILEY returned to the South and earned a law degree. He is now a federal judge in Memphis, Tennessee.

PETER BERG After retiring the Diggers, Berg got involved in environmental concerns. He helped found the Planet Drum Foundation, an environmental group that promulgates a theory of bioregionalism.

MARTY and SUSAN CAREY run a photo gallery out of their home in Woodstock, New York.

CHRIS CERF was one of the original editors of the *National Lampoon* and continues to write satirical books and television shows.

RAMSEY CLARK is now a lawyer practicing out of New York City, specializing in radical causes.

KATE COLEMAN is a journalist in Berkeley, California.

PETER COYOTE is a prominent actor. He is currently writing a history of the Diggers.

SID DAVIDOFF is an influential lobbyist operating in New York City.

JOIE DAVIDOW was the founder of the *L.A. Style* magazine and continues to do freelance writing.

RENNIE DAVIS is organizing around environmental issues and awaiting the millennium in Boulder, Colorado.

GEORGE DiCAPRIO is an underground cartoon magazine distributor in L.A. His son, Leonardo, is a prominent actor.

MARSHALL EFRON is a television writer and actor in New York.

DANIEL ELLSBERG teaches and writes and lives in Washington, D.C.

JOHN ESKOW is a screenwriter living in New York City.

BOB FASS continues to host his own radio show on WBAI-FM in New York.

DAVID FENTON owns a public relations company in Washington, D.C.

JIM FOURATT was a leading gay activist and one of the premier party organizers in New York City. After living in California for a number of years, he has returned to New York and is working for a record company.

KINKY FRIEDMAN is semiretired from performing his country songs but has gained worldwide prominence as a mystery writer.

CHARLES GARRY practiced law until he died in San Francisco a few years ago.

JOHN GERASSI is a sociology professor at Queens College in New York.

SAL GIANETTI owns a restaurant in Prague.

FATHER BERNIE GILGUN is still active in social causes in Worcester, Massachusetts.

ALLEN GINSBERG was one of America's most prominent poets and activists. He died of cancer in 1997.

JOHN GIORNO has released many volumes of spoken-word albums on his own label.

TODD GITLIN is a sociology professor in New York.

BARRY GOTTEHRER works for an insurance company in Connecticut.

WAVY GRAVY (Hugh Romney) is involved in fund-raising for many charities and runs a summer camp for children in northern California.

TOM HAYDEN got involved in electoral politics in California and was a state assemblyman from Santa Monica for several terms.

AMERICA HOFFMAN is going to college and working in the electronics field in northern California.

ANITA HOFFMAN is a dealer in rare books in northern California.

LYNN FREEMAN HOUSE is involved in environmental concerns in northern California.

OSCAR JANIGER practices psychotherapy in California.

RUBY JARRETT has retired and lives near San Francisco.

JEFF JONES is a journalist in Albany, New York.

FRED JORDAN publishes books under his own imprint in New York City.

RON KAUFMAN was released from jail a few years ago. He is working at a bookstore in northern California.

KEN KELLEY is a journalist living in the Bay Area.

PAUL KRASSNER has authored numerous books of satirical writings and continues to publish the *Realist.*

BILL KUNSTLER represented controversial and radical clients until his death in 1995.

TULI KUPFERBERG re-formed the Fugs with Ed Sanders, and publishes books and cartoons challenging the establishment.

KEITH LAMPE (PONDEROSA PINE) wanders California barefoot, preaching an ecological agenda.

IRA LANDESS is a psychotherapist practicing in New York City. He specializes in treating compulsive gamblers.

JEREMY LARNER writes screenplays and books from his home in New York City.

TIMOTHY LEARY published numerous books on neuropolitics. He died of cancer in 1997.

JEAN-JACQUES LEBEL is an artist living in Paris.

MIKE LERNER founded a radical Jewish monthly, *Tikkun,* which he continues to publish.

JAY LEVIN started the *L.A. Weekly,* an alternative weekly newspaper, and is currently working on an alternative television network.

JACQUES LEVY teaches and continues to write plays.

G. GORDON LIDDY is now a radio talk show host based in Washington, D.C.

COUNTRY JOE McDONALD continues to record albums.

ARTHUR NASCARELLA is working as a private investigator and actor.

TOM NEUMANN is a radical attorney in Berkeley, California.

JEFF NIGHTBYRD is the world's largest purveyor of drug-free urine to clients who wish to test negative after corporate urine testing.

MICHAEL O'DONOGHUE was one of America's premier satirists until his untimely death in 1995.

ROBIN PALMER teaches and is the host of a cable TV show in upstate New York.

BRUCE PASKOW was a member of the folk rock group the Washington Squares until his death from complications from AIDS a few years ago.

ABE PECK is a professor of journalism in Chicago.

GUS REICHBACH is now a judge presiding in Brooklyn, New York.

STELLA RESNICK is a psychotherapist practicing in the Los Angeles area.

JERRY RUBIN turned his entrepreneurial skills to distributing megavitamins. His last rebellious act was jaywalking across Wilshire Boulevard in Los Angeles. He was hit by a car and subsequently died from his injuries.

ED SANDERS tours with the Fugs and publishes a newspaper in Woodstock, New York.

SIDNEY SCHANBERG won a Pulitzer Prize for his reporting on the killing fields of Cambodia.

MANNY SCHREIBER is a psychologist practicing in Michigan.

MICHAEL SHAMBERG is a producer of major Hollywood films.

SUPERJOEL went legitimate and started a concrete business. He died of AIDS a few years ago.

JEROME WASHINGTON teaches creative writing in the Bay Area. He recently published his jailhouse memoirs.

LEE WEINER is a researcher working for the Anti-Defamation League of B'nai Brith.

LEN WEINGLASS continues to represent politically unpopular clients.

RANDY WICKER owns an antique lighting store in Greenwich Village and continues to be active in the gay rights movement.

BOB ZMUDA created and produces the Comic Relief shows to aid the homeless.

ACKNOWLEDGMENTS

So many people contributed to the making of this book that the acknowledgments could be a manuscript in themselves. I have to first thank my agents, John Brockman and Katinka Matson, for recommending me when Doubleday contacted them with the idea of doing a biography of Abbie shortly after his death. Thus began a nine-year odyssey that took me from coast to coast (several times) and to Europe in a search to ferret out sources for this oral biography.

In California, Veronica and Scott Smith opened their house to me. Harry Zimmerman literally gave me his apartment and introduced me to his next-door neighbor, Mercy Marquez, who helped me with my research. Michael Simmons not only let me stay at his house, he painstakingly read a two-thousand-page version of this manuscript and made many useful comments and suggestions. In the Bay Area, Ron Turner and his lovely family gave me the key to the "Bunker" downstairs and suffered stoically when I cheered the Giants on to victory over San Francisco.

Becky Wilson and Abba Roland accompanied me on research trips to Los Angeles, Denver and Chicago, and made the trips a lot more pleasant.

My trip to Abbie's hometown was shepherded by Amy Zuckerman, a talented Worcester journalist who is now a noted international trade expert, consultant and columnist. Not only did Amy participate in my interviews with Abbie's brother, Jack, but she contributed substantially to the book by conducting the vast majority of the subsequent interviews with Abbie's colleagues and friends from Worcester. Her knowledge of Worcester's interesting history and her insights into the politics of the area were most useful for my research, and I'm very appreciative of all of Amy's efforts.

A special acknowledgment must be given to Nancy Shapiro, who, on learning of this project, provided me with a wonderful set of interviews that her brother had conducted with Abbie.

Barry Shapiro was a graduate student at the University of Chicago, working on a doctoral dissertation in what he termed "political psychology," when he first met Abbie during the summer of 1972 in Miami at the Republican convention. He decided to do his dissertation on Abbie and his political philosophy, so the two met frequently over the next nine months.

Barry never finished that dissertation, turning instead to a study of the French Revolution, on which he has published a book and several articles. Today he teaches history at Allegheny College in Pennsylvania. But those 1972–73 conversations with Abbie, reproduced in part here, are the most brutally honest and intimate interviews Abbie ever granted. I am very grateful to both Nancy and Barry for allowing me to reprint them.

Over three hundred people were interviewed for this book. By the time the massive original manuscript was whittled down for publication, some of these interviews regretfully had to be omitted. I would like to thank everyone who gave of their time to contribute to this work.

These interviews yielded hundreds and hundreds of hours of tape that needed to be transcribed. Carol Realini was the person most instrumental in this daunting task. But Carol's contributions to the book went way beyond mere transcription. As an old friend of Abbie's, Carol was very helpful in suggesting sources for the interviews. Her transcriptions included annotated notes that suggested further lines of questioning. Additionally, she conducted a few interviews with New York–based FOA (friends of Abbie) while I was researching on the West Coast. Carol's own interview provided a fascinating insight into the counter-culture by a participant whose contributions were behind the scenes but substantial.

The West Coast interviews were transcribed by Allen "The Word Pro" Horne, who dispatched the finished product to me with tremendous diligence and care. When the workload got to be too much for Carol and Allen, Marguerite Dworkin came to the rescue.

Both Dawn McCombs and Tricia Bonito did valuable research for me, and I'm grateful to them for their contributions.

I relied heavily on a database program called "GOFER" that helped me organize the thousands and thousands of pages of transcripts.

But the book would never have been finished without the human touch. Harriet Rubin, my busy editor at Doubleday, had the foresight to hire Alice Rosengard, a freelance editor who did a masterful job of honing down the manuscript to an acceptable length. She, more than anyone else, is responsible for making this book a reality. Roger Scholl, who replaced Harriet, efficiently shepherded the book through the final stages of editing and production, aided by his assistant, Stephanie Rosenfeld.

I spent many hours collecting the images for this book. I'd especially like to thank Don Bowden at Wide World, Michael Schulman and Mitch Blank at Archive, and Norman Currie at UPI/Bettman for their help. Both Tuli Kupferberg and Anita Hoffman opened up their archives to me and spent hours going over the material. Jack Hoffman was gracious enough to send me a cherished family photo. Rick Meyerowitz was kind enough to lend me his valuable original *National Lampoon* issue with Abbie on the cover.

Special kudos to my good friends Kinky Friedman and Howard Stern. Kinky, in his usual poetic fashion, came up with the title of the book. Howard, the King of All Media, sacrificed a few weekends and wrote the introduction. I'm indebted to both of them.

As I am to the very special women who lived through the tumult that's occasioned when a book is born. Carmen and Rachel were there for the conception, Christy was there at the birth. I'm forever grateful for their love and support.

PERMISSIONS

Grateful acknowledgment is made to the below sources for permission to reprint the following material:

Elli Wohlgelernter for his interview with Abbie Hoffman.

The Allen Ginsberg Trust for the section entitled "How to Make a March/Spectacle" from "Berkeley Vietnam Days" by Allen Ginsberg.

Tom Buckley for the excerpt from "The Battle of Chicago: From the Yippies' Side," originally published in the *New York Times Magazine,* September 15, 1968.

David Lewis Stein for the excerpts from his book *Living the Revolution.*

Anita Hoffman for the excerpts from "To America with Love," and for her poem of August 18, 1989.

Playboy magazine for excerpts from the Abbie Hoffman interview in the May 1976 issue.

Pete Hamill for his column, "Shed No Tears for Abbie Despite Sob Sisters' Pleas," originally carried by the New York Times Syndicate.

ABOUT THE AUTHOR

Larry Sloman, aka "Ratso," was Howard Stern's collaborator on two of the fastest-selling books in publishing history, *Private Parts* and *Miss America.* Former executive editor of *National Lampoon,* he served as editor in chief of *High Times* and wrote the award-winning book *On the Road with Bob Dylan,* as well as the bestselling *Thin Ice*, an account of one season with the New York Rangers. He lives in New York City.